If
you want
to evaluate
your
library . . .

If
you want
to evaluate
your
library . . .

Second Edition

by

F. W. Lancaster

1993
University of Illinois
Graduate School of Library and Information Science
249 Armory Building / 505 East Armory Street
Champaign, Illinois 61820-6291

If
you want
to evaluate
your
library . . .

Contents

List of Exhibits

Preface

The first edition of this book, which appeared in 1988, was given very favorable reviews and received the American Library Association's G. K. Hall Award in 1989.

This second edition has been greatly expanded. Not only does it update the first edition, but it incorporates much new material, including a chapter on the evaluation of bibliographic instruction and several case studies based on investigations I have been associated with in the past five years. It has also been strengthened in the areas of cost-effectiveness and cost-benefit evaluation and in the evaluation of resource sharing. Another new chapter discusses the feasibility of continuous quality control as applied to library services. As with the first edition, it is the public services provided by libraries and information centers that are the focus of attention.

I consider that this book complements rather than duplicates the contents of my other book in this area, *The Measurement and Evaluation of Library Services*, the first edition of which was also recognized by the American Library Association when it received its Ralph Shaw Award in 1978. *The Measurement and Evaluation of Library Services* is intended as primarily a review and synthesis of the evaluation literature. This book, on the other hand, is designed to be more practical – to be used as a text in teaching the subject and to guide librarians in the selection of evaluation procedures to apply in their own institutions. While I do refer to the literature I consider most pertinent to the points I want to make, this book does not attempt to review this literature in a comprehensive way.

My thanks to my graduate research assistants, Hong Xu and Susan Bushur, for their help in gathering materials and checking references, and once more to Kathy Painter for her prowess at the keyboard.

F. W. Lancaster
Urbana, Illinois
February 1993

1. Introduction

A typical dictionary may define *evaluation* as "assessing the value" of some activity or object. Authors dealing with the subject of evaluation, however, are likely to be more precise. Some claim that evaluation is a branch of research – the application of "the scientific method" to determine, for example, how well a program performs. Others stress its role in decision-making: the evaluation gathers data needed to determine which of several alternative strategies appears most likely to achieve a desired result. Finally, some writers look upon evaluation as an essential component of management; in particular, the results of an evaluation may help the manager to allocate resources more effectively.

These various viewpoints, of course, are quite compatible. Moreover, they all tend to emphasize the *practical* nature of evaluation. An evaluation is performed not as an intellectual exercise but to gather data *useful* in problem-solving or decision-making activities.

A good way to focus on the evaluation of library services is through a generalized representation of the operations of a library as seen through the eyes of an evaluator (Exhibit 1). The long-term objective of the library,* presumably, is to produce certain *outcomes* in the community to be served.

While certain desired *outcomes* will be the raison d'être for its existence, the library is more directly concerned with the processing of *inputs* in order to generate *outputs*, which are the information services it provides. The primary input, financial resources, is used to acquire major secondary inputs, namely information resources* (mostly publications of various types), personnel to exploit these resources, and physical facilities to store materials, offer services, and so on.

The operation of the library can be considered as essentially a marriage between the information resources and the personnel: the system consists primarily of information resources and of people skilled in the exploitation of these resources on behalf of the users. Two major groups of activities are identified in the diagram as taking place within the library. The first is concerned with organization and

---

*Much of what is discussed in this book as applying to libraries could also apply to other kinds of information services. The term "library," then, is used as a shorthand for "libraries and other information centers." Similarly, "information resources" is used as a generic term to represent sources of information, inspiration, and recreation.

control of information resources. These activities – usually referred to as "technical services" in a traditional library setting – produce various tools (catalogs, bibliographies, shelf classification, and the like) that make possible the second group of activities, the public services.

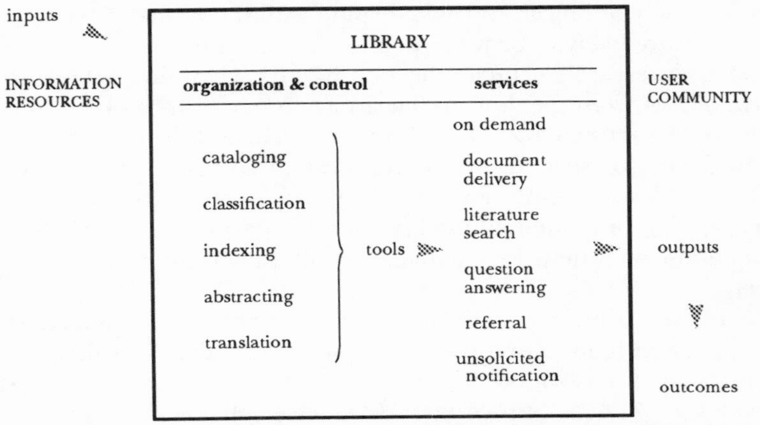

Exhibit 1
The operations of a library

The public services have been divided into two groups: "on demand" services and "notification" services. The former can be considered passive services in the sense that they respond to demands rather than initiate them. The notification services, on the other hand, are more dynamic: they are designed to inform people of publications and other information sources likely to be of interest to them. The on demand services themselves fall into two major groups: document delivery and information retrieval services. The notification services are primarily retrieval services or, more correctly, information dissemination services.

The library, then, can be looked upon as an interface between the available information resources and the community of users to be served. Therefore, any evaluation applied to the library should be concerned with determining to what extent it successfully fulfills this interface role.

Inputs, Outputs, and Outcomes

For evaluation purposes, a library can be looked at in a number of different ways. Exhibit 1 implies that an evaluation program might look at inputs, at outputs, or at outcomes. The sequence *input, output, outcome* is one of increasing complexity. One would usually like to determine to what extent the desired outcomes of a service have been attained. Unfortunately, the desired outcomes will tend to relate to long-term social, behavioral, or even economic objectives that are rather intangible and, therefore, not easily converted into concrete evaluation criteria. For example, a desired outcome in one institution might be "to improve the quality of teaching and research within the institution" while another might seek to "keep researchers and practitioners abreast with the latest developments in their fields of specialization." Regrettably, while long-term objectives of this kind should provide the justification for the existence of information services, it is virtually impossible to measure the degree to which they are achieved. Even if the measurements were possible, one could not readily isolate the contribution made by the service itself. In short, one would do well to abandon the idea of using desired outcomes as *direct* criteria for the evaluation of libraries and other information services. Drucker (1973), in fact, has suggested that this situation will apply in the evaluation of any public service institution.

In contrast to outcomes, the inputs are tangible and easily quantified. Indeed, both primary and secondary inputs are inherently quantitative rather than qualitative in nature. That is, the inputs have little value in and of themselves – they can only be evaluated in terms of the role that they play in achieving desired outputs.

The most obvious example of this, perhaps, is the collection of books and other materials that can be considered the major input to a library. Such collections cannot be evaluated in the abstract but only in relation to the purposes they are intended to serve and the actual needs existing in the population of potential users. In other words, the collection (input) must be evaluated in terms of the extent to which it satisfies the demands placed upon it (i.e., output); any other evaluation criteria would be artificial and meaningless.

The outputs of the library – i.e., the services provided – are less tangible than the inputs but much more tangible than the outcomes. The outputs are easily quantified – e.g., number of documents delivered, number of referrals made, number of literature searches performed, number of questions answered – but this is not enough. Unlike inputs, the outputs can and must be evaluated in terms of quality. Thus, for each service provided, qualitative criteria of success should be identified.

This brings us back to the outcomes of an information service. While these cannot be studied directly, the criteria used to evaluate outputs should be good *predictors* of the extent to which the desired outcomes are achieved. Take, for example, a current awareness service, such as a Selective Dissemination of Information (SDI) system. The desired outcome is to make users better informed and more up-to-date in their areas of specialization. The achievement of this objective is not easily measured directly. However, the desired outcome strongly suggests what the evaluation criteria should be at the output level. It seems reasonable to assume that the more items the service brings to the attention of users that are directly related to their interests (and, conversely, the fewer that are not directly related), the more likely it is that the users will become better informed. Further, the more of these items that are new to the user (i.e., items of which he was previously unaware), the more likely it is that the service is succeeding in keeping the user up-to-date. Thus, two evaluation criteria for this output (service) – *relevance* (or pertinence) and *novelty* – have been identified that seem also to be good predictors of the extent to which the desired outcome is reached.

Clearly, the interrelationship that exists among inputs, outputs, and outcomes has important implications for the design of information systems and services. One should begin by defining what it is that the system is intended to achieve. These are the desired outcomes. One then determines what services (outputs) are needed to produce these outcomes, and how these services can be provided most efficiently and economically. This leads to the identification of the inputs necessary to achieve the desired outputs. The criteria used to evaluate these services should predict the extent of attainment of the outcomes that guided their establishment. For document delivery services, presumably, the output measure would be the number of document needs satisfied (i.e., the extent to which the service can get publications to users at the time they are needed); for question-answering services, it would be the percentage of questions answered completely and correctly; for referral services, it would be the percentage of referrals that leads users to appropriate sources of information. Literature searches would be evaluated in terms of the relevance of the results to the information needs of the users and, for certain types of needs, the completeness of the results. It should be noted that some information services can be evaluated on a binary scale – either the user gets what he wants or he does not – while others can only be evaluated according to some form of graduated scale – for example, the proportion of items retrieved in a literature search that is directly relevant to the needs of the requester.

Just as qualitative measures of output can predict achievement of outcomes, certain input measures might be considered good predictors of desired outputs. For example, the more items that exist within the collections of the library, the more document delivery needs are likely to be satisfied; the larger the collection of reference tools, the more questions that could be answered completely and correctly, and so on.

Indeed, it is possible to use certain evaluation methods, applied to input, that are intended to simulate an output situation and thus approximate an evaluation of output. For example, in evaluating the coverage of some portion of a collection against an external standard, such as an authoritative bibliography, one is in effect estimating the ability of the library to satisfy information needs of actual users in this subject. This is a legitimate approach *if* one can be sure that the external standard fully reflects the needs of the users of this particular collection.

Costs, Effectiveness, and Benefits

A somewhat different way of looking at evaluation is in terms of costs, effectiveness, and benefits. Effectiveness relates to outputs, and the overall criterion of effectiveness is the proportion of user demands that are satisfied. The benefits of the system are really the desired outcomes. Costs are quite tangible as long as one thinks only in monetary terms. But it is easy to be myopic in this respect. One should avoid the fallacy that time spent *using* information services is free. User time is not free, at least not within the broad context of society as a whole. In point of fact, the cost of operating an information service may be quite small compared with the cost of *using* it.* For certain evaluation purposes, a realistic cost analysis of an information service should take all costs – including those incurred by users – into account. This point will be pursued further later in the chapter.

At a national level, costs incurred by all components of the system may need to be considered. Suppose, for example, that a library, *A*, requests photocopies from a particular periodical from other libraries ten times a year. From *A*'s point of view, it may be cheaper to do this than to subscribe to that periodical. However, from the viewpoint of the national system as a whole – taking the costs of all components

*See Braunstein (1979) as one example of the discussion of user costs.

into account – it may be cheaper for *A* to pay the subscription and handling costs.

Cost can be related to effectiveness or to benefits. *Cost-effectiveness* refers to the costs of achieving a particular level of effectiveness within an information service. Some type of unit cost measure will be needed. Examples of cost-effectiveness measures would include cost per document delivered to users, cost per question answered successfully, cost per relevant item retrieved in a literature search, and so on. The cost-effectiveness of a service can be improved by holding costs constant while raising the level of effectiveness or by maintaining a particular level of effectiveness while reducing the costs.

Cost-effectiveness, then, relates to optimization in the allocation of resources – the better the allocation of resources, the better the quality of service (i.e., effectiveness) that is achieved for a particular level of expenditure. In this connection, one must recognize that it is unrealistic to expect an information system to satisfy every need of every user. The concept of the "90% library" is an important one (Bourne, 1965). That is, one can design a service that will satisfy some reasonable percentage of all demands – perhaps as much as 90% – but to go beyond that would require a completely disproportionate level of expenditure. For example, 200 periodical titles may satisfy 90% of the needs for periodical articles in a particular institution, but 500 may be needed to satisfy 95% of the needs, and 1200 to satisfy 99%. The "90% library" is discussed further in Chapter 14.

A cost-benefit evaluation relates the benefits (outcomes) of a service to the cost of providing it. Again, the cost-benefit relationship can be improved by increasing benefits without increasing costs or by reducing costs without reducing benefits. In the long-term, however, a cost-benefit study attempts to demonstrate that the benefits derived from a service outweigh the costs of providing it. Because, as suggested earlier, the benefits of information services tend to be intangible, and not easily expressed in the same unit as the costs (e.g., $), true cost-benefit studies are virtually unattainable in our field. Nevertheless, attempts have been made with varying degrees of success. Cost-effectiveness and cost-benefit analysis are dealt with in Chapters 14 and 15.

While most managers would like to be able to prove that the services they provide can be justified from a cost-benefit point of view, the difficulties involved in such a study have discouraged all but a few attempts of this kind. For this reason, this book will focus on outputs and effectiveness rather than outcomes or benefits.

In general, a cost-effectiveness study is concerned with the relationship between inputs and outputs for some activity. The inputs are usually given as primary ($) or secondary resources (e.g., time of personnel) expended, while the outputs are frequently expressed as items produced or services used. In the library world, it is possible to identify input measures, output measures, and measures of the characteristics of the community to be served, and to combine these in various ways as shown in Exhibit 2.* Most libraries have many of these data, although not necessarily all of them (e.g., it is rare to have good figures on the number of items consulted within a library). Meaningful

Inputs	Outputs	Community characteristics
$	Items borrowed	Size of population served
Number of items acquired	Items consulted	Composition of population by age, gender, education and other characteristics
Number of staff	Questions submitted	
Space occupied	Searches performed	
	Persons attending library programs	
Input/community measures	**Output/community**	**Input/output**
$ per capita	Circulation per capita	$ per circulation
$ per registered borrower	Questions submitted per capita	$ per question
Books per capita	Library visits per capita	Uses per volume
Space per capita	Registered borrowers/ population served	
Staff per capita		

Exhibit 2
Some input, output, and community measures,
and interrelationships among them

input/output measures are not easily obtained because of the problem of allocating resources over a variety of activities or services. Some books purchased may be borrowed, consulted in the library by a library user, consulted by a librarian to answer a reference question, used to support some library program, borrowed by another library, used to generate photocopies, and so on, so the cost of buying and

---

*For a more complete inventory of possible measures relevant to public libraries see King Research Ltd. (1990).

owning such items cannot be attributed to any one service. To quote another example, a reference librarian may be involved in many activities – book selection, interlibrary loan, bibliographic instruction, database searching, and so on – as well as the answering of factual-type questions, so the personnel cost of answering questions of this type cannot be derived merely by relating overall personnel costs for a reference department to the number of questions handled.

While librarians have access to many of the data shown in Exhibit 2, they do not necessarily make good use of them in support of management decisions. Moreover, the output data collected tend to be purely quantitative and give a very inadequate picture of the quality of the services offered. For example, librarians know how many books were borrowed in a particular period of time but not how many times users were unable to find the items they wanted, they know how many reference questions were handled, but not how many were answered completely and correctly, and so on. Qualitative data of these types are not collected routinely in libraries; they can only be obtained through use of appropriate evaluation procedures.

Purpose of Evaluation

There exist a number of possible reasons why the managers of a library may wish to conduct an evaluation of the services provided. One is simply to establish a type of "benchmark" to show at what level of performance the service is now operating. If changes are subsequently made to the services, the effects can then be measured against the benchmark previously established. A second, and probably less common, reason is to compare the performance of several libraries or services. Since a valid comparison of this type implies the use of an identical evaluation standard, the number of possible applications of this kind of study tends to be quite limited. Examples include comparison of the coverage of different databases, the comparative evaluation of the document delivery capabilities of several libraries, and the use of a standard set of questions to compare the performance of question-answering services. A third reason for evaluation of an information service is simply to justify its existence. A justification study is really an analysis of the benefits of the service or an analysis of the relationship between the benefits and the cost. The fourth reason for evaluation is to identify possible sources of failure or inefficiency in the service with a view to raising the level of performance at some future date. Using an analogy with the field of medicine, this type of evaluation can be regarded as diagnostic and therapeutic. In some ways it is the most important type. Evaluation of an information service is a sterile exercise unless conducted with the specific objective of identifying means of improving its performance.

In what is now considered a classic article, Orr (1973) discussed the responsibilities of a manager and the need for evaluation to support the management role. To elaborate somewhat on Orr, the responsibilities are:

1. To define the goals of the organization.*
2. To obtain the resources needed to reach these goals.
3. To identify the programs and services required to achieve the goals, and to optimize the allocation of resources over these programs and services.
4. To see that the resources allocated to a particular activity are used as wisely as possible.

It is clear that at least two of these important management functions imply the use of evaluative methods.

Orr discussed the interdependency among the resources devoted to a service, the capability of the service, its use, and the benefits derived from it. He pointed out that, all other things being equal, capability increases with the resources expended, use increases with the capability, beneficial effects increase with use, and improved benefits attract greater resources (Exhibit 3). Orr is careful to point out, however, that an increase in one of these variables does not necessarily bring a comparable increase in another. For example, a 10% increase in resources will not guarantee a 10% increase in capability and a 10% increase in capability will not guarantee a 10% increase in use. Evaluation techniques are needed to measure changes in capability and in use, to predict or approximate benefits, and to ensure that resources are allocated as effectively as possible.

Evaluation Methods

An evaluation of an information service may be subjective or objective. Subjective studies – based on opinions – are not without value because it is important to know how people feel about a service. But an evaluation is of most value if it is analytical and diagnostic, seeking to discover how the service might be improved, and it is difficult to base this type of study on opinion alone. In general, then, objective criteria

---

*The more specialized the library, the more obvious are its goals and objectives. Public library objectives, which tend to be somewhat nebulous, are dealt with in McClure et al. (1987) and *Setting Objectives for Public Library Services* (1991).

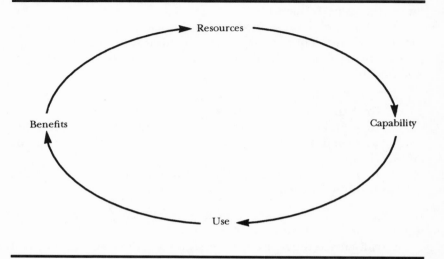

Exhibit 3
Interdependency of resources, capability, use, and benefits for some service

and procedures should be followed. The results of an objective study should be quantifiable.

Evaluation studies can involve real users in real institutional settings. Alternatively, various simulations are possible. If "real" studies are employed, the evaluator can try to get all users to participate on a voluntary basis or can use random sampling to focus on a set of representative users. The latter is much to be preferred. It is better to get reliable data from a few users than to gather less reliable data from many.

For certain evaluation purposes, too, it may be sufficient that evaluation data be anonymous while, for other purposes, this may not be good enough. For example, materials left on tables in a library may reflect materials consulted in that library but tell us nothing about who used them and for what purpose. Randomized interviews with people using materials within a library give qualitatively different data that may be essential in answering certain types of questions concerning in-house use of the collection.

If carefully designed, simulation studies can provide much valuable information without disturbing the users of the system at all. A good example is the "document delivery test" (Orr et al., 1968). A list of bibliographic references, say 300, forms the basis of a search in a particular library on a particular day. The search determines how many items are owned and how many of the items owned are actually available on the shelves. In effect, the test simulates 300 users walking into the library that day, each one looking for a single item. As long as the 300 references are fully representative of the needs of the users of that library (not too difficult to achieve in the case of a special library, much more difficult for a general library), the simulation can give excellent data on the probability of ownership and the probability of availability. Other simulations can be devised for other information services, including question-answering and literature searching.

The Five Laws of Library Science

Elsewhere (Lancaster and Mehrotra, 1982), I have described how Ranganathan's Five Laws of Library Science (Ranganathan, 1931) can guide decisions on what should be evaluated, by what criteria, and by what methods. These laws provide a fundamental statement of the goals that information services should strive for, and they are as relevant today as they were sixty years ago.

The first law, Books Are For Use, seems obvious but it is a law to which libraries do not always adhere. Ranganathan, himself, deplored the fact that many librarians seemed to be more concerned with preservation than with use, thus perpetuating the image of the librarian as a custodian rather than as someone skilled in the exploitation of bibliographic resources. The most obvious implication of the law is that one must evaluate collections and services in terms of the needs of users. Moreover, it suggests that objective, empirical investigation should replace purely subjective or impressionistic approaches.

Carried to its logical conclusion, Books Are For Use implies considerations of cost-effectiveness. Because of limited resources, $30 spent on a book that is little if ever used is $30 less available for an item (possibly a duplicate copy) of something that might be in great demand. In the operation of information services, expected "cost per use" must be of paramount concern in deciding which items to add to a collection and which not to add. This situation is changing, however, as more and more bibliographic resources become accessible through electronic networks. The obvious implication of this, of course, is that "ownership," per se, is becoming less important in the evaluation of the resources of an information service. The evaluation criterion is "accessibility": can the service make an item accessible to a requester, at the time he or she needs it, from whatever source, in whatever acceptable form?

Ranganathan's second law, Every Reader His Book, is a logical extension of the first. Data on books borrowed or used in a library have an obvious limitation: they reflect only successes and tell us nothing about failures. That is, a book used represents, in some sense, a success. But volume of use is relatively meaningless unless one can convert it into a "satisfaction rate." To do this one must determine the probability that a user, looking for a particular item, or materials on a certain subject, will find this item or these materials available at the time needed. In other words, for everything looked for, how much is found (success) and how much is not found (failure)? The second law goes beyond collection evaluation and into the assessment of *availability*. It is not enough that an item sought by a user is owned by the library; it must also be available when needed.

Every Reader His Book can be considered a generic label that really means "Every reader his need." It can be extended to other types of needs of library users – e.g., what is the probability of having a factual question answered completely and correctly? This, too, can be handled by a simulation procedure in which the evaluator tests the library through a set of questions for which answers are already known (e.g., Crowley and Childers, 1971). In this case, the reference questions may be put to the library by volunteers posing as real users. The library is evaluated in terms of the number of questions answered completely and correctly.

The third law, Every Book Its Reader, complements the second. In relation to the second law, the library's role is relatively passive. Assuming that a user makes a demand on the library's services, the evaluator is concerned with whether or not the demand is satisfied. But libraries need to be more dynamic institutions. An important function should be that of making people aware of new publications of possible interest to them. Libraries should be concerned with *exposure* as well as with *accessibility* (Hamburg, 1974).

The significance of the third law is that books need to find their potential users as well as users the books they need. One could say that, for every item acquired by the library (and even, to carry this to its logical conclusion, for every item published), there are potential readers existing in the community. A library should therefore be evaluated in terms of its ability to inform people of the materials of potential use to them.

This is not such as easy evaluation exercise and, as a consequence, it is one rarely attempted. One obvious facet is simply the extent to which the library is able to achieve penetration in the community served – the extent to which its services are known, for example. More specifically, however, evaluation should be concerned with how successful the library is in informing users of newly acquired materials. If it produces a "new book list," how widely is it disseminated? Does it produce "targeted" bibliographies (e.g., new books on gardening) and, if so, do these reach the audiences who will most benefit (in this case, perhaps, gardening clubs)?

In special libraries and information centers a more personalized level of current awareness may exist, perhaps achieved through the use of computers to match the profile of a user's interests against characteristics of newly published literature (i.e., Selective Dissemination of Information). In this case, the evaluation criteria would be:

1. How much of what is brought to a user's attention is actually relevant to his interests?

2 How much of what is relevant was previously unknown to the user?

3 What proportion of the items brought to his attention does the user ask to see?

The fourth law, Save the Time of the Reader, virtually pervades all the others. Information services must be concerned not only with satisfying needs but with satisfying needs as efficiently as possible. It is now well known that the accessibility of information services is the major determinant of their use. Someone is likely to judge a service to be "inaccessible" if it requires too much effort to use (Mooers, 1960; Allen and Gerstberger, 1966, 1968).

A defect of many evaluations of library and information services is that they look upon user time as "free." This erroneous assumption completely invalidates certain cost-effectiveness analyses that have been performed. The time of users cannot be considered free since the time they spend using library materials could be spent in other, and, in some cases, more productive ways. In their analyses of the scientific and technical communication system in the United States, King et al. (1976) showed that the cost of *using* (i.e., reading) publications greatly exceeds the cost of producing and distributing them. By the same token, the cost of *using* the library greatly exceeds the cost of the collection, staff, and physical facilities. This can be seen most clearly in the case of a library within industry or government. If a scientist or engineer visits the library to use materials for, say, one hour, it may cost the library $5 in staff time (to assist the user) and other resources expended, but it actually may cost the organization $50, when the user's time (including all overheads) is figured into the calculations.

In the evaluation of library services, the time of the user must be given sufficient weight. Moreover, in the cost-effectiveness analysis of information services, all costs, including all user costs, must usually be taken into account. To do otherwise could lead to completely erroneous conclusions. For certain types of evaluation, in fact, an information service cannot be treated in isolation but must be looked at within the context of the larger community of which it forms a part. This is particularly important in any cost-effectiveness or cost-benefit analyses.

The fifth and final law, The Library is a Growing Organism, indicates that the library must be willing to adapt to new conditions. This would include adaptability to changing social conditions and technological developments. For the evaluator, this implies examining how long the library takes to adopt innovation, including adoption of new publication forms and new forms of information distribution. Modern computer and telecommunications technologies are changing our very concept of "library." Indeed, as mentioned earlier, providing some form of online access to materials on demand seems gradually to be replacing access through "ownership" and *access*, rather than *ownership*, should be the main criterion by which a library's "resources" should be evaluated.

Libraries should also be evaluated in terms of the extent to which they are able to capitalize on the capabilities provided by technology. For example, one important advantage of automated systems is that, if properly designed, they can provide many data to aid decision-making and generally to improve the management process. Another facet is the ability of a library to exploit technology in order to provide services that it had not been able to offer earlier (e.g., a high level of literature searching support made possible by online access to a wide range of databases).

There is another aspect to adaptation that must be considered, namely the ability of the library to adapt to changing needs among its clientele. In this connection there is a danger that must be recognized and guarded against. Library services cannot be evaluated solely in relation to the demands placed upon them by present users. Such evaluation accepts demands at face value and assumes that these demands are co-extensive with user *needs*, which is not invariably true. Moreover, present users of a library may have needs for materials or information that, for one reason or another, are never converted into demands on the library's services. If evaluation activities focus only on the demands (i.e., expressed needs) of present users and fail to study the needs lying behind these demands, or if they ignore the latent needs that are not converted into demands as well as the potential needs of present non-users, the danger exists of creating a self-reinforcing situation. That is, the library is constantly improving its ability to respond to the present type of demand and, by so doing, perhaps reducing its ability to attract new users or new uses of the resources available. Such a library is far from being a growing organism.

The Need for Evaluation

Line (1979) has expressed the opinion that academic libraries (at least) do not observe Ranganathan's Five Laws. Indeed, he maintains that they tend to observe their own set of five laws, more or less diametrically opposed to Ranganathan's, namely:

1. Books are for collecting
2. Some readers their books
3. Some books their readers
4. Waste the time of the reader
5. The library is a growing mausoleum

While this may seem somewhat facetious, there is undoubtedly some truth in Line's claims. For many years libraries operated in an environment largely free from objective evaluation. If few serious complaints were received, one tended to assume that the service was satisfactory. Such an assumption was frequently erroneous but librarians, lacking objective performance measures and methods, became somewhat complacent about their services. When objective evaluation procedures were first applied to library and information services, some of the results shocked many people – e.g., the finding that a user may have less than a 50% chance that a sought item is immediately available in a library, or less than a 60% chance that his factual question will be answered completely and correctly.

The fact is that evaluation is an essential element in the successful management of any enterprise. Ranganathan's fifth law provides the major justification for evaluative activities. Healthy growth implies adaptation to changing conditions and adaptation implies evaluation to determine what changes need to be made and how they may best be accomplished. Electronic technology has already produced new forms of publications and new media for the distribution of publications and information. It is likely that the developments of the next two decades will be even more dramatic than those of the last two. The ability to distribute information rapidly and inexpensively in electronic form is threatening the entire raison d'être of the library. The library must be evaluated not only in terms of "how is it doing" but in terms of "is it doing what it should be doing?" That is, the library profession must look at its functions critically to determine if it is playing a role appropriate to the last decade of the twentieth century or one more appropriate to the first decade.

Evaluation is not an end in itself. An evaluation should only be performed with definite objectives in mind. This will usually mean that a study is designed to answer certain specific questions and to gather data to allow system improvements to be made. An evaluation can be expensive if it is diffuse and lacks well-defined objectives but need not be unreasonably expensive if it is sharply focused. Moreover, the investment made in a careful evaluative study can be fully justified if the results reveal what may need to be done to improve the effectiveness or cost-effectiveness of the service or its relevance to the present needs of the community.

Examples of decisions that might be aided through specific evaluation procedures include the following:

1. Should a program be continued? For example, should the library continue to collect film as well as videotape? To what extent should the present film collection and equipment be maintained?

2. Is the approach now used to implement some service the most cost-effective approach possible? For example, in a large public library could all questions received by telephone at a reference desk be handled initially by trained nonprofessionals, with only the more complex ones referred to the professional librarians? What effect would this have on accuracy? What effect would it have on cost?

3. Is the strategy now used the best one to achieve some goal? For example, should a library develop self-help tools to teach patrons how to use the several CD-ROM databases it now provides, or should it instead have qualified assistants available to provide personalized instruction as and when it is needed?

4. How can budget cuts best be absorbed to minimize adverse effects on service? For example, if the periodical budget must be reduced by 10 percent, perhaps to provide increased support for some other important activity, which titles can most easily be dispensed with?

5. What additional training needs exist? For example, are there certain kinds of questions that members of the reference staff tend to deal with less successfully than they deal with others?

Many readers will be able to identify other situations in which the results of some well conceived evaluation could aid in solving a management problem or in making a management decision. Evaluation should be looked upon as a practical management tool and not a mere intellectual exercise.

Diagnostic Evaluation

From the evaluator's point of view, even the simplest of library services is really quite complicated in that many factors may influence whether or not the service is successful in meeting the needs of a particular user. Consider, for example, Exhibit 4, which shows a user entering a library in order to borrow a particular item – a book, periodical article, or whatever – for which there is no substitute. The evaluator would like to know whether or not the user leaves the library "happy" which, in this case, probably means having the item in hand. Here, it is the document delivery function of the library, or at least one aspect of it, that is being evaluated.

This "known item search" situation is outwardly rather simple. Nevertheless, it is not quite as simple as it appears at first sight. In fact, whether or not the user is successful depends upon the answers to a series of questions, the most important of which are explicitly represented in the diagram. Before the user can leave the library with the item, it must be owned by the library; the user must be able to find its shelf location, which will usually mean that the item has been

Exhibit 4
The situation of a user entering a library to look for a particular bibliographic item

cataloged and that the user can find an entry for it in the catalog (or a librarian can find such an entry for the user); the book must be available to the user – "on the shelf"; and he must be able to find it on the shelf.

A convenient way of looking at this situation is to consider it as a series of probabilities. What is the probability that the item will be owned, that it will be cataloged, that it will be found in the catalog, that it will be on the shelf, that it will be found on the shelf? Clearly, the probability that the user will leave the library "happy" is the product of these five component probabilities.

This can be illustrated by means of a simple example. Suppose that the library owns, on the average, 90% of the items sought by users (i.e., the "probability of ownership" is .9), that 80% of owned items can be located in the catalog, that 75% of these are on the shelf when users look for them, and that users succeed in finding items on the shelf (when actually present there) 90% of the time. The probability that a particular user will leave the library with an item sought is, thus, .9 x .8 x .75 x .9, or .486. That is, a user of this library faces about a 48% probability that a particular item sought will be found.

One of the objectives of an evaluation is to establish probabilities of this kind. By performing a suitable study, one might determine that, of 500 bibliographic items looked for by users in a particular period of time, 450 were actually owned by the library. The success rate is therefore .9 (450/500), or 90%. Providing the sample used is truly representative of the diversity of document needs within the community, the study has established a probability of ownership of .9 for the library. In other words, a user entering the library to look for any particular item will face a probability of .9 that it will be owned. Similar studies can be performed in order to establish the other probabilities implicit in Exhibit 4: that the user can find an entry in the catalog, that an item will be available on the shelf when needed, and so on.

Unfortunately, strength in one aspect of the situation depicted in Exhibit 4 may cause problems elsewhere. The larger the size of the collection, for example, the greater the probability of ownership. But the larger the collection, the larger and more complicated will be the catalog, leading perhaps to a higher rate of failure in catalog use, at least for catalogs in card or printed form (the size factor may have a less dramatic effect in the case of an online catalog).

The questions raised in Exhibit 4 also reflect various facets of evaluation. "Is item owned?" implies an evaluation of the collection, the next two questions imply some form of catalog use study, and the last two questions refer to a study of "shelf availability." One can look at each part of the diagram separately (e.g., performing only a collection evaluation) or undertake a study to look at all parts at once (e.g., by interviewing a sample of users to establish success rate and to find where failures occur).

The probabilities mentioned earlier are based on averages for a significant number of events. A "probability of ownership of .9," for example, refers to a probability that applies to all users and uses of the library. A score of this kind, however, might vary considerably with such factors as type of user, type of document, age of material, and subject matter. In the academic environment, a particular library might satisfy 99% of undergraduate needs for publications but only 65% of doctoral student needs. The score is also likely to fluctuate with type of publication. For example, the probability of ownership might be 1.0 for U.S. patents, .9 for periodicals, .78 for books, .32 for technical reports, and so on.

This brings us to a very important point. To be useful, an evaluative study must do more than indicate what the "score" of the library is for some service. It must also provide data that indicate how that score fluctuates when conditions change. Put somewhat differently, the study should demonstrate under what conditions the library performs well and under what conditions it performs badly, thereby allowing identification of the most efficient ways to improve performance. This type of evaluation can be considered diagnostic.

The most important element of diagnosis is the identification of reasons why particular failures occur. A user might not be able to find an entry in the catalog, even though it is actually present there, because cards have been misfiled, the user does not have complete or correct information, the catalog has inadequate cross-references, the user lacks familiarity with the catalog, or any of several other possible reasons. Similarly, a book sought may not be on the shelf because another user has already borrowed it, because it is waiting to be re-shelved, because it is being re-bound, because it is missing, and so on.

If an evaluation is to be more than an academic exercise, it should be diagnostic, collecting data that indicate how a service performs and why it performs as it does, including reasons why failures occur. A diagnostic evaluation, then, should be of practical use to the librarian, providing guidance on what actions might be taken to improve the effectiveness of the services provided.

This book discusses methods that can be used to evaluate various facets of library service, both the determination of *success rate* (i.e., establishing the probabilities referred to earlier) and the identification of reasons for successes and failures (i.e., diagnosis). Those facets that relate primarily to "document delivery" (including the collection of a library and the catalog of that collection) are dealt with first, followed by reference services. The remaining chapters cover related evaluation topics, including cost-effectiveness and cost-benefit aspects.

Study Questions

1. For different types of library try to identify several desired outcomes for the services provided. What output measures might be reasonable predictors of the extent to which these outcomes are achieved?

2. Consider the library that you use most frequently. Do you have any evidence that this library observes Ranganathan's "five laws?" Do you have any evidence that Line's alternative laws are obeyed?

2. Evaluation of the Collection: Formulæ, Expert Judgment, and Bibliographic Checking

The collection of materials held is the component of library service that has been most subject to evaluation over the years. One reason is the obvious importance of the collection to all library activities. A second is the fact that the collection is something concrete and this makes it appear simpler to evaluate than the services provided through exploitation of the collection, which seem inherently more "abstract."

Nevertheless, as suggested in Chapter 1, one cannot evaluate a collection in isolation but only in terms of its value to the users of the library. At least, this is true if one accepts the fact that books are "for use" rather than "for collecting."

In evaluating a collection one is really trying to determine what the library should have that it does not have and what it does have but should not have, taking into account factors of quality and appropriateness in the published literature, the obsolescence of the literature, changing user interests, and the need to optimize use of limited financial resources. The evaluation of a collection, or part of it, can be conducted in order to improve collection development policies, to improve policies relating to loan periods and rate of duplication, or to support decisions relating to the use of space.

Based on methods used in the past, one can classify the major approaches to collection evaluation as follows:

1. Quantitative
   Size
   Growth
2. Qualitative
   Expert judgment
   Bibliographies used as standards*
      Published bibliographies
      Specially-prepared bibliographies
   Analysis of actual use

---

*Bibliographies can be used to evaluate a collection or to study the degree to which two or more collections overlap.

21

Quantitative Considerations

One obvious criterion for the evaluation of a collection is its size. All other things being equal, one would expect that the larger the collection the greater the chance that it will contain a particular item sought by a user. This is especially true in the case of libraries designed to support research. Minimum standards for collection size in libraries of various types have been put forward by different organizations, including agencies of accreditation. Standards of this type tend to be related to the size of the population served by the library. Thus, "books per capita" is a measure sometimes used, especially by public libraries. Such measures can be meaningful as long as the "books" referred to are likely to be of use or interest to the community served. However, a public library could achieve a high "books per capita" figure by buying large quantities of cheap books of low quality, by indiscriminately accepting many donations, or by never discarding books that are old and unused, none of which is likely to produce a collection of maximum value to the community.

The standards of the Public Library Association (1967) recommend 2 volumes per capita, while the International Federation of Library Associations and Institutions (1986) recommends 2 to 3 volumes and the *Standards for Public Library Service in England and Wales* (1962) recommends a growth of 250 volumes per year per 1000 population.

In any case, "books per capita" is a very simplistic formula to use in calculating the minimum or optimum size for the collection of a public library. More elaborate procedures have been proposed by various authors, including Stoljarov (1973), McClellan (1978), Betts and Hargrave (1982), and Ottensmann and Gleeson (1993). The McClellan formula, designed to help in allocating a materials budget over the various subject areas covered in a collection, is:

$$\frac{2(A \times B) - C}{D} \times E$$

where A is the number of readers expected in that subject area (McClellan used a figure for the greatest number of books in this subject charged out in any one month), B is the number of volumes needed to provide adequate reading at all levels from elementary to advanced (McClellan adopted a value of six for branch libraries and eight for central libraries), C is the number of volumes already held, D is a period of depreciation or replacement factor (ten years for science and technology and fifteen years for other fields), and E is the average purchase price per volume.

The formula is intriguing and is completely logical when broken down into its essential elements: $2(A \times B)$ is assumed to be the ideal size for a collection in this subject, $2(A \times B) - C$ is the number of volumes needed to reach the ideal, $(2(A \times B) - C)) / D$ is the number of volumes to be purchased this year, and $(2(A \times B) - C)) / D \times E$ is the amount to be spent. Such a formula could still be useful for public libraries today, although it would probably require some modification, particularly in the period of depreciation.

To put some hypothetical figures into McClellan's formula:

$$\frac{2(250 \times 8) - 600}{10} \times \$27 = \frac{3400}{10} \times \$27$$

= \$9180, which is the amount that should be budgeted for purchases in this subject area this year. Even if one is unwilling to use such a formula to arrive at actual expenditure levels, it would still be of value in determining the *relative* amounts to be spent on various subjects.

A much more sophisticated approach to the allocation of a materials budget within a public library system is described by Ottensmann and Gleeson (1993). The data considered are materials budgets, items purchased and circulation for a period of years; circulation related to budget; average book cost; and, for each branch, circulation, collection size and turnover rates (uses per item owned) for a period of approximately ten years. The primary objective of the allocation formula is to maximize circulation.

A study by Detweiler (1986) suggests that a collection of 100,000 volumes may be "optimum" for a public library when number of circulations per volume is the criterion. Between 50,000 and 100,000 volumes, a "dramatic increase in circulation per volume added" can be observed, but no such relationship is discernible in the range of 100,000 to 150,000. Above 150,000 volumes, there is some evidence of a negative correlation between collection size and circulation. On the other hand, Dolan (1991), based on data collected in England, claims that a collection of 20,000 volumes is the "least viable" size for a public library and that the "least viable" ratio of books per head of population is 3:1.

The situation is more complicated in academic libraries. It makes little sense in this setting to treat each user as equal, since faculty, doctoral students, and others engaged in research are likely to need a level of bibliographic support an order of magnitude greater than that required by undergraduates. Collection size here, then, needs to be related to the number, size, and complexity of the academic programs.

This has led to the development of various formulae for calculating the minimum size of the collection in a particular academic library.

The first such formula to be widely used was devised by Clapp and Jordan (1965). As McInnis (1972) has shown, the formula can be written as a weighted sum of several variables:

$$V = 50,750 + 100F + 12E + 12H + 335U + 3,050M + 24,500D$$ where

F = number of faculty
E = total number of students enrolled
H = number of undergraduate honors students
U = number of major undergraduate subjects
M = master's fields offered
D = doctoral fields offered
V = volumes

and 50,750 is a constant, representing a minimum viable university library in number of volumes.

Note that the Clapp-Jordan formula takes into account several factors affecting required size of collection and gives greatest weight to those likely to lead to the most stringent demands on the collection. Thus, number of doctoral fields exerts a profound influence – too much according to some critics (McInnis, 1972), especially when one considers that "doctoral field" is subject to different interpretations in different institutions.

Several variants or refinements of the Clapp-Jordan formula have been developed and used. The Association of College and Research Libraries (ACRL) has included a similar formula in its "Standards for College Libraries" (1986). It specifies a core collection of 85,000 volumes with additional increments determined as follows: 100 volumes per full time equivalent (FTE) faculty member, 15 volumes per FTE student, 350 volumes per undergraduate major or minor, 6,000 volumes per master's program where no higher degree is offered in this field, 3,000 volumes in a master's program in which a higher degree is also offered, 6,000 volumes for fields in which sixth year specialist degrees exist, and 25,000 volumes per doctoral field. Associated with this formula is a grading scheme for academic collections. A library is an A library if it owns at least 90% of the recommended number of volumes, a B library if it owns 75-89%, a C library if it owns 60-74%, and a D library if it owns 50-59%. The formula can be applied to different academic departments. Thus, a university may find itself an A library in, say, education but a D library in engineering (Burr, 1979).

Unfortunately, quantitative standards or formulae of this type can be subject to misinterpretation. Although they are intended to prescribe *minimum* requirements, some bodies responsible for funding have been known to use them against the library, reducing levels of financial support on the grounds that the library already exceeds the standards. So, some of the substandard libraries may benefit by using the formulae to show how much they need to improve, while some of the better libraries could actually suffer financially as a result of comparison with the standards.

Another problem associated with quantitative standards, of course, is the possible imprecision of the unit of measurement: "the volume." For example, should a 5-page pamphlet be given the same weight in the score as a 500-page monograph, how are microfiche to be counted, how are patents? The ACRL standards give minimum guidance on these problems.

One could also argue that the "title" is a more meaningful unit than the "volume" in comparing institutions, especially perhaps in the public library environment. Through purchase of multiple copies of bestsellers and other popular but probably ephemeral items, library A could have many more volumes than B but fewer titles. Library B, however, may have a superior collection in the sense of being richer, better balanced, and more able to meet the needs of a wide variety of users. On the other hand, a public library having several branches will need multiple copies of certain items in order to achieve a balanced collection in each location. In the academic world, some evidence exists that the larger the collection the greater the proportion of duplicates it is likely to have (Drone, 1984).

No formula has yet been developed for the size of public libraries, taking into account many factors as was done by Clapp and Jordan, although an appropriate formula could perhaps be devised based on number of people served (in various categories by age, education, ethnic group, gender), characteristics of local industry, and so on.

The size of a collection means rather little unless current rate of growth is also considered. A long-established library, while very large, could perform poorly in meeting user needs because it is no longer spending enough on new acquisitions. Piternick (1963) argues that rate of growth should be considered in terms of number of volumes rather than percentage increase in the size of the collection. In fact, he presents data that suggest that academic excellence correlates positively with size of collection and with number of volumes added but not with percentage increase in collection size. One obvious reason is the fact that percentage rate of growth tends to be much greater for newer and smaller libraries than for older, larger institutions (Baumol and Marcus, 1973). "Percentage rate of growth" is heavily affected by the weeding policies of various libraries. Voigt (1975) has presented a rather elaborate formula for calculating the rate at which university libraries should be acquiring new materials. A good review of the topic of growth of academic libraries is given by Molyneux (1986).

All other things being equal, one would expect that use of a collection (in number of items borrowed, for example) will increase with the number of items added. However, this is likely to occur only up to a point. Eventually some level of "saturation" will be reached and the addition of further items will have very little, if any, effect on use. This phenomenon was investigated by Hodowanec (1978), whose data, presented in Exhibit 5, show how circulation per student (PSC) varies with the rate at which new items are added to the collection (PSA). As the rate of PSA (per student acquisition) increases, so does the PSC (per student circulation). From the base PSC of 23.64, and base PSA of 2.65, an increase in rate of acquisition of 13% increased circulation by 6%. The PSC continues to increase up to a PSA of 8, when it levels off and a further increase in the rate of acquisition has no effect on circula-

PSC	PSA	Increase in PSC*	Increase in PSA**
23.64	2.65	–	–
25.00	3.00	6%	13%
27.70	4.00	17%	51%
29.90	5.00	26%	89%
31.60	6.00	34%	126%
32.80	7.00	39%	164%
33.50	8.00	42%	202%
33.69	9.10	42%	243%

* Percentage increase calculated from base level PSC of 23.64.
** Percentage increase calculated from base level PSA of 2.65.

Exhibit 5
Incremental increase in per student circulation (PSC) for
corresponding increase in per student acquisition (PSA)

Reprinted (in slightly modified form) with permission of the American Library Association from Hodowanec, G. V. An acquisition rate model for academic libraries. *College & Research Libraries*, 39, 1978, 439-447

tion. Hodowanec's figures, derived from data on circulation and acquisitions in 400 academic libraries in the United States, should not be interpreted as reflecting the acquisition: circulation relationship in any one library. Nevertheless, they do clearly demonstrate the saturation phenomenon. In particular, they show that rather substantial increases in rates of acquisition are needed to achieve modest increases in circulation.

Brophy (1989) also related circulations per student to books per student and to current book acquisitions per student, using data from British polytechnic libraries. He found no discernible patterns in these data.

The saturation phenomenon observed by Hodowanec (1978), based on rates of acquisition in academic libraries, and the saturation phenomenon observed by Detweiler (1986), based on the absolute size of public libraries, suggest that there may exist an optimum size for a particular type of library, at least optimum in terms of attracting circulation. The phenomenon can be related to the findings of D'Elia and Walsh (1985) that library users are unable to detect changes in the quality of the collection until it falls below some minimally acceptable level. This level may well be strongly related to size. If the collection is too small, it satisfies too few of the user needs and little borrowing occurs. As more and more books are added to the collection, assuming that they are selected to match user needs, the satisfaction rate increases and circulation rises. At some point in time, however, the library has added virtually everything it can add to meet the needs of this particular community, so adding at a greater rate or increasing the size of the collection will not improve circulation. Indeed, since larger libraries tend to be more difficult to use than smaller ones, and since very large selections of books may discourage browsing (Baker, 1985, 1986a,b), adding items beyond the optimum size may actually reduce circulation.

Carrigan (1988) presents a graph (Exhibit 6) to show the relationship between investment in a collection (or collection size) and patron satisfaction (or circulation). As the level of satisfaction increases along the curve O-Z, the resources needed to achieve an improvement in satisfaction increase at a disproportionate rate: beyond a certain level of investment, putting further resources into the collection has almost no effect on satisfaction. In fact, any increase in expenditure (collection size) beyond P (Exhibit 6) has no effect at all on level of satisfaction. This phenomenon of diminishing returns, closely associated with the idea of the "90% library," will be dealt with in more detail in Chapter 14.

In the academic environment, a positive correlation has been found between size of library and the quality of the institution, where

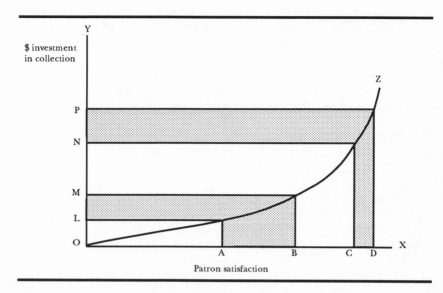

Exhibit 6
Investment in collection plotted against user satisfaction
Reprinted from Carrigan (1988) by permission of the *Library Journal*

"quality" is determined by some established scale of academic excellence (see, for example, Jordan, 1963; Piternick, 1963; and Blau and Margulies, 1974-75). This does not prove that the university or college is great because of its library, but the very fact that library size and academic excellence tend to "go together" gives some credibility to the claim that size is one criterion that has some applicability in the evaluation of collections.

Expert Judgment

One possible way of evaluating the holdings of a library in a particular subject area is to have the collection examined by a specialist in that field, a procedure sometimes referred to as "impressionistic."

The expert could be an outside consultant or a member of the institution itself; a team of specialists could replace the individual in a study of this type. The impressionistic approach has mostly been used in the evaluation of academic and other research libraries.

There are some obvious problems associated with this approach. A subject specialist may not be completely unbiased. Consequently, his evaluation may favor certain aspects or viewpoints within the field, while neglecting others. A subject specialist is not necessarily an expert on the *literature* of that subject, a situation that may be more true in some fields than in others. Moreover, as suggested earlier, the evaluation of a collection requires more than a knowledge of the literature; it requires a thorough understanding of the needs of the users of a particular library. The subject specialist may know the literature well but lack familiarity with the community the library is to serve. This seems especially likely where an outside consultant is used. Finally, if a university's own faculty members are involved in impressionistic evaluation, these may be the very individuals who were most responsible for building the collection in the first place; in this case, they would be evaluating their own efforts – a questionable practice at best.

One variant of the expert judgment approach involves the evaluation of a collection by members of the library staff, using formalized procedures to gather quantitative and qualitative data to assist in identifying areas of strength and weakness. For example, Mosher (1984) describes a method for the systematic analysis of collections, as used by a group of libraries in Alaska. For each class (e.g., economics) the following types of data are collected: number of items, variety of items (different document forms), age of materials, language, and, possibly, circulation records. At the same time, the team performing the analysis checks to see if, for example, "major" authors, works, and periodicals appear in the collection. Burr (1979) used similar methods in an analysis of the collections of an academic library. The data collected for each segment of the collection were: date of publication, language, type of publisher, and whether or not an item appears in a standard bibliography of recommended titles. Descriptive and quantitative data, if collected systematically in this way, can provide very useful input to any impressionistic study, whether conducted by librarians or outside consultants.

Bibliographies Used as Standards

In the impressionistic approach, the expert becomes a kind of "standard" used in the evaluation. In "list checking" or "citation checking," the standard used for evaluation is some type of bibliography, which is checked against the collection to determine what proportion of the items listed is owned.

The first problem faced, of course, is that of finding a suitable bibliography. A few "standard" lists have been compiled to meet special needs (e.g., of recommended books and journals for the small medical library). In other cases, authoritative bibliographies do exist (e.g., the

Cambridge Bibliography of English Literature or the *Handbook of Latin American Studies*). Comer (1981) and Hall (1985) suggest a number of published bibliographies that may be applicable to various evaluation situations.

An existing bibliographic source may be the clear choice for use in certain studies. Suppose one wanted to know how strong the medical libraries of Brazil are in their coverage of the journal literature of biomedicine. The obvious standard to use in answering this question is the National Library of Medicine's *List of Journals Indexed in Index Medicus*, which represents decisions made by a reputable and authoritative body on which journals are most worth indexing. However, even this list would need to be supplemented by a list of Brazil's own biomedical journals, since *Index Medicus* will not be comprehensive in its coverage of these. If the *List* was circulated to all important medical libraries in Brazil, and each indicated which journals they receive, one would discover:

a. what proportion of the journals on the list is accessible in Brazil,

b. how many copies of each title are to be found in Brazilian libraries,

c. which titles are not available in any of the medical libraries,

d. the comparative strengths of the various libraries in coverage of the periodical literature, and

e. the geographic distribution of the coverage (how strong the collections are in each region, each state, or each major city).

For many evaluation purposes, however, no published bibliography will exist. If one does exist, it may not be entirely suitable because it is not completely up-to-date, restricts itself to only one type of publication, has a somewhat different emphasis than that of the collection being evaluated, or for some other reason.

If no suitable published bibliography can be found, it will usually be possible to compile one exclusively for purposes of the study. Consider a situation in which one wants to know how strong is the collection of some academic library on the subject of Cuba – its history, international relations, culture, economics, and so on. One possible approach is to identify a number of scholarly books on various aspects of Cuba, recently published and reviewed favorably in reputable journals. Let us say that six such books are selected. The bibliographic items cited in them (in footnotes, chapter references, or final bibliography) can be assumed to represent the sources needed by the authors of these books in support of their research. Suppose that, once duplicates are eliminated, the six volumes yield 1350 bibliographic references. This list of 1350 items is checked against the collection to discover what proportion is owned. If 1110 of the 1350 items are found to be owned, the coverage of the collection on the subject of Cuba (more correctly, its coverage of information sources needed by Cuba scholars) has been estimated to be about 82%; put differently, the probability of ownership has been set at .82. Of course, the same bibliography of 1350 items could be used to compare the coverage of several libraries – to identify the strongest collections, the amount of duplication, and so on. The question one is attempting to answer in a study of this kind is really "could the research have been done in this library?" The "classic" study of this type is the work of Coale (1965) at the Newberry Library. More recently, Olden and Marsh (1990) have used the technique to evaluate the holdings of four academic libraries in the area of Africa studies.

The method used by Coale is most appropriate for the evaluation of collections intended to support research. However, Bland (1980) has pointed out that bibliographic references in college textbooks might be used in the evaluation of collections in small and medium sized academic libraries. The possibility of using textbooks required in various undergraduate courses as a means of assessing the coverage of an undergraduate library was investigated by Stelk and Lancaster (1990b). The setting was the University of Illinois at Urbana-Champaign and the subject selected was that of religious studies. Four courses in this area were offered during the semester in which the study was performed: in world religions, in the history of Judaism, in Christianity, and in the New Testament. For the Christianity course, there were two required texts, one in Protestantism and one in Catholicism; there was a single text for each of the other courses. All of the bibliographic references in each text were checked against the holdings of the Undergraduate Library and of the University collection as a whole. The results are presented in Exhibit 7.

In four of the five areas the Undergraduate Library consistently owns in the range of 41-46% of the items cited. The fifth area, World Religions, is better covered. This is not surprising: this is an introductory course and most of the sources cited in the text can be considered quite basic. Taken overall, the results show that a student in one of these courses faces almost a 50% chance that an item cited in a required text will be owned by the Undergraduate Library and about an 80% chance that an item cited will be owned somewhere on campus. While there are no real standards against which these results can be compared, subjectively they appear satisfactory for a subject area not given high priority at this university. Of course, these results indicate nothing more than ownership as reflected in the catalogs of the library. No attempt was made to determine the availability of the items.

The study by Stelk and Lancaster confirms that the items cited in required texts may form a useful set to use in evaluating the coverage of an undergraduate collection in some area. The results were of value in showing, perhaps somewhat surprisingly, that the university collections appear stronger in the area of Judaism than in their coverage of Christian religions and the literature of the New Testament.

For some studies, especially in scientific and technical areas, journals are better than monographs as a source of bibliographic references because such references are likely to be more up-to-date. Consider another problem: to evaluate the coverage of an academic medical library on the subject of "tropical medicine." A possible approach is as follows:

1. Identify those subject headings in *Index Medicus* that relate to tropical diseases and other aspects of tropical medicine.

2. Using the latest issues of *Index Medicus*, select a random sample of, say, 100 recently published journal articles appearing under the tropical medicine headings.

3. Acquire all of these articles, combine their bibliographies, and use this combined bibliography as the standard for evaluating the collection. If the mean number of references per article is 8, the bibliography is likely to exceed 700 items, even after elimination of duplicates, and this is large enough to give one confidence in the reliability of the results.*

The justification for this procedure is that the references appearing in recently indexed articles are likely to represent items that users will seek in a medical library. By looking for, say, 700 of these items, one is in effect simulating 700 users of the library, each one seeking a particular item.**

In Step 2, as described above, one should try to obtain all items falling in the random sample, not just those readily available. For example, of the 100 items sampled, it may happen that only 75 are avail-

---

*As an alternative to the *elimination* of duplicates, one might count the number of times a particular reference appears in the several bibliographies. The library evaluated would then get a coverage score, earning more "points" for having an item appearing in several of the bibliographies than it does for one appearing only in a single bibliography.

**Because review articles usually contain more references than other types, it might be possible to restrict the sample to review articles. For example, in biomedicine, the sample could be drawn from the *Bibliography of Medical Reviews*.

able in the library being evaluated. The other 25 should be obtained from other libraries. The reason is that a journal will tend to cite itself

Subject	Number of references	Owned by Undergraduate Library		Owned by University Library	
		#	%	#	%
World religions	136	84	62	120	88
Judaism	476	220	46	420	88
Catholicism	86	38	44	69	80
Protestantism	62	28	45	50	81
New Testament	412	171	41	301	73
Totals	1172	541	46	960	82

Exhibit 7
Results of an evaluation of an undergraduate collection
in the area of religious studies

more than it cites other journals and more than other journals cite it. By drawing sources exclusively from journals owned by the library, the possibility exists that the sample will be biased in favor of the library. This was a possible defect of the study reported by Nisonger (1983), who drew references exclusively from six major political science journals likely to be in all political science collections of any size. This may not be too important in the comparison of libraries, since the standard remains the same for each, but it is likely to overestimate the completeness of any one collection. (But see the results of Porta and Lancaster (1988), as discussed later.)

The evaluation of a library collection in a specialized subject area is much the same as the evaluation of the coverage of a database in electronic or printed form. Somewhat similar procedures could be used to evaluate the coverage of, say, *Biological Abstracts* in some specific subject. In fact, studies of this kind have been reported by Martyn and Slater (1964) and Martyn (1967).

Even if a "standard" bibliography on some subject exists, the specially-prepared bibliography has obvious advantages. This can be illustrated by another case: the coverage of an agriculture library on the subject of irrigation. An authoritative bibliography on irrigation would only cover the "core" of irrigation. But "literature of irrigation" is not quite the same as "literature needed to support research on irrigation," which is much broader in scope. By drawing samples of irrigation articles, and taking their references, one is assembling a bibliography that will include items dealing centrally with irrigation as well as items drawn from peripheral subject fields.

The situation is illustrated in Exhibit 8. Writers on irrigation will cite sources on irrigation itself, on sciences closely related (agriculture, hydraulics), on other technical subjects, and on a wide variety of very peripheral topics (e.g., mathematics, statistics). The specially-prepared bibliography, then, provides a true test of the ability of the library to supply the wide range of materials needed to support research on irrigation. This is a more realistic evaluation than one focusing exclusively on the core of irrigation itself.

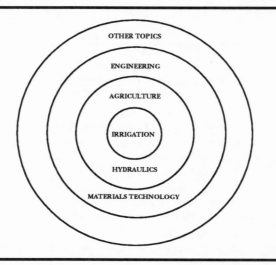

Exhibit 8
Sources cited in articles on irrigation

Many "standard" lists, besides concentrating solely on the core materials of some field, cover only those materials supposedly "the best" or "most obvious" – the kinds of things most libraries collecting in this area are likely to have. Such lists are of limited use as evaluative tools and of no use at all if they have been used by the library as tools in book selection.

It is not enough to use the list-checking approach solely to establish a probability of ownership. As emphasized in Chapter 1, evaluation should be diagnostic. In this case, the diagnostic element will involve a determination of what types of materials the library covers well and what types it does not cover well. That is, it will be necessary to compare the characteristics of the items owned with the characteristics of those not owned – by type of publication, by language, by date, by source, by subfield, by specificity – so that it will be possible to discover in what way the collection needs to be strengthened. It should be noted that diagnostic analysis of this kind requires larger samples than would be needed simply to establish a probability of ownership. A sample of 300 is quite reliable in estimating the coverage of a collection but one might need 1000 or more references to learn anything useful about what items or types of items are missing from the collection.

A more complex approach to the evaluation of an academic library collection has been used by Lopez (1983). It involves checking for ownership of a group of items, selecting references from those found, looking for these items, selecting more references, and so on, up to four or five levels of search. This method is illustrated in Exhibit 9.

Procedure	Number of references produced	Ideal score	Library owns	Possible score	Actual score
Select 5 books					
LEVEL 1 Select 20 references from each	100	5 x 100 = 500	80	500	5 x 80 = 400
LEVEL 2 Select middle reference from each of 80 found	80	10 x 100 = 1000	45	800	10 x 45 = 450
LEVEL 3 Select first reference from each of 45 found	45	20 x 100 = 2000	23	900	20 x 23 = 460
LEVEL 4 Select last reference from each of 23 found	23	40 x 100 = 4000	11	920	40 x 11 = 440
Totals	248	7500	159	3120	1750

Exhibit 9
The Lopez method of collection evaluation

The process begins with the selection of five books on some subject area. The books are chosen on the basis of their quality (as determined by reviews) and relevance to faculty research interests. From each, twenty references are selected from "different and staggered sections of the bibliographies" (Lopez is vague about how this is actually done). The 100 items thus identified are checked against the collection.

In the hypothetical situation illustrated in Exhibit 9, eighty are found. The *middle** reference in each of the eighty is then located. Of these eighty references, the library is found to own forty-five. The *first* reference in each of these is selected, and so on up to four or five levels.

Note that the "ideal score" is the one that a library would achieve if it owned every item at every level. The "possible score," on the other hand, is the maximum score a library could achieve at each level after elimination of items not found at the preceding level. The scoring system depicted in Exhibit 9 represents a doubling of values from one level to the next. This is justified on the grounds that, as one moves from level to level, the material becomes older and more difficult to trace. This method of scoring might be considered appropriate for use in the humanities and social sciences. In science and technology, however, one would reverse the procedure, giving the higher scores to the earlier levels (more recent materials).

As Lopez applied the method, "library owns" implies more than location in the catalog. It means that the item was physically located, if necessary after repeated searches over several weeks.

The method is intriguing. However, the end result is merely a numerical score for the library (Lopez refers to it as a "qualitative index") that can then be compared with the "ideal" or "possible" scores. A numerical score of this kind would only have value in comparing two different libraries, using the same five books as the starting point in each, or comparing the collections of one library in different subject fields (i.e., with the starting point varied by use of books selected from different disciplines). Its value as a tool for comparison is diminished, however, if the method fails to give consistent results when different samples are drawn using the same procedures. Nisonger (1980) has found evidence that significantly different scores can be obtained when different references are selected from the books originally chosen. Nisonger, however, used smaller samples than those recommended by Lopez.

Other criticisms can be leveled at the technique. The selection of references at each level would be better achieved by random sampling. More importantly, a possible bias exists in favor of the library being studied. The procedure would be much better if the evaluator obtained *every item at each level*, where necessary from other libraries, and drew a random sample from the complete universe of references at each level. As mentioned earlier, the tendency for self-citation (an

---

*If all bibliographic references – in footnotes, at ends of chapters, and so on – were in one list, the one selected would be the one in the middle of the list.

author tends to cite himself, a journal tends to cite itself) may cause a bias if each succeeding level of references is chosen only from items known to be in the library. In fairness, however, it has not yet been proven that these changes would make any significant difference to the library score.*

Some investigators have evaluated the collection of a university library on the basis of references contained in faculty publications or in doctoral dissertations produced in the university (e.g., Buzzard and New, 1983). This approach is of doubtful validity. Several investigations have shown that the "principle of least effort" has a major effect on information-seeking behavior: the more accessible an information source, the more likely it is to be used (Rosenberg, 1966, 1967; Allen and Gerstberger, 1966, 1968). More specifically, Soper (1972, 1976) has produced results to suggest that accessibility influences citation behavior — the more accessible the source, the more likely it is to be cited. If writers are more likely to cite sources readily available in their institutional library than to cite sources not so available, an evaluation of the collection on the basis of these citations introduces a definite bias in favor of the library. Rather than use internally generated dissertations, for example, it would be preferable to draw bibliographic references from those produced in comparable departments in other universities (i.e., departments with similar research interests). In terms of overall coverage, the difference between using internally produced dissertations and ones externally produced will not necessarily be dramatic (e.g., Popovich, 1978, estimated coverage at 88% based on the former and 84% based on the latter). Nevertheless, one is less likely to discover serious gaps in the collection, such as an important series of technical reports, from internal citation than one is from external.

Peat (1981) criticizes the procedures most frequently applied to measure in-house use of a library (see Chapter 4). He proposes that the bibliographic references appearing in faculty publications be taken as an indicator of which items added to the library's collection have received "research" use and which have not. This proposal assumes that all bibliographic items are equally "citable" and that items cited are the only ones used. The method Peat advocates has been used by McCain and Bobick (1981) in the evaluation of periodicals in a biology library.

The use of specially-prepared bibliographies is appropriate in evaluating the collection of a scholarly library on a subject by subject basis. It has little relevance, however, to public libraries because cita-

---

*See Porta and Lancaster (1988), as discussed later in the chapter.

tion is not really applicable to much of the material that public libraries deal with. For instance, cookbooks tend not to cite other cookbooks, so it would be quite difficult to compile a bibliography useful in evaluating a library's collection of this type of publication. In point of fact, the specialized or scholarly library is easier to evaluate than the popular library: user needs tend to be more sharply defined, as well as more homogeneous, and it is easier to identify appropriate standards for evaluation (e.g., scholarly bibliographies). The public library presents much more complex problems because of its generality, the heterogeneity of the user community and the demands placed upon it by that community, and the lack of clear evaluation standards.

Nevertheless, Goldhor (1973, 1981b) has developed a different form of list checking that does have applicability in the public library environment. He points out that the titles checked against a list in some subject area may represent only a small percentage of a library's holdings in this field but the checking process tells us nothing about the other items in the collection. In Goldhor's "inductive method," rather than checking a list against the collection, portions of the collection are checked against reputable book-reviewing and other selection tools. The underlying assumption is that the more of these tools a book appears in, the more desirable it is, at least if the reviews are positive. It is thus possible to give each book checked a numerical score based upon the number of sources in which it appears. This procedure gives results quite different from those obtained through the bibliographic checking procedures discussed earlier. It may give some indication of the quality of a collection, but does not evaluate its coverage or suggest how the collection might be improved. It cannot be used to establish a probability of ownership – i.e., it tells us nothing about things that should perhaps be in the collection but are not. The inductive method is more applicable to the evaluation of "popular" collections (public libraries and perhaps undergraduate libraries) than it is to collections designed to support research, although a similar procedure was used by Burr (1979) as one element in the evaluation of the collections of a university library.

A new opportunity for collection evaluation arises from the widespread adoption of online bibliographic searching by libraries. Since the searches performed reflect current information needs of certain users, the bibliographic references retrieved can be considered to represent the current document needs of these users (i.e., if a search has been successful, the items retrieved will be those the requester will seek in the library). A library could use sampling of search results (selection of searches by random sampling, selection of references by random sampling, or both) as a means for the continuous monitoring of the collection. While this might be most applicable to a special library, it could also be useful in more general libraries, including public libraries. This measure was proposed, but not elaborated on, by Cronin (1985). One example of the use of this technique can be found in an article by Seba and Forrest (1978) who compared the results of online searches with library holdings to identify periodical titles held that appeared to be nonproductive as well as productive titles not held by the library. Sprules (1983), however, has discussed some of the problems involved in trying to use online searches to assist periodical cancellation decisions in an academic library. In a much earlier study, Bourne and Robinson (1973) used printouts from a Selective Dissemination of Information (SDI) service in collection evaluation.

Some writers (see, for example, Oberg, 1988) have referred to the RLG (Research Libraries Group) Conspectus project as an evaluation method, but this is misleading. A library that applies the Conspectus criteria does not really evaluate the strength of its collection in various subjects but merely identifies its stated collection development policies in these areas.

Various possible sources from which samples can be drawn for collection evaluation purposes have been reviewed in this chapter. A summary of the possibilities is given in Exhibit 10.

Bibliographies against collection	Collection against bibliographies
Standard lists	Inductive method (Goldhor)
Specially prepared lists drawn from:	
Monographs (Coale, Lopez) College textbooks Indexing/abstracting services Selected journals (Nisonger) Faculty/student publications Results of bibliographic searches	
Collections of other libraries (overlap)	

Exhibit 10
Sources for bibliographic checking

A rather complete set of criteria for the assessment of a collection is included in the *Pacific Northwest Collection Assessment Manual* (1990). One important element in these assessment procedures is the checking of the collection against standard bibliographies to determine if the principal authors and works are adequately represented.

Comparing Different Sources for Bibliographic Checking

Porta and Lancaster (1988) have compared the results achieved when evaluating a collection on the basis of samples drawn from different types of source. The study was performed in the field of irrigation at the University of Illinois. A sample of 500 items was drawn completely at random from *Irricab*, volume 10 (1985). Of these, precisely 250 were found to be owned by the University of Illinois and 250 not. Based on this sample, then, the coverage was estimated at exactly 50%. Of the 250 items owned by the University, 174 (70%) were available in the Agriculture Library and the remaining seventy six (30%) were scattered over the other campus libraries.

A subsample was drawn from each of these sets. From the 174 items in the Agriculture Library, forty eight were selected at random. Of these, five included no bibliographic references and eight could not be located on the shelves. Six further articles contained more than fifty bibliographic references each. These six were dropped on the grounds that their inclusion would "swamp" the references from the other sources. The twenty nine items remaining (48-5-8-6) contained 396 bibliographic references. When these were checked against the holdings of the University of Illinois, it was found that the coverage was 339/396 (86%).

A similar procedure was applied to the *Irricab* items located on campus outside the Agriculture Library. There were seventy six of these and twenty five were selected at random. Among these twenty five, four included no references, three could not be located, and one contained more than fifty references (and was therefore discarded). The seventeen articles remaining yielded 154 bibliographic references. The coverage of the University of Illinois, based on this sample, was 97/154 (63%)

From the original 250 *Irricab* items not owned by the University of Illinois sixty nine were chosen at random and interlibrary loan requests were placed for these. Of these sixty nine, twenty four could not be obtained.* Of the remaining forty five, twelve included no references and two had more than fifty each. The remaining thirty one yielded 269 references. When these were checked against the University's holdings, 155 (58%) were found to be owned.

The final sample was drawn from three journals owned by the University and considered "core" journals in irrigation, namely *Advances in Irrigation*, *Irrigation Science* and *Journal of Irrigation and Drain-*

---

*Eighteen of these items could not be located in any U.S. library. The other six were incomplete citations that could not be verified.

age Engineering. Five hundred bibliographic references were drawn at random from the articles published by these journals in 1985. When these 500 items were checked against the holdings of the University, it was determined that the coverage was 388/500 (78%). Only twenty one of the 500 references were cases of journal self-citation. When these items were omitted, the coverage of the University of Illinois was determined to be 367/479, or 77%. The results of all of these methods for estimating coverage are summarized in Exhibit 11.

Sample	Source	Coverage	
1	*Irricab*	250/500	50%
2	Items referred to (cited) by *Irricab* sample		
	a) sample items in Agriculture Library	339/396	86%
	b) sample items in other University libraries	97/154	63%
	c) sample items obtained on interlibrary loan	155/269	58%
	d) combined University sample (a + b)	436/550	79%
3	Items referred to (cited) by recent articles in three core journals owned by University		
	a) self-citation included	388/500	78%
	b) self-citation omitted	367/479	77%

Exhibit 11
Comparison of coverage estimates based on different samples

The most obvious conclusion to be drawn from this exercise is that one can obtain widely divergent estimates of the coverage of a collection in some specialized subject field depending upon the source of the sample used in the study. *Irricab* was probably not a good choice to use in drawing the initial sample. While comprehensive in its coverage, it includes too many obscure items (e.g., reports from ministries in developing countries) that one would not be likely to find in any library in the United States. This was confirmed when items were sought on interlibrary loan – many could not be located anywhere.

From the *Irricab* sample one might reasonably conclude that the University of Illinois acquires about half of all items published on the topic of irrigation (not, in any case, a major focus of research at this institution). This is a little misleading. The University undoubtedly owns more than half the irrigation items that faculty and students would be likely to look for. In this case, the items cited by the original sample may be more representative of the needs of library users.

The difference in coverage estimates derived from samples 2(c) and 2(d) is not at all surprising. The University seems to own about 79% of the items cited by the irrigation items *it owns* but only about

58% of the items cited by the irrigation items *it does not own*. Two contributing factors cause this situation:

1. The items not owned by the University are in some sense more
"obscure," at least in terms of the needs of this institution. These
obscure items cite other obscure items. For example, a report from a
ministry of agriculture in some Middle East country will cite other reports from the same ministry.

2. Many journals tend to cite themselves more than they cite other
journals. The University is more likely to own a source cited by a journal it owns than a source cited by a journal it does not own.

The wide discrepancy between the coverage estimate of 2(a) and that
of 2(b) is much more difficult to explain. Since the coverage of the University libraries as a whole was considered, and not just the coverage of
the Agriculture Library, there is no logical reason why items cited by
items owned by the Agriculture Library should be covered more completely than items cited by items located elsewhere on campus (e.g., in
the Engineering Library or the Geology Library).

The most encouraging feature of these results is the remarkable
consistency that exists between the results for sample 2(d) and those
for 3(a) or 3(b). It seems that the University of Illinois Library owns
about 77-79% of items cited by irrigation publications *that it owns*.

The test of the effect of journal self-citation (samples 3(a) and
3(b)) was completely inconclusive. As it happens, these three irrigation
journals do not cite themselves very much at all. Unfortunately, two of
the three journals are quite recent in origin so the chance of self-
citation is greatly reduced. The results from this study should not be
construed to mean that journal self-citation need not be considered in
sampling for purposes of collection evaluation. Self-citation rates vary
greatly from subject area to subject area and from journal to journal.

Another interesting comparison has been performed by Oliveira
(1990). Using the subject of soil science as a test case, he compared estimates of coverage for the University of Illinois with samples of bibliographic references drawn from three sources: periodical articles,
monographs and dissertations. The major results are shown in Exhibit
12. The sample drawn from dissertations gives the highest coverage
estimate, the sample drawn from monographs gives the lowest. The
differences in coverage estimates based on the three samples are statistically significant.

It is not surprising that the dissertations yield the highest estimate
of coverage since about 66% of the references were drawn from University of Illinois dissertations: doctoral candidates are more likely to

cite locally available sources than to cite sources not available locally. Nevertheless, the library owns a high proportion of the sources cited in dissertations from other universities. Coverage based on local dissertations is estimated at 94.8%, while coverage based on external dissertations is estimated at 85.3%.

Type of source	Total # of bibliographic references	Sample size	Owned No.	%	Not owned No.	%
Monograph	10,514	1,200	923	77	277	23
Periodical	4,268	1,200	1,046	87	154	13
Dissertation	2,157	1,050	961	91	89	9

Exhibit 12
Estimates of the coverage of a university library collection based on
samples of references drawn from three types of source
From Oliveira (1991) by permission of the author

The sample based on references drawn from monographs gives a significantly lower estimate of coverage. The monographs, in this field at least, cite a higher percentage of sources that are "difficult" and thus less likely to be owned: non-English materials (17% of all references drawn from monographs as opposed to 8% and 4% for samples drawn from periodicals and dissertations), non-periodical articles (44% as opposed to 33-35% for the other two samples), and older materials. The type of source cited, in itself, can make a significant difference in the estimates since the University of Illinois, in most subject fields at least, is much more likely to own a periodical than it is to own a monograph.

Oliveira also tested the replicability of the results achieved from the three sources of references. By drawing random subsamples from his samples, he found that subsamples drawn from the monographic sources give statistically significant differences in coverage estimates (a high of 331/400 and a low of 288/400), while the subsample estimates drawn from the periodical article references were statistically equivalent, as were the estimates based on the dissertation-drawn subsamples. The sources cited in the monographs represent considerable diversity, thus one subsample is rather different from another. The subsamples drawn from the other sources, however, are much more alike. In particular, periodical articles and dissertations both cite the same set of core journals in soil science time and time again.

Oliveira's study suggests that references drawn from monographs provide the most stringent test of an academic library collection.

Nevertheless, the fact that different samples may yield statistically different results casts doubt on the value of using such samples in arriving at coverage estimates, although they may still be reliable in indicating areas of strength and weakness in the collection. It seems clear from this study that a serious evaluation of a collection in a particular subject area should draw references from both periodical articles and monographs.

While different types of samples may lead to different scores for a single library, they may not lead to different conclusions in the comparison of libraries. In comparing the holdings of four academic libraries in the area of Africa studies, Olden and Marsh (1990) found that changes in the composition of the set of items on which the comparison was based had a rather minor effect:

> It is noteworthy, however, that with extremely few exceptions the ranking of the collections in terms of percentage of items owned remains consistent regardless of whether the data were analysed for material type, publication year grouping, published in or out of Africa, or specific country of publication. (Page 186)

Checking Bibliographies Against Collections and Collections Against Bibliographies

Elzy and Lancaster (1990) have checked bibliographies against collections and collections against bibliographies (the inductive method) to determine what can be learned from each approach and how they might complement each other. The setting of the study was the Teaching Materials Center (TMC), Milner Library, Illinois State University (ISU). In support of the University's extensive education programs, Milner Library maintains a collection of books and other materials relating to all types and levels of teacher training. As an adjunct to this resource, it also provides a collection of trade books, textbooks, curriculum guides, and a variety of other media designed for use by students of preschool through grade 12 age. The present study was restricted to the nonfiction book collection of the TMC.

In principle there is no reason why bibliographies appropriate for use in the inductive method should not also be used in the reverse procedure. The difference between approaches does not relate to differences in the bibliographic sources used but to how they are applied. Four bibliographies were chosen for use in this study:

1. *Children's Catalog* (CC) (H. W. Wilson). The fifteenth edition and its supplements.

2. *Elementary School Library Collection* (ESLC): *a Guide to the Books and Other Media*. Sixteenth edition. Williamsport, Pennsylvania, Brodart, 1988.

3. *Building a Children's Literature Collection* (BCLC): *a Suggested Basic Reference Collection for Academic Libraries and a Suggested Basic Collection of Children's Books*. Third edition, ed. by H. B. Quimby and M. M. Kimmel. Middletown, Connecticut, Choice, 1983.

4. *Best Books for Children* (BBFC): *Preschool Through the Middle Grades*. Third edition, ed. by J. T. Gillespie and C. B. Gilbert. New York, Bowker, 1985.

None had been used as a book selection tool in TMC.

Systematic samples were drawn from the nonfiction shelflist of the TMC and from the four bibliographic sources, using a regular sampling interval after a random start, the objective being to arrive at a sample of approximately 400 items. Selection began with the twenty third item in the shelflist, and every forty fifth item was chosen thereafter. This procedure produced a sample of 398 items from the 18,350 items represented. To go in the opposite direction, a similar procedure was used. The total number of nonfiction items in the four sources was calculated to be about 12,000. Beginning with the seventeenth title in the combined list, every twenty eighth item was selected, giving a sample of 434 items. The 398 items in the shelflist sample were checked against the four bibliographies to determine how many included them, and the 434 items in the bibliography sample were checked against the holdings of the library to determine if they were owned or not. Only holdings of the TMC were considered and only exact matches (e.g., identical editions) were counted. All items were checked by name of author; if this failed, they were rechecked by title.

The major results of the study are summarized in Exhibit 13. The TMC owns 195/434 of the titles drawn from the four bibliographies, about 45%. Note that thirty two of the items fell into the samples for two of the sources, and eighteen of these are owned (56%), while one item fell into the samples drawn from three of the four sources; this item is owned. Coverage is best for items from BCLC (11/14, or 79%) and worst for the ESLC sample (46/114, or 40%).

Turning to the inductive sample one can see that most of the items in the TMC (310/398, or about 78%) are not listed in any of the selection tools, and only a handful of items are listed in two or more of the tools. However, this is somewhat misleading in that many of the items in the inductive sample are older items, now out of print, that might not be well covered in the four reviewing sources. In fact, CC and ESLC cover only items in print. Of the 114 items in the sample that are in print (because so identified in *Books in Print* or *Children's Books in Print*), exactly half (57/114) are reviewed in at least one of the sources. In contrast, only thirty one of the 284 out of print items (about 11%) appear in one or more of the reviewing sources.

Source	Inductive Sample				Bibliographic Sample		
	In Print	Out of Print	Total		Owned	Not Owned	Total
In all four sources	5	0	5		0	0	0
In three of the sources	19	1	20		1	0	1
In two of the sources	8	7	25		18	14	32
CC	0	1	1		50	62	112
ESLC	3	2	4		46	68	114
BBFC	12	18	30		69	92	161
BCLC	0	2	2		11	3	14
In no source	57	253	310		0	0	0
Totals	114	284	398		195	239	434

Exhibit 13
Inductive sample results compared with bibliographic sample results

These results raise the obvious question of how much the poor scores for the out-of-print books reflect the fact that the reviewing sources omit many such items or, instead, indicate that the material selected for the TMC in earlier days was of lower quality. As a test of this, items in the inductive sample were also checked against the holdings of four other large curriculum collections in Illinois – those at the University of Illinois (Urbana-Champaign), Chicago State University, Southern Illinois University (Carbondale), and Northeastern Illinois University. The results of this study are given in Exhibit 14.

If "held in at least one other center" is considered a criterion of quality, 211/398 of the items in the inductive sample qualify; i.e., about 53%. The difference between in-print and out-of-print items is not dramatic: 53/114 in-print items (about 46%) are held by at least one other curriculum center; the comparable figure for out-of-print items is 158/284, about 56%.

Exhibit 15 gives a score to each item in the inductive sample. This score represents the number of sources/centers it appears in, putting the four reviewing sources and the five curriculum centers (including

the TMC) on an equal footing. It can be seen that 44/114 (39%) of the
in-print items held by ISU and 116/284 (about 41%) of the out-of-print
items held by ISU (total 160/398, or 40%) appear in no reviewing
source and none of the other major curriculum centers in Illinois.

Curriculum Centers	In Print Items	Out-of-Print Items	Totals
Held by all four	4	7	11
Held by three centers	2	28	30
Held by two centers	21	40	61
Held by one center	26	83	109
Held only by ISU	61	126	187
Totals	114	284	398

Exhibit 14
Results of comparison of ISU's inductive sample with holdings
of four other curriculum centers in Illinois

The surprisingly high number of items owned by ISU that appear
in no bibliography and are held by no other library (160/398, or 40%)
prompted the researchers to investigate this group further. The forty
two items receiving scores of five or above in Exhibit 15 were compared to a systematic random sample of forty two items drawn from
the 160 items receiving a score of one. The two groups were compared
by age, classification, last use, and total uses. The median age of the
high-scoring sample was 1971, while the low-score median was 1972.
When broken down by classification, the group of top-scoring items is
fairly evenly scattered among subject areas, while the low-scoring
items are dominated by titles in the social sciences – the 300s in the
Dewey Decimal Classification (18/42 or 43%). The top scoring group
had only slightly higher circulation, averaging 4.1 circulations per title
as opposed to 3.8 circulations per title in the low-scoring group. A
more dramatic difference showed up in the number of titles not used
at all in each group. Those receiving scores of five or above showed
14%, or 6/42 titles, not circulating out of the building. The sample
scoring one had 10/42 not circulating, or 24%.

These data are illustrative of the different types of results obtainable from the two methods of bibliographic checking, and of the different conclusions that can be drawn from them. The TMC owns less
than half of the items recommended in the four tools. By comparing
the characteristics of the books owned with those of the books not
owned, weaknesses in the present collection – in terms of subject areas
or books of a particular type – can be identified. If these weaknesses

are considered significant, in relation to the current interests of ISU, corrective action can be taken. This would involve filling in some of the gaps by purchase of recommended books, where these still seem to be of current interest, or modification of collection development policies to avoid such gaps in the future. The inductive sample reinforces the other sample: it indicates that the TMC may include a large number of books that are not highly recommended; they are not listed in the standard selection tools and do not appear in other major curriculum collections in Illinois. This suggests the need for a rather

Score	In Print Items	Out-of-Print Items	Totals
9	0	0	0
8	2	1	3
7	4	0	4
6	11	3	14
5	12	9	21
4	15	28	43
3	12	46	58
2	14	81	95
1	44	116	160
Totals	114	284	398

Exhibit 15
Scores for items in the inductive sample when compared with
reviewing sources and holdings of other curriculum centers

thorough weeding of the collection to remove from the TMC items not appearing in the standard selection sources except where circulation records for the last few years indicate a strong and continuing demand for particular items.

As a direct result of the study a thorough weeding of the TMC nonfiction collection was undertaken. Criteria used in the weeding primarily involved currency, use, and appearance in selection sources. Over 4,000 volumes were withdrawn or, if appropriate, moved to the main collection in Milner Library. Next, a portion of the TMC book budget was set aside for retrospective collection development. Collection development efforts are focusing on those gaps in subject coverage found in this study. More than just filling in the gaps, however, the overall quality of the collection is being improved by adding up-to-date items that have won favorable reviews or have appeared in selection sources. The bibliographic sample served as a guide to areas in need of attention, while the inductive study confirmed that more attention must be given to making quality selections.

Overlap Studies

Studies of the degree to which the collection of one library over-laps those of others (i.e., of the extent of duplication of titles among li-braries) have been performed for various purposes, as discussed by Potter (1982). Most overlap studies are not performed for collection evaluation per se, although they could be. Overlap studies applied to indexing and abstracting services, in printed or online form, have been undertaken in evaluating the coverage of these services (see for example, Bourne, 1969; and Longo and Machado, 1981).

Suppose one wanted to compare the coverage of two abstracting services, both dealing with the subject of mental health. One can esti-mate the coverage of service A by drawing a random sample of items from service B and one can evaluate the coverage of service B on the basis of a random sample of items from A, as shown below:

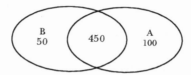

A random sample of 300, drawn from A, is checked against B and a random sample of 300, drawn from B, is checked against A. On the basis of these samples, the following hypothetical estimates are de-rived: that 450/600 (75%) are common to both, that 50/600 (8.3%) items are unique to B, and that 100/600 (16.6%) are unique to A. Another way of looking at this is to consider A as a standard for es-timating the coverage of B and vice versa: using 300 items from A as a standard, B's coverage of the mental health literature is estimated to be 66% (200/300); using 300 items from B as a standard, A's coverage of this literature is estimated to be 83% (250/300).

In principle, there is no reason why a similar technique could not be used to estimate the coverage of the collection of a library in some subject field. For example, the collection of gardening books in public library A could be evaluated on the basis of a random sample of gar-dening books from public library B. In this case, B could be a consider-ably larger library than A. The objective is to determine how complete is collection A on the subject of gardening and to identify types of ma-terials, or even specific titles, that A should have in its collection but does not.

Overlap studies can be used to compare the collections of libraries of all types and even to compare the coverage of libraries of different types. For example, for each of four Illinois communities, Doll (1980) studied overlap and duplication among the public library collections and those of two elementary schools.

Sampling techniques for overlap studies become more complicated when many databases or library collections are involved, or when the entire collection of one library is compared with the entire collection of another. These sampling problems are discussed in detail by Buckland et al. (1975).

In evaluating a collection by checking it against bibliographies, or against some other collection, one is treating it virtually in the abstract since *use* of the collection is not considered. Evaluation through use studies is dealt with in Chapters 3-6.

Study Questions

---

1. The College of Agriculture at the University of Illinois finds itself increasingly involved in supplying consultants to the less developed countries. Since many of the LDC's are situated in the tropics, demand for bibliographic support in the area of tropical agriculture is increasing. There is some feeling, however, that the coverage of the collection in this subject leaves much to be desired. You are asked to evaluate the collection in terms of its ability to support research/consulting in tropical agriculture, and to recommend how the collection in this area might be improved. What exactly would you do?

2. What procedures would you use to compare the coverage of tropical agriculture in two online data bases: AGRICOLA and CAB Abstracts?

3. A public library serving a population of about 100,000 is reputed to have an excellent collection of books on gardening. How might you confirm that this is true?

4. How would you compare a collection of science books held in the children's department of a public library with the science books held in the libraries of the local primary schools?

5. Would it be possible to derive a formula for the minimum size of a public library similar to the formulae developed for the size of academic libraries? What would be the components of such a formula?

3. Evaluation of the Collection: Analysis of Use

The approaches to evaluation discussed in Chapter 2 involve the comparison of a collection with some form of external standard. In the case of the bibliographic checking procedures, the study in effect simulates demands upon the library.

A completely different approach involves an analysis of how the collection is actually used. One objective is to identify strengths and weaknesses in the collection from present patterns of use, thus leading to modifications in collection development policies in order to increase the relevance of the collection to the needs of the users. Another possible objective is to identify little used items so that they can be relegated to less accessible (and less costly) storage areas, or even discarded completely.

The fact that one might modify a collection development policy, affecting future acquisitions, implies that present patterns of use can be taken to be good predictors of future use. Line and Sandison (1974) have expressed doubt about such assumptions. On the other hand, in a classic study at the University of Chicago, Fussler and Simon (1969) collected evidence to suggest that past use is a good indicator of present use and, therefore, present use may well be a good predictor of future use. Newhouse and Alexander (1972) support this view, which appears entirely reasonable because of the considerable inertia likely to exist in a large community of users. In the academic community, reading lists do change, new courses emerge, others disappear; sometimes completely new programs are established or existing ones discontinued. Nevertheless, changes occurring from year to year have only a minor effect on the overall patterns of need and demand; a few things change but much more remains the same. The same is true of the public library community. Unless some quite unpredictable event suddenly occurs – such as a huge and unexpected influx of some ethnic minority into the community – changes in the composition and interests of the population will occur very gradually. In the industrial environment, sudden changes of direction for the organization, as a result perhaps of a merger or the sale of a subsidiary, are somewhat more common. Even here, however, they are the exception rather than the rule.

It seems entirely reasonable to suppose, then, that one can learn much about a collection from a study of what is now being borrowed from it. This chapter will consider the use of circulation data in the evaluation of a collection.

General Patterns of Use

It has long been conjectured, and more recently demonstrated, that the pattern of use of books in a library follows a hyperbolic distribution – a rather small number of items accounts for a large proportion of all the uses and the majority of items are little if ever used. The situation is illustrated in Exhibit 16, where percentage of circulation is plotted against percentage of collection. According to this diagram, while all the collection is needed to account for all of the use, it appears that about 60% of the use is accounted for by only about 10% of the collection, and 80% of the use seems to come from about 20% of the collection.

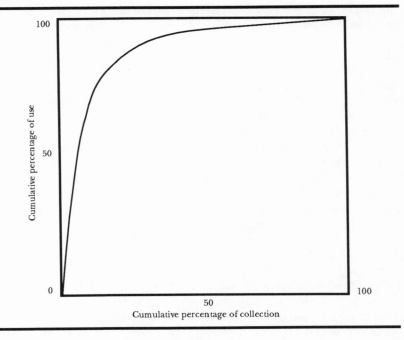

Exhibit 16
Distribution of use of items in a collection

The hyperbolic distribution of Exhibit 16 has been shown to apply to a wide variety of activities involving human selection from a finite number of possibilities (for a complete discussion see Fairthorne,

1969). The use of words in a language (Zipf, 1935) and the scatter of periodical articles over periodical titles (Bradford, 1948) – most human communication is accounted for by a very small number of the words available, most articles on a subject are concentrated in a very small nucleus of highly productive periodicals – are distributions that resemble Exhibit 16 when the data are presented as cumulative percentages. In many cases it has been found that about 80% of use comes from about 20% of the items (whatever they happen to be – words, books, airlines, consumer products), which led to the idea of an "80/20" rule. However, this is nothing more than a rough rule of thumb. While the pattern of use of any book collection will follow a hyperbolic distribution, such as Exhibit 16, the steepness of the curve is likely to vary from one institution to the next. Thus, in library A, 80% of use may come from 20% of the collection while in B it may come from 45%.

Before automation was applied to record-keeping in libraries, the analysis of circulation was based upon drawing samples. As described by Jain (1967), two approaches were possible: the collection sample and the checkout sample. The former involves selecting a random sample of items from the entire collection or from selected subject areas, usually through use of the shelflist, locating the books involved and plotting their circulation history from the earliest use to the present. This was the method used by Fussler and Simon (1969). Clearly, the method will work only if every book carries a card or slip recording the dates of each use. The main purpose of this approach is to determine the rate of obsolescence of the collection in various subject fields – that is, the rate at which use declines with the age of the materials.

The checkout sample, on the other hand, involves the analysis of all items borrowed during a particular period of time – say three selected months during the year. It is used mostly to study the subject distribution of circulation, although it can also yield an estimate of rate of obsolescence when publication dates of items borrowed are analyzed (see Chapter 6).

With automated circulation systems, however, the need for sampling disappears; data can be gathered as a continuous byproduct of the operation of the system. Records representing all circulations rather than a sample can be manipulated by computer program to produce data on subject distribution of the circulation, to identify the most heavily used titles, and (if the data are collected for a sufficiently long period) to measure rate of obsolescence.*

*An "off-the-shelf" circulation system, of course, may not have these features built into it.

The use of automated systems permits an analysis of circulation patterns based upon extensive data collected over a considerable period of time. The most complete study of this type was performed on circulation data for 86 months gathered at the Hillman Library of the University of Pittsburgh (Kent et al., 1979).

The Pittsburgh study gives us the best data available to support the pattern of use illustrated in Exhibit 16. The data are as follows:

Percentage of circulation	Percentage of collection circu- lating at all	Number of items borrowed
20	4	11,593
40	12	33,081
60	23	64,584
80	42	121,018
100	100	285,373

These data are a little misleading because they are based solely on items borrowed during the 86 month period. Approximately half the items in the collection of the Hillman Library were not borrowed at all during this period. To get the relationship between circulation and items owned, then, the values in the center column above can be roughly halved. In other words, 20% of the circulation comes from only 2% of the collection, 40% from 6% of the collection, and so on. Interestingly enough, the Pittsburgh data conform closely to the 80/20 rule.

Even more interesting, perhaps, are the data showing frequency of use of individual titles, as follows:

Number of circulations per year	Number of titles
1	63,526
2	25,653
3	11,855
4	6,055
5	3,264
6	1,727
7	931
8	497

Of those titles that circulate at all during a year, more than half circulate only once; the number that circulate frequently are very few indeed. Moreover, these data show a remarkably regular linear decline: the number of items circulating twice is almost half the number circulating once, the number circulating three times is approximately half the number circulating twice, and so on (see Exhibit 17).

By looking at the circulation data for a group of books acquired in a particular time period, Kent and his colleagues concluded that about 40% of the books added to the Hillman Library had not been borrowed even once in the first six years after they were acquired, and many others had been used only once or twice. If one applied a very modest "cost-effectiveness criterion" of two circulations or more during the lifetime of a book in the library, about 54% of the items should

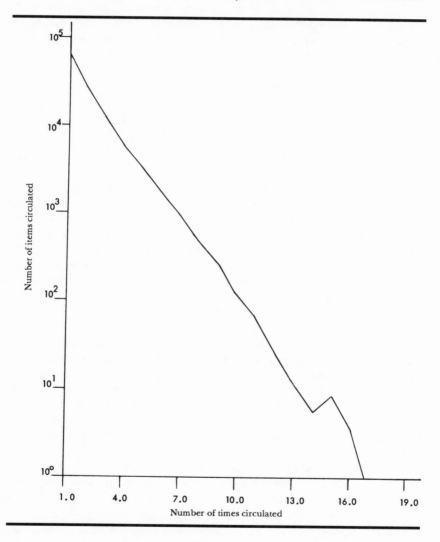

Exhibit 17
Distribution of circulation from University of Pittsburgh study
Reprinted from Kent et al. (1979) by courtesy of Marcel Dekker Inc.

not have been added (i.e., only 46% circulate two or more times). With the criterion set at three or more circulations, about 62% of the items should not have been added.

As one might expect, these findings shocked many people and many were inclined to disbelieve. Nevertheless, similar results have since been obtained in much smaller academic libraries. For example, Hardesty (1981) took a sample of 1,904 books acquired during a six-month period by a small liberal arts college and tracked their circulation for a period of five years. The data are as follows:

Number of circulations	Items circulating this many times in first 3 years after acquisition		Items circulating this many times in first 5 years after acquisition	
	Number	%	Number	%
0	843	44.3	702	36.9
1-5	911	47.8	951	49.9
6-10	118	6.2	166	8.7
11+	32	1.7	85	4.5

These data are not too different from those collected at Pittsburgh. About 44% of the items acquired had not circulated at all after three years and 37% had not circulated at all after five years. The average number of circulations per book after three years was only 1.7 and then rose to only 2.4 after five years. The data collected by Ettelt (1978) in a small community college library are compatible with those of Hardesty and Kent et al. In most subjects, less than half of the books acquired circulated at all.

Some librarians argue that the fact that a book has not been used so far does not necessarily mean that it will never be used. While this is true, it is important to recognize that the longer a book goes without being used the less probable it becomes that it will ever be used. The Pittsburgh data indicate that, when a book is added to the collection, there is little more than one chance in two (1/2) that it will ever be used. If it has not been used after the first two years in the library, the chance that it will ever be used drops to 1/4. If it has not been used after the first six years in the library, the probability that it will ever be used plummets to 1/50.*

Looked at another way, suppose that 5,000 books added to the collection of a library in 1986 have not been used up to the end of 1993 (i.e., after about six years in the library). The data from Pittsburgh

---

*However, in studies performed at a university library in England, Taylor (see Urquhart and Urquhart, 1976) discovered that the proportion of previously unused books that became used was much the same whether the books had been unused for six or for fifteen years. At least, this was true for physics, politics, and English literature. In medicine the length of disuse had a more marked effect.

suggest that only about 1/50 of these books – 100 or so – will ever be used, however long they are retained. Unfortunately, it is almost impossible to predict what this set of 100 will be. An important question for the library to consider is whether or not one can justify retaining 5,000 items for a possible use factor of 1/50.

The distribution of demand, as reflected in Exhibit 16, obviously implies that different books have different levels of "popularity" associated with them. "Popularity" need not be thought of in abstract terms. Indeed, it can be quite precise – expressed as the number of uses a book has received in a particular time period (e.g., five or more uses per year) or in terms of the time elapsing since a book was last used (e.g., not used in the past thirty six months). Buckland (1975) has presented data that suggest that the distribution of demand over the collection of an academic library, assuming six levels of popularity (say from zero uses in a year to five or more uses per year), may look something as follows:

Level of popularity	Percentage of collection	Percentage of demand
A	3	38
B	6	27
C	10	19
D	17	12
E	24	4
F	40	0

Note that, in this particular model, the 80/20 "rule" is almost observed (84% of use comes from 19% of the collection) and 40% of the collection is not used at all.

The measure of "use" discussed so far in this chapter is circulation. Obviously, some books can be used in the library without being borrowed. Total use, then, exceeds recorded circulation. The in-house use of collections is discussed in Chapter 4.

Relative Use

The most obvious application of circulation data is to produce analyses of use of the collection by subject according to the various subdivisions of the classification scheme in use in that library. The Pittsburgh data are again of interest here for they show that, in terms of subject distribution, circulation records for only a few days give results remarkably close to those gathered for the whole period of 86 months. This provides some evidence for the "inertia" mentioned earlier: patterns of use of the collection change very slowly.

It was apparently Jain (1965-1969) who first pointed out that librarians should be less concerned with establishing the absolute use of portions of a collection than with determining "relative" use. What this really means is that one should use circulation data to reveal differences between actual and "expected" (in a probabilistic sense) behavior. Suppose, for example, that books on physics occupy 12% of a particular collection. Probability alone suggests that physics books should account for 12% of the circulation. If they do, that portion of the collection is behaving exactly as expected. On the other hand, if physics books account for only 8% of the circulation, one can say that the class is "underused" (used less than expected) whereas it would be "overused" if it accounts for, say, 15% of all circulation.*

If data on the library's holdings in various classes are built into an automated circulation system, printouts can be generated to show for each class what proportion of the collection it occupies and what proportion of the circulation it accounts for. An example is given in Exhibit 18.

	Collection		Circulation	
Class	Number of books	% of collection	Number of items borrowed	% of circulation
610	172	.17	65	.45
620	309	.31	48	.33
630	524	.52	27	.19
640	602	.60	73	.52
650	144	.14	35	.25

Exhibit 18
Hypothetical "relative use" data for selected subdivisions of Dewey class 600

It is obvious from this table that circulation in 620 and 640 is close to what probability suggests it should be, while classes 610 and 650 are heavily overused and 630 is heavily underused. An automated circulation system could be used to generate such data in a more useful format. In particular, the system can identify those classes that deviate most from the expected behavior – those most overused and those most underused (see Dowlin and Magrath, 1983, for an example based on public library circulation).

The assumption is that the most deviant classes are those that need most attention. The circulation data merely highlight the deviant

---

*An overused class is one in which items are used more than expected (in a probabilistic sense) relative to the proportion of the collection occupied by that class. An underused class is one in which items are used less than expected relative to the proportion of the collection occupied by that class.

classes; they do not tell the librarian how to deal with them. One could argue that both overused and underused classes may fail to meet user needs. If a class is heavily overused (true of 610 in Exhibit 18 which gets almost three times the expected volume of use), the implication is that the library lacks the strength in this area to meet the present volume and variety of demands. The more overused a class, the lower the probability that any particular book will be on the shelf when looked for by a user. Moreover, the more overused the class, the less valuable it will be to the browser because of the phenomenon of "shelf bias."

Shelf bias is best illustrated through a simple example. Consider a brand new branch of a public library. The library has two shelves of books devoted to a popular subject, say personal computers (Exhibit 19). A user enters the new library shortly after it opens. He browses among the personal computer books and decides to borrow those that are most appealing. A second user enters the library an hour later.

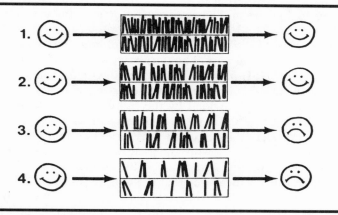

Exhibit 19
The phenomenon of shelf-bias

There is still a good selection of personal computer books available, although not quite as good as before, and this user leaves the library happy. As the day wears on, however, the selection of books available becomes less and less interesting because shelf bias is increasing. Shelf bias, then, refers to the fact that, all other things being equal, the shelves of a library will tend to display books that nobody wants to borrow. The phenomenon was identified explicitly by Buckland (1972) and Buckland and Hindle (1969), who referred to it as "collection bias." This author prefers "shelf bias" because it seems more descriptive of what is actually taking place. Buckland (1975) expresses the bias in terms of the proportion of the material absent from the shelves at a particular time. Thus, if 80 books out of 240 were absent, the bias would be 33%.

A heavily underused class may be just as disturbing as one heavily overused. The class appears not to be of much interest to the community. This may reflect changing interests over time. On the other hand, it may indicate that the selection of books is just not a good one. Perhaps the library is buying the wrong books (e.g., too technical or too theoretical) or that it owns too many books that are out-of-date and should be discarded. It is possible that use of the class would increase substantially if it were thoroughly weeded and more attractive, up-to-date items added.

As stated earlier, circulation data can do little more than bring "problem" classes to the librarian's attention. It is then the librarian's task to look more closely at such classes in order to decide why they are behaving as they are and what corrective action appears to be necessary.

The degree of discrepancy between holdings and circulation can be expressed in several ways. The simplest, perhaps, is the "circulation/inventory ratio" (C/I) used by Wenger et al. (1979), which is nothing more than the number of circulations occurring in a class during a particular period of time divided by the number of items in that class. Thus, a class with seven items and twenty circulations receives a C/I ratio of 2.9 (20/7), i.e., approximately 2.9 uses per item per x period of time (usually a year).* Dowlin and Magrath (1983) also use this but refer to it as "inventory use ratio." The Public Library Association (PLA), in its output measures for public libraries (Van House et al., 1987), uses the term "turnover rate" for the same measure (i.e., uses per item per year). Following the recommendations of the PLA, and of various state library agencies, many public libraries in the United States collect turnover data, although few seem to make intelligent use of them. In fact, the turnover rate for a complete collection is of very little interest (except, perhaps, in comparing the performance of similar libraries). What is of interest is the turnover rate for various parts of the collection. Exhibit 20 gives turnover rates for different classes of adult nonfiction for a small public library in Illinois. The turnover rate

---

*They also suggest the introduction of a time variable, incorporating in the equation the number of days the library was open during the period represented by the use data. Thus $\dfrac{20 \text{ circulations}}{(7 \text{ books}) \times (64 \text{ days})}$ yields a figure of 0.00446 circulations per book per day.

for adult nonfiction as a whole (1.11) masks the fact that the turnover ranges from a low of .51 (about one half of a use per book per year) for class 800 to 1.84 for class 400. The table shows how turnover rate correlates well with relative use. For example, class 400 has high relative use (circulation is almost twice what probability suggests it should be) and the highest turnover, and class 800, with the lowest turnover rate, is used at exactly half the level expected (10% of the collection and 5% of the use). The data from Exhibit 20 suggest that the classes in most immediate need of attention are 800 and 920 since both are heavily underused.

WEST CHICAGO PUBLIC LIBRARY DISTRICT
July 1, 1989 - June 30, 1990
Adult Non-fiction

Class	Holdings	Percentage of nonfiction collection	Circulation	Percentage of nonfiction circulation	Turnover rate
000	527	2	610	2	1.16
100	808	4	1,129	5	1.40
200	665	3	543	2	.82
300	3,339	15	3,361	14	1.01
400	250	1	461	2	1.84
500	1,022	5	1,105	5	1.08
600	4,956	22	7,702	32	1.55
700	3,585	16	4,881	20	1.36
800	2,204	10	1,133	5	.51
900	2,062	9	1,679	7	.81
910	950	4	646	3	.68
920	1,701	8	1,171	5	.69
Totals	22,069		24,421		1.11

Exhibit 20
Collection use data from a small public library in Illinois

Reprinted by permission of the West Chicago Public Library District

Nimmer (1980) has used the measure "intensity of circulation" – number of circulations per 100 titles held. Bonn (1974) proposed a simple "use factor" (renamed as "degree of use" by Gillentine et al., 1981), which is the proportion (or percentage) of the circulation accounted for by a class divided by the proportion of the collection occupied by that class. With this type of ratio, as used by Jenks (1976), the higher the figure the greater the overuse. For example, a class accounting for 3.49% of the collection and 4.79% of the circulation receives a score of 137.25 while one that accounts for .36% of the collection but only .16% of the circulation gets a score of 44.44. Metz (1983) refers to this measure as the "proportional use statistic" and Aguilar (1986) as "percentage of expected use." Aguilar derived his use of this measure from Mills (1982).

Trochim et al. (1980) use the *difference* between holdings percentage and collection percentage for each class as an indicator of overuse or underuse. Mills (1982) is critical of this: a difference of 0.2 would apply equally to a subject occupying 0.5% of the collection and getting 0.7% of the use as it would to one occupying 2.5% of the collection and getting 2.7% of use, yet the proportional discrepancy between holdings and use is very much greater for the smaller class.

Mostyn (1974) uses the term "supply-demand equality" in referring to the relative use relationship; an overused class is one in which demand exceeds supply and vice versa for an underused class.

Mills (1982) has applied the relative use principle to the problems of collection development in a film library. In a typical film library, films have to be "booked" (i.e., reserved) in advance, so it has an advantage over most other types of library in that failure rates (i.e., "denials" – cases when particular films or films of a certain type are not available to the requester) are easy to identify and record. Mills makes use of this failure rate, as well as a measure of relative use, to make decisions relating to future acquisitions. Some of his data are shown in Exhibit 21. The percentage of holdings related to the percentage of bookings gives a percentage of expected use. Thus, art films account for 1% of holdings and 0.88% of bookings, so the percentage of expected use is 88. The denial to bookings ratio brings in further data. A high D/B ratio means that films in this category are unlikely to be available when needed by a user. The worst case is "stories – holidays and seasons," where 74% of the requests for films have to be denied (D/B ratio = 0.74). On the basis of relative use data (percentage of expected use) and D/B ratio, Mills is able to make recommendations relating to future acquisitions: some classes need to be strengthened by further purchases, which might be further copies of things already owned ("add prints"), some need to be weeded, and some should be strengthened and weeded. Note that the decisions are not entirely consistent – for example, "sex education" and "stories – animal" are very similar classes in that both are underused and have low D/B ratios – yet the latter is to be weeded and the former not. This implies a knowledge of the collection, and of the users, that is not directly reflected in the evaluation data. Use data can aid decision-making but they will not make the process completely automatic.

Subject	Holdings (%)	Bookings (%)	Percentage of expected use	Denial to bookings ratio	Collection development recommendations
Art	1.00	0.88	88.00	0.12	
Dance	0.06	0.05	83.33	0.45	Add prints
Drama	.08	0.05	62.50	0.31	
Music	0.71	0.80	112.67	0.17	
Africa	0.33	0.22	66.66	0.12	
Asia	0.52	0.38	73.07	0.15	
Canada	0.14	0.11	78.57	0.18	
Europe & USSR	0.74	0.68	91.89	0.15	
Latin America	0.65	0.78	120.00	0.23	
Maps & Globes	0.24	0.17	70.83	0.33	Add prints
South Pacific	0.05	0.02	40.00	0.07	
US Geography-General	0.24	0.19	79.16	0.17	
US Geography-National Parks	0.08	0.09	112.50	0.12	
US Geography-States & Regions	0.35	0.18	51.42	0.11	Weed
World Geography-General	0.21	0.16	76.19	0.30	
Guidance	1.99	1.41	70.85	0.27	Weed
Health & Hygiene	0.44	0.27	61.36	0.22	Weed
Human Body	0.36	0.27	75.00	0.20	
Nutrition	0.22	0.27	122.72	0.17	
Physical Education	0.12	0.09	75.00	0.40	Add prints
Safety	0.56	0.35	62.50	0.18	Weed
Sex Education	0.08	0.03	37.50	0.07	
Sports	0.14	0.12	85.71	0.14	
Biography	0.12	0.12	100.00	0.24	
US Hist-General	0.34	0.30	88.23	0.22	
US Hist-Discovery & Exploration	0.10	0.09	90.00	0.12	
US Hist-Colonial & Revolutionary Periods	0.51	0.45	88.23	0.12	
US Hist-1732-1900	0.34	0.29	85.29	0.17	
US Hist-1900-Present	0.02	0.01	50.00	0.05	
World History	0.44	0.47	106.81	0.20	
Creative Motivation	0.89	0.73	82.02	0.22	
Foreign Language	0.17	0.26	152.94	0.23	
Library	0.09	0.05	55.55	0.17	
Poetry	0.17	0.12	70.58	0.09	
Reading	0.44	0.30	68.18	0.17	
Speech	0.15	0.10	66.66	0.17	
Stories-Animals	0.81	0.41	50.61	0.18	Weed
Stories-Cartoons & Comedies	0.50	0.32	64.00	0.14	Weed
Stories-General	2.01	1.65	82.08	0.22	
Stories-Holidays & Seasons	0.47	0.19	40.42	0.74	Weed & add prints
Study Skills	0.48	0.34	70.83	0.34	Add prints
Writing	0.31	0.27	87.09	0.22	
Arithmetic Operations	0.61	0.47	77.04	0.13	
Geometry	0.12	0.06	50.00	0.09	

Exhibit 21

Collection use data for a film library

Modified from Mills (1982) by permission of the author

Britten (1990) used the "80/20" rule as the basis of a study of circulation in an academic library. He found that, while the rule seemed to apply to the complete collection, substantial differences among the LC classes could be observed. For one subclass, 40% of the items are needed to account for 80% of the circulations. At the other extreme is a class in which only 1.5% of the items account for 80% of the use. He advocates that the classes that deviate most from the 80/20 distribution in a positive way (a higher proportion needed to account for 80% of the use) should be "rewarded" in future collection development and budget allocation. Clearly, this type of comparison of the performance of various categories of books is merely another variant of relative use or the turnover rate.

In order to make informed decisions, the librarian should have more than the relative use data available. It would also be important to know, for any particular class, what the level of current purchasing is and whether use of the class is increasing or decreasing over time. Consider the following hypothetical data that could be generated from a management information system within a library:

Class	% of collection	% of current acquisitions	% of circulation	Latest year's circulation compared with previous year (%)
y	2.8	3.5	0.2	-15

Class y is very much underused and use continues to decline. This would appear to be a class in which interest is waning and it seems hard to justify the fact that 3.5% of all acquisitions fall in an area that accounts for only 0.2% of current circulation. Similar data for other classes could lead to quite different conclusions. For example, if a class is underused and on the decline but percentage of current acquisitions is well below percentage of collection, the situation seems to have righted itself and no further action is called for.

The more useful data the librarian has available, the more likely it is that collection development decisions will be made wisely. In a coordinated collection development program for Illinois libraries (Krueger, 1983), the following data were collected by each participating library for each subject area of the collection: percentage of collection occupied, percentage of use accounted for, percentage of interlibrary loan requests accounted for, percentage of current acquisitions, percentage of current American publishing output (from *Publishers Weekly* and the *Bowker Annual*), median age of materials used, median age of materials owned, and an "availability" percentage (based on sampling to determine what percentage of books owned in that class was actually available on the shelf when sought). An example of the data collected is shown in Exhibit 22.

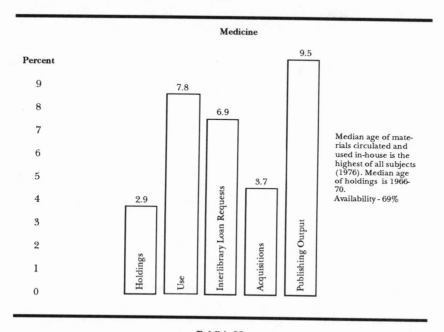

Exhibit 22
Sample of complementary data collected to evaluate the
"medicine" collection of a library

Reproduced from Krueger (1983) by permission of the Illinois State Library

Exhibit 23 gives another example of complementary data useful in collection development decisions. It shows an actual collection evaluation report, for the period July 1, 1989, to June 30, 1990, from a public library in Illinois. For each of the Dewey classes, the following data are presented: percentage of collection, percentage of circulation, turnover rate, percentage of interlibrary borrowings for the past year and percentage of acquisitions for the past year. Note here some classes that seem still to need corrective action. For example, 300 is underused and has a relatively low turnover rate, but interlibrary loans are strong (proportionally more than circulation) and the current acquisition rate is very high. The low circulation and turnover, coupled with the high rate of interlibrary borrowing, suggest that what is being purchased in this class does not fit very well the current interests of users. If better fit to user interests, acquisitions in this class might actually be reduced.

The low turnover rate and discrepancy between collection and circulation percentages further suggest that the class needs some thorough weeding. In contrast, 600 is a heavily overused class; that it now accounts for almost 28% of acquisitions indicates that this fact has been recognized and appropriate corrective action taken.

Class	Collection (%)	Circulation (%)	Turnover rate	Borrowings from other libraries (%)	Acquisitions (%)
000	1.57	1.80	1.12	3.20	2.93
100	4.00	5.10	1.26	7.40	3.90
200	3.46	2.10	0.63	5.30	2.96
300	21.80	16.40	0.738	21.30	25.94
400	0.64	0.60	0.965	1.40	0.67
500	3.75	3.40	0.89	2.60	3.30
600	14.39	25.16	1.70	21.10	27.62
700	16.09	16.69	1.01	14.60	10.98
800	12.83	5.90	0.45	8.10	3.63
900	16.30	17.20	1.03	11.90	13.37
biog.	5.05	5.47	1.06	2.57	4.60

Exhibit 23
Collection evaluation report, for the period July 1, 1989, to June 30, 1990, for a public library in Illinois

The librarian should look at fine circulation data rather than coarse to avoid jumping to the wrong conclusions. The fact that Dewey class 600 is overused does not necessarily mean that the entire class is overused; it may be that only the cookbooks are overused and all other subdivisions are actually underused. Likewise, overuse of Library of Congress class QA may suggest the need for strengthening of the entire mathematics collection when, in fact, it is only the computer science books that are affecting the results. Trochim et al. (1980) provide detailed instructions on gathering relative use data by taking circulation samples and either (a) stack samples or (b) shelflist samples.*

---

*All three samples can be considered to have some bias. Clearly, circulation samples are biased toward the more popular items while stack samples and shelflist samples are biased toward less used iems. For certain types of analysis such biases may not be important. For other types of analysis, they might be. For example, a shelflist sample is inappropriate for use in an *availability* study because it will contain too many items unlikely to be in demand.

Of course, automated circulation systems can yield data that are finer than gross use patterns; use of small subclasses or even individual titles can be examined. One example of this type of analysis can be found in Britten and Webster (1992), who analyzed MARC records for titles heavily used within an academic library in an attempt to identify common characteristics that might predict use of future additions to the collection. Common elements examined were subject heading, author, language, and imprint date.

While automated circulation systems can be used to generate more and better data than any previously available, they are not essential to the type of analysis discussed in this chapter. Before computers were applied in libraries at all, McClellan (1956) adopted an ingenious technique for monitoring use of a collection in a public library. On one selected day each month, he had members of his staff perform a count of the number of books on the shelf and the number in circulation for each subdivision of the classification scheme. The data thus collected would look as follows:

Class	On shelf	In circulation
610	128	44
620	200	109
630	321	203
640	501	101
650	89	55

These figures can serve the same purpose as the relative use figures discussed earlier. They can be converted into percentage use factors. In the case of class 650, 38% of the collection (55/144) was in use when this sample was taken, whereas only 17% of class 640 was in use.

Once more, the most deviant classes can be identified by this procedure. The hypothetical data presented, for example, suggest that considerable shelf bias may exist in class 650 but much less in 640 or 610. McClellan was able to use this method to identify classes requiring attention and then to observe the effects of his actions over a period of time – e.g., the effect of a drastic weeding of one of the subclasses or the effect of a large influx of new books. He also used the method as a key factor in allocating the book budget over the various classes. Clearly, the data collected clerically by McClellan could be generated automatically by computer. That is, if holdings data are recorded in a circulation system, printouts can be produced for any selected day to show the proportion of each subclass on loan at that time.

Last Circulation Date

Trueswell (1964-1969) has used and described an ingenious procedure for estimating what proportion of the collection accounts for what proportion of the use or, more importantly, to identify *which* books account for a specified proportion of the use. The "last circulation date" (LCD) method requires that one collect only two dates: the date on which a book is borrowed in a current circulation period and the date on which it was last previously borrowed. Suppose, for example, that "current circulation period" is defined as all books borrowed in January 1994. For each book borrowed on January 2, this date is recorded along with the date on which this book was last previously borrowed (as recorded on date slip or book card), and likewise for January 3, 4, and so on. At the end of the month of data gathering, current circulation percentages can be plotted against the time elapsing since items were last previously borrowed, as shown in Exhibit 24.

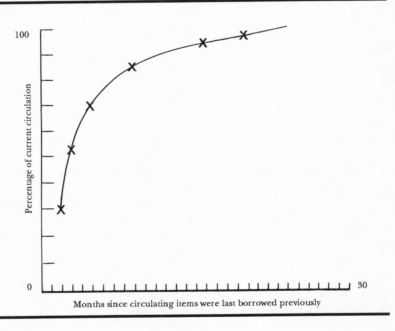

Exhibit 24
Plot of results from last circulation date method

The hypothetical data of Exhibit 24 can be interpreted as follows: about 30% of current circulation is accounted for by books that were borrowed at least once in the two months immediately preceding the current circulation, about 50% were borrowed in the preceding three months, and so on. It appears from the diagram that about 90% of the use is accounted for by items last previously borrowed within the preceding sixteen months.

If one removed from the shelves of the library all books that have not circulated within the last sixteen months, the books remaining there can be expected to account for about 90% of future circulations. The method can thus be used to establish a cut-off for retiring portions of the collection to less accessible storage areas or to identify a "core" collection likely to account for a specified percentage of future use – the 90% library, the 95% library, or whatever. Trueswell, in fact, has used the method to identify the volumes that should appear in a 99% library. In one academic library this was found to be 40% of the collection (i.e., 40% would account for 99% of the circulation); in a second it was found to be a mere 25% of the collection.

Underlying the LCD method is the fact that most books now being borrowed were previously borrowed in the fairly recent past and very few books are now borrowed that have sat unused on the shelves for a long period of time. This has been confirmed in a number of different ways, perhaps most dramatically by Metz (1980):

> At the Virginia Polytechnic Institute and State University, a collection of over one million volumes, a "rolling" or "on the fly" conversion to brief machine readable circulation records was in place for only *four-and-one-half months* before the probability that an item being brought to the circulation desk would already have been entered in the system reached .50. Only some 57,000 items had been entered in the system at this halfway point. (Pages 29-30)

Slote (1989) uses the term "shelf-time period" to refer to the length of time a book remains on the shelf between circulations.* He describes a number of methods that can be used to gather shelf-time data, depending largely on the type of circulation system in use. The shelf-time approach is essentially the same as the LCD approach. Slote claims that reliable shelf-time data for a collection can be obtained from as few as 500 consecutive transactions.

Exhibit 25 gives Slote (or LCD) data, reported by Williams (1986), for two classes of materials in an academic library. Note that 67% of the humanities items and 74% of the teacher education items returned from circulation in October 1983 had been borrowed at least once

---

*In actual fact, a distinction is made between "closed-end" and "open-end" shelf time. The former is the time elapsing between the last two recorded circulations while the latter is the time between the last circulation and the date the observation is made.

previously in 1983. Eighty-five percent of the humanities items and 94% of the teacher education items, returned in October 1983, had been borrowed previously sometime in the preceding 22 months. The "99% library" in teacher education would be those books borrowed at least once in the last five years. In the humanities, the 99% library would be those books borrowed at least once in the last nine years, approximately.

Year of penultimate date stamp	Humanities			Teacher Education		
	Total	%	Cumulative %	Total	%	Cumulative %
1983	357	67.4	67.4	369	73.8	73.8
1982	94	17.7	85.1	100	20.0	93.8
1981	20	3.8	88.9	13	2.6	96.4
1980	13	2.45	91.35	13	2.6	99.0
1979	13	2.45	93.8	1	0.2	99.2
1978	12	2.3	96.1	0	–	–
1977	7	1.3	97.4	1	0.2	99.4
1976	4	0.75	98.15	0	–	–
1975	4	0.75	98.9	1	0.2	99.6
1974	2	0.38	99.28	0	–	–
1973	0	–	–	1	0.2	99.8
pre-1973	4	.75	100.03	1	0.2	100.0
Totals	530	100.03		500	100.0	

Exhibit 25

Sample data from the Slote (or last circulation date) method

Reprinted from Williams (1986) by permission of Taylor Graham Publishing

In applying the LCD method, one would obviously have to exclude from consideration books added only recently to the library – e.g., books acquired within the past two years but not circulated, when books not circulated within the last 48 months (say) are to be retired. In a study at the University of Wisconsin, Oshkosh, Sargent (1979) applied the LCD method and discovered that 99% of the circulation came from items that had circulated at least once in the preceding 7½ years. Random samples drawn from the shelflist and catalogs, however, showed that, in this young and rapidly growing library, 56% of the collection would be needed to account for 99% of the circulation. It seems, then, that the LCD method will be more applicable in identifying a "core" in a relatively old library than it will in a very new one.

The most comprehensive application of the LCD method has been described by Trochim et al. (1980), who present results for various subject fields derived from data gathered in three college libraries.

Title Availability

So far in this chapter aggregate circulation data – e.g., on books in some subject area – have been discussed rather than data on individual titles. It is clear, however, that an automated circulation system can provide data on the use made of particular titles and can "flag" titles that are now so heavily used that additional copies should be purchased or some other steps taken to improve their availability. This aspect of evaluation will be discussed fully in Chapter 8.

Interlibrary Loan Analysis

Another approach to collection evaluation, touched upon briefly earlier, involves the examination of interlibrary loan (ILL) requests generated within a library. The justification for this is obvious: if a library is borrowing heavily in some subject field this probably indicates that the library's own holdings on this subject need to be strengthened.

Byrd et al. (1982) have described a method for determining strengths and weaknesses in a collection based on the difference in proportions between the subject breakdown of a library's acquisitions and the subject breakdown of the interlibrary loan requests it generates. The theory is that the classes needing greatest attention are those in which the volume of materials borrowed most exceeds the volume of materials purchased. This discrepancy is expressed as a "collection balance indicator" (CBI), a relative percentage, as follows:

$$100 \times \frac{\text{New acquisitions in this class}}{\text{Total acquisitions}} - \frac{\text{Titles borrowed in this class}}{\text{Total titles borrowed}}$$

A positive value on the CBI indicates a subject area relatively strong in terms of current acquisitions while a negative value indicates one relatively weak. This can be illustrated through two simple examples:

$$1. \quad 100 \times \frac{100}{400} - \frac{12}{120} = 15$$

$$2. \quad 100 \times \frac{40}{400} - \frac{30}{120} = -15$$

In the first case, 25% of the acquisitions are made in this subject field but only 10% of the titles borrowed fall in this area. The CBI is a high 15. The second case puts the proportions exactly in reverse – 10% of acquisitions and 25% of titles borrowed – and the value is a low -15.

Aguilar (1984) performed a monumental study of the relationship between internal circulation and interlibrary loan requests based on about 86,000 ILL transactions and almost two million circulation records from eighteen Illinois libraries. He found support for his hypothesis that a class that is overused (as defined earlier) in a library will be a class in which the library will borrow many items, whereas underused classes tend not to generate large numbers of ILL requests. This supports the assumption made earlier in this chapter that it is overused classes rather than underused classes that are most in need of strengthening.

As a result of his research, Aguilar (1986) developed a measure "ratio of borrowings to holdings" (RBH), which is simply:

$$\frac{\% \text{ of borrowings}}{\% \text{ of holdings}}$$

Values greatly in excess of 1 would indicate a class in which the borrowing rate is very high relative to the holdings of the library. For example, a class that occupies 8% of the collection but accounts for 15% of borrowings would have an RBH of almost 1.9. Aguilar uses the RBH data, together with relative use circulation data, to produce a collection development "model." For overused and underused classes the RBH is looked at. Decisions on the future of the class are made on the basis of relative use and RBH data. The model is shown in Exhibit 26.

Collection/Curriculum Comparisons

A number of investigators have attempted to determine the adequacy of the collections of an academic library by comparing the holdings with "classified" course descriptions. While somewhat different from the other methods described in this chapter, the method is sufficiently related to be worth considering here.

Using the classification scheme by which books are arranged on the library shelves, classification numbers are assigned to all of the course descriptions appearing in the catalog of a university. This "profile" of academic interests can then be matched against the subject profile of library holdings (as reflected in the shelflist), of current acquisitions, or of circulation.

Examples of use of such techniques can be found in the work of McGrath, Golden, and Jenks. McGrath (1968) was able to show, for each academic department, the number of circulated books relevant to the departmental profile, the percentage of the total circulation accounted for by these books, the enrollment for the department, and a circulation/enrollment ratio. Golden (1974) related the class numbers associated with a course to the number of books owned in these classes and to enrollment figures for the course in an attempt to identify strengths and weaknesses in the collection. Jenks (1976) compared circulation figures with the number of students in each department and

Class	Relative use (circulation data)	Interlibrary borrowing	Decision on the class
A	Overused	High RBH	Buy more
B	Overused	No high RBH	Continue at present levels
C	Underused	High RBH	Examine class: are right items being purchased; should it be weeded?
D	Underused	Low RBH	Curtail buying in this class

Exhibit 26
Collection development model based on Aguilar (1986)
Reprinted by permission of Haworth Press

with the number of books matching the profile of each department. He also ranked departments according to the use each made of that part of the collection matching its interest profile.

Power and Bell (1978) propose a more elaborate formula that takes into account, for each academic department, the number of faculty members, the number of students at various levels, the holdings matching the departmental profile, and circulation.

McGrath (1972) has shown that books matching the profile of institutional interests are much more likely to be borrowed than books not matching the profile, while McGrath et al. (1979) have used a subject classification approach to determine to what extent graduate and undergraduate students borrow books outside their own disciplines.

Evans and Beilby (1983) describe collection evaluation through a sophisticated management information system employed within the libraries of the State University of New York. In one machine-readable file are stored student enrollment data classified by subject field according to the Higher Education General Information Survey (HEGIS) codes. By using OCLC tapes, together with a conversion tape showing equivalencies between the HEGIS codes and Library of Congress class numbers, it is possible to relate the acquisitions data of a library to the enrollment. Thus, for each HEGIS code (e.g., 1103, German language), the system will generate a printout showing the number of titles acquired by the library, the percentage of the total acquisitions that this represents, the number of student credit hours, and the percentage of the total credit hours that this represents. Subject areas in which strong (or weak) relationships exist between student credit hours and acquisitions patterns can thus be identified, and any necessary corrections made.

Spaulding and Stanton (1976) and Kennedy (1983) describe the use of the Dewey Decimal Classification (DDC) as an aid to book selection in an industrial library network. A selection profile for each member library is constructed, using DDC numbers plus verbal descriptions. Circulation data were used in the building of the profiles. Computer-generated reports allow a manager to determine to what extent materials purchased in a particular time period match a library's profile.

Gabriel (1987) has described the use of keyword searching in online data bases, in place of the use of class numbers, to assess the coverage of a collection. Keywords associated with course descriptions are used to identify items relevant to each course.

This chapter has mostly dealt with the use of circulation and related data in collection evaluation. Circulation data, however, have two obvious limitations:

1. They tell nothing about use of materials within the library.

2. They represent successes (a book borrowed is one that a user considers at least sufficiently interesting to take from the library) but reveal nothing about failures. Put differently, number of books borrowed is not an indicator of *success rate*.

The first of these limitations is dealt with in Chapter 4 and the second in Chapter 8.

Study Questions

1. You have recently been appointed Director of a public library serving a community of 100,000. After two months on the job you have come to the conclusion that the nonfiction collection is very unbalanced. Looking around at the shelves, you feel that some subject areas are overrepresented – the collection is too strong for the needs of the community – while others seem completely inadequate. At the mo-

ment, however, this is just a suspicion. What data would you collect, over what period of time, in order to identify over-represented and under-represented subject areas, and how would you go about collecting these data?

2. You are the librarian of a small liberal arts college. A new automated circulation system is to be installed and you can now specify the data to be collected by this system. For purposes of collection development and management, which data will you collect and how will you make use of these data?

3. Look at the data of Exhibit 20 and Exhibit 23. What would you advise the directors of these public libraries in terms of future purchases in these various categories of materials?

4. In-House Use

Circulation data do not give a complete picture of a collection because they fail to take into account the use of materials within the library. This may not be too important in the case of a public library, but it is in a research library, where in-house use may greatly exceed circulation. A number of critics have attacked the studies performed at the University of Pittsburgh (Kent et al., 1979) on the grounds that they come to conclusions about use of the collection that are based largely on circulation data (see, for example, Borkowski and Macleod, 1979; Schad, 1979; Voigt, 1979).

Nevertheless, if one excludes items that are not allowed to leave the library, there is no real reason to suppose that the items used within a library will be much different from those borrowed. Indeed, evidence exists to suggest that the books used in a library are more or less the same as those borrowed.* McGrath (1971), for example, discovered a strong correlation between the subject matter of books borrowed and those used within the library, while Fussler and Simon (1969) found that the proportional use of parts of the collection was similar whether circulation or in-house use was considered (e.g., if physics materials are borrowed twice as much as chemistry materials they will tend to be used in the library twice as much). More recently, Hardesty (1981) reported a study in a small liberal arts college in which:

> . . . each book had to be physically examined, and it soon became evident that books with no recorded circulation also had remained virtually untouched within the library. Their pages were unsmudged and their spines creaked as they were opened. (Page 265)

Other evidence on the correlation between circulation and in-house use is presented by Bommer (1973) and Domas (1978). Using questionnaires placed in randomly selected monographs and bound volumes of periodicals, Lawrence and Oja (1980) discovered a statistically significant but weak correlation between the number of times a volume circulates and the number of in-house uses it receives. Hindle and Buckland (1978) point out that:

> Books that circulate little get relatively little in-house use and the higher the circulation the higher the level of in-library use. (Page 270)

---

*However, research results are inconsistent on this point. See, for example, Selth et al. (1992)

In a small academic library in England, Harris (1977) found that about 18% of the collection accounted for all in-library use, about 45% of the collection accounted for all circulation, and about 51% of the collection accounted for *all* use. In other words, only an additional 6% of the collection was needed, beyond the circulating portion, to account for all use (see Exhibit 27). As discussed later, Harris' criterion for in-house use was much more relaxed than that most frequently employed in libraries.

Selth et al. (1992), on the other hand, got quite different results at the Riverside campus of the University of California. They examined more than 13,000 volumes selected at random and concluded from available use data that more than 35% of the monographs and 25% of the serial volumes had one kind of use but not the other (circulation but no in-house use, or vice versa). In-house use was identified by means of a date stamp put in every book left on library tables, at photocopying machines, and so on, before being returned to the shelves. This count will underestimate total library use. Nevertheless, over a seven year period (the data of their study) it should give a fairly accurate picture of which items are used and which not.

In the Pittsburgh studies it was estimated that about 75% of the materials used in-house had also circulated. Assuming that a reasonable proportion of the 25% that had not circulated consisted of materials that are considered "noncirculating," it would appear that very few of the items used in the library had not also circulated.

Hayes (1981), on the other hand, performed a mathematical analysis of data from the Pittsburgh studies which, he claims, reveals that circulation is not an adequate indicator of total use.

The most obvious difference between a measure of in-house use and the measure of circulation is the ambiguity of the former. A book either is or is not borrowed, but what constitutes a "use" within a library? If a book is removed from the shelves, casually glanced at and immediately returned, has it been "used?" If it is removed, some portion of it read at the shelves, and then put back, has it been used? If it is carried to a table, along with others, glanced at and pushed to one side, has it been used?

One cannot be certain that any item is used "substantively" within a library without interviewing representative users or, at least, observing them, and neither procedure is very practical except on an extremely limited scale. On the other hand, circulation figures reflect only the activity of *borrowing* and tell us nothing about level or type of use. It is quite possible that substantial numbers of items borrowed receive no significant level of use.

The easiest way to find out what items or types of items are consulted in the library is to examine materials left on tables or desks, and this is the method most frequently used. For a particular period of time (at Pittsburgh, thirty sample days, one per week for thirty weeks)

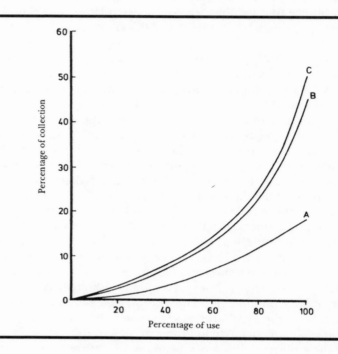

Exhibit 27
Proportion of collection needed to account for all in-house use (A)
all circulation (B), and total use (C)

Reprinted from Harris (1977) by permission of Aslib and the author

such materials are collected at regular intervals each day – say, 10 AM, 2 PM, 7 PM, and 10 PM – their identities are recorded, and they are then returned to the shelf. To ensure that, as far as possible, this procedure records all in-house uses, the library should implement an all-out "cooperation campaign." Signs prominently placed in the library will urge users not to reshelve materials they consult. These can be supplemented by notices in library bulletins, cards handed to users entering the library on the days selected for the survey, or any other procedure that seems likely to work in a particular institution.

"Table counts" of this type can be used to identify specific materials used within a library, allowing categorizations by subject, type of document, age of material, or other characteristics of interest, depending on what data are recorded before items are reshelved.

This method of measuring in-house use has been criticized on a number of counts, including:

1. However strongly one pleads, some users will reshelve materials so the method will give an underestimate of actual use.

2. Some types of users are more likely to reshelve than others so the method gives a distorted picture of actual use.

3. Some books left on tables may be used more than once while others may not have been used at all.

4. Whether books are carried to tables, or left there after use, may be influenced by physical characteristics (e.g., very heavy books may be more likely to be taken to a table but less likely to be reshelved).

The first of these criticisms is valid: total use will be underestimated. By placing "slips" in a sample of books in such a way that the slip cannot remain undisturbed if the books are removed from the shelf, Harris (1977) estimated that the complete use of materials in-house may be as much as twenty times the use reflected in materials left on tables. Clearly, Harris is saying that a book removed from the shelf, however briefly, is a book used. Lawrence and Oja (1980), using a similar technique, estimated that collection use in two University of California libraries may be six times greater than suggested by circulation data alone. On the other hand, in the public library environment, Rubin (1986) found less discrepancy between table counts and estimates of use arrived at through questionnaires or interviews. However, while the discrepancy was small when averaged over the six libraries in the study, it was quite high in some cases (e.g., in one library, table counts underestimated questionnaire results by a factor of eight).

Also, using a technique similar to if not identical with that used by Harris, Taylor discovered that about 22% of all volumes of periodicals consulted in a large academic library were left on tables (see Urquhart and Urquhart, 1976).* By specifically asking users to leave things on tables, he was able to raise this figure to 41%.

One can readily accept the fact that a count of materials left on tables will in some way underestimate amount of in-house use. However, it is not clear why this should be considered important. The pur-

---

*The slip used by Taylor (1977) is illustrated in Exhibit 28.

pose of performing an in-house study should be to discover *what* is being used, not *how much* the library is being used. Common sense suggests that, as with circulation, in-house use is heavily skewed so that most of it comes from a very small part of the collection. If the sampling period is long enough, then, the fact that some things are reshelved may not affect one's conclusions about what is being used in the library and at what levels. To take a concrete example, if five people reshelve volumes of the *Journal of Applied Physics* and twenty others do not, table counts give an underestimate of use of this item but still indicate that it is heavily used in comparison with many other physics journals which may have recorded only one or two uses over the same period.

If one *must* arrive at an estimate of total in-house use, it is possible to do so by means of "observation periods." For certain blocks of time during the sampling period, selected at random, users of the library are discreetly observed to find how many reshelve volumes and how many do not. Suppose one observes 100 users in this way. They remove 350 volumes from the shelves, leave 200 on the tables, and reshelve 150. If this is a representative sample of all users, one can conclude that volumes left on tables represent approximately 57% (200/350) of all uses (Wenger and Childress, 1977).* Metz and Litchfield (1988) estimate in-house use by counting the items reshelved and subtracting the items that have circulated, and this type of estimate may be perfectly reasonable for reporting purposes.

The second major criticism of table counts – that certain types of people are more likely to reshelve than others – rests on assumptions that have never been tested. Peat (1981), for example, claims that researchers – faculty and graduate students – are much more likely to reshelve than undergraduates but presents no evidence to support this.

Of course, there may exist certain factors within a particular library that could cause table counts to give serious distortions in terms of overall patterns of use. For example, the shelves devoted to subject *A* could be immediately adjacent to tables, while those devoted to *B* could be quite far from the nearest tables. One could argue, then, that *A* users are more likely than *B* users to carry things to tables. On the other hand, if *B* users go to the trouble of taking things to tables, they

---

*It should be recognized, however, that observation of this kind is not easily achieved and that a staff member may feel "uncomfortable" in trying to observe library users unobtrusively. Moreover, observation is costly and prone to error, as well as being nonspecific (e. g., it is not always possible to determine what is being used). Bustion et al. (1992) conclude that it is impractical for long-term use but may still be of value for calibrating results of less expensive methods.

may be more likely than *A* users to leave them there, so one factor might offset the other. Apart from factors of this type, influences associated with the layout of a library, one has no reason to suppose that (for example) economists are more likely to reshelve than metallurgists.

Unfortunately, when different methods of measuring in-house use are compared, they tend to give divergent results. A comprehensive study of in-house use of materials, involving the comparison of several methodologies in six public libraries of varying size, is reported by Rubin (1986). Questionnaires, interviews, and unobtrusive observation were all used, and counts were made of materials left on tables. Table counts indicated that, for every ten items borrowed, approximately seven were used in the library. However, library users who were interviewed claimed to use as many items in the library as they borrowed, while questionnaire data suggested that somewhat more items were used in the library than were borrowed (ratio of 1.2 to 1.0). Rubin recommends the questionnaire approach because it is relatively easy to administer yet is capable of collecting data on users as well as on materials used.

A library will usually do table counts for only a very limited period of time because of the resources needed to record data on items used before they are returned to the shelves. Shaw (1978, 1979), however, has described an ingenious method that would allow the use of a collection to be monitored continuously. In the "dotting method,"* rather than noting identifying details for a volume before it is returned to the shelf, the fact that it has been used is merely recorded by placing an adhesive "dot" on the spine. The dot, which can actually be shot onto the spine by a special type of "gun," is clearly visible when the volume is on the library shelves. If dots of different colors are used, one can distinguish items borrowed from items used in the library.

Obviously, every item must be given a dot before it is returned to the shelves, whether from circulation or in-house use. This will cause a lot of extra work for a few weeks after the procedure is initiated. But dots are not put on items coming up for reshelving that have already been dotted. After several months, the items needing a dot will be the exception rather than the rule so the procedure can go on indefinitely.

The beauty of this approach is that, merely by walking through the library, one can readily identify which volumes have been used and which not, including the earliest volumes of each periodical that have been used. Moreover, with different colors, one can identify items bor-

*Slote (1989) refers to it as the "spine-marking" method.

rowed but not used in the library, items used in-house but not borrowed, items borrowed and used in-house, and items not used at all.
Of course, the method does not reveal how frequently a particular
item has been used. Nevertheless, if one is to believe the results of several published studies, it is enough to be able to identify the items that
are not used at all.*

In studying use made of periodicals within a library, Taylor (1977)
has gone beyond use per se and attempted to determine whether or not
a reader found anything of value in a volume consulted. A survey form
(see Exhibit 28) is placed in each volume. The user is asked to place this
form in different colored folders depending on whether or not the volume was found to be of use. Because these forms are placed at known
page numbers, Taylor claims that it is unlikely for a consultation to go
undetected even if the user does not cooperate in the process.

A perfectly reasonable way to measure the in-house use of periodicals is by means of a form stapled to the front of unbound issues or
taped to the front cover of bound volumes. Exhibit 29 shows such a
form, employed by Milne and Tiffany (1991), which merely requires
the recording of a check mark when the issue or volume is used. A
rather more elaborate form, employed by Konopasek and O'Brien
(1982, 1984) in studying use of periodicals in an undergraduate library, is shown in Exhibit 30. This requires users to identify themselves
by type.

The methods described so far collect anonymous data on in-house
use – they show what is being used but not who is using it. Anonymity
can be reduced through a survey form, such as the one used by Taylor,
that asks users to supply some personal details such as, in the case of
an academic library, their departmental affiliation and status (undergraduate, master's student, doctoral student, faculty).

For more precise data, however, it would be necessary to interview
a sample of people actually using materials in the library. Random
sampling can be based on a seating pattern. Every chair in which a user
could be seated is given an identifying number. Time slots for interviewing of users (selected times on selected days in selected weeks) are
established. To each time slot a sequence of seat numbers is randomly
assigned. An interviewer approaches the first seat thus identified. If a
user is present there, the user is interviewed. If not, the interviewer
proceeds to the next seat indicated, and so on until a user is located.
The interview is conducted in order to discover relevant details on the

---

*For example, in a study of 804 journals received by an education/psychology library,
Perk and Van Pulis (1977) found that 192 titles, 24%, were completely unused.

THIS LETTER FORMS PART OF A LIBRARY SURVEY

The librarian would very much appreciate your
help in carrying out a survey of periodicals used
within the library.

A.   IF YOU HAVE FOUND AN ARTICLE OR ARTICLES IN
      THIS VOLUME OF USE TO YOUR STUDIES OR RESEARCH
      please place this form in the RED FOLDER
      located at the end of the stack.

B.   IF YOU HAVE USED THIS VOLUME BUT DID NOT FIND
      ANY INFORMATION OF USE TO YOUR STUDIES OR
      RESEARCH please place this form in the BLUE
      FOLDER located at the end of the stack.

TITLE *No 54*
       Per 612
YEAR
       17 '56

Exhibit 28
Survey form used by Taylor (1977) and how it is placed in bound volume of periodical
Reprinted by permission of Haworth Press

user as well as on the material being used. Procedures of this kind (see
Daiute and Gorman, 1974, for a detailed description) can yield data
qualitatively different from the anonymous data, including identities
of users, correlations between users and uses (e.g., who uses bound
periodicals, who uses physics periodicals, how much use is made of
physics materials by faculty and students in other departments), and
an indication of the extent to which the library's facilities are being
used without concomitant use of library materials.

Evaluation of Reference Collections

The reference collections of libraries are very rarely the subject of
any evaluation activity, presumably because it is rather difficult to col-

lect data on use of these materials. Nolan (1991) makes a strong case for the rigorous weeding of reference collections: very large reference collections are difficult to use, and a collection that is not weeded fre-

---

ATTENTION LIBRARY USERS!!!

If you have used in any way today an article or articles from this periodical issue or volume (reading, browsing, photocopying, taking out on loan), please tick one of the boxes below.

This is part of a periodicals use study. Your cooperation is appreciated.

Library Staff

Title_____

Year_____

Date begun _____

Exhibit 29
Form for recording use of periodicals
Reproduced from Milne and Tiffany (1991) by permission of
Pierian Press and the authors

quently is likely to include many sources that are not up-to-date. He suggests that more than half the items in a reference collection may not be used in any year, and almost a third in a five-year period, but these figures seem rather conservative: it seems likely that the *great majority* of sources in a very large reference collection would not be used in even a five-year period.

The dotting or spine-marking method, referred to earlier, could certainly be employed to identify those reference sources that have been used and those not. If books left on tables (or other surfaces) can be assumed to have been consulted by library users, a method using different colored dots could distinguish materials consulted by library users from those consulted by librarians. Items to which a librarian *refers* a user could receive a different colored dot – three colors in all. Nolan (1991) suggests a slightly different approach: the bar coding of reference books to allow scanning before reshelving.

TITLE:

PERIODICAL SURVEY

If you use this issue, please use the next available line to check (✓) your school status: UI UNDERGRADUATE, UI GRADUATE, or OTHER. Thank you.

#	UNDERGRADUATE	GRADUATE	OTHER	#	UNDERGRADUATE	GRADUATE	OTHER	#	UNDERGRADUATE	GRADUATE	OTHER	#	UNDERGRADUATE	GRADUATE	OTHER	#	UNDERGRADUATE	GRADUATE	OTHER	#	UNDERGRADUATE	GRADUATE	OTHER
0.	✓			25.				50.				75.				100.				125.			
1.				26.				51.				76.				101.				126.			
2.				27.				52.				77.				102.				127.			
3.				28.				53.				78.				103.				128.			
4.				29.				54.				79.				104.				129.			
5.				30.				55.				80.				105.				130.			
6.				31.				56.				81.				106.				131.			
7.				32.				57.				82.				107.				132.			
8.				33.				58.				83.				108.				133.			
9.				34.				59.				84.				109.				134.			
10.				35.				60.				85.				110.				135.			
11.				36.				61.				86.				111.				136.			
12.				37.				62.				87.				112.				137.			
13.				38.				63.				88.				113.				138.			
14.				39.				64.				89.				114.				139.			
15.				40.				65.				90.				115.				140.			
16.				41				66.				91.				116.				141.			
17.				42.				67.				92.				117.				142.			
18.				43.				68.				93.				118.				143.			
19.				44.				69.				94.				119.				144.			
20.				45.				70.				95.				120.				145.			
21.				46.				71.				96.				121.				146.			
22.				47.				72.				97.				122.				147.			
23.				48.				73.				98.				123.				148.			
24.				49.				74.				99.				124.				149.			

Exhibit 30
Form for recording in-house use of periodicals
From Konopasek and O'Brien (1982) by permission of the authors

The "slipping" of reference books – having a slip prominently displayed inside the book (see Exhibit 28) on which type of use and type of user can easily be identified – would require much more effort. Nevertheless, it should be feasible in reference collections that are not of excessive size and could also be employed to study use of parts of the larger collections.

Study Questions

1. Black University has a consolidated Science Library serving all the science faculties except that of medicine. Through an automated circulation system, it has excellent data on the use of its collection in terms of borrowings, but has no data at all on use of materials within the library. The Science Librarian suspects that the circulation data alone give a somewhat incomplete and distorted picture of the total use of the collections. She would like to do a one-time study of the in-house use of library materials. At the same time, she wants to know if it might somehow be possible to "calibrate" the in-house data to the circulation data so that, in the future, the circulation data can "predict" the distribution of in-house use. How should the study be conducted? What would you advise her on the calibration problem?

2. What are the advantages/disadvantages of knowing which volumes have been removed from the shelves of a library, however briefly, as opposed to which have been carried to tables?

3. The Undergraduate Library of a large university keeps issues of 300 periodicals in a prominent display area. For each title, the latest issue is displayed and back issues for the preceding six months are kept in adjacent storage. Space has become a problem and it is now necessary to reduce this display to half its present size. What data would you collect in order to make the best decision on how to use the reduced space? How would you collect these data?

4. The recent study by Selth et al. (1992) differs from other studies in that it suggests that significant numbers of the items that circulate may not be used in-house, and vice versa. Examine these various studies. Is there any logical explanation for the differences in results?

5. Evaluation of Periodicals

In periods of austerity, when a library finds its budget for the purchase of materials to be shrinking, subscriptions to periodicals are likely to be examined to determine which titles may be discontinued.

Duplicate titles may be the first group looked at, especially in large academic libraries. If cuts are to be made, to what extent can one justify having several periodicals duplicated in departmental libraries devoted to, say, biology, the health sciences, and veterinary medicine? But duplication need not be the paramount criterion for canceling a subscription: some titles may be heavily used in each of several locations while other titles, for which only one copy exists, may receive little or no use.

This suggests that use data should exert the most influence on cancellation decisions. Since periodicals do not circulate in many libraries, or circulate with many restrictions, the use data will have to come from some type of in-library survey as described in the previous chapter.

A major question to be considered in this chapter is whether or not data available from outside the library can substitute for actual use data in making effective decisions on which periodicals to discontinue. This could be quite important – a librarian required to reduce subscription costs by 10% might have no time to collect use data before some deadline imposed on him.

Ranking Criteria

In making cancellation decisions, it would be useful if one could produce a ranked list of titles (or several ranked lists according to discipline) reflecting retention priorities, the titles at the bottom being those one could discontinue with least disturbance to library users.

By what criteria can such rankings be arrived at? The following seem the most obvious:

1. By actual use data collected in the library.*

---

*A study by Franklin (1989) demonstrates the danger of extrapolating annual journal use from the transactions recorded during a brief survey period. The use of 145 titles was recorded for each of three academic quarters. Recorded use varied considerably from one quarter to another. For example, one title that received forty-nine uses in one quarter received only ten and five, respectively, in the other quarters.

2. By use data that have already been collected (and perhaps published) by another library. Urquhart and Urquhart (1976) suggest that, in some subject fields, periodical use data from the British Library Document Supply Centre may closely parallel periodical use data collected in a British university.

3. By opinion. For example, members of the physics faculty are given a list of periodicals received by the physics library and asked to give each a score on a scale of 1 to 4, where 4 represents "essential" and 1 "of no interest." The periodicals are then ranked according to the sum of the scores received by each title. Some support for this approach is offered by Wenger and Childress (1977), who found that a periodical was very unlikely to be little used in a library when two or more scientists recommended it. On the other hand, Bustion and Treadwell (1990) found little correlation between faculty ratings and use: journals judged "essential" were sometimes little used.

4. By citation. The *Journal Citation Reports* (JCR), published by the Institute for Scientific Information, rank periodicals in various subject fields according to the number of times they have been cited. These data are derived from the citation indexes published by the Institute.

5. Impact factor. This is another citation measure available from the JCR. The impact factor relates the number of citations received by a periodical to the number of articles published by that periodical (in a sense it is the citation equivalent of "relative use") – the more citations received per article published, the higher the impact factor. The JCR adopts a period of two years as the basis for its calculation:

$$\text{Impact factor} = \frac{\text{\# of citations received in year 3 by articles published in years 1 \& 2}}{\text{\# of articles published in years 1 \& 2}}$$

For example, if a journal publishes 115 papers in 1989 and 1990, and these papers are cited eighty one times in 1991, the impact factor would be 81/115, or 0.704.* Rankings based on impact factor and on simple citation counts will tend to differ: periodicals publishing only a few papers each year (e.g., those publishing review or survey articles) may have a low citation score but may have a high impact factor.

6. Cost-effectiveness. One of the "effectiveness" measures mentioned above (1-5) can be related to the cost of the periodical. If they

---

*Garfield (1986) distinguishes further between *cited impact factor* and *total impact factor*. The latter relates number of citations received to the number of articles published by a journal in a particular period of time, while the former relates number of citations to the total number of articles published in a particular period *that were cited*.

are available, the library's own use data should be selected. The most cost-effective journals are those with lowest cost per use.*

7. By the number of articles contributed to a particular subject area. For example, Hafner (1976) used searches in MEDLARS to identify the most productive journals in various facets of nursing and Trubkin (1982) used a variety of databases to identify the "core" periodicals in business and management. Seba and Forrest (1978) carried this further by using current awareness searches in the databases to identify the most relevant journals for the users of a special library. "Relevancy" was defined as the number of articles retrieved and judged relevant by users over the total number of articles published by a journal in a particular time period. The journals represented in the database searches were compared with the library's holdings to identify nonproductive titles held as well as productive titles not held. The most "cost-effective" journals are those having the lowest cost per relevant article published.

There are many other ways in which journals can be ranked, including "exclusivity" – the proportion of all articles published by a journal that deal with some subject of interest (Hawkins, 1979), number of subscribers, and "influence" (Narin, 1976). However, the methods listed above would seem, at least on the surface, to be those most useful to the librarian in making practical decisions on which titles to discontinue.

Line (1978) has stated categorically that no external data (e.g., from citations or from another library) are of any value in predicting use within one's own library. He suggests that, if one compared ranked lists based on various criteria (e.g., the library's own use data, citation counts, data from another library, data based on user surveys) one might very well get similar rankings *at the top of the list.* That is, the same small set of, say, physics journals will be most used in all physics libraries, most cited, most highly favored by research workers, and so on. It is not necessary to gather any data to identify these titles – any physics librarian will know which they are.

For cancellation purposes, however, one is not interested in titles at the top of such a list but only in those at the bottom. As Line points out, ranked lists produced by the different criteria mentioned earlier

---

*Holland (1976) describes a somewhat different cost-effectiveness measure. She takes into account how long a user would have to wait to obtain a photocopy from a periodical if it were not in the library's own collection. She is thus able to estimate the effects on "public service" of various levels of reduction in the budget.

are unlikely to be very similar at the bottom (journals consistently towards the bottom of all lists would have little reason to exist). Therefore, external data are of little use in making cancellation decisions.

Line's contentions make a great deal of sense. Consider Exhibit 31, which is a plot of use of periodicals in a hypothetical physics library. The distribution has been divided into three "zones" relating to degree of use of the library. Logic suggests that the titles in the first zone, most used in the library, will tend also to be most used in others, as well as being most cited and most often mentioned as important by physicists. As one moves into the later zones, however, this library's data can be expected to agree less and less with external data. Journals little used in this library will be used moderately or even heavily in others, this use varying with the different research interests of the parent institutions. Moreover, the least cited journals for a subject area as a whole will not necessarily be the least used in any particular library. Nor will they be the least cited if we narrow the subject field considerably. For example, certain journals dealing exclusively with irrigation may receive a low citation score for agriculture as a whole but they will be highly cited within the literature of irrigation and heavily used in institutions performing a significant level of irrigation research.

One is therefore inclined to agree with Line's contentions that ranked lists produced on the basis of different criteria are likely to be quite different at the bottom and that data external to the library may have little value to the librarian in making cancellation decisions. To what extent does evidence exist to support these contentions?

It has already been pointed out that rankings by impact factor are different from rankings by citation counts. One suspects that the titles at the top of the "opinion survey" list may contain a mixture of titles high on the citation count list and those high on the impact factor list. Top titles on the "use" list may also contain a mixture of high impact titles and high citation titles. Tomer (1986) argues persuasively that the impact factor alone gives a somewhat distorted picture of the importance or influence of a journal. For example, a review journal publishing very few papers may have an impact factor ten times that of some research journal publishing very many shorter papers. It does not seem reasonable to consider the former more important or influential than the latter, however, especially when the latter may be cited *in toto* some fifty times more than the former.

The cost-effectiveness ranking will probably be quite different from all the others since it is the only one that takes cost into account. At the top of this list will be the high use titles that are relatively cheap.

At the bottom will be the expensive titles that are little used. The middle of the list will include heavily used expensive titles and little used cheap ones, as well as some that are moderate on both scores.

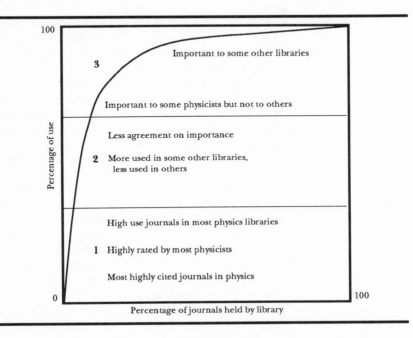

Exhibit 31
Plot of use versus percentage of periodicals held by a hypothetical physics library

In the field of physics, Scales (1976) has compared citation data from the *Journal Citation Reports* with use data derived from the British Library Document Supply Centre (BL). Little agreement was found even at the top of the two lists: only one title was common to the five most used and five most cited and only sixteen were common to the first fifty titles on each list. A low correlation was also found between the fifty physics journals most used in the MIT Science Library and the BL use data. The correlation between the MIT data and the citation data was found to be slightly better than the correlation between the BL data and the citation data.

Pan (1978) gathered use data on 169 journals from six medical libraries, including use reflected in circulation, interlibrary loan and photocopying, as well as in-house use. These were compared with citation data from the *Journal Citation Reports*. She claimed to find a statistically significant correlation between a ranking of journals by use and a ranking by citation but no significant correlation between the use ranking and one based on impact factor. However, she also found that the size of a journal – in terms of number of articles published in a specified time period – or the number of subscribers to that journal correlated as well with the use rankings as did the citation rankings.*

In the field of sociology, Baughman (1974) claimed that citation studies could be used to predict "readership." Satariano (1978), however, found differences between Baughman's list of most cited journals in sociology and a list that 526 sociologists, associated with graduate institutions, claimed to be "most read." Citation data underestimate use of popular journals and of specialty and regional journals in sociology. On the other hand, the most cited journals list includes some journals from related disciplines that do not appear among the list of titles most read.

Bennion and Karschamroon (1984) have compared the ranking of physics journals by "perceived usefulness" (based on a survey of 167 physicists) with rankings derived from multiple regression models incorporating several bibliometric values such as number of items published, citations received, impact factor, and ratio of citations made to citations received. These multivariate models are said to predict usefulness better than any single bibliometric predictor alone can do. The best single predictor was determined to be the number of subscribers to the journal. Another journal selection model that takes into account multiple criteria is presented by Oluić-Vuković and Pravdić (1990).

Wiberley (1982), using the field of social work, compared the rankings of journals derived from "national" citation data with rankings derived from "local" citation data. The national data were drawn from two leading journals and one specialized encyclopedia. The local data were the bibliographic references within publications of the faculty of a prominent school of social work. The local data were divided into two periods: 1971-1974 and 1975-1978. The national data were almost as good as the 1971-1974 local data in predicting the citation patterns of the 1975-1978 local data.

A number of other investigators have compared bibliometric data with use data or use data from one source with use data from another. There are too many to be reviewed comprehensively in this chapter. A useful summary of the earlier ones is given by Broadus (1977).

---

*Bennion and Karschamroon (1984) also found that number of subscribers correlated more closely with the results of an opinion survey than citation or any other bibliometric data did, which suggests that, if these data were readily available, they might be employed as a predictor of use in certain types of libraries.

Two other studies do deserve attention here. Stankus and Rice (1982) ranked journals by use data from an academic library (State University of New York at Albany) and compared this ranking with one based on citation counts and another based on impact factors. They found marked differences from one subject field to another. In biochemistry, excellent correlations throughout the lists were found, while in geoscience poor correlations occurred. In some fields, such as cell biology, a good correlation at the bottom of the list was discovered.

These results tend to suggest that there are some fields in which the programs of research and teaching at SUNYA are sufficiently different from the general "educational and scientific consensus" that citation is a poor predictor of use, whereas in other fields the SUNYA programs conform more closely to the general consensus. Stankus and Rice caution that use data are only likely to correlate with citation data if the use is reasonably heavy and not skewed by the eccentricities of a few frequent users.

Rice (1983) reports separately on another SUNYA study, this time in the field of chemistry. The ranking of periodicals by use in SUNYA libraries did not correlate particularly well with rankings based on *Journal Citation Reports* or the *Chemical Abstracts Service Source Index* (CASSI), the latter reflecting the number of periodical articles that various periodicals contribute to *Chemical Abstracts*. For example, *Industrial and Engineering Chemistry* ranks fourteen in use at SUNYA but appears in position sixty six on the JCR list and 770 on the CASSI list. On the other hand, two Russian journals appear among CASSI's top eight titles; by use at SUNYA, these rank in positions eighty five and eighty six. Based on a survey performed in organic chemistry, Rice claims that a good agreement exists between actual use figures and faculty judgment on which titles are important.

A somewhat different application of citation data can be found in a study by McCain and Bobick (1981). They used citations in faculty publications, doctoral dissertations, and preliminary doctoral qualifying briefs as a proxy for actual journal use figures in a departmental library. The assumption is that journals most cited by faculty and doctoral students are those most used and, more importantly, those least cited, or not cited at all, are those least used. The authors claim to have "identified a pool of less-productive journal titles which may be candidates for cancellation" but do not list these titles or indicate whether these appear to be "reasonable" candidates for cancellation according to other criteria. This procedure must be used with great caution because some periodicals (e.g., those read mostly for current news) may be heavily used but little if ever cited. Another factor to be considered is that certain titles may not be heavily used in a library because most library users have personal copies (Stenstrom and McBride, 1979). The more specialized the library, the more likely this is to be true.

In conclusion, while citation data may be of some value in identifying journals to acquire in some field – e.g., in establishing a new library – for reasons mentioned earlier they are less likely to be of much aid to deselection decisions.

Decisions Based on Multiple Factors

Wherever possible, it would seem desirable to base cancellation decisions on more than one criterion. In fact. the ideal situation might be one in which the librarian was able to give some numerical score to each periodical, the overall score being the sum of a number of component scores.

Suppose one decides that the criteria to be taken into consideration are: degree of use, opinion, cost, and the correlation between subject matter and institutional interests. Of these, only the cost figures are readily available. To gather the other needed data could require an in-house use study, a survey of user (e.g., faculty) opinion, and some form of subject classification applied to journals and to institutional interests (as in the collection/curriculum comparisons discussed in Chapter 3).

If all these data were collected, it would still be necessary to allocate a weight to each criterion and then to determine how many "points" a journal earns for each. With a maximum score of 100, one might allocate points as follows:

1. 50 for use
2. 20 for user opinion
3. 15 for relatedness
4. 15 for cost

For each criterion a scale of values, related to the allocated points, must be established, as in the following examples:

$$\frac{0\text{-}1}{0} \quad \frac{2\text{-}5}{5} \quad \overset{\textbf{Uses per week}}{\blacktriangleright} \quad \frac{30\,+}{50}$$

$$\frac{\$200\,+}{0} \quad \frac{180\,+}{1} \quad \overset{\textbf{Cost}}{\blacktriangleright} \quad \frac{\$0}{15}$$

A journal with thirty or more recorded uses per week gets the maximum score of fifty, whereas one with no uses or one use scores no points, one with two to five uses scores five, and so on. A journal costing \$200 or more to subscribe to gets no points on the cost scale while one costing the library nothing earns the maximum fifteen points.

A similar point scale would be developed for the other evaluation criteria so that each journal in the collection would eventually receive a point total, thereby allowing all titles to be ranked by numerical score. Even though use is given the lion's share of the score, one would probably apply a scoring system of this kind only to titles having some level of recorded use. Data from Pittsburgh and elsewhere (e.g., Holland, 1976) suggest that large academic libraries may receive substantial numbers of periodicals that are never used. Presumably these items would be the first to be considered in cancellation decisions.

This is all entirely hypothetical in terms of the criteria and scoring procedures; it is presented to illustrate how multiple criteria can be combined to arrive at a single score and should not necessarily be considered as a procedure advocated by the author.

This type of approach was described by Broude (1978) who combined no fewer than seven separate criteria into his "deselection model" as follows:

		Points allocated
1.	Subscription cost	13
2.	Average annual use	29
3.	Impact factor	6
4.	Number of indexing/abstracting services covering it	12
5.	Availability in another local library	6
6.	Reputation of publisher	4
7.	Curriculum relatedness	30

For two of these criteria the point scale would be reversed, with the highest score for the lowest costs and the lowest level of local availability.

One problem with this approach lies in the allocation of points. Librarians may differ as to the relative weights to be assigned to the various criteria. The allocation proposed by Broude does seem "reasonable" in that it gives most weight to the local use factors (2 and 7).

A weighting procedure of the type described by Broude is certainly intriguing. If one could also devise a procedure for "estimating" scores for newly published journals, one could compare the projected scores with the actual scores of titles owned, thus facilitating decisions on selection as well as deselection. In a zero growth situation, a title in, say, agriculture might be added if its projected score greatly exceeds the scores of some titles already held. Depending on cost, a librarian might decide to add one title and cancel two others.

With Broude's model, however, only values for criteria 1 and (possibly) 6 would be known at the time a journal was first published, although values for the important criterion of 7 could be established on the basis of a detailed description of the journal's intended scope.

In point of fact, Broude's criteria are too numerous. Moreover, some appear redundant. For example, curriculum relatedness should correlate fairly closely with use. In fact, if it does not, it has little value as an evaluation criterion. If it is found to correlate closely with use, it can substitute for the use data.*

From a cost-effectiveness point of view, the only salient criteria are 1 and 2. The journals that represent the best investment are those whose cost per use is at the low end of the scale. The cost considered can be cost of subscription only or cost of "ownership," including handling and storage costs. If curriculum relatedness correlates closely with use, a ranking based on cost per use may not differ too much from one based on all of Broude's criteria. Moreover, a numerical score for curriculum relatedness could substitute for actual use figures so the cost-effectiveness measure would relate the cost to this numerical score. The advantage of this simplification, of course, is that the score can be applied to newly published journals as well as existing ones, so that it could be used as a tool in selection as well as cancellation.

Flynn (1979) recommends that "expected cost per use" should be the criterion applied in periodical acquisition decisions. However, the only guidance he gives on how one should establish estimated use is that it be based on the "worth" of the journal. Curriculum relatedness is a little more concrete.**

A different approach to "scoring" a journal has been described by Johnson and Trueswell (1978). Journals may be ranked by a "criteria statistic score" which is merely the sum of the criteria that a particular title satisfies (a title that satisfies eight criteria gets a score of 8) or by a "weighted criteria statistic score" which takes into account the number of times a title satisfies each criterion. A title may satisfy any or all of these criteria: be recorded as photocopied in the library, be used often in the past year, be one that an individual claims to be of interest although he has not used it in the past year, be one in which library users have published in the last five years, be one that library users have

---

*A good predictor of use would have to take into account more factors that curriculum relatedness alone. For example, Holland (1976) found that foreign-language titles accounted for 10% of the periodicals budget but received only 1.5% of the use, while cover-to-cover translations consumed 22% of the budget but received only 1.6% of use. Popular news items and other periodicals not purchased in direct support of the curriculum would need to be treated differently.

**It is assumed that "curriculum relatedness" really refers to the extent to which the subject matter of the periodical matches institutional interests (research, teaching, or whatever). While this measure might be difficult to adapt to the public library environment, it should be as relevant to industrial and governmental libraries as it is to academic and research libraries.

cited in their publications, or be one citing the publications of library users. Apart from the first, all data are collected by means of a survey of users, which makes the whole process very cumbersome. It would only be viable in a relatively small research institution.

It has been assumed so far that the purpose of identifying a little used periodical is to discontinue it. An alternative strategy would be to improve cost per use by deliberately promoting the use of such items – displaying them prominently or advertising their existence in some other way.

Two Studies Relating to Periodical Use

Two studies in which the author has participated shed further light on the use of periodicals in libraries. In the first, the scatter of periodical articles over periodical titles was related to the availability of the periodicals in an academic library (Lancaster et al., 1991c).

Bradford's Law of Scattering refers to the scatter of journal articles over journal titles. If a comprehensive search is performed over a particular time period and all, or virtually all, journal articles on the search topic are discovered, it is possible to rank the journal titles by number of articles on the topic they contribute. At the top of the list might appear a single title that contributed, say, 145 articles. At the bottom of the list might appear very many journals that have only contributed a single article each to the subject. The ranked list can be divided into a number of "zones" (Bradford used three zones but four or more might be used) such that each zone contains approximately the same number of journal articles. This being so, the number of journals in each zone increases at an approximately geometric rate. This is illustrated by this simple example:

	Number of journals	Number of articles
Zone 1 (nucleus)	5	250
Zone 2	30	250
Zone 3	180	250

The first zone contains a "nucleus" or "core" of five journals that collectively contribute 250 articles on the subject, an average of 50 articles each. In the next zone 30 journals contribute 250 articles, approximately eight articles each on the average. The final zone consists of 180 journals that collectively contribute the final third (250 articles) of the literature. Clearly, most of the journals in the third zone contribute only a single article to the subject. The progression from the first to the third zone represents increasing scatter or dispersion of the literature. In comparison with the literature of Zone 1, which is very compact, the literature of Zone 2 is more scattered by a factor of six: 5 journals in the first zone, 5 x 6 journals in the second. The third zone exhibits much worse scatter: the same number of articles are spread over (5 x 6^2) journals.

These hypothetical figures represent "ideal" Bradford data in the sense that exactly the same number of articles appear in each zone and the relationship between zones in terms of number of journals is exactly a : a x b : a x b^2 (i.e., the "multiplier" between zones is exactly 6). In practice one is not likely to get data that are so exact and even Bradford's original data were very far from the "ideal."

While Bradford derived his data from a comprehensive bibliography of articles compiled on some subject, a similar pattern of scatter has been observed in other types of bibliographic data; e.g., the literature cited in a particular field (Prabha and Lancaster, 1987), requests for articles generated by a particular group of researchers (Vickery, 1948, and Neway, 1985), and the journals represented in the results of searches performed by computer in a particular database (Lancaster, 1968).

The objective of the study reported here was to determine to what extent literature scatter might be related to the accessibility of materials to library users. From the point of view of the user of a departmental library in a university, the following levels of accessibility might be identified:

1. Items in the departmental library itself
2. Items elsewhere in the university libraries
3. Items elsewhere in the state
4. Items elsewhere in the country.

Of course, this is oversimplified in several ways; e.g., participation in an online network might make the holdings of some out-of-state libraries more accessible than those of some in-state libraries, while an item immediately available in some out-of-state library can be considered more accessible than one owned by the departmental library but "missing". Moreover, the existence of telefax facilities, and the fact that the full text of some journals is accessible online, makes physical accessibility much less important than it once was. Nevertheless, the sequence listed does roughly represent accessibility, at least in a geographic sense.

One would hope that the "core" journals reflecting the interests of users of a departmental library would be in the departmental collection and that subsequent levels of accessibility (e.g., as identified earlier) would correspond roughly to levels of demand: the journals least likely to be asked for would be those least accessible. To test this, and to relate it to the phenomenon of scatter, a study was performed in the Library of the Health Sciences, which serves the University of Illinois College of Medicine and Nursing sites at Urbana-Champaign.

At the time of the study (1987) the library subscribed to about 650 periodical titles. This collection is restricted to materials in English. Duplication of titles held elsewhere on campus is minimized (the departmental libraries in applied life studies, biology, chemistry, home economics, and veterinary medicine are all rich in titles of potential relevance to the health sciences) and duplication of those held elsewhere within the site libraries for the College of Medicine (Chicago, Peoria, and Rockford) is limited to titles considered "core."

The probable demand for particular journal titles was determined on the basis of the journal titles retrieved in online searches performed for users of the library during a particular time period. The justification for this approach was simply the assumption that, if a journal appeared, say, twenty times in online search results it was much more likely to be sought by library users than one appearing only once.

The study was based on MEDLINE searches performed in the Library of the Health Sciences in June, July, and August 1987. During this period 106 MEDLINE searches were performed. Collectively, 4197 bibliographic references were retrieved, an average of about forty per search.

The scatter data are presented in Exhibit 32 in the form of a list of journal titles ranked by the number of bibliographic references they contributed to the 4197 references retrieved in 106 searches. As the table shows, the journal at the top of the list contributed forty nine items, the second journal forty seven, and so on to the bottom of the list, where 595 journals in the MEDLINE database made a single appearance each in 106 searches. In some cases, of course, several journals contributed the same number of articles (e.g., two journals contributed thirty four each and fifty seven journals contributed five each). It is also obvious that most journals in the MEDLINE database made no appearance at all among the 4197 items retrieved. In all, 1322 journals were needed to contribute the 4197 items, but most of these contributed a very small number of items each.

Suppose we divide the data from the table into five zones such that each zone contains, in a very rough sense, about one fifth of the articles retrieved. We could define the zones as shown in Exhibit 33.

In terms of number of articles in each zone, this is a crude division of the data, the crudity made necessary by the requirement that all journals contributing the same number of articles should appear in the same zone. For our purposes, however, the inexact division is not too important. What is important is that Zone 1 contains a nucleus of thirty five journals that were retrieved fairly often in the 106 searches. As one goes from zone to zone, one encounters groups of journals that are retrieved less and less frequently, until we reach the final zone containing the 595 journals that appear only once each in the combined

A	B	C	D
Number of Journals	Number of Articles	Cumulative Number of Journals	Cumulative Number of Articles
1	49	1	49
1	47	2	96
1	46	3	142
1	35	4	177
2	34	6	245
1	33	7	278
1	26	8	304
2	25	10	354
3	23	13	423
4	21	17	507
4	20	21	587
4	19	25	663
2	18	27	699
3	17	30	750
5	16	35	830
4	15	39	890
3	14	42	932
14	13	56	1114
7	12	63	1198
6	11	69	1264
9	10	78	1354
18	9	96	1516
18	8	114	1660
21	7	135	1807
33	6	168	2005
57	5	225	2290
80	4	305	2610
148	3	453	3054
274	2	727	3602
595	1	1322	4197

Exhibit 32
Scatter of periodical articles retrieved in online searches

bibliography of 4197 items. Since the 106 searches performed presumably reflect, in a broad sense, the interests of the users of this library (at least as reflected in searches requested during the summer of 1987), one would expect that the journals in Zone 1 would closely relate to the interests of the users, and that "relatedness" will decline as one goes from zone to zone, with the journals in Zone 5 least related to user interests. Looked at another way, Zone 1 journals should be requested frequently, and one would hope that most, if not all, should be in the departmental library. As one proceeds from zone to zone, demand presumably declines. Zone 5 journals should be in little demand and one would not expect many to be immediately accessible in the departmental library.

Zone	Number of Articles	Number of Journals	Cumulative Number of Articles	Cumulative Number of Journals
1	830	35	830	35
2	830	79	1660	114
3	950	191	2610	305
4	992	422	3602	727
5	595	595	4197	1322

Exhibit 33
Scatter of periodical articles over zones

To test the relationship between scatter and accessibility, the location of each of the 1322 journals was determined. Four possible locations were identified:

1. In the Library of the Health Sciences – Urbana
2. Elsewhere within the University of Illinois Libraries at Urbana-Champaign
3. Elsewhere in Illinois (including the University of Illinois at Chicago) as identifiable through ILLINET Online*
4. Not available through ILLINET Online but presumably available elsewhere in the United States.

Accessibility data for the journals appearing in each zone are presented in Exhibit 34. The data are revealing in a number of ways. Most clearly they show the strength of the library facilities. While less than a third of the journals appear in the departmental library, many of the journals in each zone are available on the campus at Urbana-Champaign.

The data are presented in a different, and perhaps more meaningful, way in Exhibit 35. For each zone the data are cumulated in the

---

*ILLINET Online is a public access catalog and circulation system providing access to the holdings of around 800 libraries in Illinois (about eight million titles).

Zone	In Departmental Library	On Campus	Located through ILLINET Online	Available Elsewhere	Total
1	21	14	0	0	35
2	42	32	4	1	79
3	60	87	34	10	191
4	95	178	122	27	422
5	91	239	178	87	595

Exhibit 34
Accessibility related to the scatter of articles

first three columns: percentage and number of journals available in the departmental library, percentage and number available in the departmental library or elsewhere on campus, percentage and number available on campus or elsewhere through ILLINET Online. However one looks at these data, accessibility declines regularly with scatter. The departmental library owns 60% of the Zone 1 journals, 53% of those in Zone 2, 31% of those in Zone 3, 22.5% of those in Zone 4, and 15% of those in the final zone. Coverage of the campus-wide libraries declines from 100% in Zone 1 to 55% in Zone 5 and ILLINET coverage declines from 100% in Zone 1 to 85% in the final zone.

The investigation was conducted to satisfy an intellectual curiosity concerning the relationship between accessibility and scatter rather than to study the performance of any library. Nevertheless, the technique could be used to evaluate the journal coverage of a departmental library, the academic library of which it forms a part, and some network to which the academic library belongs. It could also be used to

Zone	Percentage (Number) of Journals in Departmental Library	Plus Percentage (Number) Available on Campus	Plus Percentage (Number) Available through ILLINET Online	Percentage (Number) Not Available through ILLINET Online
1	60 (21)	100 (35)	100 (35)	0 (0)
2	53 (42)	94 (74)	99 (78)	1 (1)
3	31 (60)	77 (147)	95 (181)	5 (10)
4	22.5 (95)	65 (273)	94 (395)	6 (27)
5	15 (91)	55 (330)	85 (508)	15 (87)

Exhibit 35
Cumulative accessibility related to the scatter of articles

compare various departmental libraries within a university in terms of the proportion of in-demand journals they are able to supply from their own resources.

	Title	Number of courses	Total number of references
1.	Library Journal	21	307
2.	Serials Librarian	4	230
3.	Library Resources and Technical Services	12	199
4.	Illinois Libraries	13	188
5.	Library Trends	25	172
6.	College & Research Libraries	19	153
7.	Library Acquisitions	3	134
8.	Journal of Academic Librarianship	18	106
9.	Journal of Youth Services	3	101
10.	Serials Review	5	99
11.	Library Quarterly	16	94
12.	Journal of the American Society for Information Science	11	90
13.	School Library Journal	8	89
14.	American Libraries	13	88
15.	VOYA	1	87
16.	Conservation Administration News	1	78
17.	Wilson Library Bulletin	15	74
18.	Bulletin of the Medical Library Association	9	70
19.	Science and Technology Libraries	7	69
20.	Microform Review	4	67

4	journals with 60-66 appearances
6	journals with 50-59 appearances
6	journals with 40-49 appearances
11	journals with 30-39 appearances
8	journals with 20-29 appearances
11	journals with 10-19 appearances
12	journals with 6-9 appearances
31	journals with 2-5 appearances
13	journals with 1 appearance

Total number of journals appearing = 122

Exhibit 36

Journals ranked by appearance in 131 course reading lists

The second study, reported by Altuna-Esteibar and Lancaster (1993), set out to determine whether a ranking of periodicals based on "teaching-relatedness" (frequency of occurrence in course reading lists) would closely resemble rankings based on "research-relatedness" (citations in faculty publications and in doctoral dissertations). The study was performed at the Graduate School of Library and Information Science, University of Illinois. The periodicals in library and information science, subscribed to by the Library and Information Science Library at the University of Illinois, were ranked on the basis of: (1) appearance in 131 course reading lists (spring semester, 1989, through fall semester, 1990); (2) citations in 41 doctoral dissertations completed

	Title	Number of dissertations	Total number of references
1.	Journal of the American Society for Information Science	30	214
2.	Library Journal	17	115
3.	College & Research Libraries	22	100
4.	Journal of Documentation	21	92
5.	Library Quarterly	19	87
6.	Information Processing & Management	16	41
7.	Library Trends	14	39
8.	Special Libraries	13	36
9.	Aslib Proceedings	13	36
10.	Scientometrics	7	33
11.	Information Technology and Libraries	10	28
12.	RQ	6	26
13.	Bulletin of the Medical Library Association	12	25
14.	Library Resources and Technical Services	11	25
15.	Public Libraries	3	23
16.	Online Review	6	19
17.	Journal of Information Science	8	19
18.	Library and Information Science Research	13	18
19.	Social Studies in Science	6	17
20.	Online	6	17

    9   journals with 10-16 appearances
    7   journals with 6-9 appearances
  31   journals with 2-5 appearances
  32   journals with 1 appearance

Total number of journals cited = 99

Exhibit 37
Journals ranked by citations in 41 doctoral dissertations (1981-1990)

at the School in the period 1981-1990; (3) citations in 114 publications of thirteen faculty members (1986-1990). While the two rankings on the basis of research-relatedness (Exhibits 37 and 38) are quite similar

	Title	Number of faculty citing	Total number of references
1.	Journal of the American Society for Information Science	8	129
2.	Information Processing & Management	5	82
3.	College & Research Libraries	6	74
4.	Library Journal	10	67
5.	Journal of Documentation	5	55
6.	Library Trends	9	44
7.	Library Quarterly	7	41
8.	Journal of Academic Librarianship	5	33
9.	Library and Information Science Research	4	28
10.	Journal of Education for Library and Information Science	8	28
11.	Illinois Libraries	3	25
12.	Special Libraries	5	23
13.	Library Resources and Technical Services	4	23
14.	RQ	3	20
15.	College and Research Libraries News	3	19
16.	Scientometrics	2	18
17.	Bulletin of the Medical Library Association	6	18
18.	Online	6	17
19.	Information Technology and Libraries	6	16
20.	American Libraries	6	15

    8   journals with 10-14 appearances
    7   journals with 6-9 appearances
  31   journals with 2-5 appearances
  27   journals with 1 appearance

Total number of journals cited = 93

Exhibit 38
Journals ranked by citations in 114 publications of
13 faculty members (1986-1990)

(fifteen of the twenty titles in Exhibit 37 also appear in Exhibit 38), these rankings differ markedly from the ranking (Exhibit 36) based on teaching-relatedness (only seven of the titles in Exhibit 36 appear in Exhibit 37, and only nine of the Exhibit 36 titles appear in Exhibit 38). While the research emphasis seems to be in the area of information science, the teaching emphasis (at least as judged by course reading lists) seems quite different. The course bibliographies represent greater scatter than the bibliographies reflecting research interests: 122 journal titles versus ninety nine titles (doctoral research) versus ninety three titles (faculty research).

The journals were also ranked by a numerical score that takes into account both teaching-relatedness and research-relatedness. The results are shown in Exhibit 39. The unweighted score simply reflects the number of times a journal title appears in all sources — reading lists, dissertations, faculty publications. The weighted score gives much greater "credit" to the research use: a journal earns one point every time it appears on a reading list, but five points for every citation in a dissertation and ten points for every citation in a faculty publication. The weighted and unweighted rankings are fairly similar although the weighting process favors the information science area over more traditional library science.

Unweighted		Weighted	
Title	Score	Title	Score
1. Library Journal	489	1. Journal of the American Society for Information Science	2450
2. Journal of the American Society for Information Science	433	2. Library Journal	1552
3. College and Research Libraries	327	3. College and Research Libraries	1393
4. Library Trends	255	4. Journal of Documentation	1049
5. Library Resources and Technical Services	247	5. Information Processing and Management	1049
6. Serials Librarian	234	6. Library Quarterly	939
7. Illinois Libraries	228	7. Library Trends	807
8. Library Quarterly	222	8. Library Resources and Technical Services	554
9. Journal of Documentation	186	9. Illinois Libraries	513
10. Journal of Academic Librarianship	154	10. Journal of Academic Librarianship	511
11. Information Processing and Management	147	11. Special Libraries	476
12. Library Acquisitions	143	12. Scientometrics	405
13. Special Libraries	125	13. Library and Information Science Research	405
14. American Libraries	118	14. RQ	391
15. Scientometrics	117	15. Bulletin of the Medical Library Association	375
16. Bulletin of the Medical Library Association	113	16. Information Technology and Libraries	347
17. RQ	107	17. American Libraries	313
18. Journal of Youth Services	103	18. Journal of Education for Library and Information Science	304
19. Wilson Library Bulletin	100	19. Aslib Proceedings	289
20. Serials Review	100	20. Online	288

Exhibit 39
Comparison of rankings by weighted and unweighted scoring

Of the 1200 periodical titles received by the Library and Information Science Library, more than one thousand were not cited by faculty or doctoral students, in the period studied, and did not appear in course reading lists. Even more remarkable is the fact that, with tens of thousands of journals published worldwide and about 90,000 received by the University of Illinois, around one hundred titles seem to embrace the diversity of research interests of faculty and doctoral students in this school, as well as the totality of subject knowledge imparted in all courses taught over a six-semester period. More than anything else, however, the study supports the need to look at teaching-relatedness as well as research-relatedness in the evaluation of journals within an academic library.

Study Questions

1. How many different ways of ranking periodicals on the basis of bibliometric data can you identify? Which rankings are likely to be most useful to a librarian in making deselection decisions?

2. Because of severe budget cuts, the University of Illinois Library (Urbana-Champaign) must reduce its expenditure on current periodical subscriptions by 15%. How would you determine which titles to discontinue? You must have hard facts to counter possible criticisms from the faculty.

3. Do you agree with the "point allocation" associated with Broude's deselection model? If not, what allocation would you propose and why? If you were asked to develop a new deselection model for an academic library what components would you include and how would you allocate points to them?

4. What components would you include in a deselection model for an industrial library and what would be your point allocation?

5. Stankus and Rice found that a ranking of periodicals by citation impact factor agreed closely with ranking by use figures (academic library) in some subject fields but not others. What are the possible explanations for this? How would you determine which explanation is most plausible?

6. You are the librarian of a large urban high school. Because of financial constraints, the periodical collection is in a "steady state" condition. To begin a subscription to a new periodical you must discontinue enough existing subscriptions to cover the cost of the new purchase. What data would you use to compare the value of the new title with the value of existing subscriptions. The library now subscribes to 150 titles.

6. Obsolescence, Weeding, and the Use of Space

The term "obsolescence," as applied to library materials, refers to the decline in use of these materials as they get older: the words "aging" and "decay" have been used as synonyms. Obsolescence is sometimes expressed as a "half life" (Burton and Kebler, 1960). The half life of an item is that period of time up to which it receives one half of all the uses it will receive. Putting this in a library context, consider the case of ten books on various facets of biochemistry added to the collection in 1960. If circulation records for these items are available, one might find that they have collectively accounted for 180 uses by the end of 1992. But half of these circulations, ninety, had occurred after their first six years in the library – say by the end of 1966 – which puts their half life at about six years. Of course, this half life is not absolute because the books may be borrowed again in the future. Nevertheless, it will probably be a long time before enough further uses occur to change the half life, if in fact it ever is changed.

By drawing samples from portions of the collection (e.g., through use of the shelflist), and studying their circulation, one can determine the rate at which various subject fields are aging within the library. The data will usually be presented as graphs or tables, plotting decline in use over the years, although half life figures could also be used. A classic study of this type was performed at the University of Chicago, by Fussler and Simon (1969), who were able to confirm that the age of library materials is a good predictor of their use.

To draw collection samples and plot the use of these items over time can be a laborious process. Another possibility exists – taking current circulation and plotting, backwards in time, the publication dates of materials borrowed. Suppose, for example, that one takes all circulation records for agriculture items borrowed during, say, the month of April, 1993, and records the publication dates of the items borrowed. These can then be plotted as shown in the table following. The total number of items borrowed is 585, but about half of all items borrowed have been published within the last three years. The *median use age* is about three years. This is taken to be an estimate of obsolescence. The shorter the median use age, the more rapidly a field is obsolescing.

In this method, one is estimating obsolescence by working from the present into the past whereas, in the collection sample method,

Year of publication	Number of items
1993	25
1992	115
1991	172
1990	81
1989	53
1988	29
1987	17
1986	8
Before 1986	85

one is doing the reverse. Line and Sandison (1974) refer to the former as *synchronous* obsolescence and to the latter as *diachronous*. A number of investigators have assumed that synchronous obsolescence is about the same as diachronous obsolescence – for example, that a median use age of five years equates with a half life of five years. Line and Sandison dispute this, claiming that there is no reason why synchronous obsolescence should be a good predictor of diachronous obsolescence, which they regard as the "true" measure. Based on citation rather than library use, Stinson and Lancaster (1987) produce evidence to suggest that obsolescence measured synchronously should be approximately the same as obsolescence measured diachronously. The results of their study were supported, quite independently, by Nakamoto (1988) and, in a completely different subject area, by Diodato and Smith (1993). On the other hand, Rothenberg (1991), using circulation records from a large academic library, was unable to prove that diachronous and synchronous measures give equivalent results.

If obsolescence is measured on the basis of citation instead of library use, the half life of a periodical is the time elapsing from date of publication to a point at which it has received half of all the citations it will ever receive. To measure obsolescence synchronously, one takes a sample of currently published articles in some field and records the publication dates of items cited in these. The *median citation age* is the period of time, from the present into the past, needed to account for half of all the citations made in the current literature.

The librarian's interest in obsolescence is practical rather than theoretical. If use declines with age, one should be able to discard items on the basis of age or at least move older items to less accessible and less costly storage. This applies particularly to periodical titles. If one can show, for example, that 98% of the current use of a particular periodical is accounted for by volumes no more than ten years old, it might make sense to move the earlier volumes to a less accessible location in the stacks or even into some form of remote storage.

Decline in use with age will be more rapid in some subject areas than in others, although one cannot generalize much about differences among broad fields. The rate of obsolescence in the social sciences as a whole does not seem much different from that in the sciences as a whole (see, for example, Soper, 1972, and Van Styvendaele, 1981), but the humanities tend to have a much slower rate of obsolescence.* Some areas of the social sciences are undoubtedly aging more rapidly than some areas of the sciences. Even in the sciences, one field will age more rapidly than another, whether measured by citation or library use. Exhibit 40, for example, shows data for journal use gathered in six departmental libraries at the University of Pittsburgh (Kent et al., 1979). These data indicate that computer science and physics are aging most rapidly. Materials more than ten years old are still being used at significant levels in chemistry, and materials more than twenty years old are still being used in mathematics. In a study of obsolescence in the literature of music, Griscom (1983) found marked differences between musicology (slow aging) and music education and theory (fairly rapid aging).

Age (years)	PERCENTAGE USE BY AGE					
	Physics	Life sciences	Engineering	Chemistry	Computer sciences	Mathematics
0-1	67.8	34.1	41.3	36.9	54.2	23.3
2-5	82.8	66.3	73.9	65.7	83.4	56.6
6-10	90.9	84.3	87.3	82.0	87.6	63.3
11-15	94.2	91.4	93.7	93.3	95.9	80.0
16-20	96.1	95.7	96.0	94.6	100	90.0
21-25	98.2	97.6	98.3	95.2	100	96.7
26+	100	100	100	100	100	100

Exhibit 40
Decline in use of periodicals with age in six departmental libraries
at the University of Pittsburgh

Reprinted from Kent et al. (1979) by courtesy of Marcel Dekker Inc.

It is tempting for the librarian to think in terms of how far back one needs to hold periodicals to account for a specified percentage of total use. Strain (1966) refers to a *point of obsolescence*, defined as the date beyond which less than 15% of all current use occurs. Chen (1972) estimated this to be 14.5 years for physics materials used in the MIT Science Library. However, Chen's data show that one cannot generalize

---

*Studies of obsolescence in the humanities are few and far between. Soper (1972) gives data for the humanities as a whole and Longyear (1977), Grissom (1983), and Diodato and Smith (1993) present results for the literature of music.

about obsolescence even in a limited subject field: different periodicals have different aging characteristics.

To get a true picture of aging, other variables must be properly controlled. In particular, it is necessary to control for the amount of material available to be used. To give a concrete example, suppose data were collected on periodicals used in a medical library during some period in 1992. For 1991 issues, 500 uses are recorded while for 1985 issues only 250 uses occur. This seems a clear indication of decline in use with age. However, because of literature growth and other factors, the library may have on its shelves twice as much 1991 material as it has 1985 material. In this case, no evidence of obsolescence has been found: in relation to the 1991 material, the 1985 material is used exactly at the level that probability dictates. Relating use of materials to shelf space occupied can be referred to as "density of use." It can be considered the library use equivalent of the citation *impact factor.*

Sandison (1974) reworked the data published by Chen (1972) on the obsolescence of physics materials in the MIT Science Library, making allowances for the amount of space occupied by periodicals of various ages. Sandison discovered an "immediacy effect": the two most recent years were used more than probability would suggest they would be used. Beyond this two-year threshold, however, no evidence of obsolescence could be found: the materials were used at about the level expected based on amount of shelf space occupied.

Sandison's results are remarkably similar to the findings of Price (1980) on obsolescence as measured by citation. Price found this same immediacy effect: the most recent years are cited more frequently than they should be on the basis of probability, but earlier years are cited at the level expected when the amount of material published in various years is taken into account.

Quite different conclusions were arrived at by Sullivan et al. (1981). In a large academic medical library, they observed a regular decline in use with age whether or not a correction was made for shelf space occupied by periodicals of different ages.

Sandison (1981) is critical of Sullivan et al., perhaps because their results do not support his own, and points out that "use patterns for one journal or in one library can never be assumed to apply to another."

While conflicting evidence of this type exists, one can at least say that studies performed in libraries consistently show that materials with earlier publication dates tend to be used less than those with more recent publication dates, even if it is not yet proven conclusively that this is due to a true aging effect. (Rothenberg (1993) has identified and discussed a wide variety of factors that could account for changing patterns of use of materials over time.)

Weeding*

Past use can be considered the criterion of most value in deciding which books to retire to less accessible storage or which to remove from the library completely. The last circulation date method, as described in Chapter 3, can be used to establish a retirement policy likely to have a negligible effect on the overall performance of the library. For example, if all books not circulating within the past eight years were retired, this might account for no more than 1% of current use but might allow retirement of 40% or more of the entire collection. Alternatively, the "dotting" method described in Chapter 4 would identify those monographs that have received no use within a particular period of time as well as indicating how far back each periodical has been used.

The age of books has been shown to be a good predictor of actual use and might substitute for use data in the retirement of materials by broad subject category, especially when used in conjunction with other criteria such as language (Fussler and Simon, 1969).**

An effective weeding program can improve cost-effectiveness of the library by moving little used materials to less expensive storage areas, but there are costs associated with weeding itself: in identifying which materials to discard or relocate, in the alteration of catalog and shelflist records (to indicate new locations), and in retrieving materials from remote storage when requested by users. Different types of "costs" are those associated with user inconvenience, caused by delays in delivery of stored items, and possible loss of circulation due to items not being immediately available. Cost aspects of weeding are discussed by Lister (1967), Simon (1967), and Raffel and Shishko (1969), and cost aspects of storage alternatives by Ellsworth (1969) and Buckland et al. (1970), among others. The weeding of collections in libraries devoted to science and technology is discussed in Mount (1986).

McClellan (1956) has described a systematic approach to weeding the collection in a public library. When the need for the revision of a class has been established (on the basis of criteria mentioned in Chapter 3), all books published before a "period of depreciation" (ten years for science and technology, fifteen years for the humanities, five years for fiction) are removed from the shelf for examination. Books in reasonable physical condition are returned to the shelf if they have cir-

---

*A participant in a workshop conducted by the author suggested that "pruning" is a more correct analogy within the gardening context.

**Nevertheless, Douglas (1986) reported that circulation of items in an Australian academic library does not correlate well with the age of the items.

culated within the preceding two years or are judged to be of "standard value." Books in poor physical condition are replaced if they meet other criteria for retention. All other books withdrawn from the shelves are discarded or, in some cases, transferred to a "reserve stock."

Guides to the weeding of collections have been prepared. The CREW method (Segal, 1980) is popular among small public libraries. Weeding formulae are given for various classes and subclasses of materials (based on the Dewey Decimal Classification). The formulae take into account primarily the age of a book and the number of years since it was last borrowed. In addition, however, the librarian is advised to also take into account five more subjective weeding factors: is the book misleading (e.g., known to be factually inaccurate), has it been superseded by a later edition or a much better book, is the topic no longer of community interest, is the book "trivial" (having no scientific or literary merit), is the book in too poor a physical condition to retain? While the criteria taken into account in the CREW method are all valid, the formulae presented are relatively crude; for most subclasses, the age factor is either five or ten years, and a three year cutoff date for circulation (a book must have been used at least once in the past three years) is applied to virtually all subjects. Moreover, the age of items may not be really significant if use data are available. That is, if a book has not been used in a public library for the past three years, it should perhaps be discarded whether it is five, ten or twenty years old.

While it is quite possible that subjectivity cannot be removed completely, it does seem desirable to base weeding decisions on objective criteria as much as possible. Indeed, it might be feasible to come up with some method for giving a numerical score to a book, taking several criteria into account. The librarian would then examine, for probable discarding, the lowest-scoring books in each subject area. A possible scoring method is suggested in Exhibit 41. Note that last recorded use is given highest weight in this "model." While date of publication has been included as a factor, it might actually be omitted, at least in a public library, where "use" should be a paramount consideration. The factor "On recommended list" assumes that such a list exists. It will for some subject areas, but not for all. In any case, the factors that require some work for the librarian to apply them (i.e., examining items for physical condition and/or checking them against a list) would only come into play for "marginal" items – those close to some cutoff score. The items with the lowest scores according to other criteria might be discarded without further checking. The librarian could decide not to apply the scoring method to books considered "classics" – books that he feels should be in the library regardless of amount of use. Alternatively, a further criterion (Classic?) could be added to the scoring method and given a weight high enough in the scoring to ensure that all such items are retained.

Last recorded circulation date	
Last three months	60
More than three months but less than six	50
Between six months and one year	40
More than one year	30
More than two years	20
More than three years	10
More than four years	5
More than five years	0
Date of publication	
Current year (say 1993)	25
1992	25
1991	20
1990	15
1989	10
1988	5
Before 1988	0
On "recommended" list?*	
Yes	10
No	0
Physical condition	
Good	5
Fair	3
Poor	0

*Assumes the existence of some list or bibliography of books recommended in this subject area.

Exhibit 41

Possible numerical scoring method for use as a guide to weeding.
Best possible score = 100.

For the idea behind the scoring method the author is indebted to
Stephanie Kreps of St. Charles IL

The most complete guide to the weeding of collections remains that of Slote (1989). As discussed in Chapter 3, Slote's procedures are based primarily on the last circulation date criterion.

In theory, the weeding of a library collection, by getting rid of "dead" materials, should make the items displayed on shelves more attractive to readers and thus improve circulation and turnover rate. Roy (1990) did not observe such benefits in her study of four small public libraries (serving fewer than 5,000 people) in Illinois. Approximately ten percent of the adult and young adult collections (fiction and non-fiction) were discarded in each library by a combination of objective and subjective criteria. The objective criterion was "shelf time period" (how long since last recorded use). Books to be weeded by this criterion were then examined by the librarian who made a final decision to retain or discard. That the weeding was successful in identifying low-demand items is supported by the fact that only about 1% of the weeded books were subsequently requested by users in the eight months of the experiment (entries for needed items were not removed from the catalogs). Nevertheless, the weeding caused no significant increase in turnover rate or in circulation. Roy theorizes that new acquisitions to the collections tended to balance the discards (keeping the turnover rate more or less constant) and that a more radical (more than 10%) weeding, followed by weeding on a continuous basis, would be needed to increase the turnover rate.

Of course, not everyone believes in the necessity for librarians to dispose of books not being used. Indeed, W. J. West, an expert on the writings of George Orwell, has recently written a book deploring this policy, which he refers to as the "dissolution of the libraries" (West, 1991). West quotes a British librarian as claiming that the librarian's motto should be "If in doubt, chuck it out." The exact quotation (Pateman, 1990) is as follows:

> The only criterion to use in stock withdrawal is: is this book earning its keep on the shelves? If not, throw it away. (Page 491)

Use of Space

Weeding can improve the quality of a collection. When old and unused books are removed, the shelves appear more attractive to users and it is easier for them to find the newer or more popular items they are likely to be looking for. An effective weeding program has been known to increase circulation (Slote, 1989), although no evidence of this was detected by Roy (1990).

However, the main reason for weeding a collection is to save space or, more accurately, to optimize the use of space available to the library. A library may own space of varying degrees of accessibility to the public: open-access shelves, stacks, and off-site storage. From a cost-effectiveness point of view, occupancy of this space should be related to the anticipated use of materials. In particular, the materials stored on open shelves should be those likely to achieve most use relative to the space consumed.

Take, as one example, an industrial library having space to store 3000 bound volumes of 200 periodical titles on open access shelves.

Assuming an average of two volumes per year per periodical, all titles could be held for seven years back ($200 \times 2 \times 7 = 2800$ volumes). This is unlikely to be an efficient strategy. Some titles may still be used at a reasonable level when they are ten or more years old while others may hardly be used at all after five years, and a few may be virtually dead after two or three years. To use the space efficiently, density of use (e.g., use per meter of shelving occupied) must be taken into account (Brookes, 1970). This has been clearly stated by Line (1977):

> Data on the age of journals cited are of no value for discarding purposes unless they are related to the physical shelf occupancy of volumes of different ages. A volume of 1950 2cm thick which receives 20 uses is earning its keep as much as a volume of 1975 4cm thick which receives 40 uses. (Page 429)

Groos (1969) was able to show how limited space for storage of periodicals could be optimized by considering alternative strategies in which the number of titles and the number of years held are varied. His results are summarized in Exhibit 42. The number of requests satisfied in the period considered was 1172. All fifty seven periodical titles need to be held as far back as they go to satisfy all requests. But more than half of all requests would be satisfied if these fifty seven titles were held only six to seven years back. The three most productive titles alone would satisfy 48% of requests if held back to 1900. The first six titles held back to 1900 would satisfy 68% of requests and the first ten titles held back to 1946 would satisfy 69%. In terms of space utilization, the optimum strategy might be to hold the first seventeen titles back to the beginning; this would satisfy 90% of requests.

Taylor (1977) developed a "consultation factor" to account for use of shelf space. This consultation factor is defined as number of consultations per day per 1000 meters of shelving occupied:

$$Ci = \frac{1000 \times n_i}{d \times L_i}$$

where n_i = number of consultations
L_i = length of shelves
d = number of days of survey

The consultation factor is a numerical value that increases when the number of uses increases or the shelf space occupied decreases. For example, the same numerical value of ten is derived from

$$\frac{1000 \times 11}{22 \times 50} \quad \text{and} \quad \frac{1000 \times 22}{22 \times 100}$$

In the former, a title occupying fifty meters of space receives eleven uses over the twenty two day survey period. In the latter, a title occupying 100 meters of space receives twenty two uses, an average of one a day during the period of the survey.

	Number and percentage of periodical article requests satisfied related to number of titles and years held				
Years held	Titles 1-3	Titles 1-6	Titles 1-10	Titles 1-17	Titles 1-57
1960-1966	269 (23%)	444 (38%)	501 (43%)	556 (47%)	621 (53%)
1946-1966	474 (40%)	716 (61%)	809 (69%)	898 (77%)	996 (85%)
1900-1966	559 (48%)	801 (68%)	923 (79%)	1035 (88%)	1150 (98%)
0-1966	561 (48%)	803 (69%)	941 (80%)	1053 (90%)	1172(100%)

Exhibit 42

Use of shelf space related to number of periodical titles held and number of years held

Adapted from Groos (1969) by permission of Aslib

The effect of ranking journals by density of use instead of "raw use" is shown in Exhibit 43. Title *A* receives twice the use that title *G* receives but occupies six times the amount of space. Title *G* is the highest ranked journal on the basis of density of use. The journals can be ranked, according to the two criteria, as follows:

Raw use	Density of use
B	G
A	B
C, F	F, H
E	E
G	C
D	A
H	D

The top six journals in the raw use ranking account for 86% of the use but occupy eighteen units of shelf space whereas the top six in the use density ranking account for 84% of the use, yet occupy only thirteen units of space. Good examples of the practical application of density of use data can be found in the work of Mankin and Bastille (1981) and Wenger and Childress (1977). The latter carry the process further by developing a "balance index" for each subject area represented in the periodical collection. The index is obtained by dividing the subject's use per shelf space figure by the average for the collection as a whole. An index of 1.0 is said to indicate an ideal balance, a value greater than 1.0 is said to indicate that more titles should be added, while a value of less than 1.0 might indicate that some titles should be candidates for cancellation.

In some libraries retention periods for periodicals have been established on the basis of user opinion – e.g., through consultation with faculty members (Schloman and Ahl, 1979) – rather than from use or use-density data. This procedure may be acceptable if it can be shown that this would lead to decisions very similar to those made on more objective principles – perhaps rather unlikely.

Title	Units of space occupied	Number of uses	Density of use (uses per unit of space)
A	☐ ☐ ☐ ☐ ☐ ☐	18	18/6 = 3.0
B	☐ ☐ ☐ ☐ ☐	25	25/4 = 6.2
C	☐ ☐ ☐ ☐	12	12/3 = 4.0
D	☐ ☐ ☐	8	8/3 = 2.7
E	☐ ☐	10	10/2 = 5.0
F	☐ ☐	12	12/2 = 6.0
G	☐	9	9/1 = 9.0
H	☐	6	6/1 = 6.0

Exhibit 43
Hypothetical raw use and density of use data for eight periodicals

When periodicals, or parts of periodicals, are removed from primary to secondary storage (e.g., some type of warehouse), such a move need not be considered permanent. A librarian should maintain records on frequency of use of stored titles, and how far back each is used. If the use of a title exceeds some expected value after several months in storage, the title would become a candidate for return to prime storage, possibly at the expense of some other title (Snowball and Sampedro, 1973).

Douglas (1986) reports the results of removing 56,000 volumes from an open access collection over a six year period (about 8% of the open access collection per year on the average). The number of loans generated by the open access collection in this period (this collection remained more or less the same at 113,000 volumes) was relatively constant. For each 100 titles removed from stock the demand rate has been about six calls per year. The stack collection was found to account for only about 1% of total loans.

Effect of Location on Use

Mueller (1965), Harris (1966), and Pings (1967), among others, have shown that a librarian can influence patterns of use by changing the physical accessibility of various parts of the collection. In particular, the highlighting of certain books, by placing them on special displays, has been found to be rather effective as a means of promoting their use (Goldhor, 1972, 1981a). One suspects, in fact, that a colorful display on "Books that have never been borrowed" might be a great success.

Baker (1985) has tried to determine whether displays increase use because of the increased accessibility and visibility of books placed in prime locations or because the displays narrow the choice of readers by guiding them to a smaller selection of titles. Pretest-posttest experiments were performed at two small public libraries and users borrowing books were interviewed. The results suggest that the primary factor affecting use was accessibility. Selectivity was a lesser factor and seemed only to affect the larger of the two libraries.

Study Questions

---

1. Is there an "optimum" size for a book display in a public library? How would you determine what the optimum size is?

2. Using citation data, Stinson and Lancaster (1987) have produced some evidence to suggest that the rate of obsolescence of materials measured synchronously is equivalent to the rate of obsolescence measured diachronously. How would you compare synchronous and diachronous measures of obsolescence using library circulation data?

3. Sandison (1974) has presented data on decline in use of library materials with age that appear to be at odds with later data collected by Sullivan et al. (1981). Examine the two sets of data. Is there any logical explanation for the discrepancy in these results?

4. A small industrial library subscribes to 250 periodicals but has space to keep only 300 bound volumes of periodicals on open shelves. What data would you collect in order to decide how best to use this space? How would you collect the data?

7. Catalog Use

Chapters 2-6 have dealt almost exclusively with the first step of the chain of events depicted in Exhibit 4 – that is, with the question "Is the item owned?" Given that an item sought by a user is owned, it must still be found on the shelves of the library. This will frequently mean that the user must locate an entry for the item in the catalog of the library in order to determine its shelf location. This chapter deals with the next probability implied in the sequence of Exhibit 4, the probability that a user will find an entry in the catalog for an item sought.

"Catalog use studies" can be divided into two major categories:

1. Those studies designed to determine what proportion of the patrons of the library make use of the catalog. Studies of this kind may also try to distinguish between the characteristics of catalog users and those of nonusers, to determine how the catalog is used and for what purpose, and perhaps to discover why some library users never consult the catalog. A major study of this kind, involving many libraries in the United Kingdom, is described by Maltby (1971, 1973).

2. Those studies that focus on people known to use the catalog, the objective being to discover how they use it, for what purpose, and with what degree of success. Important studies of this kind have been performed by the American Library Association (1958), Lipetz (1970), and Tagliacozzo and Kochen (1970).

The first type of study will involve the use of questionnaires or interviews administered to random samples of library users. If information is needed on the behavior of catalog users, a *critical incident technique* is recommended. In this technique, an interview or questionnaire asks the respondent to focus on a particular use of the catalog rather than asking about his or her use of the catalog in general. The justification for this is that a person may be able to give fairly precise information on a single "critical" incident but might have considerable trouble in coming up with anything meaningful about his or her general behavior. The critical incident will usually be the latest incident.

If the critical incident technique is applied, the first question might well be something like "Can you remember when it was that you last used the catalog of this library?" If the respondent does remember, he is asked to concentrate on that incident and to reconstruct the event in as much detail as possible: what he was looking for, how he approached the search, and how successful he was.

The majority of "catalog use studies," however, are of the second type noted above; that is, they focus on people who are observed to be using the catalog. With an online catalog, it is possible to gather certain data on patterns of use unobtrusively – i.e., without the users knowing that their actions are recorded or observed. In general, however, one can only get useful details about how a person consults a catalog by asking him. Printed questionnaires could be employed for this purpose but interviews are likely to produce much better results. The interviewer will follow a particular "schedule" of questions.

Interviews could be conducted with a catalog user:

1. When he is observed to leave the catalog having, presumably, completed a search.

2. When he is observed to approach the catalog, before conducting a search.

3. Before and after use of the catalog.

4. Throughout use of the catalog.

Superficially, the first of these options seems most desirable. Since the subject will not know that he will later be interviewed, the data gathering process can have no influence on his behavior. If all one wants to know is whether or not the user found one or more "useful" entries, it might be sufficient to perform a post-search interview. On the other hand, for more accurate information on the success rate in catalog use, and on factors affecting this success, one will probably need to interview the user before the search begins. Of course, this may introduce some "Hawthorne effect": a user who knows he is being observed might behave a little differently than he would otherwise.

Nevertheless, a slight Hawthorne effect may be preferable to having post-search information without having corresponding pre- search information. It is important to know what a user thinks he is looking for before he consults the catalog. It is also important to know what information he brings to the search and how complete and accurate this information is (e.g., does he have title but no author, surname only, initials but not full forenames, is title correct, is author name correct?).

A catalog user will be influenced by what he finds or fails to find while performing a search. After the search, what he claims to have been looking for may not be identical with what he would have claimed to be seeking before the process began. This is most likely in the case of a subject search (e.g., before – books on athletics; after – books on the Olympic Games) but an author/title search might also be affected. For example, in a post-search interview someone might claim to have been looking for a book called *The Information Machines* by Bagdikian. Before the search, he might have said he was looking for a book by Bagdikian on the future of the newspaper industry.

After a search, too, it may be difficult to find out accurately what information the user brought with him to the catalog: he may have forgotten that he only had initials and not full forenames or that the spelling of a name in the catalog was somewhat different from the spelling he expected.

Of course, it is of little use interviewing a user before a catalog search if he is not also interviewed afterwards. Despite the Hawthorne effect, one is likely to get the most complete information on catalog use by interviewing a random sample of users before they search the catalog and again later. Before the search, the interviewer determines what the user is looking for, how he intends to proceed, and what information he has. After the search, the interviewer tries to get the user to reconstruct what he did at the catalog and to determine how successful the process has been. In a card catalog environment some supplementary information might be obtained by observing the user from a distance – e.g., which part of the catalog he goes to first, how many drawers he consults, and so on.

Studies have been performed in which the interviewer accompanies the library user throughout the search. While this is the most obtrusive of techniques, it can produce data that would be difficult to collect in any other way. For example, the user can be asked to explain why he approached the search in a particular way and the interviewer is able to record the entire sequence of events that takes place. This is particularly important in the case of a subject search where it might be valuable to know which heading is consulted first, whether the user follows up on cross-references, whether the user finds entries that suggest books relevant to his interests, and so on. The "running interview" can be valuable if it is conducted with great skill. The interviewer must be very careful to avoid influencing the searcher's behavior by helping him in any way and this is sometimes very difficult to do.

One of the most elaborate (and obtrusive) of catalog use studies was performed by Markey (1983) in one university, three public, four college, and four high school libraries in Ohio. Tape recorders were used to record the spoken thoughts ("protocols") of individuals as they performed subject searches. Where necessary, the investigator prompted the searcher to verbalize. For each search it was possible to collect details concerning the user, a statement of the search topic and the purpose of the search, the information brought to the search by the user, the tape recording of "spoken thoughts," and the interviewer's observations on the searcher's behavior.

Some investigations of catalog use have been conducted within a single institution through questionnaires mailed to a sample of the library users. One example is a study performed at the Australian National University (Wood, 1984).

Whichever method is used. it will be necessary for the evaluator to arrive at some acceptable procedure for selecting users at random for inclusion in the study. This will usually be accomplished by selecting random time slots in days that have also been selected at random. Lipetz (1970) gives excellent guidance on sampling for a large scale catalog use study.

The great majority of catalog searches will be performed either to:

1. Determine whether or not the library owns a particular book or other item – *known item search*. The user will presumably have details on author or title or both, or

2. Identify items owned by the library that deal with a particular subject – *subject search*.

Known Item Search

This type of search is much easier to deal with than the subject search. A known item search is successful if the user locates an entry for the item sought and unsuccessful if he fails to locate such an entry. For evaluation purposes, however, one needs to be able to distinguish collection failures from catalog use failures – i.e., differentiate the case in which a user fails to find an entry actually present in the catalog from the case in which he fails to find an entry because the item is not owned. For each known item search that results in failure, then, the search must be repeated carefully by one or more experienced librarians to see if the user overlooked an entry present in the catalog.

Results from previous studies suggest that the success rate for known item searches in the card catalogs of large academic libraries may be about 80% on the average. That is, the user fails to find an entry actually present for about one search in every five. This success rate is likely to vary from one library to another depending on size – the larger the library, the larger and more complex the catalog – and on characteristics of the catalog itself. It is also likely to vary with type of user. The results for online catalogs may not be much better on the average than those for card catalogs. Dickson (1984) and Jones (1986) present results that suggest that the failure rate for author/title searches in online catalogs may fall in the range of 10-20%. Seaman (1992) used a somewhat different approach, inferring failures in online catalog use from erroneous interlibrary loan requests. He found that about 9% of 1369 interlibrary loan requests made at Ohio State University were for items actually present in the catalog but not found by users.

An important element in a catalog use study will be an analysis of the reasons why users fail to find entries present in the catalog. The results of previous studies suggest that the following factors are all important:

1. The user's previous experience with library catalogs and with the one now being studied in particular.

2. The user's general intelligence and perseverance.

3. The amount and quality of information brought by the user to the catalog. For example, does he have complete and correct author information and/or complete and correct title information? It has been found that, in general, a user is more likely to have accurate information on the title of a book than he is to have complete and accurate information on the name of the author.

4. The search approach followed by the user. Most users will search under names of authors despite the fact that their title information may well be somewhat better.

5. The number of access points provided by the catalog – e.g., the extent to which title entries are included and the extent to which cross-references occur.

6. In the case of a card catalog, whether it is a dictionary catalog or one that is split and, if so, how it is split.

7. Other characteristics of the catalog, including the extent of misfiling and the quality of the guiding or labeling (for card catalogs), and the quality of the user interface (for online catalogs).

Subject Searches

In the case of a known item search, the user either finds what he is looking for or he does not. This simple binary situation does not apply to a subject search. One cannot say that such a search has or has not been successful in any absolute sense. Instead, one must be concerned with *how successful* it has been.

The evaluation of subject searches is much more difficult than the evaluation of known item searches, which explains why much better data exist on the latter situation than on the former. The main problem faced by the evaluator is to arrive at some useful measure of "success" for a subject search. In the past, many investigators have adopted criteria that are far from perfect. At the crudest level, a search is judged successful if the user is able to match his search terms with those used in the catalog. Thus, if he looks for books on higher education and finds the subject heading HIGHER EDUCATION in the catalog, the search is considered a success. In some studies a score is given to a search to reflect the degree of coincidence between the user's terms and the catalog's terms. An excellent study of the ability of users to match their terms to Library of Congress subject headings can be found in a thesis by Lester (1988). Other investigators have judged a search to be successful if, as a result, the user selects one or more books as being of possible use to him.

This latter criterion is certainly much better than the simple "matching" criterion. Nevertheless, it is not adequate. One really wants to know to what extent the items found by the user satisfy his needs and whether or not he overlooked other items that would be judged more useful than the ones actually discovered. For certain types of searches one would also be concerned with completeness – did the user find all the books owned by the library on the subject? Finally, some measure of user effort is desirable: how long did it take to satisfy an information need or how long did it take to find how many useful items?

In point of fact, the evaluation of a subject search in the catalog of a library is not significantly different from the evaluation of a subject search in any other type of bibliographic database in printed or electronic form. The evaluation of subject searches in bibliographic databases, including subject searches in library catalogs, is dealt with in Chapter 11.

Simulations

Some types of research studies relating to catalog use have been performed through simulations. One form of simulation involves the use of students or other individuals in some controlled task situation. For example, the students are asked to locate an entry for a particular title (see Gouke and Pease, 1982, for one study of this type) or to find books dealing with a particular subject. In a simpler kind of study, the subjects are asked to indicate which terms they would use to find information on some topic; these terms are then matched against the subject headings in the catalog in order to estimate the probability that a search would be successful. Useful information can be obtained in studies of this type if they are carefully conducted. The University of Chicago study of requirements for future catalogs (University of

Chicago, 1968) is a notable example of a major study based largely on various simulations.

Online Catalogs

In principle, a study of the use made of an online catalog may not differ significantly from a study of the use of a catalog in card form. To get complete information, including identification of the user and an unequivocal indication of whether or not a search is successful, interviews must be conducted with a sample of users (see Specht, 1980, for an example). Nevertheless, certain aggregate data can be collected through online monitoring, including data on volume of catalog use, use by day and time of day, use of terminals in various locations, and other data reflecting patterns of use: type of search performed, commands used, time expended, subject headings used, and so on.

It is also possible to record and print out, for subsequent study, a sample of the interactions that occur between the user and the system, or even to observe a user's search by means of a monitoring terminal. In this way, valuable information on user behavior and search strategy can be collected in an unobtrusive way. The monitoring of a user's search without the user's permission, even if anonymity is maintained, does raise ethical (and perhaps legal) issues that suggest that these techniques must be used with some caution.

Certain types of simulations can also be applied to the online catalog situation. In particular, the use of problem-solving tasks is entirely appropriate in studies of how online catalogs are used and with what degree of success (an example can be found in Gouke and Pease, 1982).

In 1981 the Council on Library Resources funded five organizations to conduct a comprehensive study of user responses to public online catalogs. The participating organizations were the Library of Congress, the Research Libraries Group, OCLC, the University of California, and J. Matthews and Associates. The study involved thirty libraries of various kinds and seventeen different online systems. Questionnaires were completed at the terminal by over 8,000 catalog users as well as almost 4,000 nonusers of online catalogs. The study also included group interviews and the analysis of "transaction logs" (i.e., machine records of interactions between users and systems). The transaction logs gave details on the commands used, the sequence of actions, errors encountered, the time spent in a search, and the types of searches performed. Summaries of this important study can be found in Ferguson et al. (1982) and Kaske and Sanders (1983).

Lipetz and Paulson (1987) studied the impact of the introduction of an online subject catalog at the New York State Library. Their work confirms the observations of Markey (1984) that the introduction of online subject searching capabilities increases the proportion of subject searches performed by library users as well as leading to an overall increase in catalog use. They also gathered data suggesting that subject searches in online catalogs may be less successful than those in other forms of catalog – at least, users of the online catalog tend to feel less certain that their searches have been successful.

A useful summary and interpretation of research on online catalogs can be found in the work of Lewis (1987).

Chapters 2-7 have discussed evaluation procedures associated with the probability that a library will own an item sought by a user and that the user will be able to confirm this ownership. The probability that a user will be able to find an item owned is dealt with in Chapters 8 and 9.

Study Questions

1. A public library in a less developed country, serving a population of 500,000, is planning to close its card catalogs and go entirely online. The online system is to be designed by an outside contractor according to technical specifications prepared by the library staff. Before the technical specifications can be prepared, it is necessary to learn more on how the present card catalogs are used, with what degree of success, and what problems users now have with the catalogs. How would you study use of the present catalogs to gather data valuable in preparing the technical specifications for the online catalog?

2. "An online catalog is merely a card catalog accessible electronically." Do you agree or disagree? Would it be possible to design an online catalog based on quite "unconventional" search approaches? Would it be useful to do so? What unconventional approaches might be used?

3. An online catalog has been in use in a small liberal arts college for a period of about two years. It has been observed that more subject searches are performed in the online catalog than was true for the card catalog it replaced. The director of the library wants to know how successful these subject searches are. Do users find materials that satisfy their needs? Do they find the "best" materials? How would you design a study to answer these questions?

8. Shelf Availability

The last steps of the chain in Exhibit 4 have to do with the probability that a user will find a book on the shelves of the library given that he has located an entry for it in the catalog. A shelf availability study can be performed through simulation or it can be achieved by a survey of library users. A review of availability studies has been prepared by Mansbridge (1986).

Simulation

Suppose one could compile a list of, say, 300 references representing bibliographic items typical of those that users of a particular library would likely be seeking. An investigator could enter the library on a selected day to see how many of these items are owned by the library and how many of the owned items are immediately available. Let us say that 212 of the items are located in the catalog and that 174 of these are found by the investigator on the shelves of the library. Three probabilities have been established (De Prospo et al., 1973):

1. The probability of ownership, which was found to be 212/300 or approximately .7.

2. The probability of availability for an item owned: 174/212 or .82.

3 The probability that the item will be both owned and available, which is the product of the two component probabilities, namely .7 x .82, or .57.

Based on a sample of 300 bibliographic references, then, the investigator has shown that a user of the library faces about a 70% chance that an item looked for will be owned, an 82% chance that an owned item will be immediately available on the shelves, and a 57% chance that an item sought will be both owned and available.

The study described can be considered to simulate a situation in which 300 users walk into the library on a particular day, each one seeking a single bibliographic item. The results indicate that fifty seven out of each 100 users can leave the library with the sought item in hand.

In performing such a study, one will want to do more than arrive at these probabilities, important though they are, and conduct an analysis to determine the whereabouts of the books that were unavailable on the shelves. Possible sources of "failure" will include:

129

1. Item on loan to another user.
2. Item in use in the library.
3. Item waiting to be reshelved.
4. Item misplaced on the shelf.
5. Item away at a bindery.
6. Item unaccounted for.

Through such an analysis, the investigator identifies all of the factors affecting the probability of availability of an item owned. For one thing, the study shows to what extent a user may be frustrated by "interference" from other users (Saracevic et al., 1977). A library functions as a kind of competitive environment in which the users compete with each other for the library's resources. As suggested in Chapter 3, because of the way that demand is distributed, most users are competing for essentially the same small group of materials.

The analysis of causes of failure may also reveal some sources of internal inefficiency. Perhaps misshelving is found to be a serious problem, or significant numbers of failures may be due to unacceptable delays in reshelving books after they are returned from circulation, or an unexpectedly large number of books cannot be accounted for, suggesting the need for more stringent security measures.

A simulation of the type described can give a very reliable estimate of shelf availability, providing that the sample of bibliographic items used can be shown to be truly representative of the document needs of the users of the library. This is relatively easy to achieve for a specialized or scholarly library but rather difficult in the case of a general or popular one.

Let us consider a study of shelf availability in an academic medical library. It seems reasonable to assume that the types of journal articles that will be looked for in the library are those appearing in *Index Medicus*, and the types of monographs are those appearing in the *Current Catalog* of the National Library of Medicine. Thus, one could use the latest issues of these two bibliographies as the source from which to draw random samples of items for a study of ownership and availability. Alternatively, one could take *Index Medicus* as a source for an initial sample and use the bibliographic references in these items as a "pool" from which a final sample is drawn.

The procedure might work as follows. Suppose 300 references are drawn at random from the latest monthly issue of *Index Medicus*. All of these journal articles are obtained (where necessary, through interlibrary loan) and their bibliographies copied. If each article contains twelve references on the average, a pool of 3600 bibliographic references has been formed. From this pool, 300* can be drawn at random to use as the sample for the availability study.

This procedure is more laborious and complicated than simply drawing the final sample directly from *Index Medicus*, but it has certain advantages: it represents items of varying ages (whereas the direct sample represents only the more recent materials) and it reflects various types of documents – articles, monographs, reports, government publications – in proportion to the way in which these items are cited in the journal literature of medicine. Because monographs tend not to be heavily cited, however, this type of sample may well underrepresent demand for monographic materials in an academic medical library. Nevertheless, by using indexing and abstracting services in this way, it should be possible to arrive at "availability samples" that are at least reasonable approximations of the document needs of users of any type of special library.

Arriving at an acceptable sample for the evaluation of ownership and availability in a public library is a much more difficult proposition. DeProspo et al. (1973) used three samples in their work in public libraries:

1. A sample of 500 books selected at random from recent years of the *American Book Publishing Record* (ABPR).

2. A sample of eighty bibliographic references drawn from periodical indexes commonly held in public libraries. Later (Altman et al., 1976) this sample was changed to one consisting of forty *journal titles* drawn from each of eight indexes commonly held in public libraries (*Applied Science and Technology Index, Art Index, Biological and Agricultural Index, Business Periodicals Index, Education Index, Public Affairs Information Service, Readers' Guide,* and *Social Sciences Index*).

3. A sample of 500 items drawn at random from the shelflist of the library.

The second of these can be considered a completely separate sample used to determine both ownership and availability of periodical articles in public libraries. It is a good sample in that it is likely to represent the types of periodical articles that users will seek in a public library.

As pointed out clearly by Bommer (1974), the other two samples have great problems associated with them. The ABPR sample is noth-

---

*As reported by Orr et al. (1968), with a sample of 300, one can be 95% confident that the results from repeated testing, with other samples of the same size and drawn in a similar way, will not vary from the original results by more than 5% in either direction.

ing more than one drawn at random from a list of everything available through normal publishing channels in North America. It is not a sample that is in any way "biased" toward the public library environment and is likely to contain a rather significant number of items of an esoteric nature that will appear in few if any public libraries. A sample of this kind, drawn from everything available, measures the size of the collection of a public library but tells us absolutely nothing about appropriateness to local needs. More importantly, since the standard used in the evaluation is drawn by random sampling, a public library would perform as well by buying books at random as it would through careful selection procedures.

This can be illustrated by considering three possible selection strategies adopted by three different public libraries:

A picks 500 books at random from the ABPR.

B selects 500 books from the ABPR that seem best to reflect the demands of the users of the library.

C picks 1,000 books at random from the ABPR.

When these three libraries are evaluated on the basis of 500 titles selected *at random* from the ABPR, probability dictates that library *A* will own about as many as library *B*, but *C* will own twice as many as either *B* or *A*. The test measures nothing more than size.

When this sample is applied to a very small public library, the number of items owned is likely to be so small that it would have no significance if used to estimate availability. It was for this reason that the shelflist sample was developed. The ABPR sample estimates ownership and the shelflist sample estimates availability. Thus, a small public library might score 31/500 on ownership and 425/500 on availability.

It should be recognized, however, that the ABPR sample could still have value in the evaluation of a library network or system, allowing estimates to be made of overall coverage as well as overlap and gaps (Clark, 1976).

At first sight, the shelflist sample appears to be perfectly valid. In fact, however, a shelflist sample used in a study of availability may significantly bias the results in favor of the library. As discussed in Chapter 3, use is more likely to be concentrated on a very small part of the collection. Most of the books will be very little used. Exhibit 44 shows a hypothetical collection divided into three levels of demand. In actual fact, most of the use comes from that third of the collection identified as "demand level one." The items in level three are almost never used. But a random sample of 300, drawn from the shelflist, will include as many low demand items as high demand items. When the sample is applied to the library, actual availability levels could be greatly overestimated.

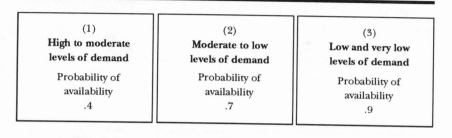

(1) **High to moderate levels of demand**	(2) **Moderate to low levels of demand**	(3) **Low and very low levels of demand**
Probability of availability .4	Probability of availability .7	Probability of availability .9

Exhibit 44
Library collection partitioned into three levels of demand

In real life, the chance that a user walking into this library will find a sought item available may be little more than .4. The shelflist sample, on the other hand, estimates availability at .66 [(40/100 + 70/100 + 90/100)/3].

In actual fact, the results of an availability study based on a shelflist sample can be adjusted mathematically to eliminate this type of bias (Kantor, 1981 and Schwarz, 1983). On the other hand, there is a much better way of arriving at the sample in the first place, namely to draw it from the circulation records of the library.*

Suppose one drew a random sample of 500 items from all those recorded as out on loan on a particular day in April. This sample could then be applied to measure availability on a selected day in, say, October. Such a sample is superior to the shelflist sample in that its composition should correspond to the various levels of demand reflected in Exhibit 44. That is, most of the items will be level one but there will also be some level two and a few level three items, this distribution reflecting the actual distribution of demand over the collection as a whole.

A study was performed by Stelk and Lancaster (1990a) to determine to what extent the availability rate calculated from a shelflist sample would differ from the availability rate calculated from a "previously used" sample. The study was performed in the Undergraduate

---

*For this idea I am indebted to Kay Flowers, Fondren Library, Rice University, Houston, Texas.

Library at the University of Illinois at Urbana-Champaign. Each sample consisted of 450 items. However, the shelflist had been discontinued in 1984 so items added to the collection after 1984 were eliminated from the "previously used" sample to make both samples comparable. The results of the study are shown in Exhibit 45.

	Sample size	On shelf # %	In circulation # %	Not accounted for # %	At binding # %
Shelflist sample	450	360 80.0	51 11.3	37 8.2	2 0.4
Previously used	450	316 70.2	130 28.9	4 0.9	0 0.0

Exhibit 45
Shelf availability for a shelflist sample and a "previously used" sample

The probability of availability for an item drawn from the shelflist is .8 while the probability of availability for an item used in the recent past is .7. The difference between these results is not as dramatic as one might expect. The same is true for the data relating to items in circulation. It is not surprising that about 30% of the previously used items were again in use but it is perhaps surprising that 11% of a completely random sample of items drawn from the shelflist would be charged out when looked for. It seems clear that the collection of the Undergraduate Library is an active one and may contain relatively few items that are in low demand. In actual fact, during the summer of 1988 the library had weeded its shelves of books that had not circulated within the preceding five years.

The shelf availability rate, whichever sample is used, is unusually high. Previous studies suggest than an availability rate of 40-50% might be more typical in an academic library. The high figure here can be explained by the sampling procedures used, which eliminated items added to the library since 1984. One can expect that the overall level of demand for items more recently acquired will exceed the level for the older items. Consequently, were the samples to be drawn from all items in the collection, including those added since 1984, the overall availability rate might well be much lower than .7. The date restriction used in sampling, however, should have no significant effect on the *comparison* of the two availability rates – i.e., it should not bias the results in one direction or another. The study suggests that availability rates calculated on the basis of a shelflist sample may not be too inaccurate in a relatively small and active library with a regular weeding program. It is likely that quite different results would have been achieved had the study been broadened to the university library as a whole.

The circulation (previously used) sample, as described, solves the problem of estimating shelf availability in a public library but not the problem of estimating ownership. Drawing samples at random from bibliographic tools designed for the public library environment (e.g., *Public Library Catalog* or the *Fiction Catalog*) is probably better than drawing from the ABPR, but carries its own dangers: if a public library uses the *Fiction Catalog* as its primary source in the selection of fiction, that source is of little use as an evaluation tool for that library.

One way to arrive at a sample for estimating ownership in a public library is to draw it from items added to another public library in a similar type of community. Consider Library *A*, serving a population of 30,000 in a predominantly agricultural community. About fifty miles away exists Library *B*, serving a predominantly agricultural community of about 100,000. A sample drawn at random from the "new book list" of *B*, assuming that such a publication is available, might be a useful sample to use for estimating ownership in Library *A*. Of course, it is better to use the larger library in the evaluation of the smaller than it is to use the smaller to evaluate the larger.

In the evaluation of document delivery, the general academic (e.g., undergraduate) library exhibits some of the same problems presented by the public library, although course reading lists or required texts might be used as a suitable source from which to draw samples. Wainwright and Dean (1976), for example, have described how undergraduate course reading lists were used in evaluation of colleges of advanced education in Australia. Stelk and Lancaster (1990b) have used textbooks in collection evaluation and the approach could obviously be extended to availability studies. Items cited in texts required for various courses should be the kinds of things that students might well be looking for in the library.

Scoring Methods

In evaluating the performance of a single library, the derivation of scores reflecting simple probabilities seems most useful. In the *comparison* of libraries, however, alternative scoring procedures are possible.

In the "document delivery test," as developed by Orr et al. (1968), the performance of a library was expressed as a *capability index* (CI), a value between zero and 100 that reflects the speed with which the library can deliver items to users. As used by Orr, the CI was derived from a five-point scale expressing "estimated delivery time," as follows:

1. Item delivered in less than ten minutes.
2. Delivery time is ten minutes to two hours.
3. Delivery time is two hours to one day.
4. Delivery time is one day to one week.
5. Delivery time is over a week.

The forms used to collect data in the availability study can be printed to indicate all possible outcomes for a search. Each of these outcomes is pre-coded with a number to indicate estimated delivery time. For example, a book immediately available on open shelves would be coded 1, the best possible case, while an item that had to be delivered to the user from controlled access stacks might be coded 2 and an item away at a bindery could be coded 5. In this scoring procedure, no binary distinction is made between items owned and items not owned. If it is thought that a non-owned item could be acquired in less than a week (e.g., through interlibrary loan), it would be coded 4; if interlibrary loan is likely to take more than a week it would be coded 5.

With a sample of 300 items, the scoring might be as follows:

$$
\begin{array}{lll}
70 \text{ items score } 1 & 1 \times 70 = & 70 \\
62 \text{ items score } 2 & 2 \times 62 = & 124 \\
44 \text{ items score } 3 & 3 \times 44 = & 132 \\
29 \text{ items score } 4 & 4 \times 29 = & 116 \\
95 \text{ items score } 5 & 5 \times 95 = & 475
\end{array}
$$

The *mean speed* derived from these results is 3(917/300) approximately. The equation for deriving the capability index is:

$$
\frac{5 \text{ minus mean speed}}{4} \times 100
$$

which, in this case, would be

$$
\frac{5 - 3}{4} \times 100, \text{ or } 50
$$

Note that a library would have a CI of 100 if all items in the sample were available in ten minutes or less and a CI of zero if no item was available in less than a week. Thus scored, the document delivery test is very discriminating in ranking libraries on their ability to deliver documents to users expeditiously (Orr and Schless, 1972).

In a study of the availability of books in Illinois public libraries, Wallace (1983) also used a scoring procedure that takes delivery speed into account. A library can earn up to ten points for a single book appearing in the test. It receives all ten points if the book is immediately available. If this ideal situation does not apply, points are deducted according to the following schedule:

Library offers to place reserve or obtain an interlibrary loan

Book obtained in 1-3 days	Deduct 1
Book obtained in 4-10 days	Deduct 2
Book obtained in 11-17 days	Deduct 3
Book obtained in 18-24 days	Deduct 4
Book obtained in 25-31 days	Deduct 5
Book obtained in 32-38 days	Deduct 6
Book obtained in 39-45 days	Deduct 7
Book obtained in 46-52 days	Deduct 8
Book obtained in 53-59 days	Deduct 9
Book obtained in 60 days or more	Deduct 10

If members of the library staff made no attempt to reserve an owned book or obtain an unowned book on interlibrary loan, the library was given a score of zero. Wallace's study involved the use of "surrogate users." In this type of study, a volunteer enters a library looking only for one or two preselected titles and records the actual outcome of this particular search.

A somewhat similar approach was used by Smith et al. (1989) in a study of the ability of university students to locate particular issues of serials: each student was given five citations to specific items in serials and was allowed one hour to locate the item and to complete a worksheet on each search. In effect, this is a problem-solving exercise devised to simulate actual use of the library.

Besides those already mentioned, simulation studies of document availability have been reported by Penner (1972), Ramsden (1978), and Murfin (1980).

User Surveys

As an alternative to the simulation method, a study of availability can be conducted through a type of user survey. One approach is simply to get users to record details of items they look for but are unable to find. This can be achieved by handing users brief questionnaires as they enter the library on those days chosen for the survey. Additional questionnaires can be made available at the catalog and other strategic points, and signs can be used to request the cooperation of users.

The survey can be designed to focus on shelf availability alone or on virtually all sources of failure. The form (it could be brief enough to fit on a small card) can be so designed that the user records: (a) details of items he is unable to find in the catalog, and (b) the fact that he was unable to locate on the shelf an item for which he had found an entry in the catalog. On the other hand, the form could be designed only to record nonavailability on the shelf of an item for which the call number is known. In the first case, obviously, it would be possible to break down the failures into collection failures and shelf availability failures. In the latter case, only shelf availability is being studied.

Users are asked to return the completed failure form to a desk at the exit, to drop it into some form of collecting box, or (in some studies) to put it on the shelf where the book is supposed to be. In this type of study, the investigator must follow up immediately to determine the reasons for nonavailability of items (as discussed earlier in the chapter).

As described, this type of survey seeks the voluntary cooperation of all users who encounter failures to find sought items. If continued for a significant period of time, reliable data can be obtained on the relative impact of various sources of failure, but no absolute value for the number of failures occurring is achieved since not everyone encountering a failure will cooperate. Moreover, the method will not give a true *failure rate* because one will not know how many successes occur for each failure recorded. The number of items borrowed on the days of the survey gives some indication of "success" but the ratio of items borrowed to recorded failures will give a very imperfect picture of failure rate.

As with many other types of study, it is usually better to focus on a random sample of users, making a strong effort to secure their cooperation, rather than trying to achieve voluntary cooperation from everyone. In this case, every *nth* user entering the library is given a form by the investigator. The cooperation of the sampled users is requested and each is asked to return his form to the investigator as he leaves the library. As an alternative, the users could be contacted as they are seen to approach the catalog.

When focusing on a random sample of users in this way, interviews can replace the questionnaires. Each selected user is interviewed as he enters the library, to find out what he is looking for, and re-interviewed as he leaves to determine whether or not he was successful. In some studies (e.g., Schofield et al., 1975), exit interviews only have been used. This is not completely satisfactory because it does not give a record of what each user claimed to be seeking at the time he entered the library.

The great advantage of the sampling method, of course, is that it gives a reliable estimate of the failure rate, as well as permitting the usual analysis to identify the reasons for failure. Suppose that 800 users, selected at random, are briefly interviewed over a period of several weeks as they enter the library. Of these, 510 claim to be looking for one or more "known items." Each records on a brief form whatever details he has on one of the items he is seeking. He is asked to use the same form to indicate whether or not he was able to locate the item in the catalog and whether or not he was able to find it on the shelves. Let us say that 450 of the 510 users fully cooperate as requested and return completed forms to the investigator as they leave the library. By follow-up procedures, the investigator is able to produce the following data:

Number of items looked for	450
Number owned	364
Number of owned items located in catalog	312
Number of located items found on shelf	209
Reasons for nonavailability of item on shelf	
In circulation	62
Waiting to be reshelved	12
Misshelved	10
At binding	8
In use in the library	2
Item unaccounted for	9

Besides determining reasons for nonavailability on the shelf, this investigator has been able to show that the probability of ownership of a sought item is 364/450 (.81), the probability of a successful catalog search for an item owned is 312/364 (.86), and the probability that an item found in the catalog will be found on the shelf is 209/312 (.67). Overall, in 209 out of 450 cases (.46) the user is able to leave the library with the needed item in his hand.

Wiemers (1981) demonstrates how a survey of this kind can be extended to cover users looking for material of a particular type. For example, one indicates that he is seeking books on Scandinavian cooking. The questionnaire then determines if he was able to confirm that the library owns books on this subject and if he was able to find books on this subject on the shelf. Jones (1991) refers to a study in which twelve public libraries in England were surveyed in a particular day to determine what selection of books they had to offer on fifteen selected topics. In 50% of the 180 cases (15 x 12), not a single book on the subject was available.

The materials availability form recommended by the Public Library Association (Van House et al., 1987) is reproduced as Exhibit 46. This form, very similar to the one developed earlier by Wiemers, covers the known-item, subject and browsing situations.

Form number _____

LIBRARY SURVEY

Library _____   Date _____

PLEASE FILL OUT THIS SURVEY AND RETURN IT AS YOU LEAVE

We want to know if you find what you look for in our libraries. Please list below what you looked for today. Mark "YES" if you found it, and "NO" if you did not find it.

TITLE	**SUBJECT OR AUTHOR**
If you are looking for a specific book, record, cassette, newspaper, or issue of a magazine, please write the title below. Include any reserve material picked up.	If you are looking for materials or information on a particular subject or a special author today, please note each subject or person below.

NAME OF WORK (Example) • Gone with the Wind	FOUND? YES NO	SUBJECT OR AUTHOR (Examples) • how to repair a toaster • any book by John D. MacDonald	DID YOU FIND SOMETHING? YES NO
1.		1.	
2.		2.	
3.		3.	
4.		4.	
5.		5.	

BROWSING If you were browsing and not looking for anything specific, did you find something of interest?

YES _____   NO _____

OTHER _____ Check here if your visit today did *not* include any of the above activities.
(Example) using the photocopy machine

COMMENTS We would appreciate any comments on our service and collections on the back of this sheet.   **THANK YOU!**

Exhibit 46
Materials availability survey form

Reprinted with permission of the American Library Association from Van House, N. A., et al.
Output Measures for Public Libraries. Second Edition. 1987

Examples of the use of the survey method in studies of shelf availability can be found in Urquhart and Schofield (1971, 1972), Gore

(1975), Kantor (1976a,b), Whitlatch and Kieffer (1978), Goehlert (1978), Smith and Granade (1978), Shaw (1980), Wood et al. (1980), Detweiler (1980), Frohmberg et al. (1980), and Ciliberti et al. (1987). Van House et al. (1987) describes some procedures and presents sample survey forms.

Latent Needs

Line (1973) went beyond the typical availability survey and designed a study to determine to what extent a university library could supply bibliographic items needed by researchers *whether they consulted the library or not.*

A study of this kind might work somewhat as follows. Suppose we identify fifty faculty members willing to participate. Each is given a set of, say, ten preprinted cards. Beginning on a selected day, a participant is to record the bibliographic details of any documents he wants or needs to consult in connection with his work at the university. One card is used for each such item and the process ends when he has used up all ten of his cards. The cards are also designed as brief questionnaires to determine whether or not the subject actually found the item he needed, where he found it, if he is still pursuing it, and so on.

If the subjects cooperate fully, and provide reliable data, a study of this type could indicate:

1. The proportion of the document needs that the library could supply if called upon.

2. The proportion of the document needs actually converted into demands on the library's resources.

3. The success rate of the library for these demands.

4. Other sources of documents used by the faculty.

5. Types of items needed by faculty that the library could not supply.

As Line discovered, there are many problems involved in a study of this kind. In the first place, the people who agree to participate may not be fully representative of the entire community. Not everyone who agrees to participate will do so, and the needs of those who cooperate may not be the same as the needs of those who do not. Line also discovered that his participants tended not to record the very simple needs – e.g., consultation of a dictionary – but only the more difficult, thus distorting the results.

This type of study is most likely to be feasible in a special library (e.g., in a small company) where the librarian knows all of the potential users. In this situation, it is possible that some form of "critical incident" technique might produce useful results. For example, a random sample of the researchers could be contacted, perhaps by telephone. Each is asked to recall the last time he needed some publication in connection with his work for the company. He is then asked if he was able to obtain it, how he obtained it, and other related questions, in an effort to determine how successful the library would be if it were the first source consulted for every need arising.

Factors Affecting Availability

The factors that affect the availability of books owned by a library have been thoroughly discussed by Buckland (1975). The most important are level of demand (popularity), number of copies, and length of loan period. It is obvious that the more popular a particular book the less likely it is to be on the shelf at any particular time. "Popularity" is not a nebulous measure in this case, but a very practical one. For example, it can be expressed in terms of a last circulation date. That is, one could say that 10% of the collection circulated at least once in the last month, 25% circulated at least once in the last six months, and so on.

It seems equally obvious that buying additional copies will improve availability. But two copies are not twice as good as one copy — sometimes both are on the shelf, sometimes one, sometimes neither — and the addition of further copies may make only a marginal difference to availability. The effect of adding an additional copy varies with the popularity of the item: if a particular book is never used it will always be available and adding a second copy does not change the situation.

If a book is off the shelf for one half of the year, one can say its availability rate is 0.5. Adding a second copy will improve availability but will not double it (Leimkuhler, 1966). Buckland (1975) presents data to show the effect of varying numbers of duplicate copies on the availability of books at different levels of popularity. With ninety eight demands per year for a particular title, if two copies will produce an availability rate of 0.5, three copies will improve availability to 0.7, and four copies to 0.8 (Freeman and Co., 1965).

Less obvious, perhaps, are the effects on availability of the length of the loan period. Suppose that every user of a library returns a book on or near the day on which it is due to be returned. There is, in fact, a strong tendency for this to occur, as reported by Newhouse and Alexander (1972), Buckland (1975), and Goehlert (1979). Then, reducing the length of the loan period from four weeks to two weeks greatly increases the probability that any book will be available on the shelf when looked for by a user. In fact, cutting the length of the period in half has roughly the same effect on availability as buying a second copy.

The librarian can improve the accessibility of books by buying more copies of popular items, reducing the length of the loan period, or both. In fact, if one wished, it would be possible to identify a desired "satisfaction level" (e.g., 0.8 – a user will find a desired item to be on the shelf in eight cases out of ten) and take steps to ensure that this level would apply to every book in the library. Suppose one divided the collection into five levels of popularity on the basis of most recent circulation date. For Level five the probability of availability could already be 0.99 and would remain there even if the loan period for this category was extended to ten years. For Level four the probability of availability might already be 0.8 with a loan period of four weeks, and no further action is required. Availability for Level three items might be increased to 0.8 by reducing the length of the loan period from four weeks to three weeks. To reach 0.8 availability for Level two, the length of the loan period may need to be reduced to two weeks. This leaves us with Level one items – the rather small number of highly popular items in the library. To ensure a probability of availability of 0.8 one might need, say, five copies of each and a loan period of one week.

Buckland (1975) has published data that show how popularity (level of demand for an item), length of loan period, and number of copies affect the probability of availability of books. His data are summarized in Exhibit 47. With a long loan period of ten weeks, the chance that one of the most popular books (class A) will be on the shelf, assuming a single copy, is only .37. This probability can be increased to .66 with two copies and .86 with three. On the other hand, reducing the length of the loan period, without buying further copies, also has a profound effect on the probability of availability. With a one-week loan period, even the most popular items in this hypothetical library have a high probability (.91) of being on the shelf when sought by a user. As Buckland's data show clearly, reducing the loan period or buying further copies are strategies that have most profound effects on the items in greatest demand. The data in Exhibit 47 should be regarded only as illustrative of the interrelationships involved among popularity, duplication rate and length of loan period. The actual probabilities of availability within this model would be determined by the different values accorded to the levels of popularity (e.g., availability values for class A if it were defined as "last circulation date = one month or less" would be different from the values were this class defined as "LCD = two months or less").

Popu- larity Class	(i)	One copy Loan Policy* (ii)	(iii)	(iv)	(i)	Two copies Loan Policy (ii)	(iii)	(iv)	(i)	Three copies Loan Policy (ii)	(iii)	(iv)
A	91	79	52	37	100	98	84	66	100	100	97	86
B	94	86	62	44	100	99	91	77	100	100	99	93
C	98	94	72	56	100	100	97	87	100	100	100	98
D	99	98	82	68	100	100	99	84	100	100	100	100
E	100	100	97	85	100	100	100	100	100	100	100	100

* (i) = one week, (ii) = two weeks, (iii) = five weeks, (iv) = ten weeks

Exhibit 47
Effect on book availability of popularity level, length of loan period,
and number of copies

Reprinted from Buckland (1975) by permission of Michael Buckland

Buckland (1975) has reported that a type of "homeostatic" effect may govern book availability. That is, if satisfaction level is pushed up from, say, 0.5 to 0.8, use of the library may increase substantially because of improved expectations of success among the community. This greatly increased demand, however, increases competition for the library's resources and forces satisfaction level down – perhaps back to 0.5. A possible solution to this would be a self-regulating library with no fixed loan period. An algorithm incorporated within an online circulation system would tell the user how long he could retain a particular book at the time he presents it for checking out. The calculation would be made on the basis of the circulation history of the book and the number of copies held, the loan period being calculated to ensure that the desired satisfaction level (say 0.8) will be maintained.

Morse (1977) shows how it is possible to calculate the probability of availability of a book given the number of circulations per year and the length of time it is absent from the shelves per circulation. He presents tables and graphs to allow one to calculate the effect on availability of increasing the number of copies or changing the loan period.

Kantor (1978) has proposed a "vitality" measure for book collections. Vitality is the ratio of the expected failure rate, based on the proportion of the collection on loan, to the actual failure rate. Consider a collection of 100,000 volumes with 5,000 out on loan at any one time. With 5% of the collection absent from the shelves, the expected failure rate would be 5%. That is, a user could expect to find a sought item on the shelves 95% of the time. However, this assumes that all books are in equal demand, which is quite untrue. In fact, most users will be looking for high-demand items and the actual failure rate could be as high as 60%. In this example, the ratio of expected failure to actual failure is 1:12 so the vitality would be a little above 8%. Kantor claims that vitality is a good measure of the "relevance" of a collection. A decrease in vitality over time would indicate "that the library is beginning to accumulate deadwood" whereas an increase would indicate that weeding procedures have successfully eliminated some of the dead material from the library.

Orr et al. (1968) and De Prospo et al. (1973) were pioneers in the application of the simulation approach to availability studies while Urquhart and Schofield (1971, 1972) and Schofield et al. (1975) were pioneers of the "failure slip" approach. The subject of availability analysis is discussed in some detail by Kantor (1976). Causes of non-availability are discussed by Saracevic et al. (1977) for the academic environment and by Kuraim (1983) for the public library environment. Other public library studies have been reported by Chester and Magoss (1977) and Wood et al. (1980). A study by Smith et al. (1989) looks specifically at the ability of students to locate required issues of serials in an academic library; a type of simulation was used – students were each given five citations to serial publications, and were allowed one hour to complete their searches and to annotate a worksheet for each search.

Chapters 3-6 deal with various aspects of collection evaluation, and Chapter 8 deals with a further facet – the availability of materials to users when needed by them. The literature on collection evaluation is very extensive and no attempt has been made to review it comprehensively in this text. An excellent annotated bibliography has been compiled by Nisonger (1992).

Study Questions

---

1. The Director of the XYZ Public Library (serving 100,000) would like to know how successful are the users of that library in finding particular books or other items that they seek. When an adult user walks into that library looking for a *known item* – whether book, periodical article, or whatever – what is the probability that the item will be (a) owned, (b) found by the user in the catalog, (c) on the shelf when looked for, and (d) found on the shelf by the user? How would you do a study to evaluate the performance of the library in its document delivery functions?

2. You are the director of the library of a research center of a large manufacturer. The library is intended to serve approximately 300 physicists and mathematicians at the research center. You report to the Vice President for Research. A new VP has recently been appointed. The VP feels that the library has not been sufficiently aggressive in its information services and believes that the scientists at the center have many document needs that they do not take to the library; they either go elsewhere or perform without the information. The VP asks you to do a study to determine how many of their document needs *could be satisfied* by the library's collection, how many *are actually* satisfied by the library, and what happens to the other needs. How will you do this study?

3. Theoretically, one could design an online circulation system based on a completely flexible loan period. Using data on the number of copies of each title and the circulation history of each, the system itself would specify for how long a particular item could be borrowed by a user. The object would be to create a situation in which, no matter what book is looked for on the shelves, the chance that it would be there would rarely drop below some desired level – say a .8 probability of availability. What would be the advantages and disadvantages of such a system?

9. Factors Determining Success or Failure in Document Delivery

Chapters 2-8 have gone systematically through the steps depicted in Exhibit 4, applying various evaluation methods to the questions raised in this diagram. The present chapter pulls together and summarizes information from the earlier chapters concerning factors that determine whether or not a user can obtain a needed item during a visit to a library. These factors, shown in Exhibit 48, are divided into two broad categories:

1. Can the user find an entry for the item in the catalog?
2. Given that he finds an entry, can he find the item itself?

Before the user can find an entry, of course, the library must own a copy of the item sought and an entry for it must appear in the catalog. The underlying factors here have to do with the library's selection criteria, the librarian's knowledge of user needs, the adequacy of the budget, and various aspects of efficiency – including the time elapsing from the date of publication of an item to the point at which it appears on the shelves and in the catalog.

Several important factors influence whether or not a library user can find an entry for an item in the catalog given that the entry is actually present. Some of these relate to the user's own characteristics: his intelligence, perseverance (e.g., how many entries he is willing to look through), and his experience in using catalogs in general and the present one in particular. Secondary influences, presumably, would include the quality of the guiding or labeling of the catalog (e.g., in the case of a card catalog, does it clearly indicate that subjects, titles, and authors appear in different sequences?; in the case of an online catalog, is the user prompted by the system in how to use it properly?) and whether or not the user has received some instruction in its use.

The single most important factor determining success or failure in catalog use is likely to be the accuracy and completeness of the information brought to the catalog by the user. Does he have the full surname of the author and is it spelled correctly? Does he have full forenames or only initials? Does he have a complete and correct title? Studies of catalog use have consistently shown that users are more likely to have complete and correct title information than complete and correct author information, although the majority will tend to

147

search by author rather than by title. A user is more likely to be able to compensate for inaccurate or incomplete title information than for inaccurate or incomplete author information. For example, he may locate the needed entry if he has at least the first significant word of the title correct, especially if this word is rather uncommon, whereas he may fail to do so if the surname is not correct (Willis rather than Wyllys) or if he has no forenames or initials.

The significance of all of these factors, of course, will be greatly influenced by the size of the catalog. The larger the catalog, the more difficult it is to use and the more important it becomes that the user should have precise and accurate information. "R. Smith" may be adequate identification for an author in using the catalog of a school library but it may be almost useless for searching the catalog of the University of Illinois.

Another factor affecting success in the location of an entry will be the number of access points provided for an item in the catalog, including the number of cross-references (e.g., from one version or part of a name to another) and whether or not added entries are given for all book *titles*. An online catalog has obvious advantages in this respect because additional access points can usually be provided easily and economically. For example, an effective online catalog should allow access to a book through any keyword appearing in its title.

Exhibit 48 also lists "filing accuracy" and "quality of cataloging" as factors affecting the success of a user in locating an entry. While unlikely to be the most important cause of failure, misfiling might occur too often in a large catalog to be judged completely insignificant. Fortunately, the problem of misfiling per se is eliminated in the online catalog. "Quality of cataloging" refers to a whole host of factors, including the ability of a cataloger to interpret cataloging rules correctly, the logic of the rules themselves, the accuracy of the cataloger, the quality of authority files, the extent of use of "analytics," and so on. In theory, "quality" of cataloging should have a profound effect on catalog use. In practice, centralized and cooperative cataloging procedures have greatly reduced the significance of "quality" as a factor affecting the probability that a particular user will find a particular entry in a particular catalog.

The second part of Exhibit 48 relates to the probability that a user will be able to find a book or other item in the library once having located an entry for it in the catalog. This has two component probabilities: the probability that the book will be on the shelf and the probability that the user will be able to find it there.

As discussed in detail in Chapter 8, the probability of availability of a book is controlled by three major factors: its level of popularity, the number of copies owned, and the length of the loan period. An additional factor is that of the level of security in the library. A very

---

Can user find entry?

Does library own copy?

Has it been cataloged?

Can user locate in catalog?

    Familiarity with catalog
    User's intelligence and
      perseverance
    Quality of cataloging
    Number of access points
    Quality and completeness of
      information brought to
      catalog by user
    Filing accuracy
    Size and complexity of catalog

Can user find copy?

    Is it on the shelf?
      Popularity of item
      Number of copies
      Length of loan period
      Security factors

Can user find it on the shelf?

    User's ability to transcribe or
      remember call numbers
    Number of shelf sequences
    Quality of guiding
    Accuracy of shelving

Amount and quality of staff assistance available

Exhibit 48
Major factors affecting success of document delivery

high rate of loss within a library could have a significant impact on availability since it is the items of greatest popularity that are most likely to be missing.

If a book is not in use, it should be on the shelf and available to be used. This is not always the case. Books may be absent from the shelves to allow them to be rebound or they may be waiting to be re-shelved. It is inevitable that some loss of availability due to these causes will occur but it can be minimized if the library operates efficiently. Books should be reshelved as soon as possible after they have been used within the library or returned from circulation, and the librarian must avoid sending materials to the bindery while they are known to be in great demand.

Even if a book is "on the shelf," this does not guarantee that the user will find it. It might be misplaced on the shelf, or the user may miss it because of a confusing multiplicity of shelving sequences, be-cause the shelves are inadequately labeled, or because of physical con-ditions – shelves too high, shelves too low, lighting inadequate in the stacks, call number on spine obliterated, and so on. Finally, a user might not find a book because he fails to remember or transcribe its call number correctly.

One other factor is given prominence in Exhibit 48. It is assumed that the amount and quality of the staff assistance available will influence many of the other factors listed: a staff member should be available to help a user who is having difficulty in finding an entry in the catalog or book on the shelves.

Chapters 2-9 have dealt in some detail with various facets of evaluation applied to document delivery. Evaluation of the major components of reference service is the subject of Chapters 10, 11 and 12.

Study Questions

---

1. Does Exhibit 48 present a comprehensive list of factors affecting success in document delivery? If not, what is omitted?

2. Try to redraw Exhibit 4 (Chapter 1) in such a way that all the factors listed in Exhibit 48 are present. Try to put the factors in the sequence in which they would affect the search for a known item.

10. Question Answering

This chapter deals with the evaluation of one major aspect of reference service in libraries – the answering of factual-type questions. This activity can be examined in several different ways: the number of questions received and their types, the distribution of questions by time of day and day of week, time taken to answer questions, staffing requirements, sources used to answer questions, and so on. However, a true evaluation would attempt to determine how many of the questions posed to the library are answered completely and correctly.*

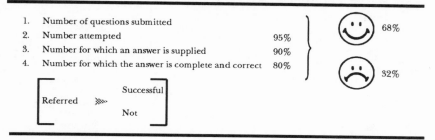

1. Number of questions submitted
2. Number attempted 95%
3. Number for which an answer is supplied 90%
4. Number for which the answer is complete and correct 80%

Referred ⟫⟫ Successful / Not

😊 68%

☹ 32%

Exhibit 49
Data needed for a complete evaluation of question-answering activities

The situation is illustrated in Exhibit 49. To get a complete picture of the quality of this service in some library, one would need to know how many questions were received in a particular period of time, how many were attempted (some might be rejected – legitimately or not – because they are out of scope, of a type that the library refuses to answer as a matter of policy, or are judged to require an inordinate amount of time to answer), for how many of the attempted questions an answer was found, and for how many of these was the answer complete and correct. If the library refers the questioner to another agency (or individual), the library can be considered success-

---

*Notice that "user satisfaction," in this situation, is a somewhat different criterion. A user may be "satisfied" with an answer that is incomplete or incorrect because he does not know, at that point, that the information received is faulty. For this reason, attempts to judge the quality of reference service on the basis of user-completed surveys (e. g., the "reference fill rate" promoted by the Public Library Association [Van House et al., 1987] are of very doubtful utility.

ful if the agency referred to is able to provide the needed information (see Crowley [1984] for results of a study on the ability of a regional referral center to answer questions posed to it by local public libraries).

In the normal course of events, the library will not have all of the data implicit in the diagram. It is most likely to record and retain data on the number of questions attempted and on the number for which some kind of answer is supplied. Certainly, it will not know how many of the questions were answered correctly. Thus, when the annual report of some library claims that the reference department "answered 95% of all questions received," it probably means merely that some kind of answer was found for 95% of the questions attempted. Never-

DATE:	DAY:			TIME:	ASKED	in person	1	PATRON:	
	M	Tu	W			by telephone	2	Undergraduate	1
	Th	F	Sa Su			by mail	3	Graduate	2
								Faculty	3
INFORMATION REQUESTED								Library staff	4
Address				1				Staff	5
Biog.				2				Other students	6
Book Review				3				Others	7
Check card cat.				4					
Critical sources:								ACTUAL TIME:	
poetry, fict., drama				5				Less than 5 min.	1
Explain ref. (in *Reader's*								5 to 15 min.	2
Guide to Periodical								15 to 30 min.	3
Literature, Book								30 to 60 min.	4
Review Digest,								1 to 2 hrs.	5
etc.)				6				2 or more hrs.	6
How to get a periodical				7					
Interpret card cat.				8					
SOURCES:									
Tel. dir.			1	DAS	11			ANSWERED:	
City dir.			2	WW	12			Yes	1
College cat.			3	WWA	13			Partially	2
Gale En. Asso.			4	Bio. Ind.	14			Hope so, patron	
HEW Dir.			5	DNB	15			to return, if not	3
Am. Men Sc.			6	Ency.	16			No	4
VF			7	Atlas	17			Referred elsewhere	5
Con. Auth.			8	Dict.	18				
Curr. Biog.			9						
DAB			10						

Patron's name and address

Exhibit 50
Reference question form used at the Walter Clinton Jackson Library,
University of North Carolina at Greensboro

Reprinted with permission of the American Library Association from Hawley, M. B.
Reference statistics. *RQ*, 10, 1970, 143-147

1. TYPE OF QUESTION Select only one category in A-D below that best fits type of answer wanted.

- Librarian
- Library Assistant
- Other Assistant

JOT DOWN QUESTION

A PARTICULAR TEXT(S) OR AUTHOR(S) WANTED

1. Is particular book, serial, etc. in our collection?
2. Smaller item in larger publication (Particular article, speech, quote, poem, law, etc.)
3. Anything (or certain type of thing) by particular author

B SHORT ANSWER WANTED (AND IS APPROPRIATE) (What, when, where, who, which, yes or no, etc.) (Answer of a few words. Includes verification and meaning of citations, bibliographical form, recommendations, etc., etc., etc.,)

C GENERAL EXPL. OF CATALOG, LIBR., OR PRINTED REF. SOURCE WANTED (Rather than short answer)

D TYPE MATERIALS OR LONGER DESCRIPTIVE ANSWER WANTED (OR APPROPR.) (Answer usually in the form of printed materials)

1. SUBJECT (Mark one)
   - a. Single subject(s)
   - b. Relate 2 subj. or concepts
2. ASPECTS (MARK ALL THAT APPLY)
   - a. Something, anything, everything
   - b. Must be cert. time period, currentness, place, country, lang., etc.
   - c. Must be cert. type ref. source, publ., materials, or format (map, pict., etc., etc., etc., etc.)
   - d. Focus on aspect, biog., hist., other.
   - e. Requests factual inf. in general (or source containing it) (names, addr., definitions, statistics, ratings, rankings, etc., etc.)
   - f. Criticism, reviews, interpr., etc.
   - g. Analysis, trends, pro/con, cause/effect, how-to-do-it, how it works, & other
   - h. Requests that you compile list of references on a subject

2A RESULTS (MARK ONE)	2B RESPONSE (MARK ONE)	2C TIME (MARK ONE)
1. Found	1. Directed and suggested only	1. 0-3 minutes (i.e. under 3 min.)
2. Partly found	2. Helped with or made search	2. 3-5 minutes
3. Not found	3. Deferred	3. 5-15 minutes
4. Don't know	4. Referred	4. Over 15 minutes

3. SPECIAL FACTORS. DO NOT OMIT MARK ALL THAT APPLY

QUESTION AND PATRON	CONDITIONS
1. Missing information or misinformation	10. Difficult to think of source
2. Concerned with foreign countr./lang.	11. Difficult to find subj. headings
3. Concerned with govt. docs	12. Books off shelf
4. Inf. needed (or citat.) very recent	13. Source difficult to consult
5. Wants no. of things	14A. Busy 14B. Very busy
6. Difficult citation	15. Cataloging or tech. problem
7. Patron in hurry	16. Collection weak in that area or out of date
8. Communic. diff. or confused question	17. Need bks. in another area or location
9A. Needs extra help 9B. Returns freq.	

4. LIB. INSTRUCT. MARK ALL THAT APPLY
   1. Expl. sources, citations, search strat.
   2. Expl. cat., computer, holdings, locations

5. NUMBER OF SOURCES USED, REC., OR INTERP. 1 2 3 4 5+

TYPE: MARK ALL THAT APPLY

1. Indexes to period.	6. Yr. own knowledge
2. Ref. books	7. Inhouse prod. tools
3. Cat. (card, online, etc.)	8. Phone bks., VF, Coll. cat.
4. OCLC, RLIN, etc.	9. Circ. bks., period., newsp.
5. Comp. database srch. or CD ROM	10. Consult someone
	11. Refer

6. QUESTION DIFFICULTY (as perceived)
- Easy
- Medium
- Hard

7. ASPECT (only if applicable)
- Stat
- Biog
- Hist.

8. SUBJECT

1st		2nd (If applic)	
	0		0
1	1	1	1
2	2	2	2
3	3	3	3
4	4	4	4
5	5	5	5
6	6	6	6
7	7	7	7
8	8	8	8
9	9	9	9

Use separate guidesheet and select subj. Mark boxes with no. of your subject.

EXAMPLE — SUBJ. No. 2: 0 / 1 1 / 2 2 — SUBJ. No. 20: 0 / 1 1 / 2 2

0862

MAKE NO MARKS IN THIS AREA

FOR OFFICE USE ONLY

Printed in U.S.A. NCS Trans Optic® M18-78712-321

Exhibit 51

Form to record reference transaction from librarian's perspective

Reprinted with permission of the American Library Association from Murfin, M. E. and Gugelchuk, G. M. Development and testing of a reference transaction instrument. *College & Research Libraries*, 48, 1987, 314-338 theless, some libraries do make serious attempts to categorize the questions received in a useful way. An excellent example of a form used to collect data on reference questions is shown in Exhibit 50. The form is designed to record details on type of question, sources used to answer it, type of library user, time spent on the question, and the reference outcome. A rather more sophisticated approach is exemplified by the reference transaction instrument (Exhibits 51 and 52) developed by Murfin and Gugelchuk (1987). The two-part form records the librarian's categorization of the question (Exhibit 51) as well as the user's evaluation of the librarian and the response (Exhibit 52).

The hypothetical data of Exhibit 49 indicate that a user asking the library to find the answer to a question faces about a 68% chance (.95 x .90 x .80) that this question will be answered completely and correctly. However, those evaluations that have been performed suggest that the actual probability of success may be lower than this – that fewer than 60% of the questions received by public libraries may be answered completely and correctly.

How can this aspect of reference service be evaluated objectively? One way would be to incorporate the study into a larger evaluation of library services based on interviews with a random sample of library users. Thus, if a user entering the library claims to be seeking the answer to some factual-type questions, that question is recorded by the investigator. On leaving the library, the user is asked to indicate whether or not he has an answer, what that answer is, and how it was found (by the librarian, by the user with the librarian's help, by the user unaided).

There is no real reason why such a procedure would not work, and it may provide valuable data that the library can use to make improvements in its services. However, it does have a number of disadvantages:

1. A lot of time would have to be spent to determine unequivocally whether or not the answer supplied is correct.

2. Members of the reference staff will know that the evaluation is taking place, and may find themselves trying harder on the survey days than they do at other times.

3. In a public library, at least, it is likely that more questions will come to the library by telephone than by personal visit. There is no way of identifying users who submit requests by telephone. Moreover, the types of questions thus submitted may not be exactly the same as those made by personal visits and the probability of receiving a correct answer may also differ.

FILL IN DOT LIKE THIS ─────────── ●

The Reference Department is doing a survey of reference use and would appreciate it if you would mark the following brief checksheet. Thank you!

(Deposit checksheet UNFOLDED in container on leaving this area or on leaving the library.)
THANKS AGAIN FOR YOUR HELP!

◄ ▭ **USE NO. 2 PENCIL ONLY** ▭

OCCUPATION (Mark one)
○ Homemaker
○ Skilled labor/trades/services
○ Secretarial/clerical/office
○ Sales/marketing
○ Professional/technical/management
○ Unemployed at present
○ Retired

AGE
○ Under 18
○ 18-40
○ 41-64
○ 65+

SEX
○ Male
○ Female

STUDENT
○ High School
○ College
○ Graduate school
○ Continuing education

SOURCE OF QUESTION
○ Work related
○ School/education related
○ Recreation related
○ Other personal project (hobbies, self-development, curiosity, etc.)

1. Did you locate what you asked about at the reference desk?
○ Yes, just what I wanted
○ Yes, with limitations
○ Yes, not what I asked for, but oth. information or materials that will be helpful
○ Yes, but not really what I wanted
○ Only partly
○ No

2. If yes, how did you find the information or materials?
○ Librarian found or helped find
○ Followed suggestions and found on my own
○ Didn't follow suggestions but found on my own

3. Were you satisfied with the information or materials found or suggested?
○ Yes ○ Partly ○ No

4. If partly or not satisfied, why? MARK ALL THAT APPLY.
○ Found nothing
○ Not enough
○ Need more simple
○ Too much
○ Need more in-depth
○ Not relevant enough
○ Want different viewpoint
○ Couldn't find information in source
○ Not sure if information given me is correct

5. How important was it to you to find what you asked about?
Very important ○   Important ○   Moderately important ○   Somewhat important ○   Not important ○

	Yes	Partly	No
6. Was the librarian busy (e.g., phone ringing, others waiting)?	○	○	○
7. Did the librarian understand what you wanted?	○	○	○
8. Did you get enough help and explanation?	○	○	○
9. Were the explanations clear?	○	○	○
10. Did the librarian appear knowledgeable about your question?	○	○	○
11. Was the service you received courteous and considerate?	○	○	○
12. Did the librarian give you enough time?	○	○	○
13. Did you learn something about reference sources or use of the library as a result of consulting the reference librarian?	○	○	○

14. Did you become acquainted with any reference sources you hadn't previously known about, as a result of consulting the reference librarian?
Yes, one ○   Yes, more than one ○   No, none ○

◻◼◼◼○◼○◼◼○○○○○○○○   0862   MAKE NO MARKS IN THIS AREA

FOR OFFICE USE ONLY

Exhibit 52

Form to record reference transaction from user's perspective

Reprinted with permission of the American Library Association from Murfin, M. E. and Gugelchuk, G. M. Development and testing of a reference transaction instrument. *College & Research Libraries*, 48, 1987, 314-338

On the whole, then, the best way to evaluate question-answering services is through some form of simulation.

Simulations

In order to perform a simulation, it is necessary to collect and use a group of questions for which definitive answers have already been established. The reference staff of the library under scrutiny can then be evaluated according to two possible criteria:

1. How many of these questions they are able to answer completely and correctly.

2. How many of the questions they answer completely and correctly out of those they *could* answer because the library is known to own at least one source containing a definitive answer.

In the latter case, the evaluator must carefully establish whether or not the library owns a source containing the correct answer for each test question.

The questions used in such a study must obviously be typical of the questions put to the library being evaluated in the normal course of events; otherwise the information gathered will not be relevant to the library under study. They will usually be real questions collected from other libraries having similar characteristics to the one being studied. If the questions are to be used to *compare* the performance of several libraries, care must be taken to ensure that they are capable of discriminating among libraries. This requires that they be pretested in another group of libraries. The questions that all libraries get correct and those that no library gets correct should both be eliminated since neither group can discriminate among libraries (Crowley and Childers, 1971). Test questions should always be pretested, however they are to be used, to ensure that they are unambiguous.

A simulation study of question answering can be performed obtrusively or unobtrusively. In the obtrusive study, the staff members participating know they are being evaluated and have agreed to take part. A librarian is given a set of, say, twenty questions and is evaluated in terms of how many are answered satisfactorily. The evaluator may be present while the librarian is working, perhaps recording the time taken to answer each question (an alternative is to establish an absolute time limit – the librarian is to answer as many as possible in the time available) and/or to observe how the librarian works, which sources are consulted, and so on.

Clearly, this approach suffers the disadvantages of obtrusive studies in general. Knowing they are observed, the subjects may not operate in quite the same way that they would under more normal conditions. Some may be excited by the challenge and do rather better than they would otherwise, while others may become nervous and perform below their true capabilities.* On the other hand, the evaluator can learn things from the obtrusive study (e.g., on search strategy) that would be difficult to learn in an unobtrusive study.

Some obtrusive studies have focused on how the reference librarian works rather than on the outcome of the task (Carlson, 1964; Torr et al., 1966). In studies of this kind, the investigator may accompany the reference librarian, as he goes from source to source, performing in effect a running interview. Alternatively, the librarian may be asked to use a microphone to record his thoughts and search strategy as he seeks the answer to a more complex question.

Unobtrusive Studies

In the unobtrusive study, the questions collected for the test are submitted to the library in such a way that they are accepted as "real" questions by "real" users. Once more, the library is evaluated on the basis of how many of these questions are answered completely and correctly.

Volunteers – for example, students of library science – are used to submit the questions to the library, usually by telephone. A schedule is established that specifies that a particular question is to be submitted to a particular library during a selected time slot on a selected day. This is to ensure that the test questions do not arouse suspicion, as they might if they were all concentrated within a short period of time, and that they are applied during a variety of "environmental" conditions (a question received during a very quiet period in the library may be treated differently from one arriving in a particularly hectic period).

The volunteers ("surrogate users") may be asked to record more than the answer they receive to a question. For example, they may record details of their conversation with the librarian, including their impressions of his or her helpfulness and whether or not they were asked to clarify the question, how long it took the librarian to find the answer, and whether or not the librarian quoted the source from which the answer was supplied.

The volunteers used in such a study must be carefully trained. They must present the question in a natural way, must understand it,

---

*Weech and Goldhor (1982) present some evidence that reference librarians perform better when they know they are being evaluated.

and must be ready to indicate why they need the answer should they be asked for this information. In the evaluation reported by Williams (1987), the volunteers pre-tested each question three times, in libraries not part of the study, in order to familiarize themselves with the question and the technique in general.

Special problems are posed when questions are submitted by a long distance telephone call, which might be necessary if the study embraces a whole group of libraries. If the librarian discovers that the call is from another town, he may legitimately ask why or even refuse to handle the question. Suspicion may be aroused when the questioner refuses to leave a telephone number and, instead, asks to call the library back. The types of problems that can arise in a study of this kind have been well reviewed by Childers (1972) and Hernon and McClure (1987a,b).

In principle, there is no reason why an unobtrusive study cannot be done by having the volunteers make personal visits to the libraries. However, for evaluation purposes this is not quite as "clean" as the telephone situation for the librarian may direct the questioner to a reference book rather than supplying the answer.

In performing an unobtrusive study, the investigator must establish clearcut rules as to how each question is to be scored. For the question "When did Christian IV of Denmark die?" the answer is unequivocally 1648. On the other hand, consider the question "When was Geoffrey Chaucer born?" One library might answer "1340," while another might respond "It is thought to be about 1340 but it is not known for sure." If the second answer is correct, does the first library get any "points" for its answer? Another factor is whether or not the librarian quotes the source from which an answer is drawn. An answer with source supplied may be considered more complete than one with no source supplied.

A number of evaluations of reference service have been performed by means of simulations in the last twenty five years, including:

Bunge (1967), an obtrusive study in medium-size public libraries in the Midwest

Goldhor (1967), an obtrusive study involving ten questions and twelve public libraries

The Institute for the Advancement of Medical Communication (Pizer and Cain, 1968), two types of obtrusive study performed in academic medical libraries

Crowley and Childers (1971), two separate unobtrusive studies of public libraries in New Jersey

King and Berry (1973), a pilot study (unobtrusive) of telephone information service at the University of Minnesota libraries

Powell (1976), an unobtrusive study involving public libraries in Illinois (see Benham and Powell) [1987])

Childers (1978), an unobtrusive evaluation of public libraries in Suffolk County, New York

Ramsden (1978), an unobtrusive study of public libraries in Melbourne, Australia

Schmidt (1980), an unobtrusive study of college libraries in New South Wales, with some of the questions posed by telephone and some by personal visit

Myers and Jirjees (1983), two separate unobtrusive studies involving academic libraries

McClure and Hernon (1983), an unobtrusive evaluation of reference service involving government documents collections in academic libraries

Rodger and Goodwin (1984), a study of accuracy of reference service at the Fairfax County Public Library

Gers and Seward (1985), a major study among public libraries in Maryland: forty questions posed to sixty outlets of twenty two public library systems (2400 questions in all, half submitted by telephone and half by personal visit)

Birbeck (1986), a large unobtrusive study involving fifteen questions and twenty four public libraries in the United Kingdom

Williams (1987), an unobtrusive test involving twenty academic libraries and fifteen questions posed by telephone (United Kingdom)

Benham, an unobtrusive study involving recent graduates of accredited library schools (Benham and Powell, 1987)

Elzy et al. (1991), an unobtrusive study involving walk-in users of a large academic library

Several of the earlier studies have been reviewed or summarized by Powell (1984) and Crowley (1985).

These various investigations display numerous differences. Some were applied obtrusively, some unobtrusively. In some, the questions were submitted by telephone, in some by personal visit, in some by a mixture of the two techniques. Some studies involved public libraries, others academic. In a few cases, the study was performed to test some hypothesis (e.g., that staff members with one type of background would outperform others or that the size of the reference collection would have a significant influence on the probability that a question would be answered correctly).

At the same time, all the studies have something important in common: they show that the user of a library faces a surprisingly low probability that his factual question will be answered accurately. Overall, the studies tend to support a probability in the range of 50 to 60%, with some libraries or groups of libraries doing much worse than this, and a few doing rather better.*

Weech and Goldhor (1982) were able to compare the obtrusive and unobtrusive approaches in five public libraries in Illinois, using two sets of fifteen questions, each set being considered comparable in terms of difficulty. They recorded an overall score of 70% accuracy for the unobtrusive study and 85% for the obtrusive study, both scores measurably higher than those recorded in other studies of public libraries. In the academic environment in the United Kingdom, Williams (1987) reported an average success rate of 64% for questions posed unobtrusively and 86% for questions posed obtrusively.

The Weech and Goldhor study was performed at the Library Research Center, Graduate School of Library and Information Science, University of Illinois at Urbana-Champaign. For a number of years this center also performed an annual survey of selected public libraries in Illinois, using students from the University to put two questions to their own libraries while at home on vacation, one question in person, and one by telephone. The results were incorporated with other results (e.g., on document availability) in an annual Index of Quality for Illinois public libraries (Wallace, 1983).

The answering of factual-type questions is not the only aspect of reference service that can or should be evaluated. Olson (1984) points out that, in addition, reference librarians should be evaluated on their responses to questions involving knowledge of library services,* on their performance in providing instruction in use of reference sources, and on their ability to "negotiate" a question. She goes on to suggest how such studies might be performed. Another reference service that is becoming increasingly important and prevalent involves the conduct of literature searches for users via databases accessible online. The evaluation of literature searching is discussed in the next chapter.

A special type of obtrusive test involves the evaluation of the reference librarian on his ability to correct an incomplete or erroneous bibliographic citation (Orr and Olson, 1968).

Evaluation of Question-Answering in a Large Academic Library

This section of the chapter presents a case study in the evaluation of reference service in an academic setting. Conducted at Milner Li-

---

*In Childers' study of twenty questions in fifty-seven libraries (Childers, 1978), one library got only 15% right while another scored as high as 75%.

**The Fairfax County, Virginia, study reported by Rodger and Goodwin (1984) found evidence that reference librarians do not always display adequate knowledge of library services.

brary of Illinois State University (ISU), it has several features that make it unusually interesting, including the fact that it involved a large number of "surrogate" walk-in users and that it seems to be the largest unobtrusive study so far performed within a single library (Elzy et al.,1991, Lancaster et al., 1991a).

The environment

ISU is a comprehensive university with over 22,000 students. Milner Library is a central facility organized into five subject divisions with five separate reference service points: Education/Psychology, General Reference and Information, Social Sciences/Business, Science/Government Publications, and Humanities/Special Collections. The five divisions are staffed by twenty members of the library faculty, nineteen classified employees, and a complement of student assistants. Each floor or division also has attached to it one auxiliary "special" collection (e.g., music, maps).

Methods

The study was performed unobtrusively. Students were trained to walk into the various libraries, seeking a particular librarian by name (librarians are identified by nameplate and the students were given schedules of who would be working on which reference desk at which time), and to pose questions for which answers were already known by the investigators (but not by the students). They recorded what the librarian did for them and the answer supplied or found, and answered various questions about the librarian's behavior and attitude. The test questions used were drawn from many sources: reference textbooks, earlier studies, and the knowledge and experience of the project staff. From a pool of several hundred candidates, fifty-eight were eventually selected. All were checked against the holdings of the Milner Library to be sure that they could be answered there. The evaluation, then, was not of the library's resources but of the ability of the staff to exploit the resources available.

Twenty-one undergraduate students participated in the study. A group session was used to give the students preliminary training in how to pose the questions, and to pass out the necessary schedules and forms. The students, who were paid for their participation in the investigation, were asked to keep details of the study completely confidential; they were not to discuss it with anyone until the project was completed. Individual interviews were scheduled later with each participant to give final instructions and to answer questions they might have. Exhibit 53 shows the first page of the evaluation form designed for use in the study. It identifies questioner, question, librarian, time spent by the librarian, time question asked, answer provided, and source used. The rest of the eight-page form consisted of twenty-eight attitudinal questions, the first two of which appear on Exhibit 53, and space for student comments. As the exhibit shows, the student judged the librarian for each attitudinal element on a ten point scale.

Questioner: _____

Librarian/Floor: _____

Question: Number:_____   Short phrase: _____

Time question asked: Date: _____   Hour: _____

Time spent with Librarian in minutes: _____

Answer (actual answer, directions given. Sources or floors provided by librarian): _____

_____

_____

_____

Source:

      Title: _____

      Date or edition: _____

      Volume: _____

      Page: _____

Attitude and Demeanor

  1. Looks approachable

Not at all	Seldom	Some of the time	Mostly	To a large extent
1 2	3 4	5 6	7 8	9 10

    Comments:

_____

_____

_____

  2. Acknowledges user's approach to desk

Not at all	Seldom	Some of the time	Mostly	To a large extent
1 2	3 4	5 6	7 8	9 10

    Comments:

_____

_____

_____

Exhibit 53
First page of evaluation form used in unobtrusive study of reference
in an academic library

All questions were posed over a three-week period in April 1989, and few problems were encountered. Almost all were posed to more than one librarian, sometimes in different divisions if appropriate to more than one. The students were conscientious and all forms were completed with very few missing data. Students attended a group debriefing session to share their experiences and observations on the study.

The study was designed so that each floor and each librarian could be evaluated on both attitude and accuracy of their responses to the students. The attitude score was easy to arrive at. For each of 190 "incidents" (the posing of a particular question to a particular librarian), the attitude score was the mean of the values earned on the ten-point scale for each of the twenty-eight attitudinal aspects.

The accuracy score was more of a problem. Scoring a question posed by telephone is relatively easy, at least for factual questions: either the correct response is given or it is not. (Actually, this is an oversimplification since some questions can be partially answered.) The situation is more complicated for a walk-in question, particularly in the case of an academic library, because a variety of responses are possible from the librarian – everything from providing the answer to pointing the questioner to some possible sources.

In actual fact, of course, one can score the response to a question in various ways depending on what one considers an appropriate response to be. In an academic setting, librarians frequently consider that the most important component of reference service is that of teaching students how to find information; librarians should direct students to appropriate sources rather than provide an answer for them. In this study, however, it was deliberately decided to look at the activity from a student's more short-term view. In general, it was felt that a student would rather be given an answer than shown where to find it. The scoring scheme used (see Exhibit 54) reflects this. The best score for a reference incident was awarded when a student was given a complete and correct answer. Scores were reduced when the student was *led* to an appropriate source, and reduced further when *directed* to an appropriate source. The worst score – zero on a fifteen-point scale – was awarded for the case in which the student was given an incorrect answer, the assumption being that a wrong answer is worse than no answer at all.

The ranking of responses, as reflected in Exhibit 54, seems logical, although the numerical values and the intervals between them are rather arbitrary; in retrospect, it would have been more logical to assign a zero to the "no answer" situation and a minus value to an incorrect response. Using the fifteen-point scale, it was possible to give an accuracy score to each incident and to average the accuracy scores to arrive at an overall accuracy score for each librarian and each division.

	Points
Student <u>provided</u> with complete and correct answer	15
Student <u>led to a single source</u> which provided complete and correct answer	14
Student <u>led to several sources</u>, at least one of which provided complete and correct answer	13
Student <u>directed to a single source</u> which provided complete and correct answer	12
Student <u>directed to several sources</u>, at least one of which provided complete and correct answer	11
Student given an <u>appropriate referral to a specific person or source</u> which would provide complete and correct answer	10
Student provided with <u>partial answer</u>	9
Student is given an <u>appropriate referral to the card catalog or another floor</u>	8
Librarian <u>did not find an answer</u> or suggest an alternative source	5
Student given an <u>inappropriate referral</u> to catalog, floor, source, or librarian unlikely to provide complete and correct answer	3
Student is given <u>inappropriate sources</u>	2
Student is given <u>incorrect answer</u>	0

Exhibit 54
Scoring method used in unobtrusive study of reference service

Exhibit 55 shows the accuracy score for the first fifteen (of fifty-eight) questions, along with the mean time spent by the librarian with the student. As the data reveal, the scoring method was quite discriminating. For example, questions four and fourteen, each posed twice, received a maximum score of fifteen, while question six, posed four times, received the very low score of 5.5.

Exhibit 56 shows the breakdown of scoring for the 190 reference incidents. The best possible score, fifteen, was awarded in almost one-third of all cases. Clearly, how many incidents are judged "satisfactory" is entirely dependent on what one is willing to accept in the way of service. If one is willing to accept any of the outcomes down to "appropriate referral," then any incident scoring ten or above would be considered acceptable – about fifty eight percent of the incidents, according to Exhibit 56.

Question	Times posed	Accuracy	Mean # of minutes spent on question
1	2	12.0000	13.5
2	2	13.0000	5
3	2	7.5000	4
4	2(1)*	15.0000	3.25
5	2	14.0000	6.5
6	4(1)@	5.5000	6
7	–	–	7
8	2	8.0000	9
9	5	10.2000	4.2
10	2	14.0000	3
11	4	9.7500	4.2
12	4	13.2500	8
13	2(1)*	14.0000	5
14	2	15.0000	3.5
15	2	11.5000	3

* Accuracy data missing for one case
@ Timing data missing for one case

Exhibit 55
Question by question results (first 15 questions out of 51)
from an unobtrusive study of reference service

Exhibits 57 and 58 show that accuracy and attitude scores were quite discriminating in separating the performance of different divisions and of different librarians. A study of this kind can identify various types of problems (e.g., librarians who tend to spend too little time with a user, librarians who are perceived to be unhelpful, types of questions that tend to be poorly handled, important reference sources that seem to be little known by the staff) allowing library managers to take action to improve the overall quality of the service.

User Expectations and Satisfaction

To obtain detailed evaluation results that would allow a library manager to identify specific problem areas in reference service, and suggest possible solutions, there is probably no substitute for the unobtrusive study. Nevertheless, if an unobtrusive study is impossible, more subjective approaches can be useful in revealing the perceptions and attitudes of users towards reference services in a particular library.

Score of answer	Frequency	Percent
15	58	30.5
14	24	12.6
13	13	6.8
12	5	2.6
11	8	4.2
10	3	1.6
9	7	3.7
8	10	5.3
5	18	9.5
3	10	5.3
2	16	8.4
0	10	5.3
Missing*	8	4.2
	190	100.0

*Some students failed to provide enough information upon which to base judgments, or asked the question in such a way as to change the expected response, thus invalidating the question.

Exhibit 56
Accuracy of answers provided in an unobtrusive study of reference service

A good example of this type of study can be found in Dalton (1992). The survey was undertaken at the University of South Africa (UNISA) and was intended to assess the satisfaction of postgraduate students with the services provided by the Subject Reference Division.

Division	Questions	Accuracy	Attitude
A	30(3)*	10.4074	8.2100
B	30	12.7333	8.2067
C	20(2)*	11.7778	8.5200
D	71(2)*	9.6377	7.7141
E	39(1)*	8.1053	7.1256
Mean	190(8)*	10.1538	7.8342

* Missing data for accuracy scores.

Exhibit 57
Accuracy and attitude scores by divisions in an unobtrusive study of reference service

A questionnaire was administered to a random sample of 500 of the 2954 postgraduate students, and 367 completed questionnaires were received. (The instrument was designed to determine the attitudes of

Librarian	Number of questions asked	Attitude	Accuracy	Mean minutes spent
1	10(1)*	8.1900	10.3333	4.35
2	10	7.0000	7.6000	5.45
3	10	7.6300	7.5000	6.975
4	9(1)*	7.6000	7.1250	5.65
5	10(1)*	8.7500	13.8889	7.88
6	10	8.2100	13.0000	4.85
7	10	7.7200	11.8000	6.7
8	10	8.2300	10.8000	6.3
9	10(1)*	8.2900	9.6667	4.3
10	10	7.8000	9.5000	7.6
11	10(1)*	5.7400	7.2222	2.15
12	10(1)*	7.3600	11.8889	3.95
13	10(1)*	7.7800	11.2222	6.95
14	10	7.8700	8.6000	8.05
15	10	8.1800	9.7000	5.85
16	12	7.0750	8.5833	4.75
17	10	8.6900	13.4000	7.30
18	9	8.2444	10.2222	8.05
19	10(1)*	8.6600	9.6667	8.5
Mean	190(8)	7.8342	10.1538	

*Missing data for accuracy scores.

Exhibit 58

Accuracy and attitude scores for each librarian in an unobtrusive study
of reference service

students towards various services of the Subject Reference Division, towards the librarians, and towards the library collections (see Exhibit 59). For each element in the study (e.g., availability of librarian, relevance of materials received) the students compared their expectations with their perceptions of actual service received, according to the following scale:

much less than I expected – value of 1 (unacceptable)
less than I expected – value of 2 (minimum tolerable)
about as much as I expected – value of 3 (expected/neutral)
more than I expected – value of 4 (deserved)
much more than I expected – value of 5 (ideal)

The measure of user satisfaction is the difference between the service expectations and the perceived performance. This measure (actual performance minus expected performance) is derived from the *disconfirmation of expectations model* used in consumer satisfaction studies.

Demographics
1. Sex
2. Age
3. Home language

Educational characteristics
4. Previous undergraduate study at Unisa
5. Previous post-graduate study at Unisa
6. Degree
7. Faculty
8. Years registered
9. Language of study

Library usage
10. Personal use of library service
11. Use of subject reference service
12. Role of study supervisor/ promoter

Awareness of service
1. Source of awareness

Subject reference librarian skills
2. Availability
3. Attitude (friendliness, courtesy
4. Negotiation skills
5. Subject specialisation
6. Knowledge of library's services, policies & procedures
7. Expectations

Subject bibliography service
8. Relevance of references
9. Amount of references
10. Academic level of references
11. Timeliness
12. Expectations

Current awareness service
13. Relevance of references
14. Amount of references
15. Academic level of references
16. Currency
17. Expectations

Inquiry and advice service
18. Accuracy of information
19. Timeliness
20. Expectations

Library collections
21. Reference
22. Research collection
23. Journals collection
24. Expectations of reference works
25. Expectations of research collection
26. Expectations of journals collection

Overall service quality
27. Overall performance
28. Expectations of overall performance

Exhibit 59
Factors considered in a questionnaire on user expectations and experiences regarding reference services

From Dalton (1992) by permission of the
South African Institute of Library and Information Science

Clearly, an instrument of this kind can be valuable to managers in identifying elements of reference service with which users express least satisfaction

Capital Planning Systems (1987) looked at user reactions and staff self-assessment for questions received by the business departments of two large public libraries in the United Kingdom. Staff at one of these libraries believed they had answered 79% of all questions completely, with another 18% answered partially, leaving only 3% not answered satisfactorily. At the other library, the corresponding figures were 71%, 19% and 9% (this last includes some categorized as "unable to answer"). Between 80% and 90% of users, contacted by telephone, claimed to be completely satisfied with the service they received, but these figures were derived from rather small samples. The high rates of success reported in this study can be partly attributed to the fact that a very large number of questions (22% in one library, 31% in the other) were of a simple name/address type that could be answered from the British electoral registers.

Performance Factors*

If the staff of a library is evaluated, obtrusively or unobtrusively, on its ability to answer reference questions, the study should be performed with the intention of improving the service and not as a mere intellectual exercise. That is, the evaluator should attempt to identify the most important factors influencing the quality of the reference service in order to make recommendations – relating to the collection, training of staff, recruitment of staff, allocation of staff time, or whatever – on how the service might be improved. The remainder of this chapter will be devoted to factors affecting the quality of question-answering services in libraries.

Exhibit 60 relates to the probability that questions will arise in the minds of members of a community and that these individuals will approach a library to have their questions answered. An underlying assumption is that a library is readily accessible to members of the community.

It seems reasonable to suppose that level of education and intelligence, as well as diversity of professional and personal interests, will strongly affect the probability that questions will arise in the minds of individuals, information be needed by them, and information needs

---

*This section is a somewhat modified and expanded version of an article that first appeared in *The Reference Librarian* in 1984 and is published here with the permission of Haworth Press.

actually be recognized.* These same factors also seem likely to influence motivation, i.e., whether or not an individual actually seeks to find the answer to some question.

Sequence of events	Factors affecting probability that event will occur
1. Question arises in the mind of some individual.	Individual's education, background, interests, experience, and level of intelligence and literacy.
2. Individual recognizes that he needs to have question answered.	Individual's education, background, interests, experience, and level of intelligence and literacy.
3. Individual is sufficiently motivated to seek answer.	As for Event 1, plus: (a) the value of the answer to the individual, and (b) the individual's perception of the probability that the question can be answered by some source.
4. Individual approaches library to have question answered.	Is individual aware of existence of library? Is individual aware that library provides this service? Is library perceived to be appropriate and convenient source to use? Has individual had good or bad experiences with libraries in general and this library in particular? Is the library open at the time answer is needed? Can individual visit or contact library at time answer is needed?

Exhibit 60
Probability that a question will arise and be submitted to a library

There are at least two other factors likely to influence motivation. The first is the perceived value of having a question answered. In many cases, an answer will have no financial value. Nevertheless, it will have some intangible value to the questioner, such as curiosity satisfied or mind set at rest. Even if the reward is intangible, when an individual seeks the answer to a question, he or she is making a type of value judgment: that the answer is worth the effort (a cost) of pursuing.

---

*These factors seem to apply more to an individual in a "home" environment. In a business environment, presumably, somewhat different factors will apply.

In some instances, of course, an answer will have financial value. In these situations, the amount of money involved will probably determine the motivation. For example, in buying a major appliance, such as a refrigerator, one could save $100 or more by finding that some consumer magazine judges one brand as effective as another. In buying an electric toaster, on the other hand, one may decide that the potential savings are so small that the consumer information is not worth the effort of seeking.

Finally, although no hard evidence exists on this, one suspects that the motivation to find an answer to some question will be influenced by the individual's perception of the probability that an answer exists, is recorded, and can be found. The answers to many questions may never be sought because the individuals, in whose minds the questions are raised, believe (perhaps quite erroneously) that no recorded answers exist.

The next step illustrated in Exhibit 60 relates to the probability that an individual, once decided to seek the answer to some question, will go to a library rather than to some other source. Clearly, he must know that a library exists, that he is qualified to use it, and that the library does attempt to find answers to many types of question. If these conditions apply, the library will presumably be selected if (a) the questioner perceives the library to be the most convenient information source to use, (b) he retains favorable impressions if he has used the library in the past, and (c) the library is open at the time the information is needed.

Given that it is approached by some member of the community, will the library seek to find the answer to his question? Clearly, the question must first be understood by the librarian receiving it. Whether this occurs will depend on the ability of both librarian and questioner to communicate. If the question is understood by the librarian, will it be accepted? Perhaps the questioner will be refused because he is not a qualified user (e.g., in the case of some industrial library). If the questioner is acceptable, the question may not be. It could be of a type that the library, as a matter of policy, refuses to answer (e.g., homework questions, quiz questions, or certain kinds of medical questions). See Exhibit 61.

For some questions, while an answer may be considered to "exist," at least in a theoretical sense, it has not been recorded or even, perhaps, determined. This might apply, for example, to a question on the height of a relatively obscure building or one on the thermal conductivity of some uncommon alloy. Given that an answer has been recorded somewhere, the question arises as to whether or not the librarian can locate it. Six groups of factors influencing this probability are identified in Exhibit 62 and elaborated on in Exhibits 63-68.

---

1. Communication factors:
   Questioner
   Librarian

2. Policy factors:
   Is questioner acceptable to library?
   Is question acceptable to library?

Exhibit 61
Will library attempt to find answer?

---

1. Is answer recorded somewhere?

2. Can librarian find answer?
   Policy factors
   Collection factors
   Librarian factors
   Question-related factors
   User factors
   Environmental factors

Exhibit 62
Will questioner receive a complete and correct answer?

Most questions can be answered if one is willing to put enough time, energy, and money into the endeavor. Whether a particular user gets a non-routine question answered completely and correctly will partly depend on how much time the librarian is willing and able to devote to it. This will be determined in part by library policy. But other factors also come into play: how busy the librarian is at the time the question arises, how important the librarian perceives the questioner to be, how interested the librarian is in the question (and, under certain circumstances, the questioner!), and so on.

There are other library policies affecting the probability that a question will be answered completely and correctly. An important one relates to how money can be spent. In some cases, the most up-to-date or accurate information could be obtained through a long-distance telephone call. In other cases, such a call might save many minutes of the librarian's time. Exactly the same could be said of access to online databases. Library policies are very shortsighted if they do not allow

1. How much time is librarian willing and able to spend?

2. What expenditures can librarian incur?
   Long-distance telephone
   Access to online services

Exhibit 63
Policy factors

1. Does the library own a source that contains the complete and correct answer.

2. How many sources does the library own that contain a complete and correct answer?

3. How accessible are these sources to the librarian?

4. How well organized and indexed are these sources?

Exhibit 64
Collection factors

1. Knowledge:
   Of collection
   General knowledge
       Current awareness
       Language abilities

2. Ability and willingness to communicate

3. Decision-making abilities

4. Perception of professional responsibilities and commitment
   to these responsibilities

5. Efficiency:
   Speed
   Accuracy

6. Education and training

7. Experience as a librarian and as a reference librarian

Exhibit 65
Librarian factors

reference librarians to use the most cost-effective approach available. Regrettably, in many libraries, ownership still represents a more legitimate expenditure of public funds than access does.

It seems fairly obvious that a question is more likely to be answered if the library owns a source that could provide the answer than if it does not. Some of the other collection factors identified in Exhibit 64 may be somewhat less obvious.

It is hypothesized (without any hard data to offer in support*) that the probability that a question will be answered completely and correctly increases with the number of sources owned by the library in which the answer is recorded. This is really a matter of probability: the more substitutable sources that exist, the greater the probability that the librarian will use one of them. This probability is related to the relative obscurity, or otherwise, of the question. "What is the capital of Argentina?" is a question that could be answered by any one of several hundred sources in some libraries. On the other hand, consider the following question: "What is the origin of the name Tigre, a resort close to Buenos Aires?" This question can be answered by few (if any) sources in even a large library. The probability that this question would be answered correctly is very low.

Another hypothesis, untested as far as this author is aware, is that the physical accessibility of the information source to the librarian influences the probability that an answer will be found. In many libraries, a "quick-reference" collection exists immediately adjacent to the reference desk. If the correct answer to a question is contained here, it seems highly probable that the librarian will find it. This probability is likely to decrease successively when: the answer exists elsewhere in the open-access reference collection, the answer exists in reference materials in closed-access stacks, the answer exists in circulating materials, the answer exists in a circulating item that is now on loan, the answer exists in an item in a remote storage facility.

Finally, the organization of the information source needs to be taken into account. For example, for a particular question the only answer may exist in one history of art. The probability that this answer will be found by a librarian, given that the book itself is looked at, will depend on how the book is organized and how well it is indexed.

In Exhibit 64, collection factors are considered from the aspect of a single factual question. Primary factors, rather than secondary, are

---

*Powell (1976) studied the relationship between collection size and success in answering questions in the aggregate. He did not determine number of possible sources for each question.

identified. Such factors as "size of collection" are purely secondary since, viewed at the level of the individual question, these factors merely influence the primary factors (e.g., the probability that the library will own multiple information sources that are equally complete and correct).

A number of librarian factors are identified in Exhibit 65; some are more important than others. First and foremost, the librarian must have a detailed knowledge of the information sources available. However, general knowledge is not insignificant. In particular, the librarian should have a good grasp of current events. Without this, he may well give an answer that is no longer accurate (e.g., to the question "Who is the world record holder in the 1500 metres?" when the record was broken two days before the question was asked). Ability to read foreign languages may be important in some libraries but, for most questions, is not likely to be a major factor influencing the probability that an answer will be found.

The ability of the librarian to communicate effectively influences his understanding of the question in the first place as well as his ability to convey a correct answer to the user. Decision-making abilities affect the efficiency of the librarian's search strategy. Other important decisions include when to refer to an outside source and when to give up completely.

The librarian's perception of his professional responsibilities may influence whether or not he accepts a question (e.g., questions should not be rejected out-of-hand because they seem too difficult) as well as how much time he is willing to devote to it.

The efficiency of the librarian is another important factor. The more quickly he finds answers to the routine questions, the more time he can devote to the nonroutine. He must also be accurate, in checking indexes, in reading text or tables of data, and in relaying answers to users.

Certainly one would expect that, all other things being equal, the more experienced the librarian is in reference work, the more likely it is that the question will be answered completely and correctly. To a lesser extent, one might also expect this probability to be related to the education and training of the librarian, although a study by Bunge (1967) tended to indicate that reference librarians without formal education (i.e., without attending library school) were no less likely to answer questions correctly than those with formal education in librarianship.*

---

*However, the less trained staff members took longer to answer questions.

The complexity of a question (Exhibit 66) will affect the probability that the librarian will understand it, that a complete and correct answer can be found, and that the answer can be transmitted successfully to the user. The obscurity of the question will affect the number of sources in which an answer appears and, thus, the probability that an answer will be found. The subject matter involved, since this relates to the strengths and weaknesses of particular collections, as well as of particular librarians, is another significant factor.

1. Subject

2. Obscurity

3. Complexity

4. Stability of answer (in particular, how recently did answer change?)

Exhibit 66
Question-related factors

More important than all of these, however, may be the stability of the answer and, more particularly, how recently the answer changed. The question "When was Smetana's *The Bartered Bride* first performed in the United States?" is obviously easier to answer correctly than "When was *The Bartered Bride* performed most recently by a major opera company in the United States?" The first answer, presumably, cannot change while the second may have changed as recently as yesterday.

While some librarians may deny it, it is hard to believe that "human" factors do not enter into this picture (Exhibit 67). In an industrial library, a vice president receives more care and time than a

1. Status

2. Personality and attitude

3. Ability to comprehend answer

Exhibit 67
User factors

design engineer recently appointed. In an academic health science library, the same situation applies to the dean of the medical school. But status is not the only "human" influence. Whether consciously or unconsciously, it seems reasonable to suppose that a librarian will try harder for the questioner judged "simpatico" (or, for that matter, "simpatica") than for one considered rude, arrogant, or ignorant.

Finally, although an answer may exist, and the librarian can comprehend it, the user may not be able to. This might apply, for example, in the case of a questioner who is a child. Alternatively, the librarian may locate a source for the answer but neither the librarian nor the user can understand it. For example, the user may be a practicing engineer and the answer, appearing in the literature of applied mechanics, is incomprehensible to him because it is too mathematical.

---

1. Stress

2. Physical/mental health of librarian

3. Pure environmental:
   Temperature
   Humidity
   Lighting

Exhibit 68
Environmental factors

Environmental factors (Exhibit 68) may be more important than they seem at first. If a questioner calls at 9:05, shortly after the library has opened, it may be more likely that his question is answered correctly than if he calls at 12:05 at which time two of the three reference librarians are at lunch, five people are waiting at the reference desk, and two telephones are ringing. Stress can be expected to influence the accuracy of the librarian, his effectiveness, and his perseverence.*

Quite apart from these stress factors, the efficiency of librarians varies from one day to the next depending on health factors, how much sleep they have had, whether or not they have quarrelled with their spouses that day, and a whole host of related factors that are frequently overlooked and are difficult to categorize. Also frequently overlooked is the fact that human efficiency diminishes as physical environmental conditions deteriorate. In a building without air conditioning, time of day may significantly influence the probability that a question will be answered correctly.

---

*Nevertheless, based on a study of public libraries in Maryland, Gers and Seward (1985) claim that degree of "busyness" seems not to influence the probability that a question will be answered correctly.

Exhibit 69 relates to the probability that a librarian, unable to answer a question himself, will refer the library user to another source. One factor has to do with the librarian's own self-assurance. Some librarians seem reluctant to refer a questioner elsewhere, especially to another professional colleague or department, because they feel that such an action is a sign of their own inadequacy. Others may refuse to refer because they adopt a tenacious and proprietary interest in a particular question. Tenacity is an admirable quality but not if it results in failure to answer an answerable question.*

1. Is librarian willing to refer question
   (a) to a colleague in the library,
   (b) to an outside source?

2. How extensive is the librarian's knowledge of the resources, abilities, and interests of individuals or institutions?

3. Do referral directories appropriate to this question exist, does the library own them (or can access them online), and does the librarian know of them?

4. Is the questioner willing to be referred?

Exhibit 69
Referral factors

If the librarian is willing to refer, the quality of his referral will depend on his knowledge of primary or secondary information sources, as well as the relevance and accessibility of these sources and the willingness of the questioner to be referred elsewhere. Once the question is referred, of course, all of the performance factors previously identified will tend to apply to the new situation.

Not all the factors listed, obviously, are of equal importance. Their range and diversity do indicate, however, that the effectiveness of question-answering activities is governed by a rather complex set of variables. Moreover, chance enters into the situation: if one telephones a public library, for example, the probability that one's factual question will be answered completely and correctly may depend on the time selected and how the reference librarian happens to be feeling that day. It is little wonder that several studies have indicated that the probability of complete success in this situation may not be much more than .5 to .6. On the other hand, it should also be recognized that the factors

---

*In a study of public libraries in Illinois, Wallace (1983) discovered some reluctance to refer a question to system resources when the reference librarian was unable to answer it locally.

identified imply some redundancy and counterbalancing. For example, that a particular question can be answered correctly from several sources might tend to compensate for the fact that a librarian may not be feeling at his very best on a certain day.

As a result of a large study performed among public libraries in Maryland, Gers and Seward (1985) report that "behavioral factors" seem to exert more influence on reference performance than any other type of factor. As Travillian (1985) notes, four behavioral factors correlated with completeness and correctness of response:

1. The level of negotiation of the question.

2. Whether or not the librarian used a follow-up question to determine if the questioner was satisfied with the response.

3. The degree of interest shown by the librarian.

4. The extent to which the librarian seemed to be "comfortable" in dealing with the questioner.

Correctness of response did not seem to correlate with size of collection, size of staff, or the extent to which the staff appeared to by "busy" at the time the question was received.

In terms of factors affecting the performance of reference service, the results of the Maryland study must be viewed with considerable caution. More than half the questions used could be answered from a single source (*World Almanac*) and 87.5% could be answered using only seven basic reference tools. It is hardly surprising, then, that size of collection did not correlate with quality of reference service.

As electronic information sources are increasingly used to support question-answering activities, the importance of some of these factors will decline. Clearly, access will be more important than ownership and the size and redundancy of the collection will no longer be significant variables affecting the quality of reference service. Moreover, online indexes to the contents of electronic resources will tend to ensure that a librarian will choose the best source for any particular question. At the same time, the ease with which an electronic source can be updated will tend to ensure that the information is the most current available.

Study Questions

1. When a student or faculty member walks into the Reference Room at the University of Illinois Library, looking for an answer to a factual

question, what is the probability that he or she will find or receive a complete and correct answer? How would you determine this probability?

2. The Nevada State Library wishes to establish a "state reference library" to act as a backup for reference services provided by public libraries throughout the state. The proposed state-supported library would be the first source each public library would contact for most factual reference questions they are unable to answer from their own resources. Rather than establishing a completely new library, the State Library has decided that the new reference resource should be located within an existing public library and that State funds would be spent to strengthen the reference collection of the library chosen, as well as to provide additional staff. There are two problems:

1. Which public library should be chosen? The contenders are those in Las Vegas and Reno.

2. To what extent should the collection be expanded? From a cost-effectiveness viewpoint, how large should the reference collection be? The goal is a service capable of answering 95% of the questions referred to it by other libraries.

What data would you collect, and how would you collect them, in order to advise the State Librarian on which public library to choose and on the optimum size for the expanded reference collection?

3. Have *all* the factors affecting success/failure in question answering been identified in this chapter? If not, what is omitted? Try to draw a diagram (similar to that of Exhibit 4) in which all of these factors are presented. Can they be presented in a sequence that reflects the order in which they might affect the probability that a particular question will be answered completely and correctly?

11. Database Searching

This chapter discusses the evaluation of those information services that respond to a user's request for "information" on some topic by searching databases (printed or electronic) to identify bibliographic items that appear to deal with this topic. Such services are variously referred to as "bibliographic searching," "information retrieval," "literature searching" or "database searching" services.

It is only in the last twenty years or so that information services of this kind have become fairly common in most types of libraries. Earlier, they could be found only in certain special libraries, particularly those in industry. In general, public, school, and academic libraries lacked the resources to attempt anything but the simplest of bibliographic searches for their users. Instead, they generally directed users to appropriate printed sources in which they could perform their own searches, instructing them in the use of these sources if necessary.

This situation has changed dramatically since early in the 1970s. The use of online networks to search bibliographic databases is now commonplace in academic and special libraries of all sizes as well as in some of the larger public libraries, and databases have reached even many of the smaller libraries in CD-ROM form.

A rather complex set of interrelationships now exists among the various actors – individual and institutional – on the online searching scene. A somewhat simplified view of these relationships is presented in Exhibit 70. The *producer* plays key roles in the whole operation as compiler and publisher of the database. Compilation involves the acquisition of published materials within the stated scope of the database (which implies careful selection criteria) and the processing of these to form bibliographic representations (records) within the database. This may involve descriptive cataloging, subject indexing (perhaps using terms drawn from a controlled vocabulary such as a thesaurus), and sometimes the writing of abstracts. In some cases, however, the intellectual processing is minimized: keywords in titles and abstracts are used as access points in place of humanly assigned index terms. Most frequently today, the database is distributed in two versions: in machine-readable (electronic) form and as a printed index (with or without abstracts) roughly equivalent to the electronic form.

Machine-readable databases are acquired by various *computer centers*. These centers have developed software to convert all databases to a common processing format, to make them accessible online via various telecommunications networks, and to allow them to be interrogated by remote users. *Libraries* generally access the databases through one or more of these computer centers although, in some cases, the database producer may also make online access possible through computers of its own.

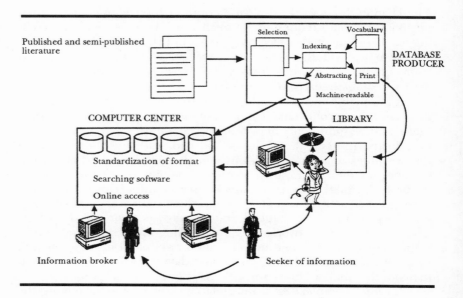

Exhibit 70
Database searching situation in the United States

The *seeker of information* may visit a library to ask the librarian to perform a search on his behalf; this will usually be done online although it could also involve use of databases in printed or CD-ROM form housed within the library itself. Alternatively, the user could visit the library to perform his own search in printed tools, CD-ROM resources, or (less commonly) to use the library's terminals to access remote databases. As terminals become increasingly available in offices and in homes, more and more individuals perform their own searches without the help of a librarian. Indeed, some libraries now prefer to train users to perform their own searches instead of performing searches on their behalf. In the academic world, the trend to self-service has been greatly facilitated by the emergence of Internet, which is considered a major step toward a National Research and Education Network.

Finally, rather than going to a library or performing searches for themselves, some individuals or institutions may prefer to use the services of an *information broker* who will conduct the searches of databases on a fee basis.

For present purposes it will be assumed that a library user asks a librarian to perform an online search to satisfy some *information need*. The obvious evaluation question is "To what extent do the results of the search satisfy the information need?"

Evaluation Criteria

The criteria that are appropriate to the evaluation of the results of a literature search will vary somewhat depending on the type of information need. Three broad types can be identified:

1. The user wants to find out if anything has been written on a particular subject and will be satisfied to find a single item on the subject.*

2. The user wants to retrieve a selection of representative items on a subject but does not need to find everything.

3. The user wants a comprehensive search – everything on the subject should be retrieved.

A fourth type of need also exists but occurs very infrequently: the user believes that nothing has been published on some topic and sets out to prove it. Of the three principal types of need enumerated above, the second is probably more common that the third and the first is least common.

An obvious evaluation criterion, applicable to all of these cases, is whether or not the search retrieves one or more items that the requester finds useful in satisfying his information need. For the second type of need and, more particularly, the third, the criterion is extended to "how many useful items were found?" The term *pertinent* will be used henceforth to refer to an item that is useful to the user in that it contributes to the satisfaction of his information need. (Considerable discussion exists in the literature on the meaning of the terms *pertinence* and *relevance* and on the difference between the two – see, for example, Swanson (1986) and Lancaster and Warner (1993) – and this will not be repeated here.)

---

*A search of a database may also be performed in order to answer some factual question. In this case, the evaluation criteria are the same as those applying to other question-answering situations (see Chapter 10).

The retrieval of pertinent items from the database is frequently referred to as *recall* and the extent to which pertinent items are retrieved as a *recall ratio*. Thus, if a database contains twelve items pertinent to a particular need and a search in this database retrieves nine of the twelve, one could say that the *recall ratio* is 9/12, or .75.

Recall alone gives a very incomplete picture of how efficient a search has been. For example, it might be acceptable to find nine pertinent items among twenty items retrieved but quite unacceptable to find nine among 200. The former search has performed at a much greater *precision* than the latter. A *precision ratio* is frequently used in conjunction with the recall ratio to give an indication of how efficient or discriminating a search has been. Thus, in the examples used earlier, one could say that .75 recall had been achieved at .45 precision (probably quite acceptable) or at .045 precision (probably unacceptable).

In a sense, the precision ratio provides a rather indirect measure of the "cost" of a search to a user: it will take much more time to examine a printout of 200 items to find nine useful than to find nine among twenty. Clearly, if the user is paying for the search, a more direct measure of cost can be used, namely the cost per pertinent item retrieved. Suppose that the search that achieved a precision of 9/20 cost the user $12, while the search that achieved a precision of 9/200 cost $30. In one case the cost per pertinent item is $1.33; in the other it is $3.33.

The cost per pertinent item retrieved is related to both the recall ratio and the precision ratio. Obviously, a search that retrieves eighteen pertinent items at $12 is "twice as good" as one that retrieves nine at $12, assuming, of course, that all items are equally useful. Less obvious, perhaps, is that a precision ratio of 9/200 implies a greater cost than a precision ratio of 9/20. This is because the higher precision suggests a more direct search approach requiring less time at the terminal. It also indicates lower printout costs, especially when a charge is levied for each citation printed. In other words, the better the search, in terms of recall and precision, the lower the cost is likely to be per pertinent item retrieved.

In the discussion so far it has been assumed that a librarian performs a search for a user and delivers the results in the form of a printout of bibliographic references. The cost per pertinent item retrieved will be equally applicable to a situation in which the library user performs his own search, even if no printout is made. In this case, also, recall and precision will affect the cost per pertinent item retrieved.

So far, three different performance measures have been mentioned: recall ratio, precision ratio, and cost per pertinent item retrieved. Many others have been suggested or used (Robertson, 1969), including the complements of the recall ratio (which can be thought of as a *miss ratio*) and the precision ratio (*a noise ratio* or *noise factor*) and the *expected search length*(W. S. Cooper, 1968). Some of these other measures are more "mathematically acceptable" than recall/precision, and are especially valuable in experimental situations in which different retrieval systems or retrieval approaches are being compared (Sparck Jones, 1981). Nevertheless, the three measures discussed are those that most directly indicate the value and/or acceptability of a search in the eyes of the library user.

Application of the Criteria

Suppose one wants to evaluate the literature searching activities of a particular library, say a departmental library within a university. It will be important to get feedback on a continuous basis from all users of the service so that some form of quality control is in effect. A brief evaluation form should accompany each search printout delivered to a user, the user being urged to return the completed form when the results have been examined. The form should obtain the user's subjective assessment of the value of the search as a whole, using some scale (such as: of great value, of value, of little value, of no value), as well as an indication of the reasons for the value decision – particularly important for cases in which the search is judged to be of little or no value. The user should also be asked to indicate how many items retrieved were useful in contributing to satisfying his information need (i.e., pertinent items). A distinction should be made between major value and lesser value items, perhaps along these lines:

1. Very important. I would not want to have missed these.
2. Pertinent to my interests but not so important.
3. Pertinent but of marginal value. The search would not have suffered much if these had not been retrieved.

It might also be useful to find out how many of the pertinent items are *new* to the user (i.e., items brought to his attention for the first time by the search) and to have the user give some blanket statement on why some items retrieved may not have been pertinent to his interests. Finally, the user could be asked to give bibliographic data on items he felt should have been retrieved, because known to be pertinent, but were not. An evaluation form along the lines of Exhibit 71 might be suitable.

Search Evaluation

The printout attached presents the results of the search recently undertaken for you on the subject of _____.
To help us monitor and improve our services would you please study the search results and answer the following questions:

1. Would you judge this search to be:

              Of great value _____   Of value _____
              Of little value _____   Of no value _____

2. Give a brief statement to explain the reason for your value judgment.

3. The search retrieved a total of _____ items. Please indicate how many were useful in contributing to the satisfaction of your information need according to the scale presented below. (NOTE: in judging the importance of an item do *not* take into consideration whether or not you were previously familiar with it. Indicate how many items you were previously familiar with in the final column.)

		Number of items	Number previously familiar to you
A.	These items are very important to me. The value of the search would have been greatly reduced had these been missed.	_____	_____
B.	These are pertinent to my interests but of lesser importance. Nevertheless, it is good that they were retrieved.	_____	_____
C.	These are pertinent but of very marginal value. The search would have been just as valuable without them.	_____	_____
D.	These are not at all pertinent to my interests.	_____	_____

4. For the items judged D above please give some explanation as to why they were not pertinent:

5. If you are aware of any pertinent items that were not retrieved in this search, but probably should have been, please give bibliographic details below:

               *   *   *   *   *   *   *

Exhibit 71
Draft of search evaluation questionnaire

Based on data supplied on the evaluation form, the library can calculate a precision ratio for the search and also a cost per pertinent item retrieved. These figures can be based on items of any degree of pertinence or only on those judged more important (e.g., cost per "very important" item retrieved). It would also be possible to derive a *novelty ratio* for the search, i.e., the number of new and pertinent items retrieved over the number of pertinent items retrieved, which would be especially useful in evaluating a search performed for current awareness purposes.

These performance figures can be used to monitor the service and to observe if its quality appears to improve over time (e.g., as the searchers gain more experience or after some change has been made in the service, such as adopting a new form to record the user's request). They must be used with considerable caution, however, because they do not provide a complete picture of the results of a search: the number of pertinent items missed is not known.

To obtain an estimated recall ratio requires considerable effort (and some cost) and a librarian will not want to go to this trouble for all searches performed. On the other hand, he should be willing to estimate recall for a sample of searches in order to get a more complete picture of the quality of this service. There are two practical ways in which the recall of a literature search can be estimated.

The first method involves the conduct of "saturation" searches by other members of the library staff. Suppose, for example, that the library employs three librarians who conduct searches for users. The "real" search for a particular user, performed by searcher A, retrieves a total of forty references, of which eighteen are judged pertinent by the user (precision is .45). Searcher B is asked to perform the same search. He is given the search statement of the user but not allowed to see the search strategy used by A. Presumably B may have a slightly different search approach and will thus retrieve a somewhat different set of references. Any items retrieved by B but not by A must be submitted to the requester of the search to be judged on the same scale of pertinence as before. If searcher B finds two pertinent items not found by A, A's recall can be estimated at 18/20 (i.e., $A/(A+B)$), or .9. The process can be repeated with searcher C. In this case the recall estimate would be based on $A/(A+B+C)$. If A's recall is to be based on the additional pertinent items found by B and C, the two sets of results (B or C items not found by A) should be combined for submission to the requester. Moreover, the additional searches by B and C should not be held up pending receipt of the user's evaluation form, otherwise the later searches might be conducted after the database has been updated by several thousand items, greatly complicating the comparisons. For this reason it might be desirable to establish in advance that the user is willing to cooperate in the evaluation.*

---

*It is highly desirable, of course, that little time be allowed to elapse between the requester's first and second set of assessments.

The estimate of recall established in this way is really an upper bound value. For example, if A/(A + B + C) gives a value of 18/21, A's search could not have achieved better recall than 18/21, and the true recall may be somewhat less than this (A, B, and C combined might not have found *all* pertinent items, perhaps because of indexing errors). Nevertheless, for most purposes, the method will give perfectly acceptable results.

The second method of estimating recall is easier than the first although it is more difficult to explain clearly. It involves a "parallel" search in one or more databases other than the one in which the search to be evaluated was performed. Consider again the hypothetical search that retrieved forty references, of which eighteen are judged pertinent by the requester. Suppose the search falls in the field of electronics and has been performed in the INSPEC database. It would be possible to do a second search in another database that also covers electronics, such as COMPENDEX.* Let us say that the second search (which need not be comprehensive since it is the original search, not the second, that is being evaluated) retrieves twelve pertinent items. This set of twelve items can be used as a *sample* of pertinent items by which to estimate the recall of the original search. First, the twelve items must be compared against the forty originally retrieved to see how many are duplicated in the two searches. This comparison may show that, of the twelve, ten were retrieved in the original search (eight judged pertinent and two not pertinent), leaving two about which nothing is known. Suppose that both of these new items are judged pertinent by the user. It must now be established that they appear in the INSPEC database – e.g., by performing author searches. If they do, the estimated recall for the INSPEC search is 8/10, or .8. That is, of the *sample* of pertinent items found in the COMPENDEX database (and also known to be in INSPEC), 8/10 were retrieved by the original search in INSPEC. Another way of looking at this result is that the eighteen pertinent items retrieved in the INSPEC search are estimated to represent about 80% of the total of pertinent items in the INSPEC database. This second method of estimating recall is likely to give a more accurate result than the first: if certain pertinent items have not been adequately indexed in the first database they may not be retrieved however many people search for them but they might very well be exposed by a search in a second database.

---

*For this purpose the equivalent printed tool, in this case the *Engineering Index*, might be used in place of an online search; or, the original search, the parallel search, or both might be performed in CD-ROM databases.

The evaluation form developed by the American Library Association's Machine-Assisted Reference Section (Blood, 1983) is illustrated in Exhibit 72. The form addresses precision and novelty but not recall (e.g., the requester is not asked if he is aware of important items that were not retrieved). The form could be improved by asking the requester to explain why certain items are not relevant, since this information could be useful in determining what went wrong with a search or how it could be improved.

Establishing performance results for a sample of searches (whether these results be recall ratios, precision ratios, cost per pertinent item, or whatever) does not in itself tell the librarian how the service might be improved. If one is serious about achieving improvement, one must undertake some analysis of reasons why failures occur in searches. Examples of *precision failures* (items retrieved that the user judged not to be pertinent) can be identified from the search evaluation form. Why were such items retrieved? The most likely explanation will be one of the following:

1. The searcher did not clearly understand what the user wanted.

2. The search was performed more broadly than it should have been.

3. The vocabulary of the database (e.g., thesaurus terms) was not specific enough to allow this search to be conducted with high precision.

4. Errors of indexing occur in the database.

Examples of *recall failures* can be identified through the procedures used to arrive at the recall estimates. Recall failures will usually be due to one of these causes:

1. The searcher did not clearly understand what the user wanted.

2. The searcher did not explore all reasonable search approaches.

3. The structure of the vocabulary (e.g., thesaurus) did not give the searcher enough help in identifying appropriate terms.

4. Errors of indexing occur in the database.

It is clear that some factors affecting the performance of a literature searching service in a particular library are outside the control of the library itself (i.e., under the control only of the database producer or, possibly, the computer center making the database accessible). Nevertheless, the librarian can use evaluation procedures to identify problems that *are* under local control and can be corrected – perhaps by further training in search techniques or by changing the procedures by which the library staff determine the needs of users (e.g.,

Search number _____

Since only a limited sample of users is asked to evaluate the results of their computerized literature searches, the validity of the sample results depends on subsequent follow-up of nonrespondents. The search number was entered by a member of the library staff in order to identify users who return their questionnaires and to eliminate them from a subsequent telephone follow-up of nonrespondents. If you prefer to complete and return this questionnaire without indicating your name in order to remain anonymous, the search number will *not* be used to identify your response. Whether or not you choose to remain anonymous, your response will be kept strictly confidential.

Name: _____

Address: _____

Telephone number(s): _____

Status: (Categories vary by type of library--local option phrasing)

    e.g. *Academic Library*:   Faculty _____   Graduate student _____

                             Undergraduate _____   Staff _____

                             Other (specify) _____

    e.g. *Special Library*:   Administrator _____   Salesman _____

                             Laboratory technician _____

                             Other (specify) _____

1. What was your main purpose in requesting this search? In other words, at the time you submitted your search request, what had you planned to do with the results?
     (Local option--provide list of possible responses, e.g. term paper, Ph.D. dissertation, faculty research, grant proposal, etc.)

2. Was the purpose of this search to determine that no previous work had been done on this topic?
     Yes _____   No _____

3. Does this search provide enough *relevant* citations for the purpose for which you submitted the search request?
     Yes _____
     No, but didn't expect to see anything _____
     No (please comment) _____

4. Among the total citations provided by this search, what percentage appears *relevant* to the specific question or topic for which you submitted a search request?
        0% _____
        1 to 25% _____
        26 to 50% _____
        51 to 75% _____
        76 to 100% _____

Exhibit 72

Search evaluation questionnaire recommended by the American Library Association's Machine-Assisted Reference Section Committee on Measurement and Evaluation of Service

Reprinted with permission of the American Library Association from Blood, R. W. Evaluation of online searches. *RQ*, 22, 1983, 266-277

5. Among the total citations provided by this search, what percentage appears *relevant* to your overall information need, rather than simply relevant to the specific question submitted as a search topic or question?

    0% _____
    1 to 25% _____
    26 to 50% _____
    51 to 75% _____
    76 to 100% _____

6. Among the *relevant* citations provided by this search, what percentage is new to you, or, in other words, was unknown to you at the time you examined the search results?

    0% of the *relevant* citations are new to me _____
    1 to 25% of the *relevant* citations are new to me _____
    26 to 50% of the *relevant* citations are new to me _____
    51 to 75% of the *relevant* citations are new to me _____
    76 to 100% of the *relevant* citations are new to me _____

7. Do you feel that the citations that are both *relevant* and previously *unknown* to you are worth the cost that you paid for the search?

    Yes _____   No _____
    If "No," please comment.
    (Optional question--may be omitted if library does not charge)

8. Was the time lapse between submitting your search request and receiving your search results reasonable?

    Yes _____   No _____
    If "No," please comment.

9. Were the results of the search of value to you?

    Yes _____   No _____
    If "No," please comment.

10. The major reason for the Search Evaluation Questionnaire is to obtain your comments and suggestions for improving the computerized literature searching service. If you have suggestions as to how *any aspect* of the search service can be improved, please comment *in detail*:

Exhibit 72 *continued*

improved interviewing methods or a redesigned form for capturing the user's request statement). The evaluation of database searches, and factors affecting the success of such searches, is dealt with in greater detail in Lancaster and Warner (1993).

Database Selection

The discussion so far in this chapter has dealt with the evaluation of a search performed in a particular database. While certain library users may specify which databases they want searched, it is probably more common (at least in a general library) for a librarian to decide which one to use, based on the subject matter of the request. From the user's point of view, as well as from that of the library manager, another legitimate evaluation question is "Was the database used the best one for this particular subject?" The best database is probably the one that contains most literature on the topic, although other criteria could also come into play – the type of literature covered, its "level" (elementary, intermediate, advanced), the language of the material, and so on.

With the number of databases now readily accessible online, the selection of the most appropriate one to use for any particular application is no longer a trivial task. Moreover, a danger exists that a librarian will tend to use a small number of databases – those with which he is most familiar – exclusively, or to always select the "obvious" database without considering other possibilities. The ERIC database is not necessarily the best source for *all* education-related topics; nor is AGRICOLA, ipso facto, the best one for *all* searches in agriculture. The "most obvious" database is not always the most productive. For example, Lancaster and Lee (1985) were surprised to find that the Energy database (Department of Energy) contained more items on acid rain than did Enviroline, and Hu (1987), in her study of database selection, discovered that some searches that seemed obviously "agricultural" would probably get better results in other types of databases – perhaps in biology or chemistry. Databases that are frequently overlooked are those whose scope is defined by type of document rather than by subject. Obvious examples are databases that deal with technical reports and/or conference papers; yet these sources are especially important for newly developing and rapidly changing subject areas.

In large academic libraries, and others in which many online searches are performed in a wide range of subject areas, the library manager should take steps to determine whether or not those responsible are selecting the databases most appropriate, all other things considered,* to the needs of library users. Hu (1987) produced evidence to suggest that database selection might be considerably improved in a significant number of cases in an academic library.

While one would not want to evaluate the database selection in every search, it would certainly be desirable to undertake a periodic check on some random sampling basis. For a sample of searches performed, the selection process could be evaluated in one of three ways:

1. Subjectively by a panel of experienced searchers.

2. By using one of the "database indexes" such as Dialindex (Dialog Information Services) to indicate which of the available databases appears to contain most items on a particular topic.

*There are other factors, such as differences in costs, that must also be taken into account.

3. By using some form of "gateway" system that performs the database selection process "automatically."

Of these possibilities, the second may well be the best (see Hu, 1987), although a combination of the first and second approach might be even better. The third approach may not be very satisfactory since the systems that perform database selection "automatically" appear to use relatively unsophisticated procedures (Lancaster and Warner, 1993).

Nondelegated Searching

The delegated database search – one in which a librarian performs a search for a library user – presents a relatively simple evaluation problem in the sense that the librarian can keep copies of all items needed for the analysis (search request form, search strategy, printout of items retrieved) and can urge library users to participate in the evaluation by completing the necessary forms and doing whatever else is required. The nondelegated search, on the other hand, is considerably more difficult to study. Unfortunately for those concerned with performance evaluation, nondelegated searching is becoming increasingly prevalent and will continue to grow in importance as more and more databases become available in CD-ROM form.

The nondelegated search, by a library user, in some database – whether in printed, CD-ROM or other form – presents similar evaluation problems to the search in the library's catalog, as discussed in Chapter 7. One can interview a sample of users – for example, as they are observed to leave a CD-ROM terminal – to find out what they were seeking, how they searched, and with what degree of success, but such activities are very labor-intensive.

An alternative approach would be to design a form (a modified version of that shown in Exhibit 71) to record some or all of the following: (a) user search topic, (b) user's overall assessment of the value of the search performed, (c) user's perception of how many useful items were retrieved, (d) identification of the user, (e) how long the user spent on the search, and (f) which terms, or term combinations, were searched upon. These forms would be displayed alongside CD-ROM or other terminals and prominent signs would urge users to cooperate with the library by filling in the necessary data. It would be even better, of course, if the user could be induced to leave with the form a duplicate copy of his dialogue with the database and a record of the items retrieved.

Regrettably, it is extremely difficult to find users who are willing to go to this amount of trouble, so the number of completed forms, or at least the number completed satisfactorily, may represent only a very small percentage of the searches performed. The less asked of the user, the greater the cooperation is likely to be (items (a), (b), (e) and (f), as identified above, may be the minimum needed in order to draw any useful conclusions), and cooperation may also increase if certain incentives can be offered to the user (e.g., a search performed by an experienced searcher on the same topic) if they agree to cooperate fully.

Despite the difficulties, the evaluation of searches performed by library users cannot be ignored by the library manager who is concerned with the effectiveness of the services provided. It is not enough merely to make databases available; users must be able to exploit them effectively. Indeed, they could easily become disenchanted with the capabilities of database searching if they get poor results the first few times they try to search on their own. Only through some well planned evaluation exercise can the library manager determine how successful users are, what types of problems they encounter, and what types of mistakes they make, thus allowing some appropriate corrective action (e.g., through user-instruction programs or the implementation of user-friendly interfaces).

Probably the best approach to this evaluation problem is the use of forms alongside the terminals, on a continuous basis, coupled with periodic interviews with users performed through sampling procedures. In some situations alternative approaches could be used. For example, in an academic environment, tests of database use (problem-solving tests in which the student's search results are evaluated against some standard) could be incorporated into programs of bibliographic instruction to identify the types of problems most prevalent in database searching in general or in the use of particular databases.

Subject Searches in the Catalog of a Library

It should be noted that the criteria and procedures used to evaluate a subject search in an online database would be equally applicable to the evaluation of a subject search in a printed index. With some modifications they would also apply to the evaluation of subject searching in a card catalog.

The efficiency of such a search can be expressed in terms of the cost *in time* per pertinent item found. Thus, if a user spends fifteen minutes at the catalog to find three books he wishes to consult or borrow, the cost per item is five minutes of the user's time. An equivalent of the precision ratio could also be applied to this situation, but it would be a rather artificial measure based on the number of cards the user must examine to find the three items he judges pertinent. A recall ratio could be established by having searches on the user's topic performed by experienced librarians, but this measure would only be meaningful for the (probably rare) case in which the user wants to find everything the library owns on some topic.

In evaluating a subject search in an online catalog, the performance criteria would be (a) cost, in time, per pertinent item found (or, less desirable, number of entries examined and number judged pertinent), and (b) some estimate of recall or, better, a determination of whether or not the best items were found. Pertinent items overlooked by the user can be identified by searches performed by experienced librarians.

Subject Searches in the Catalog of a Library: a Case Study

As reported in Chapter 7, criteria used in the past to evaluate subject searches in library catalogs have been rather crude. The simplest approach (and the one still most commonly used – see Lester, 1988, and Hancock-Beaulieu, 1990) is to judge a search successful if the user is able to match his subject terminology with the terminology of the catalog. Clearly, this is a crude measure of success, since it gives no indication of whether or not a user would find *anything useful* in this way, much less whether he or she would locate the most relevant items.

In a somewhat more sophisticated approach, a subject search is judged successful if the catalog user selects one or more items (and presumably borrows them) as the result of a search. This is an improvement, certainly, but the evaluation criterion is still very unsatisfactory.

The quality of subject access in library catalogs cannot be improved from the results of studies based on such imperfect criteria. A subject search in the catalog of a library cannot be considered fully successful unless the user is able to locate the material that is, in some sense, the "best," i.e., the most complete, the most up-to-date, or the most authoritative.

A study reported by Lancaster et al. (1991b) used a series of simulations to determine the probability that a skilled catalog user would retrieve "the best" materials available in a library on some subject and, if they are unable to retrieve the best materials, to determine what changes would be needed to ensure that future catalogs would allow more successful subject searching (i.e., searching that produces more of the better materials).

Fifty-one bibliographies representing recommended readings on selected topics were assembled from faculty members of the Univer-

sity of Illinois and neighboring institutions and from the recommended readings appearing in recently published articles in encyclopedias or encyclopedic dictionaries. For each bibliography thus
obtained, the following steps were taken:

1. Journal articles were eliminated, since traditionally these have
not appeared in library catalogs (a situation that is now beginning to
change).

2. A search on the topic was performed in the "full" online catalog
of the University of Illinois, the Full Bibliographic Record (FBR), containing about 4.5 million entries. These could be searched by author,
title, keywords in title, subject headings and subheadings, and other
access points. A limited Boolean searching capability exists in the
catalog. The searches were performed by two members of the research
team who had studied the capabilities of the FBR and had become
highly proficient in searching this tool. They performed each search
on the basis of the title of the encyclopedia article (or other source)
only and did not see the bibliography until after the search was completed.

3. For items in the bibliography not retrieved by this subject
search, author/title searches were performed in the FBR and the full
bibliographic records for these items were printed out. At this point,
items not appearing in the FBR, and presumably not owned by the
University of Illinois, were eliminated from further consideration.

4. An analysis was performed to determine why items presumed
to be relevant to a particular topic, and judged sufficiently important
to be cited by the author of an article on this topic or listed by a faculty
member, were not retrieved in the original subject search, and how the
search strategy or characteristics of the catalog would have to be
changed to allow these to be retrieved. Some items could have been retrieved by the use of alternative subject headings that were in some way
related to the headings used by the searcher. Others could have been
retrieved by expanding the search to other elements in the existing
bibliographic record, such as title words. However, many could only be
retrieved by the expansion of the existing records to include the contents pages of books and/or their indexes, and some could only be retrieved if the full text of the book were available to be searched. In
many cases, then, the book itself had to be located to allow these deter-
minations to be made. In this step of the analysis, it was found that
some of the items appearing in the bibliographies were not fully relevant to the subject of the encyclopedia article and, thus, to the subject
search. When members of the team agreed on this, such items were
eliminated from the search. In many cases the item thus rejected

covered only one facet of a multifaceted topic. For example, the author of an article on education of the handicapped might cite a book that deals with education but not the handicapped or one that deals with the handicapped but not with education; in situations of this kind, the item was omitted from the study. In some other cases, the item in the bibliography had been cited by the author (e.g., for methodological reasons) but fell clearly outside the subject domain of the article.

It is important to emphasize two facts about the investigation: it was not intended to evaluate the FBR per se or to evaluate the performance of particular searchers, but to determine what characteristics an online catalog would need to have in order to permit the retrieval of the "most important" literature on some topic as defined earlier. The entire study could have been performed without the conduct of any subject searches. That is, author/title searches could have been performed for all items in the bibliography, and the analysis could have been achieved by looking at the full bibliographic records and the books themselves. The disadvantage of this, of course, is that a decision would have to be made on each subject heading involved as to whether an experienced searcher would be likely to use it. The use of an actual searcher in the first step of the process avoided this dilemma and provided a more realistic approach.

The results of the fifty-one searches are summarized in Exhibit 73. In the first search, for example, sixty-six of the items in the bibliography were confirmed to appear in FBR, but only fifteen of those were retrieved in the subject search, giving a recall ratio of 22.7%. As the table shows, the results varied from eight cases having 100% recall to two searches with zero recall. The mean recall ratio for the fifty-one searches – the average of all the individual ratios – is 59.4%.

On the surface, 59% recall could be considered a respectable, if not exactly inspiring, result. However, this is very misleading, for several obvious reasons:

1. The searchers were students of library science who had acquired considerable experience in searching the catalog. The results they achieved would not be duplicated by a typical library user.

2. They studied the *Library of Congress Subject Headings* (*LCSH*) with some degree of intensity before beginning a search, a situation not likely to be true for the typical catalog user.

3. They were instructed to perform broad searches, to achieve maximum recall, *with no concern given to the precision of the search*. For example, a search on feminist methodology in scholarly inquiry

achieved a recall of more than 90%, but only through the use of the term *Feminism*, which retrieves bibliographic records for close to 1,200 items, almost all of which are completely irrelevant to the precise topic of the search. If the search had been restricted to more specific terms,

Search #	Recall		Search #	Recall	
		%			%
1	15/66	22.7	26	5/5	100.0
2	6/12	50.0	27	10/10	100.0
3	12/23	52.2	28	4/13	30.8
4	0/6	0	29	21/36	58.3
5	2/13	15.4	30	14/15	93.3
6	4/7	57.1	31	12/15	80.0
7	3/5	60.0	32	6/11	54.5
8	4/17	23.5	33	2/4	50.0
9	6/8	75.0	34	11/23	47.8
10	5/7	71.4	35	5/10	50.0
11	0/1	0	36	8/9	88.9
12	4/8	50.0	37	4/4	100.0
13	11/19	57.9	38	13/13	100.0
14	2/5	40.0	39	3/7	42.9
15	3/4	75.0	40	12/17	70.6
16	3/9	33.3	41	5/7	71.4
17	3/6	50.0	42	6/6	100.0
18	11/12	91.7	43	4/6	66.7
19	2/9	22.2	44	2/3	66.7
20	22/47	46.8	45	1/1	100.0
21	10/10	100.0	46	4/5	80.0
22	6/21	28.6	47	2/5	40.0
23	13/22	59.1	48	7/7	100.0
24	6/15	40.0	49	2/5	40.0
25	8/13	61.5	50	1/2	50.0
			51	2/3	66.7

Exhibit 73
Recall ratios achieved in fifty one searches in an online catalog

such as *Women in science*, or *Women scientists*, recall would have been much lower – only about 42%. To get a high recall in a search on the Gumbel distribution, which relates to the statistics of extremes, requires use of such broad terms as *Mathematical statistics* and *Stochastic processes*, which retrieve records for more than 1,200 items. The same situation applies to other searches. While recall was high in a few of the fifty-one searches, these results would not be achieved under real-life conditions because a library user would just not be willing to look through hundreds of records to find a handful of relevant items.

The results are misleading in one other respect: a significant number of the items in the bibliographies are journal articles, which have not traditionally been included in library catalogs; thus, the results really represent only 59% recall of part of the literature.

There are relatively few searches in which a high recall could be achieved at an acceptable level of precision. This tends to occur only in situations where the subject of the search coincides closely with a subject heading or headings. For example, a search on the image of women in the Bible achieved 75% recall on the single term *Women in the Bible* and could have achieved 100% recall by use of the additional term *Women (theology)*, and a search on queuing theory achieved 90% recall on *Queuing theory* alone. Such a close match between a subject heading and the topic of a search was rare and may well be rare in real life.

The main purpose of the study was to determine what might be done to library catalogs to make them more effective tools for subject access. Exhibit 74 sheds light on this by showing how nonretrieved items could have been retrieved. The fifty-one bibliographies collec-

Total number of relevant items in FBR for 51 searches	607	
Number of relevant items retrieved in 51 searches	327	
Recall ratio (327/607)	53.9%	

Possible improvement	Additional Items Retrievable	Revised Recall (%)
Elements in existing bibliographic record		
Other closely related subject headings	38	60.1
Closely related and somewhat related headings	51	62.3
Other parts of record	10	55.5
Subtotal	61	63.9
Enhancements to record		
Indexes of books	125	74.5
Contents pages	86	68.0
Full text	58	63.4
Subtotal	211*	90.3
Not retrievable even on full text	8	

* The categories "indexes of books" and "contents pages" are not mutually exclusive.

Exhibit 74
How results could have been improved for the fifty one searches
represented in Exhibit 73

tively contained 607 items included within FBR and, of these, 327 were retrieved in the subject searches. If we simply average these numbers (327/607) we get an average recall of 53.9% – a slightly different figure from the 59% achieved by averaging the individual ratios.

The exhibit shows clearly that the best "hindsight" approach to searching the existing bibliographic records could only improve the average recall from 53.9% to 63.9%. If the searchers had used *all* subject headings that could be considered closely related to the subjects they were dealing with, recall would only have improved about six percentage points, from 53.9% to 60.1%. The addition of subject headings considered "somewhat related" would push recall only to 62.3%. Of course, the decision that a heading is "closely related" or "somewhat related" to a topic is a subjective one, but the decisions reflected some degree of agreement among members of the project team. In general, these decisions were generous to the existing bibliographic records in that the investigators considered as "related" headings that were only loosely connected to the search topic. For example, *Glossolalia* was accepted as closely related to "spirit possession" (*LCSH* does not link them) and *Numerical taxonomy* (a very broad term) as somewhat related to "the classification of birds."

If the searches had been broadened to include other parts of the existing bibliographic records, beyond the subject headings, little improvement in recall would have occurred. Only ten of the 229 items not retrievable on subject headings could have been retrieved on other parts of the bibliographic record, in this case titles or subtitles. That extending a search from subject headings to titles/subtitles has minimal effect on recall suggests that the subject headings assigned are very "close" to the terminology of titles and that there is little complementarity between titles and subject headings.

As the exhibit shows, the average recall for the fifty-one searches could not have exceeded 63.9% even if the searchers had used all subject headings of any degree of relevance to the sought topics and had extended the search to keywords in titles. Had they done this, of course, precision would have been even worse than it was with the approaches actually used.

Unfortunately, there is very little that can be done to improve the situation on the basis of existing bibliographic records and cataloging practice. Searches performed in databases that are the electronic equivalents of printed indexes can achieve better results (i.e., a reasonable level of recall at a tolerable level of precision) through flexible capabilities for Boolean search, but even the most sophisticated of capabilities would have had little effect on the results of the present study. The reason, of course, is that a typical catalog record has too few access points to make it likely that a search combining terms will get an acceptable level of recall: a record having two or three subject headings is quite different from one including ten or twelve descriptors and/or a 200-word abstract. This is illustrated clearly in a search dealing with photosynthesis in biotechnology. *Photosynthesis* and *Biotechnology* are both *LCSH* headings, but not one of the records for the eleven relevant items contains both headings. In fact, in four of the six records for relevant items having the heading *Photosynthesis* this is the *only* term assigned. It seems likely that most real information needs are multifaceted: censorship in the Soviet Union (not all of censorship or everything on the Soviet Union), crazing of polymers (not everything on polymers), humor in child development (not all of humor), and so on. Such multifaceted topics can be handled in library catalogs as long as they coincide with existing subject headings or subject heading/subheading combinations (e.g., *Censorship — Soviet Union* and *Humor in children*) but there is little hope that in other cases two or more facets of a search topic will be represented in existing catalog records (by combinations of subject headings, keywords, or both).

This study was not intended as an evaluation of a particular online catalog, and FBR has many limitations that make it far from an ideal tool for subject searching. Nevertheless, with existing bibliographic records, even the most powerful of searching capabilities would offer only marginal improvement.

The results of this study strongly suggest that a sophisticated and experienced searcher in an online catalog is unlikely to retrieve, on the average, more than 50-60% of the items appearing in subject bibliographies prepared by experts, and that this level of recall could only be achieved at quite intolerable levels of precision. The results achieved by a less experienced searcher would be much worse. Moreover, there is no way that the situation can be improved significantly (e.g., by mapping of user vocabulary to subject headings or parts of subject headings in various ways) within the constraints of existing catalog records.

There are still those who cling to the belief that the use of classification schemes can lead to significant improvements in subject access in online catalogs (e.g., Drabenstott et al., 1990). This was not investigated systematically in the study because it was recognized that the scatter of related material would be too great to make this approach worth pursuing. That this assumption was correct is borne out by the fact that the sixty-six items considered relevant to censorship in the

Soviet Union were scattered over forty-one numbers in the *Dewey Decimal Classification*.

In summary, some records known to be present in the catalog were not retrieved by subject because the searcher did not exhaust all subject heading possibilities and because the particular catalog used offers little in the way of searching aids. However, these factors had a very minor effect on the results. Overwhelmingly, the subject search failures in this study were caused by the fact that the subject matter of items included in library catalogs is represented in a completely inadequate way in the traditional bibliographic record.

The lower part of Exhibit 74 illustrates what is possible through various forms of enhancement of the catalog records. In the analysis, preference was always given to retrieval through the existing bibliographic records. That is, if the record for an item could be retrieved on a further subject heading or title keyword, no attempt was made to determine if it was also retrievable through the terms found in its index, contents pages, or full text. Thus, as an example, records for the 125 items retrievable through the terms in back-of-the-book indexes could *not* have been retrieved using any part of the existing bibliographic records.

The data that relate to the enhanced records are not cumulative with the data from existing records. For example, searches on terms from the book indexes would retrieve records for 125 items more than the 327 actually retrieved (i.e., would raise recall from 53.9% to 74.5%) and 125 more than the 388 (327 + 61) potentially retrievable through the existing records. In other words, existing records plus book indexes could raise recall to 513/607, or 84.5%.

Note that the results for indexes and contents pages are not mutually exclusive: records for some items could be retrieved using terms from either component. Recall is potentially greater for the indexes than for the contents pages, even though more books have contents pages than have indexes, because indexes tend to offer many more access points than contents pages do.

Exhibit 74 shows that records for some fifty eight of 607 items could only be retrieved on words occurring in the full text of the book and eight are not even retrievable on full text. These items are relevant "by analogy" but the words needed to retrieve them *do not appear in the text*.

The results shown in Exhibit 74 might suggest that the problems of subject access in library catalogs could largely be solved were the text of contents pages and/or indexes stored in a form suitable for searching. Nothing could be further from the truth. Even if this were economically feasible, it would make little practical difference to the retrieval capabilities of a large catalog because the resulting precision would be completely intolerable. It is almost impossible to calculate how frequently a particular term or term combination might occur in indexes or contents pages for a collection of several million items, but it is safe to say that many searches on such extended records would retrieve thousands of items rather than the hundreds that were retrieved in many of the searches on existing records alone. Only in the case of an atypically specific search, involving a rather rare word or name, might the enhanced record improve search results. In other cases, any improvement in recall would be accompanied by a disastrous decline in precision.

Moreover, records for some items could be retrieved using terms from index or contents pages only through some ingenuity on the part of the searcher. For example, Rescher's book *Scientific Progress*, highly relevant to growth of the literature of science, refers (contents page) to growth of the "scientific enterprise" and to growth in "scientific progress," but makes no explicit reference to the literature of science.

Of course, one could reach a different conclusion from the results of this study: that the solution to the problem lies in the adoption of a detailed level of analytical subject cataloging, with twenty or thirty subject headings per item rather than the two or three more typical of present practice. This would be enormously expensive. Moreover, it would have less effect than Exhibit 74 might suggest, since these results are arrived at by hindsight. For example, the memoirs of Shostakovich has some relevance to censorship in the Soviet Union, as well as to many other specific topics. But there is no guarantee that a cataloger or indexer would recognize the relevance of this work to all of these topics even if he or she were allowed to assign an unlimited number of subject headings. Twenty different scholars might all find in this work certain portions that have some relevance to their areas of specialization, but it is by no means certain that relationships of this kind would be recognized by any but the subject specialist. Of course, this is not to imply that indexers or catalogers should be able to recognize every possible context to which a publication may apply but, rather, that subject experts can see relationships that others would fail to see.

The fact is that library catalogs permit only the most superficial of subject searches. In the first place, they rarely include periodical articles, which are the most important sources of information for many topics. Further, they tend to provide access only at the level of the complete bibliographic item rather than at the level of the subitem (a particular chapter, article, conference paper, or paragraph). A book that deals substantially with topic X is not necessarily a more important contribution to that topic than an article in a journal, encyclopedia, or handbook; a conference paper; or a chapter in another book. The catalog fails the searcher by providing access to only a small part of the literature that exists in the library on a particular topic. Moreover, the literature for which it does provide some level of subject access is not necessarily the best available in the library on any particular topic. The library catalog, as it now exists, may provide adequate subject access for a small collection – for example, in a school or small public library – or lead to a few items, not necessarily the best, on some topic but it is quite inadequate for a large, multidisciplinary library, especially one that attempts to support educational or scholarly needs.

Despite popular belief, the transformation of the card catalog into an online database has not significantly improved subject access. Indeed, it may have made the situation worse because it has led to the creation of much larger catalogs that represent the holdings of many libraries. Merging several catalogs into one, when each component catalog provides inadequate subject access, exacerbates the problem, since the larger the catalog the more discriminating must be the subject access points provided. But catalogs have grown much larger without any significant compensatory increase in their discriminating power. The application of the most sophisticated of searching software to any large catalog of the type traditionally used in libraries would make little difference to its performance: the records stored are completely inadequate representations of the subject matter with which they deal. In a database providing subject access to periodical titles, such as MEDLINE, a five-page item might be represented by ten or twelve subject headings, as well as keywords in titles and abstracts. In contrast, a 400-page book on the same subject might only be accessible in the catalog of an academic library by two subject headings, the title words, and perhaps a classification number.

This investigation was begun in the hope of identifying practical ways in which online catalogs could be made more effective tools for subject searching. However, the results suggest that significant improvements are not possible within the constraints of existing subject cataloging practice. The conclusion that emerges most clearly is that, if one wants to know the best things to read on some topic, there is no substitute for consulting an expert, either directly or indirectly (e.g., through an expert-compiled bibliography). Rather than trying to turn the present imperfect tool into an effective mechanism for subject access, the library profession might do better to concentrate on producing a subject access tool, of a different type, more useful to library users. Lancaster et al. (1991b) have suggested what such a tool might look like.

Searching of CD-ROM Databases: a Case Study

The study described compares the results achieved by library users searching a CD-ROM database with results achieved by a skilled librarian searcher and those obtained by a team of skilled librarians.* The investigation had several interrelated objectives: (1) to determine, at least for one database and sample of users, what kind of results library users achieve when searching a CD-ROM database, (2) to determine whether a team approach to searching gives results that are significantly better than those obtained by a single experienced searcher, (3) to discover what might be learned about search strategy in general by an analysis of the interactions taking place in the team discussions, and (4) through all of this, to try to identify ways in which end-user searching of CD-ROM resources could be made more effective (e.g., what types of training, instructions or interface might be needed).

The study was conducted within the Milner Library at Illinois State University. It involved real users of the Education/Psychology/Teaching Materials Center at ISU. Searches used only the ERIC database in CD-ROM form.

This decision was taken for several reasons:

1. It was desirable that the comparisons be based on searches in a single database to avoid extraneous variables associated with differences among subject areas and among databases.

2. Education is an obvious strength of ISU. There are about 115 faculty members in education and 760 graduate students, including about 160 doctoral students.

3. The ERIC database in CD-ROM form is heavily used by faculty and students at ISU.

4. Within the Milner Library it was possible to assemble a team of four librarians all of whom have both an academic background in education and experience in database searching.

5. The staff of the Milner Library was enthusiastic about the study and made a full commitment to it.

---

*This study was supported by the Council on Library Resources. A more complete account can be found in Lancaster et al. (1992).

6. The author had participated in projects with the professionals of the Milner Library in the past and had established a good working relationship there.

The choice of an education database for this study had no particular significance beyond the fact that it happens to be one already used heavily in CD-ROM form by faculty and students who lack training in database searching.

The first step in the study was to advertise it in such a way that enough real library users would agree to cooperate in the way required. Searches representing real information needs of faculty and graduate students at ISU were wanted, not artificial searches devised for the purpose of the study. In other words, real users were to evaluate search results according to the degree to which they satisfied real information needs.

To promote the study, a placard was designed and placed next to the CD-ROM terminal in the Education/Psychology Library. This asked CD-ROM users for their help in the study and told them what this would entail. Forms giving more detailed instructions were also placed at the terminal.

A letter was sent from the Milner Library to all members of the education faculty at ISU. The letter invited faculty members to participate in the study and asked them to make the study known to their graduate students. The instructions and a specially designed search request form were included with each letter.

A library user who agreed to cooperate in the study:

1. entered personal identification data and subject-related information on the search request form,

2. performed his/her own search in the ERIC database on CD-ROM, making, for purposes of the study, a copy of the search strategy and of the records retrieved in the search,

3. completed the search request form by entering the time taken in performing the search, and

4. placed the request form, search strategy and search results in an ERIC Study box at the Information Desk in the Education/Psychology Library.

A member of the Milner Library staff collected the materials thus deposited and separated the request form from the user's search results. A copy of the request form (but not the search results) was delivered to (a) a librarian highly experienced in searching the ERIC database (the same searcher participated over the two years of the project) and (b) the coordinator of the team search.

Within a short time after the user's search, the experienced searcher (designated "education librarian" hereafter) performed a search on the same topic using only information on the search request form as a guide to the search. Within the same general time frame, the team of searchers met at Milner Library, discussed the request, and performed a CD-ROM search interactively during the team meeting. The team's discussions were recorded on tape for later transcription. To the researchers were delivered, at the same time:

1. the search request form.
2. results of the user's search (plus search strategy).
3. results of the education librarian's search (plus search strategy).
4. results of the team search (plus search strategy).
5. a tape of the team interaction.

Note that neither the education librarian nor the team was allowed to contact the library user to discuss his/her need further.

The team comprised four members, all with considerable experience in database searching in the education area. Two were division heads, one a reference librarian, and the fourth was a cataloger responsible for cataloging all education materials at Milner. Because of scheduling problems, not all members of the team were present at all sessions. Team size varied from two to four members. Each team member brought different skills and perspectives to the discussions.

When the three sets of search results were received by the investigators, they were combined into a single set. That is, through a process of "cutting and pasting," a single composite set of retrieved items, without duplicates, was compiled. This entailed a rather considerable amount of work. The results of the team search were in the form of citation plus abstract, but the patron and librarian searches were citations only. Since results were to be judged on the basis of abstracts, the research assistants had to locate abstracts for any items not retrieved by the team and print these out.

Three copies were made of the composite search results. One copy was retained by the investigators. This was marked to show who had retrieved each citation – patron, librarian, team, any two of these, or all three. The other two copies were mailed to the patron. One copy was to be retained by her/him, the second was to be returned to the investigators marked to indicate the pertinence of each item to her/his information need. The patron was asked to judge each item according to the following set of codes:

A. A very important item. The value of the search would have been greatly reduced if this had been missed. *I was NOT aware of this item before I performed my ERIC search.*

B. A very important item as defined above. *I WAS aware of this item before I performed my ERIC search.*

C. Pertinent to the subject of my search but of less importance. Nevertheless, it is good that it was retrieved.

D. Pertinent but of marginal value. The search would have been just as useful without it.

E. Not at all pertinent to the subject of my search.

The set of completed search evaluations was subsequently transmitted to the investigators for tabulation and analysis of results, and the tapes of the team discussions were transcribed and summarized.

The study does have limitations that should be mentioned. The library user was asked to fill out the request form before undertaking the search, rather than later, but this could not really be enforced so it is possible that some of the request statements used by the librarian searchers represented the user's post-search interpretation of his/her needs rather than the pre-search interpretation. If this were true, it would give the librarian searchers an additional advantage over the library user. However, there is nothing on any of the request forms to suggest that they had been completed after the search was performed.

A more serious problem is that delays of several days, or even sometimes weeks, occurred between the time a user performed a search and his/her receipt of the composite printout representing the combined results of all three searches. Clearly, the user had seen his/her own results at the earlier time so his/her evaluation of the composite results would be influenced by this. Moreover, the assessments of the value of retrieved items, if they had all been made at the time of the user's search, might have differed somewhat from the delayed assessments that actually occurred in the study. Since this was a real-life evaluation, and not a contrived experiment, it was impossible to avoid this situation. In actual fact, it probably had little, if any, effect on the *comparison* of the results of the three searches.

Quantitative results

In all, thirty five searches were included in the study. For each of these cases, there were actually three searches – by library patron, education librarian and team – and recall, precision and novelty ratios were calculated for each.

The numerical results of the searches are extracted and presented in Exhibit 75 (recall ratios), Exhibit 76 (precision ratios), and Exhibit

77 (novelty ratios).* Exhibit 78 gives the summary figures based upon the arithmetic mean for each set of ratios. These results are not at all surprising. In terms of recall, the librarian was able to find more than the library user and the team was able to find even more. Note that these figures do not represent absolute recall. Rather they are figures for *relative recall*. That is, the total number of items considered to be pertinent in each search is the number found by the user plus additional items found by the librarian plus additional items found by the team: the patron's recall ratio is $A/(A+B+C)$, the librarian's is $B/(B+A+C)$ and the team's is $C/(C+A+B)$.

Results from other studies (e.g., Wanger et al. (1980) and Saracevic et al. (1988)) strongly suggest that the half dozen searchers involved in the present study will not find everything of value to the user. So the figures in Exhibit 78 are not very impressive. At best, the patron is finding only about one third of the items judged useful in relation to the information need and, more significantly, only a third at best of the A items (the very important ones that the patron was not previously aware of).

As predicted when the study was devised, the education librarian was more successful than the patron in retrieving items that the patron would consider useful, and the team was more successful still. Nevertheless, the results are not really inspiring: the best search, one based on ideas generated in a discussion involving several experienced librarians, only retrieved about half the items that the patron considered useful, and only half of the really important ones. However, one must bear in mind here that both the education librarian and the team were functioning under very unfavorable conditions since they had to operate only on the basis of the information on the patron's request form and could not contact the patron for clarification of the request. Some of the requests recorded were very unclear.

It is well known that recall and precision tend to vary inversely. That is, a strategy designed to achieve high recall will tend to get low precision, and vice versa. As Exhibit 78 shows, this phenomenon is well illustrated in these results: the patron has the worst recall but the best precision, the team has the best recall and worst precision, and the education librarian falls in between these two extremes. The relative performance of the three searches is illustrated more clearly in Exhibit 79.

---

*The novelty ratio, as defined for purposes of this study, is the number of A items (the ones judged very important by the user) that were new to the user over the number of A items retrieved in the search.

Patron				Education librarian				Team			
T	A-C	A-B	A	T	A-C	A-B	A	T	A-C	A-B	A
33.3	40.0	0	0	0	0	0	0	91.7	100.0	100.0	0
13.8	17.6	23.3	23.8	25.3	32.4	39.5	40.5	74.7	67.6	60.5	59.5
36.5	34.6	32.8	52.6	71.1	72.3	68.8	78.9	27.7	31.5	45.9	36.8
15.5	15.0	25.5	27.4	17.5	18.0	16.4	15.7	71.8	72.0	60.0	58.8
1.0	1.0	1.0	1.0	51.7	53.5	55.1	54.5	49.2	47.4	46.1	46.6
18.0	22.4	26.9	22.2	82.0	79.6	80.8	88.9	37.7	38.8	42.3	38.9
0	0	0	0	80.0	80.0	75.0	75.0	20.0	20.0	25.0	25.0
76.7	80.0	75.9	100.0	30.0	25.0	34.5	25.0	56.7	57.5	65.6	62.5
9.1	10.3	25.0	25.0	27.3	20.7	16.7	16.7	66.7	72.4	66.7	66.7
28.6	39.3	40.0	30.0	38.1	50.0	66.7	60.0	50.0	35.7	26.7	30.0
18.6	22.9	34.2	37.1	64.0	59.0	52.6	54.3	34.9	42.6	44.7	40.0
15.5	6.2	8.3	8.3	13.1	18.7	16.7	16.7	75.0	56.2	83.3	83.3
5.3	6.0	0	0	73.3	86.0	88.5	100.0	26.7	16.0	19.2	18.2
31.2	27.9	28.8	38.7	39.6	41.1	30.3	35.5	33.1	34.9	45.5	29.0
59.4	59.8	61.5	6.7	32.8	32.6	31.9	52.5	43.4	45.3	43.8	64.2
50.0	57.1	100.0	100.0	87.5	92.9	100.0	100.0	45.8	64.3	87.5	100.0
57.4	59.6	40.9	40.0	41.0	42.3	68.2	66.7	52.5	57.7	54.5	66.7
30.4	30.7	30.6	30.0	76.3	76.2	79.3	79.1	61.9	60.8	69.4	69.1
21.1	22.3	25.0	14.3	56.6	51.2	31.2	57.1	55.4	62.0	68.7	71.4
9.7	9.1	15.4	0	91.9	93.2	88.5	100.0	53.2	47.7	53.8	45.4
37.3	40.5	46.2	41.2	46.7	50.0	53.8	52.9	100.0	100.0	100.0	100.0
54.3	58.0	70.7	68.2	44.7	43.5	34.1	36.4	9.6	10.1	7.3	4.5
17.7	21.5	25.9	13.8	47.6	49.5	48.1	51.7	87.1	87.1	88.9	82.8
69.3	69.2	72.0	70.8	34.2	34.6	32.3	31.2	14.0	15.0	11.8	12.5
48.5	47.6	48.8	48.1	35.2	35.2	34.6	24.7	41.2	40.7	42.5	44.2
77.3	78.9	78.6	65.5	20.6	21.0	21.4	34.5	11.3	11.8	10.7	10.3
10.5	14.5	17.0	8.7	11.4	13.0	17.0	21.7	79.0	73.9	66.0	69.6
42.8	39.5	34.9	29.4	34.2	37.2	41.5	29.4	47.4	51.2	53.8	60.3
71.6	71.4	68.5	66.7	32.8	35.2	39.7	40.6	86.2	90.5	97.3	100.0
8.8	10.0	13.2	16.7	54.9	53.1	52.8	33.3	39.7	40.8	37.7	56.7
26.7	28.6	75.0	0	80.0	78.6	50.0	0	93.3	92.9	75.0	0
24.4	17.7	22.2	25.0	20.5	19.3	16.7	21.4	56.4	62.9	61.1	53.6
46.8	45.0	53.6	66.7	34.0	35.0	35.7	33.3	61.7	62.5	64.3	60.0
19.6	19.5	18.3	0	34.9	33.5	37.8	12.5	59.8	60.5	68.3	87.5
43.7	38.5	33.3	100.0	75.0	69.2	66.7	0	68.7	61.5	66.7	0
1130.4	1162.2	1183.3	1177.9	1605.8	1632.6	1622.9	1540.7	1883.5	1891.8	1960.6	1754.1

* T (total) takes all items considered pertinent into account, A-C excludes items that are pertinent but of marginal value, A-B are the very important items, and A are the very important items that the patron was not previously aware of.

Exhibit 75
Recall ratios for thirty five searches in a CD-ROM database

The novelty ratios of Exhibit 78 are a little difficult to interpret. The patron's ratio, 51.8, indicates that about half the items judged very important were new to the patron – i.e., brought to his/her attention for the first time by the ERIC search. The education librarian and the team were able to find proportionally more new items among those considered very important by the user, presumably because they were able to think of less obvious search approaches.

The last item of quantitative data is search time. The library users averaged around fifty five minutes per CD-ROM search, with a range of ten minutes to 210 minutes. There seems not to be any positive correlation between length of search and performance. The four longest

Patron				Education librarian				Team			
T	A-C	A-B	A	T	A-C	A-B	A	T	A-C	A-B	A
44.4	22.2	0	0	0	0	0	0	23.4	10.6	2.1	0
92.3	92.3	76.9	76.9	84.6	84.6	65.4	65.4	60.7	43.0	24.3	23.4
100.0	77.6	34.5	17.2	100.0	83.2	37.2	13.3	100.0	93.2	63.6	15.9
94.1	88.2	82.3	82.3	94.7	94.7	47.4	42.1	98.7	96.0	44.0	40.0
100.0	100.0	100.0	100.0	100.0	100.0	80.3	78.7	100.0	93.1	70.7	70.7
91.7	91.7	58.3	33.3	52.1	40.6	21.9	16.7	82.1	67.9	39.3	25.0
0	0	0	0	10.8	10.8	8.1	8.1	6.2	6.2	6.2	6.2
90.2	62.7	43.1	15.7	85.7	47.6	47.6	9.5	91.9	62.2	51.3	13.5
17.6	17.6	17.6	17.6	52.9	35.3	11.8	11.8	26.5	25.3	9.6	9.6
80.0	73.3	40.0	20.0	76.2	66.7	47.6	28.6	45.7	21.7	8.7	6.5
88.9	77.8	72.2	72.2	67.1	43.9	24.4	23.2	56.6	49.1	32.1	26.4
29.5	4.5	2.3	2.3	50.0	27.3	9.1	9.1	60.6	17.3	9.6	9.6
100.0	75.0	0	0	83.3	65.2	34.8	16.7	48.8	19.5	12.2	4.9
84.2	63.2	33.3	21.1	100.0	86.9	32.8	18.0	92.7	81.8	54.5	16.4
100.0	99.5	98.0	4.0	100.0	98.2	91.8	57.3	100.0	97.4	90.3	50.0
92.3	61.5	61.5	15.4	84.0	52.0	32.0	8.0	84.6	69.2	53.8	15.4
53.0	47.0	13.6	9.1	73.5	64.7	44.1	29.4	50.0	46.9	18.7	15.6
100.0	98.3	57.6	55.9	100.0	97.3	59.5	58.8	100.0	95.8	64.2	63.3
100.0	73.0	10.8	2.7	100.0	62.6	5.0	4.0	100.0	77.3	11.3	5.1
60.0	40.0	40.0	0	62.0	44.6	25.0	23.9	62.3	39.6	26.4	18.9
68.3	41.5	29.3	17.1	79.5	47.7	31.8	20.4	61.5	34.4	21.3	13.9
62.2	48.8	35.4	18.3	57.5	41.1	19.2	11.0	22.5	17.5	7.5	2.5
78.6	71.4	50.0	14.3	69.4	54.1	30.6	17.6	74.0	55.5	32.9	16.4
79.0	74.0	67.0	34.0	59.1	56.1	45.5	22.7	57.1	57.1	39.3	21.4
66.7	57.5	51.7	30.8	76.3	67.1	57.9	25.0	70.1	60.8	55.7	35.0
69.4	55.6	40.7	17.6	66.7	53.3	40.0	33.3	64.7	52.9	35.3	17.6
91.7	83.3	66.7	16.7	23.5	17.6	15.7	9.8	65.9	40.5	24.6	12.7
64.4	50.5	36.6	19.8	69.3	64.0	58.7	26.7	55.0	50.4	43.5	31.3
100.0	90.4	60.2	55.4	100.0	97.4	76.3	73.7	100.0	95.0	71.0	69.0
100.0	72.2	38.9	27.8	97.4	60.0	24.3	8.7	88.0	57.6	21.7	18.5
44.4	44.4	33.3	0	75.0	68.7	12.5	0	70.0	65.0	15.0	0
67.9	39.3	28.6	25.0	34.8	26.1	13.0	13.0	37.9	33.6	19.0	12.9
73.3	60.0	50.0	33.3	66.7	58.3	41.7	20.8	32.6	28.1	20.2	10.1
100.0	87.8	36.6	0	100.0	84.9	42.5	2.7	100.0	89.6	44.8	11.2
58.3	41.7	16.7	8.3	46.2	34.6	15.4	0	47.8	34.8	17.4	0
2642.4	2183.8	1483.7	864.1	2498.3	2037.2	1250.9	808.0	2337.9	1885.9	1162.1	708.9

Exhibit 76
Precision ratios for thirty five searches in a CD-ROM database

Patron	Education librarian	Team
0	0	0
100.0	100.0	96.2
50.0	35.7	25.0
100.0	88.9	90.9
100.0	97.9	100.0
57.1	76.2	63.6
0	100.0	100.0
36.4	20.0	26.3
100.0	100.0	100.0
50.0	60.0	75.0
100.0	95.0	82.4
100.0	100.0	100.0
0	47.8	40.0
63.2	55.0	30.0
4.1	62.4	55.4
25.0	25.0	28.6
66.7	66.7	83.3
97.1	98.9	98.7
25.0	80.0	45.4
0	95.7	71.4
58.3	64.3	65.4
51.7	57.1	33.3
28.6	57.7	50.0
50.7	50.0	54.5
59.1	43.2	63.0
43.2	83.3	50.0
25.0	62.5	51.6
54.1	45.5	71.9
92.0	96.6	97.2
71.4	35.7	85.0
0	0	0
87.5	100.0	68.2
66.7	50.0	50.0
0	6.4	25.0
50.0	0	0
1812.9	2157.5	2077.3

Exhibit 77
Novelty ratios for thirty five searches in a CD-ROM database

searches – 150 minutes, 120, 120 and 210 – on the average achieved a recall of less than 25% of the A items, compared with the figure of around 33% for the average of all thirty five searches. At the other extreme, the six shortest searches – between ten and twenty minutes per

	Patron	Education librarian	Team
Recall			
Total	32.3	45.9	53.8
A-C	33.2	46.6	54.1
A-B	33.8	46.4	56.0
A	33.7	44.0	50.1
Precision			
Total	75.5	71.4	66.8
A-C	62.4	58.2	53.9
A-B	42.4	35.7	33.2
A	24.7	23.1	20.3
Novelty	51.8	61.6	59.4

Exhibit 78
Average performance figures (average of the individual ratios)
for thirty five searches in a CD-ROM database

search – achieved a recall of around 27%. In other words, the best re-call results were achieved in the searches that were neither very long nor very short. However, one cannot draw any useful conclusions from this since the searches vary considerably in difficulty and in the number of pertinent items involved.

The average time spent by the team – in discussion and performance of the search – was around eighteen minutes per search, with a low of five and a half minutes and a high of forty minutes. This is based on timing for twenty nine searches. These times are likely to be a slight underestimate, however, because the tape recording ran out for a few of the searches (meaning that the search took more than thirty minutes) and it was not possible to estimate the time for these very precisely. The average for a team search, then, may well be in the twenty to twenty five minute range, rather than the eighteen minutes recorded. Unfortunately, there are no comparable data for the education librarian because these times were not recorded.

Qualitative results

It is often reported that library users have a lot of trouble searching databases because they experience problems in use of Boolean search logic. In this study, search logic was not the major problem encountered. The greatest problem faced by users was the fact that they do not identify and use all of the terms needed to perform a more complete search, frequently because they search too literally. To improve patron searches of CD-ROM databases, it is necessary to find some way of leading the patron from the terms first thought of (which are frequently literal translations of the terms appearing on the request form) to other terms needed to achieve more comprehensive results.

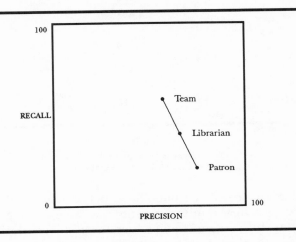

Exhibit 79
Performance points for three searches (patron, education librarian, team)
based on thirty five completed searches in a CD-ROM database

Analyses of the transcripts of the team interactions did not shed as much light on the cognitive behavior of database searchers as the investigators had hoped. At least, they seem not to reveal much that is unexpected. Primarily, the team operated through a heuristic approach that involved effective exploitation of the thesaurus plus use of retrieved records to suggest additional search approaches.

The fact that members of the team have some familiarity with the thesaurus seemed to strongly influence their approach to searching. After examining the request, they appeared to focus first on that facet most likely to be directly translatable into thesaurus terms. Frequently this is the facet that is most "concrete." They then made very effective use of the thesaurus structure to identify useful search terms.

Compared with the user's own search and with the search of the education librarian, the team search achieved by far the best recall in this study. This is hardly surprising: several experienced librarians, pooling their knowledge, are able to identify more potentially useful

terms than any one searcher alone. These results confirm those of
Saracevic et al. (1988) – different individuals can come up with quite
different search approaches.

The results do support one of the hypotheses underlying the
study: that a team search approach might be valuable in certain limited settings, perhaps for searches in which positive results could be of
great monetary value to a company or searches performed in certain
critical health care situations. In the present study, the cost per pertinent item retrieved can be estimated at $6.07.*

This figure is arrived at as follows. The hourly salary rates for the
four team members is $21.34, $27.52, $25.26, and $13.10. Assuming
all four members present at all team interactions (not really true but a
worst case situation for the cost analysis) the cost per hour would be
$87.22. If personnel benefits are calculated at 20%, cost per hour
would be $104.66. At eighteen minutes per search on the average, and
thirty five searches, total cost of the team searches would be
$10,987.20. Over the thirty five searches, the team retrieved 1810
items judged pertinent by the library users, making the cost per pertinent item $6.07. The cost per team search is approximately $314.

For the most valuable items (those of major value not previously
known by the requesters) the per item cost is $18.31 ($10,987.20/600).
For the "critical" search situations alluded to earlier, a cost of about
$18 per item does not seem unreasonable, especially if many of these
items would not be found in any other way.

CD-ROM and end-user searching

A substantial body of literature has already accumulated on user
acceptance of CD-ROM databases and user satisfaction with the results of searches in these databases. Almost all of this is purely subjective, based on user impressions rather than objective evaluative data.
Even the extensive studies of MEDLINE on CD-ROM (Woodsmall et
al., 1989) do not include any true evaluations. User response to CD-
ROM databases has been overwhelmingly enthusiastic. For example,
Steffey and Meyer (1989) report that the majority of the comments of
their users were of the "Wow! This is fantastic!" type. Nevertheless,
some evidence exists to indicate that the initial enthusiasm of some
users does decline with increased use of the medium (e.g., Allen,
1989; Miller, 1987).

---

*This is based only on costs in staff time. Actual costs would be slightly higher because
the cost of leasing the databases would have to be included in the calculations, plus costs
for materials consumed and space occupied.

It is rather disturbing that so many library users seem completely uncritical in their evaluation of CD-ROM. Many express satisfaction even when they achieve very poor results. For example, Nash and Wilson (1991) found that undergraduate students were generally satisfied with their search results even when very few of the citations retrieved were useful to them.

An extreme example of this misplaced enthusiasm is cited by Dalrymple (1989):

> As we got further into the study, we became more and more concerned about the reliability of using the idea of satisfaction and what it really meant when somebody said that they were satisfied. Most everybody loved the system. They liked using it. It's fun. They get in and they get something out, but we can tell from our observations that a lot of them are not using the system terribly well and perhaps not getting what they think that they're getting. This is a real concern for us. I had an extreme example of a woman who never got the hang of combining terms. So she would go in with a couple of search terms and she would print out her citations and then she would put in the next term and print out her citations. Then she would walk out with her two printouts, really happy, really satisfied. She loved the system. She was there a couple of times a week. (Page 30)

People exposed to CD-ROM databases overwhelmingly prefer these to printed indexes even when there is rather little difference in the search results achieved (e.g., Stewart and Olsen, 1988).

Putting electronic databases into the hands of large numbers of library users is an exciting development but it has its dangers. As Charles and Clark (1990) report:

> In our enthusiasm to embrace CD-ROM technology, librarians have neglected to make patrons aware of its drawbacks. (Page 327)

They were specifically referring to the fact that CD-ROM databases tend not to be very current, but a greater danger lies in the fact that they give some library users a false sense of security – the feeling that, because the source is "technological," they are finding everything or, at least, finding the best materials. This even extends to the fact that some users feel they can do better than experienced searchers:

> "Using the disc," said one Columbia student, "is much better than having someone else search and give you useless information." (Miller, 1987, p. 207)

The dangers have also been highlighted by Kirby and Miller (1986):

> It is well known that user-friendly online search systems are enthusiastically received. End users are well satisfied because they enjoy being able

to find relevant references with simple techniques, with little expenditure of time, perhaps in the convenient location of their own offices. They are in danger, however, from "unquestioned answers." At demonstrations of user-friendly systems, when a simple search has retrieved only a few references, the comment may be heard: "Well, that's all there is in the computer!" End users sometimes do not realize that the computer finds only what they specify, not necessarily what they want. (Page 27)

Perhaps the most disturbing aspect of this false confidence syndrome is the fact that most CD-ROM users find these products to be so easy to search that they feel no need for instruction in their use (Lynn and Bacsanyi, 1989; Schultz and Salomon, 1990).

Some investigators have come closer to true evaluation. For example, they have at least asked users to indicate the proportion of the retrieved references they consider useful (one such study is LePoer and Mularski, 1989). But these indications of search precision give an incomplete picture of the success of a search. Some estimation of recall is needed. Also, it is necessary to make some distinctions among items retrieved (or not retrieved) in terms of their relative value to the user. For example, a user may find five or six "useful" items but may miss one so much more valuable that it makes the retrieved items almost redundant.

Kirby and Miller (1986) performed a rare evaluation in which the search results achieved by end users were compared with results for searches on the same topics performed by experienced intermediaries. The searches were performed online, using the BRS/Saunders Colleague system, rather than on CD-ROM, but this is not really significant. It was found that users were generally satisfied with their results even when they were very incomplete relative to the intermediary's search.

The results of the present study provide some hard data to support the conclusions of other writers. For example, Ankeny (1991), reviewing end-user searching in general, concludes:

Evidence is accumulating that actual success rates of end-user searches are quite low . . . (Page 356)

The user search results in the present study are quite compatible with the sparse evaluation results reported previously: 20% of the users in the LePoer and Mularski (1989) study reported a precision of only 25%, and 22% of the users reported a precision of around 50%; 46% of their users reported a precision of 75% (the average for the searches in our study).

The present findings also agree closely with those of Kirby and Miller (1986); it is not so much logical errors that produce poor searches as inadequate search strategies, especially the inability to identify all useful search terms.

In the long-term, libraries may do a disservice to their users by making CD-ROM databases available and giving the impression that such sources can be used with little or no training. Schultz and Salomon (1990) suggest that CD-ROM, as presently used, may be fine for the student who needs to find two or three references for a paper, but is inadequate to support more serious research. To improve the results achieved by library users requires adequate user instruction in some form (a simple manual, personal or classroom instruction, or computer-aided instruction) or, alternatively, use of effective search interfaces.*

Study Questions

1. The research department of a small pharmaceutical company employs twenty five research scientists and one technical information specialist. The company is very information-conscious and much of the time of the information specialist is spent in searching online databases to provide references needed to support the work of the researchers. In fact, it has reached the point at which the demand for searches is beginning to exceed the capacity of the information specialist. He requests that a second information specialist be appointed. The Director of Research thinks he has a better idea. Since terminals are readily available throughout the department, he proposes that the information specialist, in conjunction with some outside information consultants, should train each of the twenty five scientists in the techniques of online searching. Once trained, the scientists will do their own searches directly. The information specialist argues that this is undesirable from the viewpoint of effectiveness (*he* is better at searching than the scientists will ever be) and cost-effectiveness (his salary is ap-

---

*The results of some studies (e.g., Stewart and Olsen, 1988) suggest that instruction in use of CD-ROM databases may not have as much positive effect on results as one might expect. However, a lot more evidence is needed before one can generalize on this. Clearly, a lot depends on the quality of the instruction. Allen (1990) presents the results of a survey of library users, experienced and inexperienced in use of CD-ROM products, to determine what type of training they felt they needed to aid their use of the databases.

proximately half the average salary paid to the research scientists). The Director of Research, however, is convinced that, once trained, scientists can satisfy their own information needs more effectively by searching directly. He asks an outside consultant to conduct an objective evaluation that will prove or disprove his point. You are the consultant. How will you do the study?

2. The searching of databases has been increasing rapidly throughout the departmental libraries of a large university. The University Librarian is pleased with this. Nevertheless, she has a doubt: with the large number of databases now accessible, how can one be sure that a librarian selects the "best" database for any particular information need? How could you evaluate the present database selection among the departmental libraries?

12. Evaluation of
Bibliographic Instruction*

Bibliographic instruction, which has become an extremely important element in the services provided by libraries, especially academic libraries, poses evaluation problems that are rather different from those presented by the other library activities discussed in this book.

The evaluation of a program of bibliographic instruction is an evaluation of an educational program. It therefore seems appropriate to deal with the subject within the broader context of a discussion of evaluation in education in general. Bibliographic instruction can be formal (e.g., an actual course in a college or university curriculum on how best to exploit the resources of the library) or informal (e.g., reference librarians may constantly try to teach library users how to find information rather than finding it for them); this chapter deals primarily with the evaluation of some formal program of instruction. While the literature of library science contains quite a few accounts of how to evaluate bibliographic instruction programs, few descriptions of actual evaluations and their results can be found. Exceptions include Fjällbrant (1977), King and Ory (1981), Hatchard and Toy (1984), Kaplowitz (1986), Tiefel (1989), and Lawson (1989).

Several levels of evaluation that can be applied to an educational program are suggested in Exhibit 80. The illustration indicates that:

1. The imparting of knowledge of some type to a particular community has been identified as desirable. This recognition is based on some form of *needs assessment*.

2. A program to impart this knowledge is designed and

3. It is implemented.

4. The program changes the knowledge, skills or attitudes of the participants.

5. Their participation in this program has some effect in changing their behavior or performance. For example, as a result of participating in a bibliographic instruction program, a group of university students may experience greater success in locating materials needed to complete course work effectively.

---

*This chapter draws heavily on guidelines prepared by the author for UNESCO (Lancaster, 1983).

6. This change of behavior produces its own benefits. Hopefully, students who use the library more effectively will learn more and perform better academically.

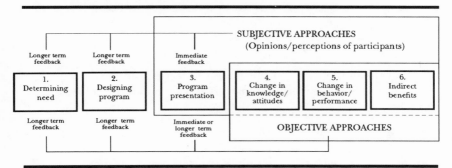

Exhibit 80
Levels and types of evaluation applicable to bibliographic instruction

From an evaluation standpoint, this situation can be examined at several different levels. An obvious concern is the quality of the presentation of the program: were the instructors satisfied with it; were the students? At the next level, an important evaluation question would be "did the program impart the knowledge, skills or attitudes it was designed to impart?" This can be considered in a narrow way – do students perform well on tests involving use of information resources? – or from a broader perspective – do they use library services more effectively than before? The ultimate evaluation criterion, however, is presumably whether or not the academic work of the students improves as a result of participation in the program.

Moving in the opposite direction, some other evaluation questions emerge: was the program well designed, was this type of instruction the best method to use in meeting this particular need, was the need a real one, are there other instructional needs that are more pressing and that should have been given higher priority? Evaluation procedures can apply to all the steps involved in a particular educational activity. Moreover, they should be regarded as essential elements in any educational program.

The distinctions made earlier in the book between evaluations of effectiveness, of cost-effectiveness, and of cost-benefit, as well as the distinctions between macroevaluation and microevaluation, apply equally to the bibliographic instruction situation. Being most tangible, the *costs* of the activity tend to be easiest to determine. It is usually more difficult to judge the effectiveness of the activity and more difficult still to assess its benefits. An evaluation to determine how well the program is satisfying the needs of those for whom it was designed is an evaluation of *effectiveness*, one that determines whether the needs are being satisfied as efficiently and economically as possible is a *cost-effectiveness* evaluation, and one that determines whether or not the benefits of the activity exceed its costs is a *cost-benefit* study.

The evaluation of effectiveness may itself be subdivided into:

a. evaluation of *how well* the activity is carried out.

b. evaluation to determine *how* it is carried out and whether or not it can be improved.

The first level, which has been referred to as *macroevaluation*, is concerned with the overall assessment of performance (i.e., how well the objectives of the activity are being met). Macroevaluation in itself tells us *how well* an activity is performing, but not why the performance is at this level, what failures occur in the operation, or how the operation might be improved. Macroevaluation alone is a relatively sterile task since, presumably, the principal objective of any evaluation is to produce improvement in the activity being studied. In order to improve an activity one must undertake a more detailed level of analysis to determine how it is carried out, how much failure occurs, why this failure occurs, and what might be done in the future to raise the overall level of performance. This analytical level of evaluation can be referred to as *microevaluation*. Microevaluation is essentially diagnostic, the objective being to improve the performance of the activity under review.

This categorization of evaluation is as applicable to educational activities as to any other. The effectiveness of a bibliographic instruction program could be evaluated, at the macro level, by asking the participants how satisfied they were with the methods of presentation. Alternatively, the impact of the program could be evaluated more objectively; e.g., by using some kind of test instrument to determine how well the participants perform on appropriate tasks before and after the program. Microevaluation would go beyond this, however, and would seek to discover, in detail, why 38% (say) of those participants were not satisfied with the program or why it had no significant impact in increasing the knowledge of a certain proportion of those participating. The objectives of the microevaluation would be to improve this program or others of this type in the future. A cost-effectiveness analysis would attempt to determine whether the objectives of the program (e.g., showing students how to use basic information sources more effectively) could have been achieved more efficiently or economically in some other way. One form of program would be more cost-effective than another if it could be shown to be less expensive to implement but equally effective in transmitting the needed knowledge or, alternatively, if it could be shown to be more effective as a means of transmitting this knowledge while costing no more than the alternative form of presentation. Finally, a cost-benefit analysis would be concerned with program justification. Do the benefits of this particular endeavor outweigh the cost of providing it? In this case, should the library be spending this much of its resources on bibliographic instruction or would it in fact be more valuable (in terms of benefit to the community at large) to spend the money in some other way? Cost-benefit studies are concerned with value per dollar invested. But the long-term value of many activities (and education is certainly no exception) is exceedingly difficult to express in absolute terms and, thus, cost-benefit studies are highly complex undertakings if approached in a systematic way. In actual fact, most cost-benefit "analysis" is highly subjective: a decision is made by an individual, or group of individuals, that a particular program is worth carrying out. They decide subjectively that the benefits of the program outweigh the cost of providing it.

A distinction must again be made between subjective and objective approaches to evaluation. Subjective evaluation is based on opinions: of participants, of instructors, or of independent observers. Objective evaluation, on the other hand, attempts to move away from opinion, pure and simple, and to arrive at an assessment that is more standardized and perhaps more quantifiable. An obvious example of an objective evaluation is one in which the success of a program is measured by testing the knowledge or abilities of the students before and after their participation. Some standardized test may be applied before the program and again when it is completed, the purpose being to measure the *change* in the students as a result of their participation. Presumably, if the educational experience has been successful, the students will achieve significantly higher "scores" on the second test than they did on the first. A variation on this is the use of some standard test applied to two matched groups of students, each group having been exposed to a different method of presenting the same material, the object here being to compare the success of one approach with that of the other.

Subjective approaches to evaluation are potentially applicable to all the steps identified in Exhibit 80. That is, one can ask program participants for their reaction to program content and the way it was presented. One could also ask them whether they feel that their knowledge and/or attitudes have changed as a result of participation. Subsequently, questionnaires or interviews could be used to determine, from the participants themselves, whether they feel that participation in the program has changed their behavior or performance or has had any indirect benefits. There is nothing wrong with getting the opinions of participants in this way. Nevertheless, a more objective approach may be preferable in evaluating the program in terms of knowledge acquired, attitudinal or behavioral change, or indirect benefits. Objective approaches, of course, are more difficult to implement than those that are purely subjective.

Scriven (1967) was first to make the important distinction between *formative* and *summative* evaluation. Later, Studebaker et al. (1979) differentiated among preformative, formative and summative evaluations. A *formative evaluation* of a program is one designed to improve it before its conclusion. "Dry run" activities, to test out aspects of the program before it is presented to the intended audience, can be considered formative. Formative evaluation can also be applied while the program is going on, the objective being to improve this particular educational experience before it is completed. It is obvious that formative evaluation is more feasible with programs of relatively long duration. Formative evaluation is not necessarily purely subjective. It is perfectly possible to have a formative test of the learning acquired by students. Such a test might, for example, determine whether or not students can demonstrate the achievement of certain behavioral objectives. In the case of a program to be repeated several times, an evaluation performed at the end of the activity can also be regarded as formative if it is intended to improve the quality of future offerings in the series.

Summative evaluation, on the other hand, is evaluation of a finished product. It is not intended to improve an activity but to demonstrate what it can do (i.e., show its worth). Summative evaluation gathers information for administrators – to aid a decision concerning the future of a program (e.g., adoption, continuation or termination decisions).

The *preformative evaluation* that Studebaker et al. (1979) identify refers to needs assessment, program planning, and any other evaluative activities that take place before or early in the development of a program. Preformative evaluation would include:

1. evaluating the need for various types of activity to allow the establishment of meaningful priorities.

2. evaluating the goals and objectives of proposed activities to determine if they are, in fact, realistic.

3. evaluating plans for the achievement of stated goals and objectives.

The distinction between formative and summative evaluation illustrates the fact that evaluation of bibliographic instruction can be conducted from a number of different viewpoints, the most important being those of:

a. the students

b. the instructors

c. those responsible for planning, administering or funding the program.

The instructors should be most interested in formative evaluation, the object being to improve the quality of program content and their own teaching methods. Participants should also be concerned with formative evaluation; they will want to provide feedback to the instructors in order, where necessary, to change the direction or emphasis of the program and thereby make it more responsive to their own requirements. Participants will also want to know how well they are progressing (in terms of their own objectives or the objectives set by the instructors) and how they might be able to apply the learning gained. Planners and administrators are likely to want evaluations that are more comprehensive and far-reaching. They are likely to be concerned with the total impact of a program on participants as well as with program costs.

One of the clearest expositions of approaches to evaluation in education is that given by Hampton (1973) who identified four possible "steps" proposed earlier by Kirkpatrick (1967). These steps are:

1. evaluating *reaction* of participants.

2. evaluating *learning* acquired.

3. evaluating *behavioral change*.

4. evaluating *program results*.

Clearly, these steps are all illustrated, explicitly or implicitly, in Exhibit 80. Evaluation of *reaction* (of students, instructors, observers) is easiest to accomplish. Such evaluation is completely subjective, although the data may be gathered in some systematic way and in a consistent form. These data may also be quantifiable in some sense (e.g., 80% of the participants were satisfied with the approach used). Evaluation of *learning* is best achieved through some objective procedure, usually some form of test. More difficult is the evaluation of *behavioral change* in the participants. This goes beyond learning as such into the application of the learning acquired. It is possible for someone to "learn" some body of knowledge (in the sense of passing some test which may be based on memorization) but still not be able to apply it in a practical situation. One approach to the evaluation of behavioral changes is by the measurement of the performance of an individual before participation in some program and again some time after participation. Preferably this evaluation should be objective. Another possible method of measuring behavioral change is by the use of a test of problem solving or decision making abilities. *Program evaluation* differs from the types mentioned earlier in scale rather than in approach or form. The evaluation of an educational program is of concern to those who plan and administer it. Program evaluation implies the existence of a set of program objectives. The evaluation is conducted to determine how well these objectives have been met. Clearly, a complete program evaluation could involve studies of reaction, learning or behavioral changes, or all three of these, depending on what the objectives of the program happen to be.

Participant Reaction

One important element in the evaluation will be the reaction of the students attending the program. Studies of participant reaction will tend to be subjective. Methods will be used to determine the *opinions* of the participants relating to the program in general and, possibly, certain specific features of it. At the most general level, an evaluation of reaction seeks to determine how "happy" the students are with the way a program is progressing or with the way it was conducted. In fact, the type of data collected in this form of evaluation has been referred to as "happiness data" (see, for example, Knowles, 1970) or as a "happiness index."

Evaluation of student reaction has definite value. As Hampton (1973) points out:

> It is important to know how people feel about the programs they attend, for it is reasonable to expect that participants who enjoy a program are more likely to obtain maximum benefit from it. (Page 107)

Knowles (1970) has stated that:

> On the whole, this kind of feedback is most useful in providing a general sense of trends in morale and satisfaction, but it frequently turns up specific and practical suggestions for improvement in the general program or in specific activities; and it may reveal problem points that call for deeper evaluation. (Page 224)

"Reaction data" can be gathered for the purpose of formative evaluation or for summative evaluation. Both formal and informal procedures can be applied. At a more informal level, instructors can ask participants for their unstructured, "off the cuff" impressions of the program. With a relatively small group this could possibly be achieved through an informal discussion with the entire group at the end of a session.

A more formal approach to the collection of reaction data will use some type of structured instrument for data gathering. Usually this will be a questionnaire completed by each student, probably anonymously, although interviews may be used in place of the questionnaire. If interviews are used, it is important that they be conducted in some consistent manner, following an interview guide of some kind. Questionnaires, although widely used and accepted as survey instruments in social science research, are criticized by some investigators, usually for two major reasons:

1. Questions may be misinterpreted by respondents and it is sometimes difficult to know whether or not the respondent has interpreted a particular question in the way the designer of the instrument intended.

2. There is sometimes some doubt as to whether a respondent has answered truthfully or accurately and there may be no convenient or practical way to check the validity or accuracy of a response.

The first objection is unlikely to be too serious if the number of people attending a program is sufficiently small. It will be possible to have someone in attendance while questionnaires are being completed within the group. This person (perhaps one of the instructors) will be available to "interpret" the questionnaire to participants and to answer any questions they may have on how to complete it.

The question of veracity or validity of responses is unlikely to apply to a student evaluation of an educational program. This is a problem that is more likely to apply in a situation in which the respondent is, in some sense, evaluating himself. For example, there may be a tendency for a respondent to overestimate the number of journals read, the number of hours spent reading, or the number of his own publications. This is a matter of prestige and of the desire of the respondent to appear "in the best light." There is no reason to suppose, however, that the participants in an instruction program would want to be untruthful or otherwise inaccurate in the completion of a questionnaire – the nature of the questions asked virtually precludes the possibility of this problem occurring.

Interviews seem to have three major advantages over question-naires as methods of data gathering:

1. the presence of the interviewer tends to ensure that all questions are correctly interpreted by the respondent.

2. it may be possible, by means of "probing" questions, for the interviewer to check on the accuracy of responses;

3. the interviewer may be able to collect unsolicited observations from the person interviewed; data unanticipated in the interview schedule may thus be collected.

As previously indicated, the first two of these advantages are unlikely to be very significant in the evaluation of bibliographic instruction, and the third benefit does not seem sufficiently important to warrant the use of interviews in place of questionnaires. Interviews are more expensive and time-consuming. They require scheduling of participants, which may not be at all easy to arrange. Moreover, interviews cannot be completed anonymously, unlike questionnaires, and they would probably require use of an independent interviewer. Members of the teaching staff should not conduct such interviews. They are unlikely to get completely candid responses and they may, perhaps completely unwittingly, influence the responses by the way they pose the questions. For formal measurement of student reaction, then, the printed questionnaire is likely to be the preferred instrument for gathering data. Nevertheless, where a skilled, independent interviewer is available, there is little doubt that interviews can elicit more detailed and revealing responses.

Group interviews with students can also be of value in getting feedback designed to improve the program although, as Freedman and Bantly (1986) have pointed out, it may be preferable to have such interviews performed by someone other than the instructors. Some problems of the group interview are dealt with by Martyn and Lancaster (1981).

To allow meaningful evaluation, on the basis of reaction data, it is important that some statement of the objectives of the program be available to participants. One important facet of the evaluation will be the students' assessment of how well the program has met its stated objectives. If no stated objectives exist, or are available to students, the possibility exists that they will evaluate the program in relation to goals that the organizers never intended. While it will also be important to learn of the personal objectives of students, and their judgment on how far these have been met, a wide discrepancy between the objectives of the students and those of the organizers would tend to indicate a failure in the design or promotion of the program or, possibly, the selection of participants.

Nevertheless, evaluation should not be conducted on the basis of stated objectives alone because a program may have benefits to the participants that were not anticipated by the organizers. It is possible that a program might receive a rather poor score in relation to its stated objectives but still be a valuable educational experience for some other reason. It is important, therefore, that the evaluation should be sufficiently open-ended that it will take account of benefits that are apparent to the students although not anticipated by those responsible for planning and organizing the endeavor. Parenthetically, it is worth mentioning that certain educational experiences may also have undesirable consequences that were unanticipated by the organizers or the teachers. For example, it is conceivable that a course on "literary appreciation" may cause certain students to hate reading, especially if the course requires the student to read a large body of literature in which he may have little or no interest. Harmful effects of this kind are more likely to occur with children or young people, and less likely in the education of an adult population. Nevertheless, at all levels, a poorly designed and boring program could conceivably turn certain participants against library use.

An ongoing formative evaluation of a program need not be a very elaborate procedure. To be sure that it is "reaching" its audience, however, some feedback should be obtained as early as possible. Indeed, there is much to be said for the use of brief reaction questionnaires completed by the students at the end of each session. The participants should not object to this as long as they know that the data are to be used, as necessary and possible, to improve the program as it progresses. Of course, this requires a commitment that the data will be reviewed promptly and that every effort will be made to respond to them.

For ongoing formative evaluation purposes, participants should be asked their opinions on some or all of the following points:

1. The importance and relevance of the materials covered up to this point. If the program can be divided into a series of discrete sections, an assessment of the relevance of each would be appropriate.*

2. The quality of the teaching in terms of how the material has been presented. If a number of different instructors are involved, stu-

---

*Instructor perceptions of what is relevant and important may not coincide very closely with the perceptions of the participants (see, for example, Hatchard and Toy, 1984).

dents should be asked to rate the performance of each, particularly if they are to perform again later in the program or if they may be under consideration for use in later programs. If a number of different teaching approaches or teaching materials have been used, students should indicate how successful each has been.

3. The novelty of the information presented. A student will normally attend an educational offering in order to learn something new. One should, therefore, be interested in discovering how much he or she is really learning (i.e., what proportion of the material he has been exposed to is new). Relevance and novelty are both important in evaluation. The subject matter may be relevant to a student's interests but not new to him or it may be new to him but not directly relevant to his needs.

4. The "level" of the material presented. It will be important to know, as a program is progressing, whether the material presented is at a level appropriate for the particular audience addressed. It should not be too simple. The students must not feel that they are being "talked down to." Simplicity may also be related to novelty – the students may be learning nothing new because the instructors have underestimated their prior knowledge of the subject matter and are treating the material at too basic a level. Neither, of course, should the material presented be "over the heads" of the audience. This matter of level of treatment is extremely important in formative evaluation: instructors must know, early in the program, whether or not they are "reaching" people. There is no point in waiting until the end only to discover that the majority of the participants have been completely bored, either because the material has been redundant or because they were unable to follow it.

5. How well the student feels that he is progressing toward satisfying his own objectives in participating.

6. An indication of which features of the program, as conducted so far, have been most valuable or interesting and which have been least valuable or interesting.

7. If outside projects or readings have been used, the students' assessment of the value and relevance of these experiences.

8. Any suggestions the students have as to how the program might be changed, in later days, to make it a more valuable educational experience.

9. The overall rating of the program, on some scale, by all participants.

10. Any other observations or comments the students would like to make.

A formative evaluation does not necessarily have to be this highly structured. There may be something to be said for a more free-form approach. Woodward and Yeager (1972), in a different type of setting (industrial), used daily logs in which students recorded general impresions of each day in an anecdotal, free-response form. In this they were guided only by very general headings such as "problems encountered."

In all of this data gathering the evaluator must try to discover *why* various responses are made. If students express dissatisfaction, one must learn the precise nature of this dissatisfaction in order to make changes designed to improve the program. Thus, one must discover exactly why a student feels he is not making satisfactory progress in the program, which parts of it he has found too complex, which parts repetitious, and so on. This implies that the questionnaire should be designed in such a way that, whenever the student indicates some form of dissatisfaction, he is asked to describe the precise nature of the problem.

The kinds of data needed to conduct an ongoing formative evaluation of some educational offering are summarized in Exhibit 81. The tabulation is undoubtedly incomplete. In particular, each program may have some special features that require emphasis in the evaluation questionnaire. Nevertheless, these data seem to be those of greatest overall importance and they should be generally applicable in the formative evaluation of most of the educational activities with which libraries will be involved. Of course, not all the items listed will apply to every possible situation. Moreover, not everything need be collected at once. A fairly simple daily log (see Exhibit 82) or check sheet completed after each session (Exhibit 83), for example, could be supplemented by a more detailed weekly review form. Several examples of questionnaires used in formative evaluation are given in Lancaster (1983). A more detailed discussion on the design of questionnaires is given in Martyn and Lancaster (1981).

A terminal evaluation of a program may have formative and summative elements. The librarian may need to make decisions concerning its future — whether it will be offered again, with how much change, for what type of audience, and so on — and such terminal evaluation may also be used to gather more specific information that may assist the instructors in improving details of the program if it is to be given again.

In the terminal evaluation one may want to ask some of the same questions that were used in the ongoing evaluation, this time addressed to the program as a whole rather than just a part of it, but some additional types of questions may also be included. Some of the

1.   Importance and relevance of subject matter.
2.   Quality of the presentation
     a) by individual instructor
     b) by form of presentation used.
3.   Novelty of the information transmitted.
4.   Intellectual "level" of the material presented.
5.   Students' assessment of their own progress.
6.   Most and least valuable features of the program so far.
7.   Value of outside projects and/or readings.
8.   Student suggestions for improvement of the program.
9.   Overall student rating of the program
10. Any other observations the student wishes to make.

Exhibit 81

Types of data to be collected in the ongoing formative
evaluation of an educational program

	Excellent	Good	Fair	Poor
Lectures	☐	☐	☐	☐
Demonstrations	☐	☐	☐	☐
Practical exercises	☐	☐	☐	☐
Other elements (as appropriate)	☐	☐	☐	☐

Comments/explanations. Use the back of this form to record any comments you would like to make on
what has occurred in this program today. We are particularly interested in learning of any problems you have encountered, or if you have been dissatisfied with some aspect of the program. We welcome any suggestions you care to make
on how the program might be made more useful for you.

Exhibit 82

Daily evaluation log

major questions to be answered are presented in Exhibit 84. Most of
these are self-explanatory. At this point it will be necessary to ask students to view the program in its entirety as an educational experience,
including various factors that may have contributed to an atmosphere
conducive to learning. In this terminal evaluation one is concerned
with looking back on the program, to determine how successful it was
in toto and to identify any failures or problem areas that may have occurred. On the basis of this experience one may be able to make valuable changes in the future or draw on this experience in the planning
and execution of future offerings.

In bibliographic instruction programs at the university level it is
important that the participants feel that they are being treated as

adults. Bryant (1979) has emphasized the importance of several principles of adult education enunciated by Knowles (1970):

1. Learners must feel the need to learn.

2. The learning environment is characterized by mutual trust and respect.

3. The learners must perceive the goals of the learning experience to be theirs.

4. The learners accept a share of the responsibility for planning the learning experience.

Name:_____ Date:_____

The following questions are intended to obtain a quick summary of your
impressions of the last session.

Please place a check mark (X) to represent your opinion along each scale.

1.   How important was the topic for you?

----
quite   neutral   extremely
unimportant   important

2.   How helpful was the session to a student trying to learn more about how
to use the resources of the library more effectively?

----
extremely   somewhat helpful   extremely
unhelpful   somewhat unhelpful   helpful

3.   How interesting was the session?

----
extremely   neither, or some   extremely
boring   of both   interesting

4.   If the session were repeated, how would you want to see it changed?

----

5.   Have you any other comments, criticisms, suggestions?

Exhibit 83
Single session check sheet

5. The learners participate actively in the learning process.

6. The learning process is related to and makes use of the experience of the learners.

7. The learners must have a sense of progress toward their goal.

---

1. Have students' objectives been met?
   Have overall program objectives been met?

2. How valuable has the program been to participants in terms of their own goals?
   What were the main benefits gained?

3. How do students rate the quality of the instruction
   a) by individual instructor
   b) by type of learning experience (lecture, practical demonstrations, and so on)?

4. Size of group participating–too large, too small, about right?

5. Was the level of treatment of the subject matter "correct" for the majority of the audience?

6. Was coverage of subject matter comprehensive or were there notable gaps in coverage?

7. Were the various educational experiences well integrated into a meaningful and complete program, or were they disjointed and overlapping?

8. Was most of the material presented "new" to most of the participants, or was it repetitive and redundant?

9. Which features of the program were most valuable and which least valuable to those attending? Another way of putting this is in the form of features that participants would like to add or delete.

10. Were the physical and related arrangements (e.g., lecture or demonstration rooms) satisfactory?

11. Would participants recommend this program to others and would they attend another, similar program if it were offered?

12. Any other ways the program could be improved?

Exhibit 84
Some important questions to be answered in the terminal evaluation of a program

The opinions of participants may be considered "soft" evaluation data but the questions asked can and should be quite concrete. One way in which evaluation data can be made more concrete is through focusing attention on the objectives of the students or of the instructors. Instructors must develop a set of *behavioral objectives* for the program, with one or more behavioral objectives associated with each segment. If, at the conclusion of the program, each participant is asked to indicate how far he feels these objectives have been met, this can legitimately be regarded as part of the evaluation of reaction. If, on the other hand, some "demonstration of achievement" is developed for each of the objectives, and some testing procedures used to determine how far the objectives have been met, it is really the *learning* of the students that is being measured and this form of evaluation then falls legitimately in the category "evaluation of learning acquired," as discussed later.

Meyer and Jenkins (1979), in the evaluation of a minicourse, had students use a four-point scale to indicate the extent to which they considered the course objectives were met. The format used is shown in Exhibit 85. While the content here is quite different, it should be possible to use this as a model for the development of behavioral objectives for a module in bibliographic instruction (e.g., learning about CD-ROM databases), as well as for a possible evaluation instrument. The students, presumably, will have objectives of their own. An important element in the terminal evaluation will be the determination of how well the objectives of the students have been satisfied. To do this one must discover, for each student, what his or her objectives were in participating, and how far these objectives were actually met. For this purpose, it might well be desirable to use some very brief "pre-program questionnaire" to determine student objectives before the instruction begins. At the end of the program, each participant can be presented with the objectives specified before it began. They are then asked (a) to modify this statement of objectives if they feel that, in retrospect, it was too narrow, too broad, or otherwise inappropriate, and (b) to judge the success of the program in meeting their original or revised objectives. It will also be desirable to include a statement of the objectives of the program as prepared by the organizers and to ask students how far they feel that these general objectives have been met.

The California State Department of Education (1979) recommends that, at the beginning of an educational program, each student be asked to prepare his own set of goals. As the program progresses, he is invited to modify this list and the terminal evaluation should include some questions of the following type:

1. What were your goals when you entered the program?

2. Have you changed your mind about any of these goals? If so, how?

3. Which of your goals have been achieved?

4. If you did not achieve some goals, what could have been done to help you accomplish them?

5. What do you intend to do with your knowledge, skills, and capabilities; that is, what are your goals for the future?

In evaluating an institute for the training of librarians, held in the Caribbean, Chang (1976) approached this situation through a very

Objective	Rating			
At the conclusion of this minicourse you should be able to:	0	1	2	3
1. identify the steps involved in planning and implementing a curriculum project within a school;				
2. work effectively as a member of a curriculum development team within a school;				
3. describe and discuss various factors influencing the determination of aims and objectives for various levels of the curriculum within a school;				
4. apply stategies for: (i) collecting information (ii) making effective decisions (iii) improving communications both vertically and horizontally within the school administrative structure in relation to curriculum development;				
5. produce a practicable plan of action for improving the process of curriculum development in your school				

Rating key: Extent to which each objective has been attained.
3 = Sufficiently for all practical purposes
2 = Adequately, but some room for improvement
1 = To a minimum extent only
0 = Not at all

Exhibit 85
Student evaluation of the extent to which program objectives were met
From Meyer and Jenkins (1979) by permission of
the Association for Educational and Training Technology

simple pre-test and post-test. The pre-test instrument posed the following question:

Please list *specifically* what you expect to learn from attending the Institute for Training in Librarianship.

The corresponding post-test question was put as follows:

On your pre-test, you were asked to list specifically what you expected to learn from attending the Institute. Below please indicate *whether or not your expectations have been met* by the Institute. Please give examples. If your expectations have not been met, please indicate in what way(s) they have not been met.

Note that Chang seeks to discover the causes of failure or dissatisfaction. As emphasized earlier, it is important to discover *how* and *why* a failure occurs if such failures are to be corrected or avoided in the future.

A summative evaluation may not be entirely structured. It is sometimes illuminating, for example, to have each student list the things that they themselves feel they have learned as a result of their participation.

It should be pointed out that some writers are critical of the kind of terminal evaluation typified by such questions as "How much of the material was new to you?" Misanchuk (1978), for example, refers to this as *justificative evaluation* (an attempt to justify the event after it has been completed) and claims that this type of evaluation should not take place at all. He states that such evaluation asks participants for information that should have been gathered prior to the design of the program as part of the "needs assessment" or in the selection of participants. To a certain extent he is correct. Nevertheless, he is referring to a rather ideal situation. In fact, it may be quite difficult to gather reliable information concerning the knowledge and objectives of students before the program is actually underway.

Both Dixon (1977) and Misanchuk (1978) indicate that the subjective opinions of students may not always correlate well with objective measures of learning taking place (i.e., the student may express greater satisfaction than he really should). It is possible that one should only give opinion great weight if it agrees well with other measures. Dixon, in fact, suggests that the opinions and perceptions of students may have more validity if collected later, perhaps six months or a year after participation in the program, so that the students have had some opportunity to apply what they learned.

Trail and Gutierrez (1991) offer a rare example of an approach to determining student attitudes toward a bibliographic instruction program. If evaluations of this type are common in libraries, they seem rarely to appear in the literature.

Independent Observers

So far, only the reaction of students has been discussed. While student reaction is obviously of great importance, it is not the only data of interest. Wherever it can be arranged, it may be highly desirable to have some independent observer present at some of all of the presentations. Such an observer can: (1) mix with students and obtain feedback and reaction that may be more "candid" and impromptu than the reaction data obtained by the teaching staff through more formal procedures, and (2) observe the instructors in action and thus arrive at his own assessment of the quality of the program, both in terms of its content and of the methods of presentation. This second function may be regarded as a form of "peer review"; thus, it requires the use of an individual who is knowledgeable in the subject matter covered in the program and at a level of seniority and professional experience beyond that of the instructors. It is probably desirable to provide this outside observer with some type of checklist on which to record, in standardized form, observations on program content, teaching methods, student interest, and whatever else one may be concerned about. On the other hand, an observer may be encouraged to make less structured diary-type observations as illustrated in Exhibit 86.

Houge (1981) has described the use of "participant observers" in evaluation. A participant observer is a bonafide registrant in a course who, before the course begins, agrees to act as a kind of official observer of what transpires. Such an observer will become familiar with the goals and objectives of the program, will meet with the instructors, make observations on teaching techniques, and interact with the other students in order to collect their perceptions. Houge claims that this method complements and is consistent with more conventional methods of getting participant reaction. Patton (1990) points out that participant observation is essentially a combination of observing and informal interviews.

Observation can be a powerful evaluation method if properly used. Patton, for example, has claimed:

> To understand fully the complexities of many situations, direct participation in and observation of the phenomenon of interest may be the best research method. (Page 25)

His book presents an excellent account of evaluation through observation, including the use of participant observers.

Valuable as observer input can be, it must be recognized that one bibliographic instruction librarian may not be a good evaluator of another because some investigators have found that colleagues tend not to be good evaluators of instruction.

Reaction of Instructors

Another "reaction study" will involve the teaching staff. It will be valuable to have the instructors evaluate the program from their point

May 18, 1975

Today we completed the last of our observations in the ABE

program. Some rather interesting things have emerged in these

observations which we'd like to try to summarize.

There appears to be some contradiction, or at least

discrepancy, between what the teachers say they think the ABE

program ought to be about and what actually seems to be happening

as we were able to observe it.

For example, in our interviews with teachers, most said they

felt the program was so oriented toward reading that other

important things were being slighted. The most common thing

teachers referred to was the whole idea of coping skills or the

things people need to know how to do to get along in the world.

Teachers felt these skills were essential and said it was likely

that the ABE program was the only place these adults were able to

learn these skills.

In practice, however, there is little evidence to suggest

that these same teachers are able to do much with teaching coping

skills. Classroom observation indicates that up to 95% of

instructional time is spent in reading or language skills areas.

Exhibit 86
Excerpt from the diary of an evaluation observer

of view, and to prepare a summary of this evaluation once it is over. A
good instructor will constantly be evaluating himself. He is likely to
recognize the fact that certain material was not presented as clearly or
as completely as he would have liked, that a different sequence of presentation would have improved the situation, that certain types of information could be better presented in an alternative way, and that
certain topics might be omitted entirely in the future, because they
were redundant, of only marginal relevance or interest, or because
they were clearly boring to the audience. The instructors' evaluation

should also include their observations on the students – their quality, degree of interest in the subject matter, the intelligence of the questions asked, their diligence (e.g., in completing assignments), and their general suitability for participating in a program of this type. It is possible that a program may fail to meet part of its objectives because some of the students did not have the background necessary to benefit fully from the experience.

Knowles (1970) has mentioned that instructors have great shortcomings as observers because they

> . . .are personally involved in the outcome of the evaluation, so that it may be difficult for them to be objective. They may tend to overlook instances in which desired changes are not being produced and to emphasize minor successes. (Page 237)

On the other hand, it could be argued that the reverse situation might also be true. Some instructors may be too sensitive, too self-critical. They may find faults where none really exist. Whatever the limitations of the instructor as an evaluator, however, it is clear that he has an important role to play. His input will be analyzed and interpreted along with the input from students, independent observers and other individuals who are involved in some way with the educational experience. It is important that a complete evaluation should be based on input from a number of individuals representing different levels of involvement and points of view.

Evaluation of Learning

While the opinions of participants can be considered an important element in evaluation, more objective measures of the success of an educational program may be desired. In particular, the organizers may want a more precise measure of how much the participants have learned. Clearly, this is more difficult than simply assessing student reaction.

The use of behavioral objectives was alluded to earlier. An instructor should develop behavioral objectives for each segment of a program and identify an appropriate "demonstration of achievement" for each objective. How precise these objectives and demonstrations can be depends largely on what is being taught. *Psychomotor* skills (e.g., how to assemble a piece of equipment) can usually be reduced to rather precise objectives and demonstrations. *Cognitive* objectives may be quite precise if they relate to the imparting of factual knowledge but will tend to be much less so if they relate to the improvement of analytical and problem solving skills. *Affective* objectives, having to do with changing the attitudes or opinions of a group, tend to be least easily converted to concrete demonstrations of achievement. In the case of bibliographic instruction, the objectives will mostly be cognitive, although some affective objectives may also be involved (e.g., giving students a more positive attitude toward the library in general).

In developing behavioral objectives one can be guided by much sound advice in the literature of education (see Wilsing (1979) for one example). A good example of objectives for a program in the BI area can be found in Olsen and Coons (1989). The Association of College and Research Libraries (1987) has published a draft model statement of objectives for academic bibliographic instruction (approved at the ALA Annual Conference in 1988) and Jackson (1989) has discussed use of the model. To the extent that an objective can be made precise and converted into an immediate demonstration of achievement, it may be possible to test a student's learning during the program itself. For example, a possible objective might be:

To teach students how to perform an effective search in the ERIC database in CD-ROM form

and an appropriate demonstration of achievement might be:

The student performs a search on the topic of X. The following important items should all be retrieved: a, b, c, d, e, f. No more than thirty items should be retrieved in total.

In some cases, however, the objective and demonstration will be of a longer-term character, as in the following example:

By the end of the academic year, 90% of participants will have searched the ERIC database in direct support of at least one of the research papers they are required to write in this college.

Clearly, the extent to which this objective is reached could only be determined through some follow-up procedure.

If one objective of an educational program is to produce some attitudinal change among participants, it may be possible to assess the success through some form of pre-test and post-test of attitudes. A series of attitudinal statements makes up the test. Respondents indicate their agreement with each statement on a scale such as: Strongly Agree, Agree, Disagree, and Strongly Disagree. Such a method has been used by Smith (1974), Postlethwait et al. (1974), and Penn (1978), among others. Postlethwait et al. used such statements as:

I approach biology with a feeling of hesitation.
I really like biology.

I have always enjoyed studying biology in school.

It makes me nervous to even think about doing a biology experiment.

I feel at ease in biology and like it very much.

I feel a definite positive reaction to biology; it's enjoyable.

in evaluating an undergraduate course in biology; and similar statements could be devised relating to student attitudes towards the library, library tools or specific types of resources. The measure of success, then, would be the extent of movement in student attitudes (before and after the program) toward the desired objectives.

A more elaborate type of evaluation would involve the use of a control group. The attitudes of students who had taken the program would then be compared with the attitudes in a matched control group (see, for example, Mehlinger and Patrick (1970)).

Silver (1981) has warned that the attitudes of participants toward the subject matter of a program may influence their opinions on its quality. He describes an experiment in which, before a course, the knowledge and attitudes of participants were measured. After the course, tests of knowledge and of attitudes, as well as a questionnaire relating to the quality of the course, were applied. Silver found that attitudes did not change significantly before and after the course and were found to be directly related to opinions on the quality of the course. That is, those participants with the more positive attitudes towards the *subject* of the course were more likely to judge it of high quality. On the other hand, opinions on quality did not seem to correlate with changes in the participants' *knowledge* of the subject matter.

In the case of programs designed to impart factual knowledge (e.g., how to use particular reference tools), some test of mastery of subject matter can be applied to students before and after the program. This type of test is very appropriate to the bibliographic instruction situation: students can be tested on their ability to find answers to factual questions (and to document the sources they use).

In a pre/post situation involving factual-type questions, there are several possibilities for bias in one direction or another. If the instructors prepare the set of questions there is a danger that, consciously or unconsciously, they will give particular emphasis to questions of this type in their actual presentations. If the same questions are then used at the end of the program, the "evaluation of learning" may be somewhat biased in favor of the program since it is possible that other types of questions, although equally important, might not be answered nearly as well. It is also possible that the students themselves, remembering the questions asked in the pre-course exercise, will concentrate on these in their study of library resources, possibly to the exclusion of other topics of equal or greater importance. This could be true even when the student is given no indication that he will be tested again at the end of the program, a condition essential to the conduct of an evaluation of this type. Tiefel (1989) encountered this phenomenon in her evaluation of a bibliographic instruction program at Ohio State University: groups that completed the posttest without the pretest scored significantly lower than groups that had completed both.

There are ways in which some biases can be reduced (e.g., the questions may be compiled by an independent evaluator or use may be made of a crossover test, in which students and questions are divided into two-groups so that group A answers A questions before the program and B questions after it, while group B answers B questions before and A questions afterwards) but these may introduce new biases.

It can be seen, then, that it is somewhat difficult to arrive at a test design that has no possibility of bias in one direction or another. From the viewpoint of experimental design, it would be better to use a control group of people who have not participated in the program but are otherwise well "matched" with the student group in terms of other characteristics, especially in their educational background and level of experience. The use of a control group in this way would eliminate the need for the use of pre-course questions. The two groups would simply answer the same set of questions when the course is completed, and the two sets of results can then be directly compared, the assumption being that the student group should get significantly better scores than the control group. This type of measurement of learning should be possible within a university environment. The use of control groups in this way in the evaluation of library instruction programs is illustrated in Dykeman and King (1983), Nielsen and Baker (1987) and Lawson (1989).

Another possibility is to develop a rather large set of questions that range over the entire subject matter of the program. One half of these questions are then selected at random to form the pre-course test and the other half form the post-course test. The "at random" is important here. As Braskamp et al. (1983) have pointed our, an instructor could achieve very good results by choosing difficult questions for the pretest and easy ones for the post-test.

It is well to recognize, as Linn (1981) discusses, that the difference between a pre and post score for an individual is typically an unreliable indicator of actual change in knowledge. The reliability improves considerably, however, when scores for an entire group of individuals (e.g., all participants) are considered in the aggregate.

Mehlinger and Patrick (1970) point out that an evaluation instrument that tries to measure learning must satisfy three basic requirements to be valid: test items must be specifically related to the stated objectives of the program, experts must be able to agree on what is the "correct" or "best" answer to a question, and most students who have not participated should not be able to respond correctly to the test items.

Tiefel (1989) describes a pretest/posttest approach to evaluating a bibliographic instruction program in an academic library. The instrument used, which included ten questions designed to test the student's ability to use library resources and five questions of an attitudinal nature, is reproduced as Exhibit 87. The evaluation results indicate that the instruction program was successful in improving the attitudes of students toward libraries as well as in improving their ability to use library resources. The pretest/posttest approach was also used by Kaplowitz (1986), Ware and Morganti (1986), Lawson (1989), and Edwards (1991). Lawson compared the library knowledge of college freshmen who had taken a computer-assisted instruction program with that of freshmen who had been given a traditional "library tour." It was concluded that the former was as effective as the latter in providing library orientation and teaching the use of basic reference tools.

An example of a post-test only approach can be found in Johnson and Plake (1980), who compared the traditional library orientation tour with a computer-assisted instruction (CAI) program. Two groups of students, one exposed to the tour and one to the CAI, were tested for knowledge and attitudes after the instruction, as was a control group of students who had not been subject to any instruction.

Feinberg and King (1992) discuss the use of a workbook/workshop approach to bibliographic instruction at the State University of New York at Stony Brook. They give a sample of the questions used to test students in various information seeking skills.

It is important to test participants in a BI program to find out what they have not learned (thus allowing improvements in future programs) as well as what they have learned. Tiefel (1989), for example, discovered that the program at Ohio State had not succeeded in informing freshmen of the limitations of the library catalog (e.g., that it does not include journal articles).

Stewart and Olsen (1988) studied the effect of formal instruction on the success of students using the ERIC database in printed and CD-ROM form. Students were judged on whether or not they retrieved items previously identified as "relevant" and on the cost in time per relevant item found (e.g., the group of students instructed in search-

For each question, circle the letter corresponding to the best answer.

1. Search strategy involves
    a. Planning your approach to searching for information on a subject
    b. Using an encyclopedia first to find general information on your subject
    c. Starting your research by going to a magazine likely to have an article on your topic
    d. a and c are correct
    e. a and b are correct

2. The Library of Congress Subject Headings books (red books)
    a. Indicate which subject headings are used in the subject card catalog and on LCS
    b. List books in the Library of Congress
    c. a and b are correct

3. You need to find a magazine article about child abuse.
    You should go directly to
    a. Time Magazine
    b. The card catalog
    c. *Readers' Guide to Periodical Literature*
    d. Library Control System

4. You are in the West Campus Learning Resources Center.
    To find out if the LRC has a copy of *Ordinary People* by Judith Guest, you would check
    a. Book stacks
    b. Subject card catalog
    c. Author-title catalog
    d. LCS
    e. c and d are correct

5. What is the call number you would need to locate the book *Rock 'n' Roll Woman*?
    a. ML 3561
    b. ML R62
    c. ML3561 R62 07
    d. 73-9374

ML 3561 R62 07	ROCK MUSICIANS
	Orloff, Katherine. *Rock 'n' Roll Woman* / by Katherine Orloff. Los Angeles: Nash. Pub., 1974, 199 p., ports, 28 cm. Interviews with Nicole Barclay, Toni Brown, Rita Coolidge, and others.
OU	OSNdc 73-93974

The following is a citation from a periodical index:

a _____ FOOTBALL, College
b _____ Beautiful Rose, even for Bama: USC vs. Ohio State
c _____ D.S. Looney.   Sports Illus 5:28-33 Ja 14, '80

6. Which of the above letters identifies the date of publication?

7. Which of the above letters identifies the title of the magazine?

Exhibit 87

Test of library skills and of attitudes toward libraries

Reprinted with permission of the American Library Association from Tiefel, V.
Evaluating a library user education program. *College & Research Libraries*, 50, 1989, 249-259

8. Which of the above letters identifies the volume number of the magazine?

9. In the Ohio State University Libraries, Library Control System (LCS) is a
    library computer system which can be used to
    a. Find out if the OSU Libraries have Jaws by Peter Benchley
    b. Find out at which library or libraries Jaws is located
    c. Determine which OSU Libraries have Time Magazine for 1970
    d. a and b only
    e. a, b, and c

10. At OSU, you can accomplish the following tasks by calling the library center at 422-3900.
    a. Check a book out
    b. Renew a book
    c. Have a book sent to you on campus address
    d. Find out if OSU has Mein Kampf by Adolf Hitler
    e. All of the above are correct

Circle the letter that expresses your feelings about OSU Libraries:

		Positive		Neutral	Negative	
11.	Telephone Center	a.	b.	c.	d.	e.
12.	Computerized Card Catalog (LCS)	a.	b.	c.	d.	e.
13.	Search Strategies	a.	b.	c.	d.	e.
14.	Using OSU Libraries	a.	b.	c.	d.	e.
15.	Librarians	a.	b.	c.	d.	e.

Exhibit 87 *continued*

ing the CD-ROM version consumed, on the average, 2.8 minutes of
time per relevant item retrieved while the group using the print version, and not instructed in its use, consumed 17.6 minutes per relevant
item retrieved.) The users of CD-ROM did much better, on the average,
than the users of print, but the effect of instruction on search performance was not as dramatic as one might have expected.

More sophisticated tests of learning in library instruction programs
are also possible. Dykeman and King (1983), for example, found that
undergraduates who were instructed in research techniques by a reference librarian produced better research papers (better written and containing more pertinent research material) than undergraduates, taking
the same sociology course, who had not had this instruction. Kohl and
Wilson (1986) compared two approaches to bibliographic instruction in
terms of quality of the bibliographies in student term papers; their
method was also used by Ackerson et al. (1991).

Behavioral Change

If evaluation of learning is difficult, evaluation of behavioral change in students is even more of a problem. This phase of evaluation is concerned with the long-term effects of an educational program. It goes beyond learning as such into the application of the learning acquired. The obvious consideration in this evaluation is to find out how the students have benefitted, in the long run, from participation. The potential benefits of a program of bibliographic instruction could be considered at various levels: greater use of the library, use of a wider range of library resources, more sophisticated use of the resources, and greater success in applying library resources in the participant's own research or studies. The evaluation of user instruction in terms of changing patterns of library use was one approach used by Fjällbrant (1977) in her studies at Chalmers University Library. Unfortunately few details are given in her article.

It is clear that the long-term success of a program can only be measured by some type of follow-up study, conducted perhaps six months to a year after the end of the program. A follow-up questionnaire can be used in this situation to determine whether or not the participants have been able to make use of the material presented and, if they have used it, with what degree of success. At the same time, the participants can be asked to look back on the program and to assess its value within the longer-term perspective. Unfortunately, it is not easy to get a high response rate in follow-up surveys of this type.

Nadler (1976) contends that evaluations performed some time after the conclusion of a program are likely to achieve more reliable results. One reason is the possible existence of a "halo effect" (e.g., the latest experience may exert most influence even if it is atypical of the program as a whole), so the evaluation data provided at the immediate conclusion of a program may be somewhat misleading. He suggests that, before the conclusion of the program, all participants should be asked to write a brief memorandum indicating specifically what they intend to do as a result of participating. Three copies are made: one retained by the student and two by the instructors. Some months later, the instructor mails one of these copies to the student to provide "linkage" to the program. While not specifically suggested by Nadler, this occasion could be used to ask the recipient to what extent the planned actions have actually taken place.

Jaster (1981) gives an example of the use of follow-up telephone interviews as a way of assessing the impact of a seminar on written communication skills. Telephone follow-up has much to commend it (not least of which is the fact that it establishes another form of "linkage" with program participants). Patton (1990) is a strong believer in the use of interviews with participants – before the program, at the end, and as a means of follow-up. An example of a follow-up interview is given in Exhibit 88. Note how it attempts to get reaction directly related to the course and its impact (including behavioral changes resulting from the course) and also probes for attitudinal changes (the participants were interviewed before the course so pre-course and post-course responses can be compared). While the subject matter dealt with is quite different, it is easy to see how this particular approach could be modified to take in the types of questions that would be important in a follow-up to a program in bibliographic instruction.

Evaluation of Program Results

The "evaluation of program results," as the expression is defined for the purpose of this chapter, is concerned with the assessment of a complete educational program, which may involve a whole group of components (e.g., courses at different levels of depth for students at different levels or bibliographic instruction emphasizing different subject areas). The library director should be interested in discovering how successful the program has been as a complete entity. This is a level of evaluation that is of broader scope than the type of evaluation considered so far. As an example, one could evaluate as distinct units several courses that comprise a complete program. It is conceivable that each course could be quite successful but that the entire program fails to achieve its objectives, possibly because it is incomplete or emphasizes the wrong things. For example, a program could make a student more skilled in the use of library resources but might completely fail to encourage the student to use the resources more frequently. It is clear from this that there must be *program objectives* (in the broader sense) as well as objectives for individual components in the program, and that criteria and procedures should be developed whereby the results of the program can be evaluated against the program objectives. Evaluation of the program is the responsibility of the program planner rather than the individual instructors, although instructors and students may both have important roles to play in the assessment of the program.

A series of general objectives should be developed for any educational program. For any specific educational activity within this program it will be important that precise objectives, relating to the overall program objectives, be developed. These objectives must clearly deal with *who* is to be instructed, *what* information is to be imparted, and what the end results are intended to be. The educational activities

This interview is being conducted about six months after your Outward Bound course to help us better understand what participants experience so that we can improve future courses.

1. Looking back on your Outward Bound experience, I'd like to ask you to begin by describing for me what you see as the main components of the course? What makes an Outward Bound course what it is?

   a. What do you remember as the highlight of the course for you?

   b. What was the low point?

2. How did the course affect you personally?

   a. What kinds of changes in yourself do you see or feel as a result of your participation in the course?

   b. What would you say you got out of the experience?

3. For nine days you were with the same group of people, how has your experience with the Outward Bound group affected your involvement with groups since then?

FOR DISABLED

   (*Check previous responses before interview. If person's attitude appears to have changed, ask if they perceive a change in attitude.)

4. We asked you before the course to tell us what it's like to be disabled.
   What are your feelings about what it's like to be disabled now?

   a. How does your disability affect the types of activities you engage in?
   (Clarification): What are some of the things you don't do because you're disabled?

   b How does your disability affect the kinds of people you associate with?
   (Clarification): Some people find that their disability means they associate mainly with other disabled persons. Other people with disabilities find that their disability in no way limits their contacts with people. What has been your experience?

   c. As a result of your participation in Outward Bound, how do you believe you've changed the way you handle your disability?

FOR ABLE-BODIED

4. We asked you before the course to tell us what it's like to work with the disabled. What are your feelings about what it's like to work with the disabled now?

   a. What do you personally feel you get out of working with disabled persons.?

   b. In what ways do you find yourself being different from your usual self when you are with disabled people?

   c. As you think about your participation in the course, what particular feelings do you have about having been part of a course with disabled people?

5. About half of the people on the course were disabled people and about half were people without disabilities. To what extent did you find yourself acting differently with disabled people compared to the way you acted with able-bodied participants?

Exhibit 88

Example of interview with participants six months after conclusion of a course

From M. Q. Patton. *Qualitative Evaluation Methods*. Second edition.
Copyright 1990, Sage Publications Inc.
Reproduced by permission of the publisher

6. Before this course we asked you how you typically face new situations. For example, some people kind of like to jump into new situations even if some risks are involved. Other people are more cautious, etc. How would you describe yourself along these lines right now?

   a. To what extent, if at all, has the way you have approached new situations since the course been a result of your Outward Bound experience?

7. Have there been any ways in which the Outward Bound course affected you that we haven't discussed?

   (If YES): How?
   Would you elaborate on that?

   a. What things that you experienced during that week carried over to your life since the course?

   b. What plans have you made, if any, to change anything or do anything differently as a result of the course?

8. Suppose you were being asked by a government agency whether or not they should support a course like this. What would you say?

   a. Who shouldn't take a course like this?

9. Okay, you've been very helpful. Any other thoughts or feelings you might share with us to help us understand your reactions to the course and how it affected you?

   a. Anything at all you'd like to add?

Exhibit 88 *continued*

themselves must obviously be planned with these objectives clearly in mind.

Evaluation must be integrated into educational activities from the very beginning and it must occur at various stages in the complete process. The following sequence is recommended:

1. Establish objectives for a particular program.

2. Evaluate the objectives. Are they really the objectives one wishes to achieve? Are they reasonable and viable? Modify the objectives if they fail to stand up to this examination.

3. Develop plans for a training program that is likely to satisfy these objectives as efficiently as possible, addressing all of the various questions mentioned earlier.

4. Develop *criteria* by which the program can be evaluated in terms of the achievement of its objectives.

5. Develop *procedures* for program activities.

6. Have each element in the program evaluated. Evaluation of a program element could include reaction evaluation (formative and summative), evaluation of learning acquired, and evaluation of behavioral changes in the students.

7. Analyze and interpret the results of these evaluation activities. This should be a continuing and current activity. Programs may be slightly modified, expanded, drastically changed or abandoned completely on the basis of results gathered through these evaluation activities. It is, of course, important that the evaluation data be considered in relation to the *criteria* developed earlier; i.e., the criteria identified as significant in measuring the degree to which the program objectives have been met.

8. On the basis of all the evaluation data available, consider whether or not the program objectives have been satisfied, conducting whatever further surveys (e.g., follow-up studies with students) may be needed to complete the overall evaluation of program results.

9. Identify weaknesses or failures and the causes of these. Use the knowledge thus gained in the planning of future, improved programs.

As Steele (1973) has pointed out, program evaluation goes beyond instructional evaluation. It is concerned with the additive effects of a whole series of instructional units. Instructional evaluation deals primarily with impact on the individual whereas program evaluation deals more with impact on some group or community of individuals. Program evaluation is concerned, among other things, with the establishment of priorities.

In this chapter, various broad levels of evaluation applicable to educational programs have been identified. An example of a very thorough and multi-faceted approach to the evaluation of a training course is given in a report from the U.S. Civil Service Commission (1970). In the course, the behavioral objectives were carefully specified and the degree of attainment of each objective was determined by pre- and post-testing, by post-assessment by each student and by the student's supervisor, and by "observations" made by peers and the teaching staff using a checklist. The pre-and post-test in this evaluation made use of two sets of fifty questions each, approximately matched as to difficulty. All of these questions were of the true/false or multiple choice type. An interesting technique employed in this evaluation was the use of a self-assessment questionnaire completed by the students before and after the course. This questionnaire was designed to determine, for each element covered in the course, the student's assessment of its importance to him and his present understanding or skill in the area. With a self-assessment instrument of this type, used before and after the program, one can determine (a) how far it has changed the attitudes of participants toward the importance of various program elements and (b) how far the students themselves feel they have progressed in their knowledge. The authors of this report are careful to point out that, when so many approaches are taken to the evaluation of a single program, there is a very real danger that students will find the evaluation "oppressive" and will rebel against it.

Lechner (1989) performed a rare type of study in which the effects of a bibliographic instruction program (written materials supplemented by two lecture/discussion sessions) were studied from four different perspectives: content knowledge, performance on library search tasks, attitudes towards ease of use of libraries, and patterns of library use. When those receiving the bibliographic instruction were compared with a control group, no significant differences could be detected by any of the four evaluation methods.

Cost-effectiveness

This chapter has largely been restricted to the evaluation of an educational program in terms of its *effectiveness*. Cost-effectiveness

	Traditional Small Group Instruction	Conventional Large Group Lecture-Lab	Individualized Instruction	
			Locally Developed Materials	Commercially Developed Materials
Effectiveness				
Posttest Achievement	Depends on instructional strategy, materials, and management system; could be high if a mastery learning model were used	Not as high as the individualized course which uses a mastery model	Significantly higher than the conventional course	
Unit Achievement	Could be high if a mastery learning model were used; this would be difficult to manage in this mode	Probably not as high as the individualized course which uses a mastey model; a mastery model here would be difficult to manage given the usual manpower resources	Average unit performance was 90% or higher for 3 successive quarters	
Student Satisfaction	Generally highly positive	Least positive of all the alternatives	Generally highly positive	
Efficiency	Average in-class time is 42 hours per term	Average in-class time is 42 hours per term	Average in-class time for self-paced students is 32 hours per term	

Exhibit 89
Effectiveness considerations relating to four instructional alternatives

From A. D. Grotelueschen et al. *Evaluation in Adult Basic Education*
Copyright 1976, Interstate Publishers Inc. Reproduced by permission of the publisher

	Traditional Small Group Instruction	Conventional Large Group Lecture-Lab	Individualized Instruction	
			Locally Developed Materials	Commercially Developed Materials

Feasibility

	Traditional Small Group Instruction	Conventional Large Group Lecture-Lab	Locally Developed Materials	Commercially Developed Materials
Instructor Receptivity	Highly receptive; most aspire to teach small, intimate classes	Receptivity varies; some like the lecturer role; student-oriented instructors dislike lecturing to large groups	Few are willing to devote the extra time to develop the required system and course mate rials; changes in-instructor's role to one of manager of learning	Few are willing to adopt or adapt complete systems developed by others; more would be willing to adopt than to develop an entire course; changes instructor's role to manager of learning
Student Receptivity	Highly receptive even though most 100-level teachers are lower ranked faculty	The expected mode for 100-level lecture-lab courses; reactions vary according to student's preferences	Students who enroll are receptive; enrollment data suggest that the course is perceived as too time consuming even though the result is a high grade	
Conditions for Learning	Tends to be instructor paced and controlled; students proceed with group regardless of performance; some opportunities for individualization in pacing and feedback	Large group requires it be instructor paced and controlled; students proceed with group regardless of perform-ance; difficult to provide opportunities for indi-vidualization in packag-ing and feedback	Materials learner controlled; progress is individually paced; mastery learning approach provides multiple trials to demonstrate proficiency and receive optimum feedback	
Facility Requirements (assumes en-rollment of 200)	Seven classrooms, 30 seats, one hour, three days per week; seven lab sections, 30 sta-tions, two hours per section one day per week	A lecture room (200 seats), one hour, three days per week; seven lab sections, two hours per section one day per week	A lecture room (200 seats), one hour, one day per week, an individualized learning lab with 14 carrels to handle 200 students if open 50 hours per week	
	Present lab space can accommodate 25% of enrollees; incremental costs required for construction if lab work were required of everyone		Facilities not a problem because integration of lab and lecture permits flexible scheduling thus optimal facilities use	

Exhibit 90

Feasibility considerations relating to four instructional alternatives.

From A. D. Grotelueschen et al. *Evaluation in Adult Basic Education*
Copyright 1976, Interstate Publishers Inc. Reproduced by permission of the publisher.

| | Traditional Small Group Instruction | Conventional Large Group Lecture-Lab | Individualized Instruction | |
			Locally Developed Materials	Commercially Developed Materials
Costs[a]				
R & D Investment: Replacement[b]			$ 49,059	$ 13,385
Operation: Per Term[c]	$ 8,701	$ 3,043	$ 3,804	$ 3,804
Operation: Ten Years[c]	$348,040	$121,720	$152,152	$152,152
Total Dollar Costs: Ten Years	$348,040	$121,720	$201,211	$165,537
Unit Costs[d]				
50 students per term	$ 15.25	$ 18.67	$ 25.15	$ 20.69
100 students per term	$ 15.30	$ 9.36	$ 12.57	$ 10.35
200 students per term	$ 13.38	$ 4.68	$ 6.29	$ 5.18
400 students per term	$ 13.48	$ 3.30	$ 3.14	$ 2.59

[a] All direct costs inflated 5% per year for ten years.

[b] These are the existing operational modes: R & D, investment, etc., are assumed to be non-incremental sunk costs.

[c] Operation costs are based on a student enrollment of 200 which is the capacity of present lecture hall.

[d] Unit costs include operation, R & D, investment, and replacement costs; depreciation is based on a ten year schedule.

Exhibit 91
Cost analysis of the four alternatives listed in Exhibit 90.

From A. D. Grotelueschen et al., *Evaluation in Adult Basic Education.*
Copyright 1976, Interstate Publishers Inc.

studies in evaluation are less frequently performed. Such a study would normally be conducted in order to *compare* the effectiveness and costs of alternative approaches to achieving some desired educational objective. Given three approaches, all shown to be equally effective, the cheapest alternative will be the most cost-effective. Given three approaches, all costing the same amount, the most effective approach (in terms of achieving the desired objectives) will also be the most cost-effective.

A rare example of cost-effectiveness analysis is given by Grotelueschen et al. (1976). Four alternative instructional approaches were compared in terms of their likely effectiveness and feasibility or ease of implementation (Exhibits 89 and 90). The costs, including unit costs per student, were then computed for all four approaches (Exhibit 91). If all four methods can produce roughly equivalent results (i.e., they are equally effective), the second approach is the most cost-effective, at least until the number of students per term reaches 400, when the fourth approach becomes more cost-effective. This example is put forward as a useful model for a cost-effectiveness analysis relating to educational programs.

Cost-effectiveness analyses applied to bibliographic instruction in libraries seem virtually nonexistent. Even comparisons of different instructional methods are not easy to find. Bostian and Robbins (1990) did compare four methods of instructing students in the use of CD-ROM databases. However, students were evaluated on the basis of their reactions and on subjective assessments of their search approaches, rather than on actual results achieved, and costs were not compared.

Hallak (1981) and Wolf (1990), among others, have discussed the analysis of costs associated with educational programs. Wolf also presents some general guidance on cost-effectiveness and cost-benefit analysis.

Further reading

Besides the items already referred to, useful discussions of various aspects of evaluation applied to bibliographic instruction can be found in Glogoff (1979), Hardesty et al. (1979), Werking (1980), and Association of College and Research Libraries (1983).

Study Question

---

1. You have just been appointed Bibliographic Instruction Librarian at a small liberal arts college. The college librarian is also rather new — he is enthusiastic about BI and you are the first BI librarian. You have to design a BI program. Identify the desired *outcomes* for the program.

Is it possible to determine the extent to which these outcomes are met? If not, can you identify some *outputs* that could be used as predictors of the extent to which the outcomes are achieved? How will you evaluate the success of the program?

13. Resource Sharing

Libraries cooperate with each other by sharing resources in a variety of ways. Interlibrary lending is the most obvious example but other cooperative programs are also possible, including those for the acquisition of materials, for the storage of less used materials, for the support of regional reference libraries, and so on. Libraries share resources in order to improve their cost-effectiveness. This is demonstrated in Exhibit 92. A library may be able to satisfy 80 to 90% of the needs of users from its own resources. It cannot go much beyond this point economically because it would require a completely disproportionate expenditure to do so. For example, a library may be able to satisfy 90% of the needs for periodical articles by subscribing to 200

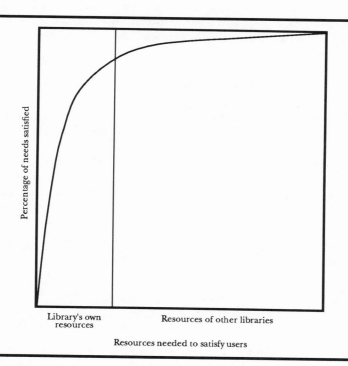

Exhibit 92
Cost effectiveness justification for sharing resources

titles; to satisfy 95% may require 700 titles, and 98% satisfaction may entail use of as many as 2,000. A similar pattern of diminishing returns affects other services provided by libraries.

Because library cooperation is now in such an advanced state in much of the developed world, a librarian can reasonably assume that almost any item can be acquired from another library if needed by a user. The decision on whether or not to purchase a particular item, then, is governed by the expected volume of use of the item and its cost. This can be seen most clearly in the case of a subscription to a periodical (Williams et al., 1968): for a title costing $50 per year, a level of demand as low as four uses a year may make it more economical to own the item than to acquire photocopies or tearsheets when user needs arise. For a title costing $500, of course, the level of demand would need to be very much greater to justify an annual subscription.*

The growth of electronic publishing over the last twenty years, together with the development of telecommunications networks to allow access to remote information sources, means that the tradeoff factors suggested in Exhibit 92 can be extended beyond the conventional concepts of "resource sharing." That is, acquisition decisions now involve two general alternatives:

1. To make a capital investment in the ownership of a particular item and a continuing investment (e.g., in handling, storage) to keep it on the shelves. This can be considered as an investment in "access" – a book or other item is purchased in order to make it readily accessible to users.

2. To acquire access to the item, or part of it, as and when the need arises. This access could be achieved by borrowing, acquiring a photocopy/tearsheet/reprint, or (for some publications) accessing the item online.

To carry this to its logical conclusion, one could say that the *primary* collection of any library consists of those items that will be used so many times that they are worth buying outright, while the *secondary* collection is every other information resource, in whatever form, that can be acquired or accessed when needed. The corollary to this, of course, is that the "materials budget" of a library should become

---

*See King (1979) for a concise analysis of the buy versus borrow situation. The discussion in this paragraph is simplistic in that it fails to take copyright restrictions into consideration.

instead an "access budget" and that a librarian should be given a free hand to decide whether an item should be owned or access made available in some other way.*

Evaluation Criteria

Many studies of the costs and the effectiveness of resource sharing activities, especially interlibrary lending, have been carried out, although few true cost-effectiveness analyses have been performed. The criteria for evaluating the effectiveness of these activities seem fairly straightforward. For interlibrary loan the obvious criterion is fill rate or, more precisely, the number of items supplied in time to be of use to the requester (Cronin, 1985). Some procedures for collecting such data are given by Zweizig and Rodger (1982) and Van House et al. (1987).

Possible criteria for the evaluation of various resource sharing activities can be found in a report by Peat, Marwick, Mitchell & Co. (1975). For interlibrary loan they advocate the collection of data on fill rate, delivery speed, transactions per request (i.e., the number of sources approached before a deliverable item is located), labor hours per request, and total cost per request. For cooperative reference services, data should be sought on the proportion of referred questions that are answered completely and correctly, on elapsed time, and on cost per question. Throughput time and cost per item are the obvious criteria to use in the evaluation of programs designed for cooperative cataloging and other types of cooperative processing.

Tools designed to facilitate resource sharing must be evaluated in terms of their effects on resource sharing activities. For example, the cost of building and maintaining an online union catalog must be balanced against the effect this tool has on fill rate, response time, and cost per transaction. A more subtle criterion is the contribution that the union catalog might make toward achieving a more equitable distribution of demand over participating libraries – insuring that the largest library in the system is the "source of last resort" rather than the source that all libraries automatically turn to.

To evaluate the success of some resource sharing activities, of course, the criteria will be less direct, and perhaps less obvious. One example is a program for coordinated collection building among a group of libraries. If such a program works effectively, the group presumably will be able to satisfy more demands from group re-

---

*I am greatly indebted to T. C. Dobb, University Librarian, Simon Fraser University, for the ideas encapsulated in this paragraph.

sources than was possible before the program existed. At the same time, use per item purchased should increase and cost per use decline within the group as a whole. It is clear, then, that the true effects of resource sharing can only be determined when reliable quantitative and qualitative data exist to describe the situation before the resource sharing activity was initiated. Unfortunately, good "before" and "after" data rarely exist.

Evaluation Procedures

Many of the techniques described elsewhere in this book are as applicable to the resource sharing situation as they are to individual libraries. For example, the collection of a network of libraries can be evaluated by the methods discussed in Chapters 2-3 and availability rate within the network by the procedures described in Chapter 8. Studies of network resources are easily accomplished if the network makes use of a combined catalog/circulation system capable of showing the circulation status of any item owned by member libraries. Mansbridge (1984) has undertaken one of the few studies of availability within a network. The availability of items in the network to a particular library and the availability to the network of items in a particular library were both considered.

More often than not, resource sharing is assumed to be a desirable activity, to be taken on trust, and comparatively few evaluation studies have been conducted. The only exception to this is the area of interlibrary lending (ILL), where numerous studies of fill rate and delivery times have been undertaken. Recent examples include Medina (1988), for academic libraries in Alabama, and Horton (1989) for a single academic library in Saudi Arabia.

Studies of why interlibrary loan requests are made, and what use is made of the materials thus obtained, are quite uncommon. An exception is presented by Porter (1990). The form used to collect data, shown in Exhibit 93, was designed for use in a nursing library but could be modified for use in other types of library.

Lowry (1990) looks at ILL, from the lending institution's point of view, as loss of investment. He quotes figures of $106 and $181 for purchase and "shelving" of monographs and serial volumes respectively. The owning library, he points out, loses on its investment when it lends to another library – in two ways: (a) an item lent may not be on the shelf when sought by the library's own users, and (b) books, as physical items, have a finite life and each use reduces this life. Pursuing this latter aspect further, he points out that, if a typical publisher's book binding lasts for 25 circulations, one loan to another library costs

**PLEASE HELP NORMANBY LIBRARY TO PROVIDE A BETTER
SERVICE TO YOU BY FILLING IN THIS SHORT QUESTIONNAIRE !!!**

All information received will be strictly confidential.

1. Why did you request this book/article?

   - essay/project/study/seminar
   - work interest
   - personal interest
   - other (please specify) ....

2. What date did you receive this book/article? ....

3. How much of the book/article was relevant to you?

   none ... up to 25% ... 26%-50% ... 51%-75% ... over 76% ...

4. How much of the book/article did you read?

   none ... up to 25% ... 26%-50% ... 51%-75% ... over 76% ...

5. Please tick the phrase(s) which apply to you (you may tick more than one):
   I made a reference to this book/article in my essay
   The book/article gave me something to think about
   I would like to find out more on this subject
   I will put the ideas of this book/article into practice
   The book/article arrived too late to be of use
   The book/article did not contain the information I expected
   The library staff did not keep me informed about problems
   Other (please specify) ....

Please add any comments which you feel may improve the inter-library loans/book
reservation service of Normanby Library (continue on the other side if necessary).

Thank you for taking the time to complete this questionnaire

Exhibit 93
Form used to collect data on use of interlibrary loan service
From Porter (1990) by permission of the Canadian Library Association and the author

$4.24 ($106 ÷ 25) in reduced life. It is difficult to understand the
rationale here since decline in life expectancy is related only to the
binding and the cost of rebinding the item is not likely to equal the
cost of the original purchase.

The cost of interlibrary loan activities, from the viewpoint of the
individual library, is obviously dependent on how many activities of
various types are engaged in. For example, the cost of supplying an
item is not the same as the cost of obtaining one. Bonk and Pilling
(1990) identify six different activities:

1. Applying for an item that will subsequently be returned.
2. Applying for an item that will be retained.

3. Applying for an urgent item (one that requires special handling).

4. Supplying an item that will be returned.

5. Supplying an item that will not be returned.

6. Applying for an item (or receiving a request for such an item) that cannot be supplied.

In the study reported, libraries were asked to calculate costs of each activity, based on 100 transactions of each, by recording staff time involved and adding non-staff costs (e.g., materials) associated with the activity.

MacDougall et al. (1990) compare the cost of obtaining interlibrary loans from a national center (in this case the British Library Document Supply Centre) with the cost of setting up a local network (of five academic libraries) for that purpose. Clearly, the decision on which mode of operation is preferred is heavily dependent on the BLDSC charges, on estimated local costs, and on the proportion of total demand that can be satisfied locally. In this particular situation, with present BLDSC charges and the proportion of demands that can be satisfied locally at only 26%, the local network approach is not considered a viable option.

It is difficult to evaluate cost-effectiveness of resource sharing activities because it is not always obvious what the measure of effectiveness should be. For example, how should one look at the cost-effectiveness of membership in an interlibrary loan (ILL) network? One way is to compare the cost of borrowing a book through the network compared with the cost of circulating a book from the library's own collection. As Kavanagh (1988) points out, the ILL cost is likely to be very high. She suggests that, since ILL makes available to users items that the library does not own, it makes more sense to compare the acquisition cost of a book, rather than the circulation cost, with the ILL cost. Kavanagh claims that the cost of membership in a network is justified even for a library that lends four times more than it borrows. For example, it may cost a library $6000 to lend 2000 items, but the 500 books it borrows would cost the library $15,000 in purchase price alone (without considering storage and other costs). This comparison is biased towards the resource sharing situation because a book purchased will presumably generate more than a single use. Another way of looking at the situation – not used by Kavanagh – is in terms of access to resources. For a modest annual investment, a small public library might acquire ready access to two million volumes. In comparison, the same amount of money would add only a very small number of books to the library's own collection. There is yet another comparison that could be made: the annual cost to the library of maintaining access to its own limited resources compared with the cost of annual access to the network resources; the unit cost (per item made accessible) for network participation would presumably be a very tiny fraction of the unit cost of ownership.

Another example of this type of problem can be found in Rutledge and Swindler (1988), who discuss the advantages to an academic library of belonging to the Center for Research Libraries. One obvious way of measuring the return on investment is to divide the annual membership costs to a library by the number of items acquired from the center in a year. As Rutledge and Swindler report, such a figure could be in the range of $200 to $400 per use. This is obviously a very myopic way of looking at the situation since it ignores the fact that, without the CRL, a library would probably need to purchase for its own collections some of the items it is able to obtain when needed from the center. Rutledge and Swindler suggest other ways of looking at the economics of this situation, including the cost per library user served. They point out that the annual cost of maintaining one academic library is about $600 for each faculty member and student served; in contrast, annual membership in the CRL is a little more than $1 for each person served.

Cooperative Collection Development

Cooperative approaches to the building of collections assume increasing importance as library budgets continue to shrink. Evaluation procedures can be applied to this situation in a number of different ways. One possible application relates to the selection of libraries for participation in the program – that is, the identification of which libraries should collect comprehensively in particular areas because they already demonstrate strength in these areas. The example described here relates to the design of a collection assessment tool for fiction to be used in a cooperative collection development context.

The collection assessment tool considered has two distinguishing characteristics: (1) it deals with fiction rather than nonfiction, and (2) it is to be used for the purposes of cooperative collection development. For evaluation purposes, fiction has properties somewhat different from those of nonfiction. Most obviously, it does not become obsolete in quite the same way (a novel is never really superseded or replaced by a later edition) and is not subject to the more "scholarly" evaluation criteria (e.g., citation counts) that can be applied to certain types of nonfiction. The assessment of a collection for the purposes of cooperative collection development is somewhat different from the assessment of that collection at a purely local level: measures of local use become less important and measures of quality and depth of collection become more important.

To develop a plan for cooperative collection development one must have a way of identifying collections that are "strong" in certain genres of fiction (mysteries, espionage, historical novels, and so on). Moreover, one must be able to compare *different* libraries in terms of their strengths; this requires that the collection assessment tool be the same for all libraries.

Within this context, "strength" has two dimensions: (a) extent of coverage, and (b) quality of coverage. What one needs to develop is a bibliographic instrument that can be used to compare the coverage and the quality of different public library collections in terms of various genres of fiction. One approach to such a tool can be illustrated through a simple example.

Suppose one compiles a sample of ten espionage novels published within the past five years and checks book reviews to see how they have been reviewed. Based on the reviews, one can give every book a mark of "quality" (or desirability). Stars can be used in much the same way they are used to rate hotels and restaurants: five stars for a novel favorably reviewed in all sources checked, one star for a book negatively reviewed in all sources. The result is a list like the following:

1	*****	6	***
2	*****	7	***
3	****	8	**
4	***	9	**
5	***	10	*

Two libraries, *A* and *B*, check the list against their holdings. *A* owns six of the ten items and *B* only four. By this standard, then, *A* owns 60% of the representative espionage novels while *B* owns only 40%. Perhaps more importantly, *A* scores four on a "quality" scale for its espionage collection, while *B* scores only three on the five-point scale (i.e., on the average, *A*'s books earn four stars and *B*'s only three).

Clearly, one has little confidence in a comparison based on only ten titles. What would be needed is a more valid comparison tool containing, say, fifty titles in each genre, published within a particular period of time. Such a tool, if properly constructed, could be used to identify libraries within a particular public library system that have relatively strong collections (both in terms of extent and quality of coverage) in various fiction genres. The tool thus developed could be applied statewide or even nationally.

The development of a tool of the type proposed is not without its difficulties. In the first place, one must agree on a valid and useful classification of fiction (Sapp, 1986; Baker and Shepherd, 1987; and Baker, 1988). Moreover, it must be recognized that a "miscellaneous" category will be needed since some fiction will defy classification. Furthermore, literary classics (such as Dickens, Bronte, Hardy, and Cooper) must be handled differently – perhaps on an individual author basis (e.g., to identify strong Dickens collections).

Considerable effort will also be needed to identify the book reviews. While many can be found through the standard book review indexes, it may also be necessary to search more obscure sources not covered by such indexes. It will also be necessary to develop a credible method of weighting the scoring of the quality of the books based on the quality of the reviewing source – for example, a glowing half-page review in the *Times Literary Supplement* should carry more weight than ten favorable lines in *Library Journal*.

Another problem to be addressed is that of "historical depth." One library may be very strong in espionage novels published within the last ten years, but another may be much stronger in the older and perhaps more "classic" espionage novels. One way to solve this problem might involve compiling two samples of titles for each genre – one for recent titles and another for older titles. Using the "median age" of the holdings of the library might be another way to develop an indicator of historical depth of a library's collection in a particular genre.

While the collection assessment tool envisaged is based primarily on the bibliographic checking method described, its uses could be supplemented by some measures of local use (turnover rate, relative use, or in-use ratio), some measure of interlibrary activity (the extent to which the library borrows fiction of a particular genre, the extent to which it lends in the genre), and other appropriate measures (e.g., median age of holdings, median age of use).

Clearly, the tool developed must be tested in some prototype stage to make sure that it does what it is supposed to do, perhaps through an initial evaluation, based on a single genre in two or three libraries, as well as a more comprehensive test of the complete instrument in, say, ten libraries after any adjustment suggested by the initial evaluation. Testing the bibliographic tool envisioned, and even applying it on a broad scale, would be greatly simplified if the holdings of the libraries involved are accessible through an online catalog.

The tool itself could be prepared in the form of a manual, incorporating simple instructions to be followed by the local libraries, forms to be used, formulas for simple calculations, and so on. Models can be found in Trochim et al. (1980); Krueger (1983); and Van House et al. (1987).

In the long run, resource sharing activities must be evaluated in terms of the extent to which they increase the effectiveness of library services or reduce the cost of providing an effective service. Some cost-effectiveness aspects of resource sharing have been discussed in this chapter. The subject of cost-effectiveness analysis is dealt with in more detail in the next chapter.

Study Questions

1. A legislative committee has questioned the value of state support to cooperative library "systems" in Illinois. The committee wants an in-depth evaluation performed on one of the systems, the objective being to show that the funds expended are justified, either (a) in terms of greatly improved library and information services to the community or (b) in actual savings to the participating libraries. How would you perform such a study?

2. Two adjacent towns, serving populations of 35,000 and 65,000, have independent school systems. The education authorities in these communities believe that greater cooperation in educational activities would be mutually beneficial. You have been employed as a consultant to advise them on what types of cooperation might be possible in the area of school library services. What would you advise?

14. Cost-Effectiveness Considerations*

The term "cost-effectiveness" implies a relationship between the cost of providing some service and the level of effectiveness of that service. Throughout this book, *effectiveness* has been considered in terms of objective measures of success in satisfying user needs – proportion of factual questions answered completely and correctly, proportion of sought items immediately available to users, and so on. The cost-effectiveness of an operation can be improved by holding the level of effectiveness constant while reducing the cost of providing the service or by improving the effectiveness while holding costs constant. For example, it might be determined that the reference department of a public library is able to answer correctly 80% of the questions put to it. If it were possible to reduce costs of this service (perhaps by discontinuing subscriptions to some reference sources that are infrequently used), without affecting success in answering questions, the cost-effectiveness of the service would be improved. Of course, some service might be so inefficient that it would be possible to increase effectiveness while reducing costs, but this type of situation is rather rare.

Cost-effectiveness analyses can be thought of as studies of the costs associated with alternative strategies for achieving a particular level of effectiveness. To take a very simple example, suppose that the parents of two young children decide to buy an encyclopedia to help them with homework. A test with a few sample questions suggests that any one of three encyclopedias would be equally effective. If one of the encyclopedias costs less than the others, it can be considered the most "cost-effective" purchase.

It is relatively easy to think in terms of the cost-effectiveness of a single service but much more difficult to do so at an institutional level. Here, cost-effectiveness has to do with the optimum allocation of resources. Unfortunately, the different services provided by a library are competing with each other for limited funds. Moreover, effectiveness measures differ from service to service. If more resources are put into answering factual questions, the diversion of resources from elsewhere may reduce the effectiveness of other services. If success in question-answering goes from 80 to 85%, but that in document delivery de-

---

*Various aspects of cost-effectiveness have been discussed throughout the book. The present chapter tries to pull these together.

clines from 60 to 55%, it would be difficult for the librarian to claim that the reallocation of resources has improved the effectiveness of the institution. In a theoretically ideal situation, the allocation of resources would be so perfect that no amount of reallocation would improve the library's services to users. However, it is highly unlikely that such an ideal would ever be reached. Moreover, the existence of competing services, to which different effectiveness measures apply, would make it impossible to determine that the ideal had been achieved.

Cost factors

Several cost-effectiveness and cost-benefit measures will be discussed in this chapter and in Chapter 15. Clearly, in order to derive such measures, it is necessary to calculate the cost of each product or service.* While it is not my intention to present a detailed discussion of cost analysis (see the following sources for that: Mitchell et al., 1978; Griffiths and King, 1983; Citron and Dodd, 1984; Roberts, 1984, 1985; Rosenberg, 1985; Kantor, 1989), it does seem appropriate to suggest some relevant principles here. In order to calculate the cost of a library service, all components of the cost must be identified. Exhibit 94 lists the most obvious of these components.

Personnel costs

The largest component in the cost of operating a library is likely to be the cost of the staff. To perform cost-effectiveness or cost-benefit

---

Personnel
    Full time on this service
    Part time on this service
Materials consumed
Equipment use
Space occupied
Mailing and other delivery costs
Telephone and facsimile transmission
Cost of online access
Leasing of databases
Purchase and maintenance of collection
Other costs

Exhibit 94
Components of the cost of a library service

---

*Getz (1980), an economist, has accused librarians of ignoring costs in their evaluative studies. He, on the other hand, ignores effectiveness except in terms of circulation and other quantitative measures of use.

analyses relating to a particular service, it is necessary to calculate the personnel costs associated with it. Note that personnel costs will usually be more than salaries and wages paid – allowance must also be made for personnel overheads incurred by the employer, including such elements as contributions to insurance and retirement plans.

Hours	Activities				
	A	B	C	D	E
1					
15					
30					
45					
2					
15					
30					
45					
3					
15					
30					
45					
4					
15					
30					
45					
5					
15					
30					
45					
6					
15					
30					
45					
7					
15					
30					
45					
8					
15					
30					
45					

Exhibit 95
Elements of a daily activity log

Where the entire time of an individual is devoted to a single product/service, the entire salary and benefits will be charged to that activity. However, some members of the staff will contribute to more than one service and it will be necessary to estimate the time devoted to each. Probably the best way of achieving this is to have these staff members complete daily activity logs for a period of time: two weeks would be enough as long as these weeks are typical of the individual's work throughout the year. The elements of such an activity log are illustrated in Exhibit 95. Within an assumed eight hour working day, fifteen minute intervals are identified on the log, along with five possible services or products to which the staff member could contribute. He or she marks the log to show how many of the fifteen minute blocks of time are devoted to each activity.

The activity log allows one to apportion to the various services the cost of staff time consumed. Thus, if 30% of one person's time is devoted to Activity A, 30% of his/her salary (including personnel overheads) must be charged to Activity A.

The daily log will probably show that staff members spend some time on activities not directly associated with any service – attending meetings, participating in conferences, and so on. This time should be charged to the services/products in the same proportions as the other time. If Activity A consumes 60% of the time a staff member contributes directly to service activities, 60% of his/her time not committed to any particular service should also be charged to Activity A.

Of course, the work of some members of the staff is not directly devoted to any single service. This includes, most obviously, the time of managers, but it may also include other types of personnel whose work is associated solely with the library – such as, perhaps, guards, messengers, and so on. The cost of all such staff members contributes to the cost of the operations, so their time has to be charged in some way to the various services/products. Probably the best way of doing this is to charge in proportion to the other costs incurred by the various services/products. Thus, if service A is estimated to consume 15% of the center's other resources, 15% of the personnel costs not directly associated with any one service should also be charged to this activity. The justification for this is that a service that consumes 15% of the resources is perhaps three times more complex than one that consumes 5% of the resources so it will also require proportionally more of the management and other time.

There is still one important personnel cost that has not been accounted for – the cost of those individuals whose time is devoted to the "technical service" activities that support the public services. These significant costs will be dealt with later under the heading "Purchase and Maintenance of Collection."

Materials consumed

For each service/product it will be necessary to calculate the costs of all materials consumed: paper, office supplies and so on. Library materials purchased for general use would not be included here unless actually *consumed* in the operation (e.g., cut up in the production of some form of press clipping service).

Equipment use

The cost of equipment use must also be allocated. This requires records to be made of how much use each service makes of each item of equipment. For equipment leased, the annual leasing costs will be charged to the services/products in proportion to the use made. For equipment owned by the library, the purchase price of the equipment needs to be amortized over a period of time that is assumed to represent its useful life. The greatest equipment cost is likely to be the cost of computer processing. The total cost of computer processing, including personnel costs and the purchase price of the computer amortized over a period of, say, five years, must be allocated to the several services and products in proportion to their consumption of computer time. Similar allocations must be made for other equipment such as terminals and photocopying machines. Equipment use that cannot be attributed to any one service should be spread over the services in proportion to the other resources they consume as was done for uncommitted personnel costs.

Space occupied

Buildings occupy space and space costs money (to purchase or to rent). Presumably, there is a space cost that has been calculated for the buildings occupied by the library. This should be calculated on a unit basis, such as the cost per square foot, and the calculation can include a component for general building overheads such as the costs of lighting, heating and of maintenance.

Given that such a space cost has been calculated (e.g., for university property), the cost of the space occupied by the library can be calculated. This cost should then be apportioned over the various services and products offered. There are various ways in which this can be done. One possibility is to apportion the cost of space in proportion to the number of people engaged in an activity. The justification for this is simply that the use of space is likely to be directly proportional to the number of people. Thus, a service that consumes the time of six people is likely to occupy roughly four times the space occupied by a service involving one and one half people. Note that number of people is not the same as personnel costs since the amount of space occupied by a person does not necessarily correlate well with the salary paid.

Of course, a significant part of the space may be occupied by people not contributing *directly* to the services and products, including the technical services staff, the managerial staff and the personnel associated with computer processing, and by the collection of materials. One way of handling this would be to calculate the cost of the space occupied by each of these components and to add this cost to the overheads of each component. Thus, the cost of computer processing would include a space cost component as well as equipment and personnel costs. A simpler method, which would probably suffice for most purposes, would be to allocate the *indirect* space costs to the services and products in proportion to the calculated *direct* space costs. So, if Service A employs 20% of the personnel associated directly with the services offered by the library, this service will be assigned 20% of *all* space costs.

It may be that space occupied can be ignored by some libraries in the calculation of the costs of its services. This could be so if the cost of the space does not come out of the library's own budget. Nevertheless, it can be considered a true cost to the parent organization and thus, from the organization's viewpoint, is a legitimate charge to library activities.

Mailing and other delivery costs

These costs are obvious. They need to be calculated for each of the services and products.

Telephone and facsimile transmission

The cost of facsimile transmission should be calculated for each of the services since, presumably, document delivery could consume a disproportionate amount of the total fax costs. The same applies to telephone charges if one or two of the services are likely to account for most of the cost (perhaps because of the need for many long distance calls).* On the other hand, if communications use is widely distributed over the various services, it may be difficult to apportion these costs

---

*Note, however, that telecommunications costs associated with access to remote databases are dealt with differently (see Cost of online access).

accurately. If this is so, some allocation formula must be used, as described earlier – e.g., cost allocated in proportion to other resources consumed.

Cost of online access

This refers to charges incurred in accessing remote databases through commercial vendors or through library networks. All costs (telecommunications charges, database royalties, and so on) directly incurred need to be accounted for and charged to the various services. Presumably, most of these charges would be incurred by the database searching services but some might be incurred by SDI or question answering services or even document delivery (e.g., if online facilities are used to request a photocopy). Costs should be charged to the services that incur them – e.g., 80% to bibliographic search, 10% to SDI, 5% to question answering, 5% to document delivery.

Leasing of databases

Databases in CD-ROM form are usually leased rather than purchased outright. The cost of this leasing must be charged to the various services making use of the databases. Presumably, the proportions would be very similar to the allocations discussed above for "Cost of online access."

Purchase and maintenance of collection

The biggest problem associated with the costing of library services is that of allocating the costs of the collection of books and other materials that support these services. At the same time, the costs of the staff members responsible for building, organizing and maintaining the collection – the technical services staff – must also be allocated. The problem is simply the fact that materials purchased can be used to support a number of activities. Thus, periodicals acquired by, say, an industrial library could support document delivery activities, certain reference services, and various current awareness services – a contents page service, an abstracting service, selective dissemination of information, and so on. How much of the total cost of acquiring and maintaining the collection of periodicals should be assigned to the costs of each of these services?

The total annual cost of the collection building and maintenance activities can be taken to be the cost of purchase of the materials themselves plus the cost of the staff who process them – those involved in acquisitions, cataloging and classification, checking in of periodicals, and maintenance of the collection (including the shelving of materials, binding and repair). It will be necessary to calculate the total personnel costs for these technical services, using the daily activity log illustrated earlier (Exhibit 95) to determine the technical services component for those staff members whose activities may encompass both technical services and public services.

Since subscriptions to periodicals tend today to be a very substantial component in the total cost of a library collection, it is probably necessary to separate the annual materials costs into (a) cost of periodical subscriptions and (b) cost of acquiring all other materials. The cost of the technical services personnel can then be allocated to these components in the same proportions. For example, if 70% of the materials budget goes to acquire periodicals, 70% of the personnel costs for technical services can also be allocated to periodicals. The justification for this is that, while books and other nonperiodical items require more effort in selection, ordering, cataloging and classification, a lot of time is expended in checking in periodical issues, following up on missing issues, shelving and reshelving periodicals, and so on.

Let us say that periodicals consume 70% of the current collection costs and other materials consume 30%. We are still faced with the problem of allocating these costs over the various services and products. Some general formula, such as those proposed earlier for the allocation of space or management costs, does not really seem appropriate here because some services will draw upon the collection much more heavily than others.

It is clear, in a typical library, that the collection supports the document delivery service more than any other service, so a large part of the materials costs should be allocated to this activity. But the periodicals may also heavily support some current awareness service. The entire collection can be considered to support question-answering activities, although those items generally categorized as "reference books" will be the most obvious contributors to this service. Printed indexing and abstracting publications will largely support literature searching activities, but they may also support some current awareness activities.

To arrive at an allocation formula for the collection, it will be necessary for senior members of the library staff to arrive at some consensus on this matter. Nevertheless, by way of illustration, a purely hypothetical allocation of collection costs is given in Exhibit 96.

While the distribution illustrated is hypothetical, it may not be too unrealistic. Note that there are significant differences between the allocations for periodicals and for other materials, at least as they apply to certain services. For example, the distribution assumes that most factual-type questions are answered from reference books and that databases within the library (in printed or CD-ROM form) substantially support the bibliographic search activity.

Service or product	Percentage distribution of collection costs (including staff time associated with collection building and maintenance)	
	Periodicals	Other materials
Document delivery	40	40
Question-answering	1	25
Database search	5	10
Referral	1	2
Contents page service	20	0
Recurring and special bibliographies	5	8
Abstracts bulletin	15	10
SDI	5	2
Information analysis activities	8	3

Exhibit 96

Hypothetical distribution of collection costs over various services and products
of an industrial library

It must be recognized, of course, that the cost analysis applied to collection building has been deliberately oversimplified. It takes into account only the costs of the materials acquired in a particular year and puts all of these costs as charges to the services in the same year. A more sophisticated analysis would take into account the fact that some materials – such as bound periodicals and certain reference books – will continue to be used year after year, so the costs of acquisition would be spread over several years for some of the information services. For example, it would make sense to say that the total percentage of the periodical costs attributed to the contents page service should be charged to the year the periodicals are acquired. On the other hand, some of these periodicals may still be contributing to document delivery services five or more years from now, so periodicals costs for this service should relate to past purchases as well as current acquisitions.

While such an analysis would be more realistic in some respects, it may be unnecessary for most purposes. The cost analysis discussed here is intended as a means to arrive at cost-effectiveness and cost-benefit ratios for the various services and products rather than to establish absolute cost figures. The ratios referred to would be used only to compare different services or to record changes in a single service over a period of time. For these purposes, it is more important that the cost figures be derived in a consistent manner than that they be "absolute."

Other costs

As Exhibit 94 indicates, a library may incur other costs, such as travel expenses, that do not fall under the other categories. These should be treated separately, and charged to the services that incur them.

To illustrate the cost analysis, as applied to a single service, a purely hypothetical example is presented in Exhibit 97.

Components	$ per year
Personnel costs	
Staff devoted full-time to service	50,000
Staff devoted part-time	12,000
Managerial and related costs	3,000
Equipment use	10,000
Space occupied	3,000
Materials consumed	3,000
Mailing and other distribution costs	5,000
Telephone and fax	1,000
Purchase and maintenance of collection	8,000
Other costs	2,000
Total Costs	**$97,000**

Exhibit 97
Cost components of a hypothetical library service

In the performance of cost-effectiveness studies it is important that all appropriate costs be taken into account. The danger exists that less obvious costs may be overlooked. Two examples serve to illustrate the point:

1. In comparing the cost of performing searches in a printed tool, such as *Chemical Abstracts*, with that of performing searches in the online equivalent, the cost of owning the printed tool must be accounted for. A major element in the cost of an online search will be the cost of *access* to the database (including computer costs, telecommunications costs, and database royalties). The equivalent cost of access to the printed tool is the cost of the subscription, the cost of handling it (checking it in and so on), and the cost of the space it occupies. Thus, if it costs $5,000 a year to own a particular database in printed form, and the database is used 500 times each year, the cost of performing a search in this tool must include $10 for "access cost." Not to do so would give a completely distorted picture in the comparison of "manual" versus online searching (Elchesen, 1978; Lancaster, 1981).

2. Consider a comparison, within a particular company, of the cost of online searches performed by librarians with the cost of searches performed by company scientists on their own behalf. Suppose that, on the average, it costs $80 per hour to interrogate the databases used by the company (all costs except personnel costs) and that, on the average, a librarian spends fifteen minutes online per search while the scientist spends twenty minutes. The librarian costs the company $20 per hour, while the scientist costs $30 per hour. Taking these factors into account, then, the average cost of a scientist search will be about $37 while the average cost of a search by the librarian will be $25. This comparison has overlooked the costs associated with the delegation of the search by scientist to librarian. For a scientist to describe an information need to a librarian may consume fifteen minutes of the time of each party. Thus, for the delegated search situation one must add a further $7.50 in scientist time and $5.00 in librarian time, bringing the cost up to $37.50. Even this analysis is incomplete. If one assumes that the librarians have already been trained in online searching, but the scientists have not, it will be necessary to build into the calculations the cost of training the scientists – and this cost must be amortized over some period of time.

These figures are purely hypothetical and certain assumptions underlie the analysis (e.g., that all scientists have suitable terminals in their offices). The whole situation has been deliberately oversimplified in order to illustrate what can happen when significant costs are overlooked. A more sophisticated analysis would need to take into account how librarians and scientists would spend their time if they were not online to databases.

Cost-effectiveness Measures

A cost-effectiveness study looks at return on investment. As implied earlier, the "return" on a library's investment (in material, personnel, and facilities) can be measured in service to users. More precisely, a good cost-effectiveness measure is one that balances cost against some unit of user satisfaction. The database searching situation provides a good example. As discussed in Chapter 11, the success of a bibliographic search can be expressed in terms of the number of pertinent items retrieved. An appropriate cost-effectiveness measure, then, is the cost per pertinent item retrieved. Returning to an example used earlier, one could compare online searching by librarians with searching by scientists on the basis of (a) cost, (b) effectiveness, or (c) cost-effectiveness. Consider the following data:

	Librarian	Scientist
Cost	$37 per search	$40 per search
Effectiveness	15 pertinent items retrieved on the average	20 pertinent items retrieved on the average
Cost-Effectiveness	$2.47 per pertinent item retrieved	$2 per pertinent item retrieved

The cost comparison favors the librarian, but the effectiveness and cost-effectiveness comparisons both favor the scientist. A more sophisticated analysis would distinguish between "major value" and "minor value" items; e.g., the scientist might find more than the librarian but the librarian finds the ones that the scientist judges more valuable, perhaps because it is these that are "new" to him.

It seems that very few studies have looked at the true cost-effectiveness of end-user searching versus librarian searching, although Nicholas et al. (1987) have touched upon some of the issues.

The literature searching situation is unusual in that the cost-effectiveness measures seem relatively clearcut and easily defended. For other components of library service, it may be less clear what the best measure of cost-effectiveness should be. Take the case of a subscription to a periodical. One possible measure of return on investment would be the number of articles it publishes annually that are likely to be of direct interest to the library's users. This is more obviously appropriate in the case of a highly specialized library. For example, based on past performance, journal A can be expected to publish about twelve "irrigation" articles each year, while journal B can be expected to publish about twenty. A costs $120 to subscribe to while B costs $250. In return on investment, A is a somewhat better buy for an irrigation library, always assuming that an article in A is "as good" as one in B. In the case of a more general library, however, such a measure of "yield" seems much less appropriate and would be exceedingly difficult to apply.

The most obvious measure of return on investment for an item purchased is the number of uses it receives. In a very superficial sense, a book that costs $75 to acquire and make ready for the shelves is a more cost-effective purchase, if used twenty times in its lifetime in the library, than one that costs $30 and receives six uses. The problem with this, of course, is that all uses are presumed "equal," which many librarians are quite unwilling to accept. If cost per use were the only consideration, a public library could improve its overall cost-effectiveness by buying more and more of the highly popular items at the expense of materials in categories of lower demand. Such a strategy is sometimes advocated (see, for example, Newhouse and Alexander, 1972) although it completely ignores the need to build a "balanced" collection and to serve the needs of a wide variety of users, some of whom might be quite atypical of the majority. In an academic library, of course, amount of use is even less acceptable as a measure of success in book selection (see Voigt, 1979, for example); indeed, some university librarians seem to place more value on potential use than they do on actual use.

Nevertheless, cost per use cannot be dismissed entirely. As Kent et al. (1979) have shown, the cost-effectiveness of a collection of periodicals can drop dramatically when titles receiving no use at all are retained in the collection. Cost per use or expected use will be an obvious criterion governing many decisions – whether to subscribe to a new periodical, whether to discontinue some publication for which an online equivalent exists, whether to purchase some expensive reference tool, and so on.

The Pittsburgh study (Kent et al., 1979) presents cost per use data for the periodical collections of several departmental libraries. Cost per use data for a special library is given by Sridhar (1988). Franklin (1989) also presents cost per use data for 145 serials considered as possible candidates for cancellation in an academic library.

One example of a cost-effectiveness analysis, based on cost per use, can be found in the work of Chrzastowski (1991), who studied journal use and costs at an academic chemistry library. Uses – circulation, in house use (determined through reshelving counts), and interlibrary loan – were counted over a six-month period and costs were the 1988 subscription costs. She found that only 9% of the 682 journals subscribed to (sixty one titles) were never used in the six-month period, but an additional 164 titles (24%) were used only once or twice. The journals not used at all account for only 3% of the total journal subscription costs. Average cost per use for all 682 journals was calculated to be $3.53. Even among the twenty most frequently used journals, substantial differences exist in cost per use, ranging from a high of $5.74 to a low of $0.05. The ten highest and ten lowest cost per use titles are shown in Exhibit 98. The study permitted cancellation of enough titles to save $40,000 a year.

A more sophisticated approach to the same problem is reported by Milne and Tiffany (1991). They compare the cost of subscribing to a serial with the cost of cancelling the subscription and relying on obtaining copies from other libraries when needed. The study was performed at the Memorial University of Newfoundland. Uses were determined by means of a form fixed to the front cover of unbound issues and to bound volumes. Users were asked merely to put a check mark on the form if they employed the issue or volume in any way (read, browsed, copied, borrowed). The method was mentioned earlier in Chapter 5 and the form illustrated in Exhibit 29. The survey was conducted for a full year.*

Ten Lowest Cost per Use Titles	
Title	Cost per use
1. Analytical Chemistry	$ .05
2. Journal of the American Chemical Society	$ .06
3. Journal of Chemical Education	$ .10
4. Science	$ .12
5. Journal of Organic Chemistry	$ .13
6. Chemical Engineering	$ .14
7. Industrial and Chemical Engineering	$ .15
8. Pollution Engineering	$ .18
9. Accounts of Chemical Research	$ .19
10. Chemical and Engineering News	$ .26

Ten Highest Cost per Use Titles	
Title	Cost per use
1. Solid Fuel Chemistry (translation)	$585.00
2. Mendeleev Chemistry Journal (translation)	$575.00
3. Mass Spectrometry Bulletin	$440.00
4. Kinetika I Kataliz	$412.00
5. International Journal of Enviromental Studies	$411.00
6. X-Ray Spectrometry	$375.00
7. ChemInform (Chemischer Informationsdienst)	$354.39
8. Chemistry In Ecology	$258.00
9. Fluid Mechanics - Soviet Research	$227.00
10. C1 Molecule Chemistry	$226.00

Exhibit 98

Differences in cost per use for journals in an academic special library
(high and low end of the scale for 682 titles)

From Chrzastowski (1991) by permission of Haworth Press

It was estimated from a pilot study that two out of every three users made correct use of the form (i.e., checked a use when it occurred) so a correction factor of 3/2 was applied to the use figures collected from the forms.

An important element in the Milne and Tiffany study is the calculation of the *lifetime use* of a serial. That is, for each serial, an estimate was made of how many uses it would receive in its lifetime in the library; for example, the 1989 issues of a serial will be used in 1989, in

---

*The study was actually spread over four years with one quarter of the serials collection studied each year.

1990, 1991, 1992, and on into the future. Actual use figures for a serial were collected for only the latest five years of that serial. Lifetime use was calculated from the use data supplemented by data on patterns of citation drawn from the *Journal Citation Reports* associated with the citation indexes. That is, the pattern of decline in citation with time for a particular periodical was assumed to approximate the pattern of decline in use with time for that periodical within the library. The cost per use of the serial was the current subscription cost of the serial (note that other costs of ownership were not considered) divided by the total number of estimated uses that this year's issues will receive over their lifetime in the library.

Cancellation decisions were based on two criteria: (a) cost per use, and (b) amount of use. Cost per use was related to the cost of obtaining a photocopy of an article when needed (calculated to be $14 Canadian at the time). If cost per use exceeded $14 the serial was considered a potential candidate for cancellation unless the total number of uses of the serial per year was estimated to be twenty four or more. About one half of all the commercially-published serials in the library in scientific and technical disciplines did *not* satisfy the cost-effectiveness criterion (i.e., cost per use exceeded $14) at their 1989 subscription costs. However, only one third of these could be cancelled because of the other − amount of use − criterion. Nevertheless, the study allowed the cancellation of 21% of 5800 serials, at a recurring annual saving of $291,000 Canadian (about 26% of the previous total subscription costs). The $291,000 saved per year represents gross savings. Clearly, the net savings will be less since the costs of additional interlibrary loan activities must be deducted from this total. Milne and Tiffany estimate that added interlibrary loan costs could reduce the annual savings by 25-40%. The one-time cost of the survey itself was about $30,000.

Very few analyses of cost-effectiveness aspects of participation in network or consortium activities have been published, although Mandel (1988) uses hypothetical data in a model of costs and benefits associated with membership in cataloging cooperatives.

A very unusual cost-effectiveness analysis can be found in the work of Brownson (1988) who compares costs and effectiveness of book selection by expert bibliographers and by "mechanical" processes (blanket orders, standing orders, approval plans). Cost per book added to the collection tends to be lower for mechanical selection procedures. However, the mechanical procedures add to the collection certain titles that are not really wanted, whereas expert selection will fail to acquire certain titles that should be acquired. The cost of the "missed" titles can be assumed to be the cost of borrowing them from other libraries when needed, or the cost of acquiring them at a later date in the out-of-print market, while the average cost of acquiring a wanted book through mechanical procedures is inflated by the costs associated with the acquisition of unwanted items. Of course, the validity of such a comparison assumes that a clear difference exists between wanted and unwanted titles. For the purpose of his analysis, Brownson makes the distinction on the basis of the number of reviews in major reviewing media.

Huang and McHale (1990) have put forward a "cost-effectiveness" model to aid the decision on when to discontinue a printed source and to rely entirely on online access to that source. They develop an "online/print threshold" which relates the cost of making the printed source available in the library to the average cost of an online search in that database. The "average yearly cost" of a printed source (yearly subscription rate) is used to derive an "average daily cost," which is the subscription cost divided by the number of days the library is open (estimated at 260 in this corporate library setting). If the average cost of the online search is equal to or less than this daily cost, it is assumed to be desirable that the print source be discontinued. While this is an original approach to the analysis, it is rather simplistic. It is difficult to see why average daily cost is used in place of cost per use of the printed source, other than the fact that some survey must be performed to estimate annual use whereas average daily cost is easily derived (except that cost of ownership exceeds subscription cost). The "model," in fact, is not a true cost-effectiveness model since search effectiveness is not considered (i.e., it is assumed that searches in print or online databases are equally effective).

Today, of course, librarians are concerned with print versus CD-ROM and online versus CD-ROM, as well as with print versus online. Welsh (1989) gives an example of the online versus CD-ROM comparison based on use of the NTIS database – estimated at 162 searches or sixty four hours per year in his library. Welsh estimates the CD-ROM cost per hour to be $35.17 (annual subscription cost to the database, $2250, divided by sixty four) as opposed to per hour costs of $80 for DIALOG/Dialnet access. At the rate of sixty four hours of searching per year, annual savings from CD-ROM acquisition are estimated to be $5120-$2250, or $2870. As Welsh himself recognizes, this is a rather simplistic cost comparison. Not considered for the online access mode are the costs of printing bibliographic records ($.30 online, $.45 off-line), which can be a substantial component in the overall cost of a comprehensive search. On the CD-ROM side, however, some allowance must be made for the cost of the paper consumed. More importantly, some part of the cost of acquisition of the CD-ROM equipment must be allocated to each hour of CD-ROM use. Assume equipment purchase costs (workstation and CD-ROM drive) of $2195, that the lifetime of this equipment is estimated to be five years, and that it is used for 1600 hours of searching in the five-year period (this estimate is based on five CD-ROM databases, each one used an average of sixty four hours per year). Then, one must add about $1.40 ($2195/1600) to the cost of each hour of CD-ROM searching for equipment use, plus a little more for paper consumed and for the space occupied in the library by the equipment (which would be more or less comparable for CD-ROM workstation and online terminal). So, the actual cost of an hour of CD-ROM searching may be closer to $37 than the $35 that Welsh estimates, although this is still considerably less than the cost for online searching.

But this analysis is obviously based only on database access costs and ignores the extremely important element of human costs. From the library's own point of view, the CD-ROM database has the obvious advantage that most library users will perform their own searches, whereas online searches in Welsh's library (in a government agency) are performed by professional librarians. From the agency's viewpoint, however, the situation may be quite different: users searching the CD-ROM database may be paid more, on the average, than the librarians and they will probably spend more time on a search than the more experienced librarians (indeed Welsh himself points out that users of CD-ROM tend to spend more time on a search because they know they are not paying for connect time), so the actual cost per search to the agency, taking salaries and overheads into account, could be very much greater for the CD-ROM situation.

Of course, this comparison takes into account only the cost side of the cost-effectiveness equation or, at least, it considers cost per search as the unit of cost-effectiveness rather than cost per useful item retrieved. If the librarians can find many more useful items, through the online facilities, than the library users can from the CD-ROM databases, the cost per useful item retrieved (the true cost-effectiveness measure in this situation) may well be less for the online access alternative. On the other hand, the most cost-effective alternative, from the agency's point of view, might well be the one in which the librarians perform CD-ROM searches for library users. It is clear that this comparison is quite complicated. The decision on which is the better alternative cannot be made solely on the basis of costs, but must take search results (the effectiveness) into account. Moreover, a different decision would probably be made if total agency costs are considered instead of only the library's costs.

As suggested earlier, cost-effectiveness analysis can also be applied to address input/output relationships. Mandel (1988) looks at one manifestation of the relationship between input costs and search performance. In this case, she relates various levels of detail in cataloging to (a) the probability that users will search on the access points provided and (b) the probable number of searches that would be successful given different levels of detail in cataloging.

Since the space occupied by a library is not "free," one type of cost-effectiveness analysis has to do with the optimum use of space, especially the space occupied by materials. Some aspects of this were discussed in Chapter 6. As suggested there, use per unit of shelf space occupied is a criterion that should be considered in deciding which materials to dispose of or to relegate to less accessible storage areas.

Cost-effectiveness analyses of alternative storage policies have been discussed by several writers, including Ellsworth (1969), Buckland et al. (1970) and Stayner and Richardson (1983). These last authors compare four different storage options: (1) extending the existing library building, (2) acquiring one's own remote storage facility, (3) joining a cooperative storage facility, and (4) using compact storage and/or microforms to optimize use of space in the existing building.

The Stayner and Richardson study also includes a comparison of various approaches to the weeding of serials. Four different strategies were identified: (1) weed all *titles* for which no volumes published in the last fifteen years have been used in the last five years (15/5 rule); (2) weed all closed *titles* (i.e., titles for which current issues are no longer received); (3) weed all *volumes* published before a certain date; (4) weed all *volumes* published before a certain date that have not been used in the past X years. Note that "weed" here could mean either (a) dispose of, or (b) retire to a storage facility. Exhibit 99 shows the results of these strategies, when applied to the collection at Monash University, in terms of number of volumes and titles weeded and estimated effects on serials use (circulation and in-house). The third strategy, based on age but not use factors, will retire most volumes but could have a significant negative effect on user satisfaction. The strategies that take use, as well as age, into account are more efficient in that they retire fewer volumes but are less likely to have a negative impact on user satisfaction. This can be considered a cost-effectiveness analysis even though the cost is not expressed in monetary units. In this case, the cost is considered in terms of inconvenience to users or, possibly, lost circulations. Inconvenience and lost circulations can probably be translated into monetary terms, but it is not easy to do so.

Weeding rule		No. of volumes or titles weeded	% of sample	% of 1975-80 circulations affected	Estimated % of total in-house use affected
1)	Weed low-use titles '15-5 rule'	228 titles 2097 volumes	44.7 23.1	0	1.6
2)	Weed all closed titles	240 titles 2661 volumes	47.1 29.3	6.2	3.3
3)	Weed all pre-1965 volumes	4643 volumes	51.1	11.9	2.5
4)	Weed low-use pre-1965 volumes:				
a)	'75-'80 use = 0	a) 131 titles 1798 volumes	a) 25.7 19.8	0	0.28
b)	'70-'80 use = 0	b) 99 titles 1318 volumes	b) 19.4 14.5	0	0.14

Notes: If we require a criterion to weed 2100 volumes (i.e. about the same as the 15-5 rule):

(a) We could select pre-1960 volumes which had attracted the least use in 1975-80, starting with those not used at all during that period, until we have 2100 volumes. We calculated that only twenty eight circulations in the period 1975-80 would have been affected.

(b) We could select pre-1965 volumes in the same way, and only twenty five circulations in the period 1975-80 would have been affected.

Exhibit 99

Comparison of four strategies for the weeding of serials

From Stayner and Richardson (1983) by permission of the
Graduate School of Librarianship, Monash University

The weeding of serials by one of these strategies can reduce library costs in that they remove volumes to storage areas that are less costly to maintain. Nevertheless, they do have other costs associated with them: records need to be altered and there must be some way of informing library users of the effects of the strategies adopted (e.g., where earlier volumes of serials have been moved to).

Diminishing Returns

The phenomenon of diminishing returns is of great importance when the cost-effectiveness of any operation is taken into account. Many manifestations exist. One, mentioned earlier, relates to the special library situation in which the cost of subscribing to periodicals is balanced against their potential yield of papers directly related to the scope of the library.

If the journal titles contributing papers on a particular subject are arranged in descending order of their yield, the familiar "scatter" phenomenon (Bradford, 1948) will be observed: a small number of journals (the "core" or "nucleus") will contribute a disproportionately large number of papers, but much of the literature will be widely scattered over very many titles (this phenomenon was dealt with in Chapter 5). Exhibit 100 shows some hypothetical data covering a period of, say, three years. The journal at the top of the list has contributed 314 papers on the subject in this period, the second has contributed a further 265 papers, and so on down to 130 journals that have published only one paper each on the subject in three years. In all, 252 journals are needed to contribute all 1757 papers on the subject, but almost one-third of the papers appear in the first two journals only.

Besides the scatter data, Exhibit 100 presents subscription costs associated with each line of the table. It costs almost $12,000 to acquire

Journals	Articles	Cumulation Journals	Cumulation Articles	Cost ($) (cumulative)
1	314	1	314	450
1	265	2	579	525
1	223	3	802	550
1	48	4	850	785
2	37	6	924	809
1	29	7	953	874
1	23	8	976	902
1	22	9	998	916
1	21	10	1019	964
2	19	12	1057	994
1	17	13	1074	1271
2	15	15	1104	1431
2	14	17	1132	1451
4	13	21	1184	1479
2	12	23	1208	1503
1	11	24	1219	1516
2	10	26	1239	1576
7	9	33	1302	1629
5	8	38	1342	1829
2	7	40	1356	1869
8	6	48	1404	2245
11	5	59	1459	2762
12	4	71	1507	3326
18	3	89	1561	4172
33	2	122	1627	5723
130	1	252	1757	11833

Exhibit 100

Periodical titles ranked by decreasing yield of articles on some specified topic over a three year period all 252 journals but about a third of the literature can be obtained by subscribing to only the first two on the list, which will cost $525.

Exhibit 101 presents the data in graphical form. One-third of the periodical literature can be acquired at subscription costs of $525 but it would cost about three times this much to acquire two-thirds. The law of diminishing returns is demonstrated with a vengeance after about the 80% level. It costs more to go from 80% to 90% than it does to go from 0 to 80%.

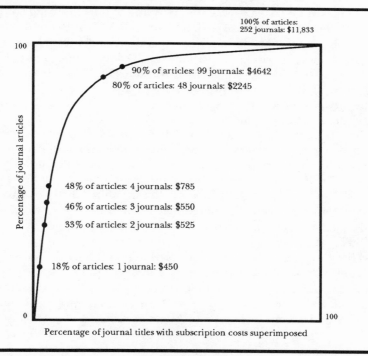

Exhibit 101
Yield of periodical articles in a specialized subject
related to subscription costs

The data of Exhibit 100 suggest several possible selection strategies. For example, it might be decided to subscribe only to titles that yield seven or more papers per year. If this were so, the top ten journals on the list would be purchased at an annual cost of $964. The top ten journals can be expected to yield about 55% of the relevant articles. If the cutoff was put at five papers per year, the number of journals goes up to fifteen and the subscription cost to $1431. This would yield about 63% of the relevant articles.

Another possible strategy would be to leave out the more expensive medium-yield journals. For example, the journal ranked thirteen costs $277 a year yet yields only about six articles per year. If this title were omitted, the top fifteen titles would yield 1101 papers (about 63% of the total) at a subscription cost of only $1,164. This would probably be the preferred strategy if the library had only about $1,200 to spend or if cost per article is the criterion governing the decision.

It is obvious that a special library trying to build a strong collection in this subject area can only acquire about 60-70% of the periodical literature by direct subscription. Not only would it be uneconomical to try for much more, it would be virtually impossible: as one goes down the table (Exhibit 100), the predictability declines rapidly with the decreasing yield. That is, the most productive journals for this subject are likely to be the most productive for some time to come, whereas the 130 journals at the bottom of the list, which have only contributed one paper each in the last three years, may never contribute again. As one proceeds down past the middle of the table, one is less and less confident that a journal contributing a few papers each year will continue to do so. For the 30-40% of the periodical literature that cannot be acquired by direct subscription, this special library must turn to secondary sources – *Current Contents*, printed indexing/abstracting services, or regular searches in online databases.

This discussion of the special library problem has been a little oversimplified in that it takes into consideration only the subject matter central to the library's interests. The data might relate, say, to the subject of agricultural communications. A library devoted to this subject will collect materials in related areas, including agriculture in general and communications technology. Looked at in this broader context, somewhat different subscription decisions might be made. For example, some journals yielding only three or four papers per year on agricultural communications might still be wanted if these are key journals in the broader fields.

A ranked list of the journals contributing articles on some subject, such as Exhibit 100, can be valuable in a number of ways. Having such a list can bring to the attention of a librarian high-yielding journals that may have been overlooked including, perhaps, some inexpensive journals that might add significantly to coverage at little extra cost.

Hyperbolic curves of the type shown in Exhibit 101 completely typify the phenomenon of diminishing returns. The phenomenon was encountered in earlier chapters. Most obviously, the curve is similar to that derived when the number of volumes in a collection is plotted against the number of circulations (see Exhibit 16). In fact, the 80/20 rule applies well to these scatter data: 80% of the papers come from 19% of the journals.

Another example of diminishing returns has been presented by Powell (1976). In studying the size of reference collections in Illinois public libraries, Powell discovered (Exhibit 102) that a collection of around 3,000 volumes seemed about "optimum." A collection of this

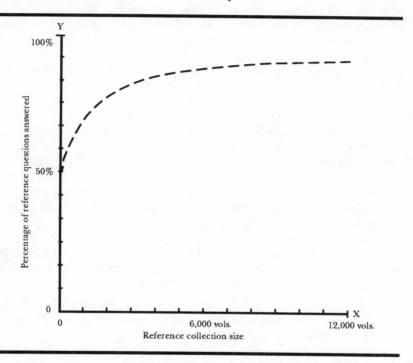

Exhibit 102

Relationship between the size of a reference collection and percentage of test questions that a library can answer correctly

Adapted from Benham and Powell (1987) by permission of Scarecrow Press Inc.

size might answer 90% or so of a selected group of questions. To raise this to 95% might entail a leap to as many as 12,000 volumes. Exhibit 102 illustrates once more the phenomenon of unpredictability. It is possible that a very large proportion – perhaps 70% – of the questions received by a small public library could be answered by as few as twenty or thirty well selected tools – one encyclopedia, one dictionary, an almanac, local directories, two or three major biographical sources, a book of quotations, and so on. This is because many of the questions received are of the same general type and quite predictable. After, say, the 70% level, the predictability greatly declines. One might need several hundred volumes to answer 80% of the questions and several thousand to answer 90%. Exhibit 102 provides a dramatic demonstration of the advantages of resource sharing. A public library might need many thousands of volumes to answer 90-95% of the questions it receives in a year but it might be able to answer 80% with a small fraction of these. From a cost-effectiveness point of view, it would make sense for each public library to lower its sights – to aim to answer, say, 80% of the questions from its own resources but to have ready access by telephone or online network to a regional or statewide reference library designed to answer the more obscure and less predictable questions.*

The 90 Percent Library

The law of diminishing returns leads naturally to the idea of the 90% library. The idea (Bourne, 1965) is simply this: it is possible for a library service to satisfy some large proportion – say 90% – of all demands efficiently and economically, but it would take a completely disproportionate amount of money and/or effort to raise this by as little as another 2 or 3%. This is due to the unpredictability problem mentioned earlier. (For example, Abbott (1990) considers it realistic for an academic library to try to satisfy 90% of interlibrary loans in ten days. The ideal of 100% is not realistic because "some requests would always be obscure.") Some examples of the phenomenon, several of which have already been mentioned, are as follows:

1. Ninety percent of the factual questions received might be answered from 3,000 volumes. Ninety-five percent may require an increase to 12,000 volumes.

2. Ninety percent of the periodical articles requested by users of a special library may come from eighty periodical titles. To raise this to 95% may require an increase to 300 titles.

3. Ninety percent of the circulations in a public library may come from 20% of the collection but 95% of the circulations are accounted for by 60% of the collection.

---

*From a cost-effectiveness point of view it makes little sense for an individual library to attempt to satisfy more than some specified percentage of total demands (of any type) from its own resources. It is this fact that justifies resource sharing and makes such activities central to library service. In this the author differs from those librarians (e. g., Ballard, 1985, 1986) who regard resource sharing as a peripheral activity, or even one that is unjustified.

4. Ninety percent of the demands for periodical articles may be satisfied by journal issues no more than five years old. To satisfy 95% of the demands may require that one go back fifty years (Exhibit 103).

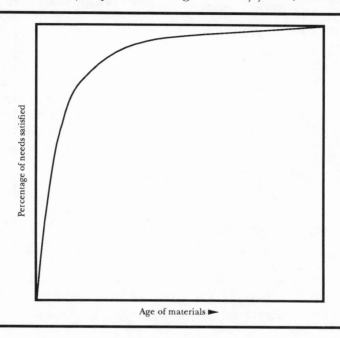

Age of materials ►

Exhibit 103
Decline in use with age

A generalized representation of the 90% library phenomenon is presented in Exhibit 104, which shows that, in terms of satisfying user needs (for documents, for answers to questions, or whatever), the resources needed to go from 90% satisfaction to 95% may exceed the resources needed to go from zero to 90%. The greater the success rate demanded, the more disproportionate becomes the required expenditure of resources. Librarians must recognize the fact that one can satisfy all of the users some of the time, or some of the users all of the time, but not all of the users all of the time.

Some writers in library science fail to distinguish clearly between cost-effectiveness and cost-benefit studies.* The latter, quite different from the former, are dealt with in the next chapter.

---

*For example, Schauer (1986), while he points out that a cost-benefit study is not the same as a cost-effectiveness study, fails to distinguish clearly between the two.

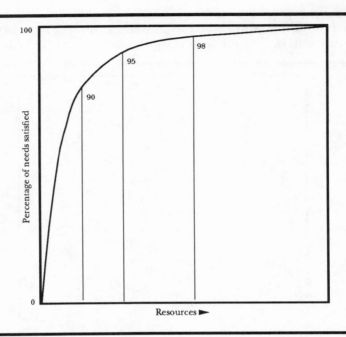

Exhibit 104
Generalized representation of the 90% library phenomenon

Study Questions

1. You are the Undergraduate Librarian in a large university. A new periodical on popular science has been brought to your attention. It is within scope and will cost $80 a year to subscribe to. You know that another periodical on popular science, also costing $80, is so heavily used that it is rarely available when sought by users. How will you decide on whether to spend the $80 on the new title or on a second copy of the heavily used one?

2. A small college library has been holding on to its subscription to *Chemical Abstracts* despite substantial increases in costs. Although chemistry is part of the curriculum, a new librarian is reluctant to maintain the subscription any longer, preferring to pay for access to chemistry is part of the curriculum, a new librarian is reluctant to maintain the subscription any longer, preferring to pay for access to the database online when necessary. What data should he collect in order to be able to justify his decision on cost-effectiveness grounds?

3. The National Institutes of Health is establishing a new information center on the subject of Acquired Immunodeficiency Syndrome (AIDS). You are the first librarian. You have $8,000 to spend on periodical subscriptions. How will you decide which periodicals to acquire in order to get the best return on your investment?

15. Cost-Benefit Studies

Although the terminology is used rather loosely, a cost-benefit analysis is quite different from a cost-effectiveness study. "Cost-benefit," clearly, refers to a relationship between the cost of some activity and the benefits derived from it. In effect, a cost-benefit study is one that tries to justify the existence of the activity by demonstrating that the benefits outweigh the costs. Ideally, the benefits should be expressed in the same units of measurement as the costs, that is in $, £, or some other currency. Unfortunately it is exceptionally difficult, if not completely impossible, to express the benefits of library service in monetary units. Indeed, it is not easy to think of the benefits derived from a library in any but subjective terms.

As suggested in Chapter 1, the benefits of a library relate to outcomes or impact. In a sense, the very existence of a library in a community or institution implies that some individuals at some time made the decision that the cost of supporting the library is justified by the expected benefits.

It may be possible to look at impact of an information service at various levels, as follows:

1. Existence
2. Awareness
3. Trial
4. Adoption
5. Referral
6. True impact or benefit

These six levels of impact, which are not unlike the stages usually associated with the diffusion of innovation (Rogers and Shoemaker, 1971), are presented in a sequence of increasing significance. They are best explained within the context of a particular type of information service, say an employment agency.

The first level, "existence," may be thought rather trivial. One might argue, however, that the mere establishment of the employment agency, where no such agency existed previously, must have some impact in and of itself, although it is not known how much the impact will be.

"Awareness" is a more significant measure of impact. It seems reasonable to suppose that the more people who are aware of the existence of the agency (determined through some type of survey) the

294

greater its impact; it can hardly have much impact if no one knows it exists.

One step beyond awareness is "trial." The potential impact of the agency increases with the number of employers and job seekers who make some use of its services. "Adoption" goes further. It implies that some companies are sufficiently satisfied with the service that they become regular customers. The greater the number of regular customers, the greater the impact.

The more satisfied the customers of the agency are, the more likely they will be to recommend its services to others. The number of referrals that occur can thus be considered another measure of impact. The true impact, however, has to do with the real objective of the agency, which is to match employers with job seekers. The agency benefits the community it serves to the extent that individuals can use its services to locate suitable jobs and companies to find suitable employees.

In theory, these levels of impact could be applied to, say, a public library. Its potential impact increases with the number of people in the community who are aware of its existence and of the services it provides. "Trial" can be expressed in terms of the number of individuals in the community who register for a library card and "adoption" in terms of the number who have used the library at least X times in the past year. Referral would be more difficult to measure.

The public library differs most from the employment agency in the final level of true impact. It is clear why the latter exists, what its objectives are, and in what terms its benefits should be expressed, but it is much less clear what the desired outcomes of the public library are.

Approaches to the Measurement of Benefits

In the cost-benefit context, industrial libraries differ somewhat from public, school, or academic libraries. On the one hand, it is more likely that librarians in industry will be asked to justify the library's existence in monetary terms. On the other hand, it is a little easier to think of the benefits of the library in the same terms – i.e., the extent to which the library contributes to the profit-making activities of the company. It is hardly surprising, then, that more attempts at cost-benefit analysis have been applied to industrial libraries than to libraries of other kinds.

Various approaches to measuring the benefits of an information service have been discussed or tried.* In order of increasing sophistication, these are:

---

*A number of examples of these various approaches can be found in a report by Plate (1983).

1. Net value approach
2. Value of reducing uncertainty
3. Cost of buying service elsewhere
4. Librarian time replaces user time
5. Service improves organization's performance or saves the organization money:
    a. duplication avoided
    b. loss of productivity avoided
    c. cheaper solution suggested
    d. invention stimulated

The "net value" approach is extremely simplistic. The net value of an information service to a user is considered to be the maximum amount he is willing to pay (gross value) minus the actual cost. For example, suppose a small company asks an information broker to find a particular item of information – say to determine if data exist on the thermal conductivity of a particular alloy. The company gives the broker authority to spend up to $5,000 to locate the data (*gross value*), which implies that the data are worth at least this much to the company. In fact, the broker is able to find the data at a cost of $200. The *net value* of this incident to the company is thus calculated at $4,800.

The value of information to an individual can often be thought of in terms of the extent to which it reduces his or her uncertainty. This is most clear in the situation in which the seeker of information could make a good decision or a bad decision, especially if there are actual costs associated with these decisions. Consider, for example, a man who has decided to buy a particular model of video recorder. At the time this decision is made, three stores in his community carry the model and offer it at widely different prices:

Store	Cost ($)
A	225
B	282
C	214

Clearly, the best decision would be to go to store C and the worst would be to go to B. The *maximum potential benefit* to be derived from this information is $68, which is the difference between the most that could be paid and the least that could be paid ($282 − 214 = 68$). Suppose that a database exists that provides information on the current prices of products within local stores (offered perhaps by some videotex service), and that the consumer can obtain the information noted above at a cost of $12. The *net benefit* to the user of having this information can be considered to be $56 (the maximum potential benefit, $68, minus actual cost).*

Consumer information is perhaps the prime example of information to which a monetary value can frequently be given. Take a somewhat different example. A young woman wants to buy a particular kind of exercise machine. A consumer magazine has tested these machines and found three models to be equally acceptable. The models are priced at $327, $344, and $405. The maximum potential benefit of this information to the consumer in this case is $78. It might well be worth her while to visit the local public library to check the consumer ratings. For a less expensive purchase – say a toaster – similar ratings may be considered less important.

Some industrial librarians have attempted to justify the existence of their services by calculating how much it would cost the company to buy equivalent services from elsewhere – another library within the organization itself, an external library, or a commercial information service (see, for example, Magson, 1973). In this case, the underlying assumption is that the service is worthwhile. The question being considered is whether it is better for the company to provide the service through an in-house library or some other way.** The entire range of services offered by the library can be considered in such a study. Alternatively, a single service can be the focus of attention. For example, it might be determined that the total cost of providing online literature searches through the library, at a level of 500 searches a year, is $35,000. To buy this level of service from a commercial agency might cost $50,000. Thus, the net benefit to the company of providing the service in-house is $15,000.

In many ways this is a reasonable approach to justifying the existence of a library of this type, although there are certain problems associated with it. Some services may not be suitable for delegation to an outside contractor for reasons of practicality or of industrial security. There might be a certain "convenience" factor associated with the in-house facility that the outside agency could not duplicate, although it would be difficult to give this factor any real monetary value. A more practical problem is the fact that the collection of materials owned by the library is likely to contribute to many different services – docu-

---

*For a more complete discussion of this type of approach see Wills and Christopher (1970).

**One could argue perhaps that this is more a cost-effectiveness study (comparing alternative strategies) than a cost-benefit study.

ment delivery, literature searching, question answering, preparation of an information bulletin – and, as discussed in the previous chapter, it is not always easy to allocate the costs of the collection over the various services in a completely satisfactory way. Nevertheless, if corporate management is satisfied with this approach to the justification of services, it has a lot to commend it from the librarian's point of view.

A somewhat similar approach compares the cost of the librarian providing some service with the cost of the librarian's customers undertaking the activity for themselves (Rosenberg, 1969; Mason, 1972). To take a very simple example, suppose that the average cost of a literature search provided by the librarian is $140 and it is calculated that the average cost of an equivalent search undertaken by a customer (e.g., a research scientist) would be $195, because of salary differential. It could be argued, then, that the librarian saves the company $55 for every search performed.

Of course, there are some underlying assumptions here: that the scientist would do the search if the librarian was not available and that the scientist's results would be qualitatively equivalent to those of the librarian.

Rosenberg (1969) tried to carry this method further by having users "weight" the results of a literature search performed by the librarian, according to the scale.

0   Useless (e.g., because not relevant or received too late).
1   Adequate. User would have spent same amount of time as librarian.
2   Good. User would have spent twice the amount of time spent by the librarian.
3   Excellent. Results could not have been achieved by user or could not have been achieved at an acceptable cost.

These weights may be built into a "savings" equation, (A × B × C) − A, where A is the cost of the librarian's time, B a multiplication factor to account for the difference in salary between librarian and engineer, and C the assigned weighting factor. Thus, if a literature search costs $75 in librarian time, the salary differential is 1.5, and the weight given by the user is 2, the savings would be calculated as ($75 × 1.5 × 2) − 75, or $150.

Clearly this is very subjective, for one can have little confidence that a user could arrive at any realistic estimate of how much time it would take to perform some information retrieval task. Several other investigators have tried to justify an information service by estimating potential cost savings attributable to having these services available. It is assumed that, were the library not available, engineers or scientists would spend more of their own time in information seeking and that this would be costly to the organization. Analyses of this type are only as good as the validity of the estimates of time saved.

Nightingale (1973) provides an example of one approach. He calculated that it cost £2500 per year to produce a company abstracts bulletin. By means of a survey, he determined how many journals were regularly scanned by the recipients of the bulletin and had them estimate how many additional journals they would want to scan for themselves if the bulletin was discontinued. A median value of six additional journals per user was obtained. Nightingale calculated that it would take a user ten minutes, on the average, to scan a journal in order to identify items of interest. The cost of this activity was estimated at 18.5 hours per user per year (six journals x ten minutes x number of issues), which worked out to £74. With 400 users, the cost of the extra scanning would be £74 x 400, or £29,600. The bottom line of the cost benefit analysis, then, is a saving annually of £27,100 (£29,600 less the cost of producing the bulletin).

Blick (1977) used a somewhat different approach. He judged the value of a current awareness bulletin to a pharmaceutical company by whether or not researchers would have found valuable information without the bulletin. He determined that 59% of the items judged "vital" would have escaped the attention of users if the bulletin did not exist, along with 50% of the items judged "important," while a further 35% of the "vital" and 15% of the "important" items would have been found too late through other channels. Estimates were made of how much time scientists would spend directly scanning journals if the bulletin did not exist. Savings of scientist time were calculated at £102,000 per year – 4.6 times the cost of producing the bulletin. However, neither Blick nor Nightingale seems to have calculated the cost of scientist time in scanning the bulletins themselves.

These analyses seem reasonably conservative. Much less conservative are data reported by Kramer (1971), based on a study performed at Boeing Aerospace. Kramer estimated the savings for the company attributable to having the library perform literature searches and answer factual questions, as opposed to having the engineers do this for themselves. Questionnaires returned by 153 engineers, for whom literature searches had been performed, estimated that 9,479 hours of engineering time would have been consumed had the engineers conducted the searches themselves. The librarian time to perform these searches (in printed sources) was calculated to be 1,071 manhours (about seven per search). Clearly, even if the librarian is paid at the same rate as the engineer, the savings would seem to be considerable. About 8,000 hours of engineer time at present rates (and including all overheads) might work out at well over $300,000.

Kramer also used follow-up telephone interviews with 215 engineers for whom the library had answered factual questions. While the librarians averaged twelve minutes per question, the engineers estimated that it would have taken them an average of 5.42 hours per question to find the answer! For 215 questions this represents another 1,166 hours of engineering time saved.

Benefits in the Literature Searching Situation

It was pointed out in Chapter 1 that the evaluator tends to look at an information service in terms of inputs, outputs and outcomes. It should be obvious to the reader of this book that most evaluations in the library/information service area look at inputs and outputs rather than outcomes. Most evaluations of literature searching activities, as discussed in Chapter 11, deal in output measures (general indicators of "user satisfaction" or such predictors of satisfaction as recall, precision and novelty), but some investigators have attempted to study the outcomes or benefits of literature searching or SDI (Selective Dissemination of Information) activities, sometimes expressing the benefits in monetary terms.

Kramer's study looked at the benefits of literature searches, but searches based on printed sources. Since access to electronic databases has become so prevalent, many more studies of the benefits of database searching have been performed.

In a corporate research environment, Mondschein (1990) has looked at the benefits deriving from use of Selective Dissemination of Information (SDI) facilities; costs were not discussed. The measure of benefit adopted was improved productivity as measured by publications produced. Mondschein discovered that regular users of SDI services appear to be more productive than nonusers or those researchers who use the services infrequently.

Several studies of the benefits of database searching have been performed in the health care field. For example, Schnall and Wilson (1976), Greenberg et al. (1978), and Scura and Davidoff (1981), all of them dealing with services provided by "clinical medical librarians," asked the clinician users of the services to what extent information provided had directly influenced patient care. Operating in a hospital library setting, King (1987) asked users of information or documents supplied to judge their clinical value, cognitive value (i.e., contribution to user's health care knowledge), quality, currency, relevance to the clinical situation that had prompted the request, and impact on clinical decision making. Marshall (1992) built upon the methodology used by King, focusing more clearly on the impact of information on clinical decision-making and patient care.

Ideally, of course, one would like to go even beyond this – to attempt to determine to what extent a clinical information service might contribute to reducing morbidity and mortality, the length of time a patient stays in hospital, or the costs of the medical care. Wilson et al. (1989) present the results of a study in which the critical incident technique was used to evaluate the benefits of searches performed in the MEDLINE database. More than 500 health professionals, known to be MEDLINE users, were interviewed by telephone. The subjects of the study were asked to focus on a recent MEDLINE search. Besides attempting to determine impact on medical decision-making, the investigators also tried to identify longer-term outcomes. They report that "information obtained via MEDLINE has had important beneficial, even life-saving consequences" and were able to document eight life-saving cases.

Estabrook (1986) asked engineers to estimate time savings associated with the use of a search/document delivery service, and to put a dollar value on the information retrieved. She concluded that, by the most conservative estimates, the company saved two dollars for every one expended on the service. In best-case terms, however, the company might save almost fifty dollars for each one dollar invested in the information center. This latter information was arrived at by including two extreme cases in which the recipients of information estimated potential savings of one million dollars and two and one half million dollars.

Collette and Price (1977) present another example of justifying the cost of literature searching activities in terms of engineering time saved and other elements of the dollar value of search results. Based on results from a user survey, they arrive at benefit estimates that they consider to be "ultraconservative." Benefits per online search were calculated to be $315 on the average, while per search costs were estimated to be $112. They also make a point that is frequently overlooked: even a library search that produces no relevant items may have value to the company since it would probably be much more expensive for the engineers to undertake these searches themselves.

One of the better studies of the benefits of online searches is reported by Jensen et al. (1980). Telephone interviews were conducted with a sample of users of the NASA Industrial Application Center at the University of Southern California. Each was asked to estimate the

benefits of an online search performed for them in terms of hours
saved (compared with having to perform the search themselves or obtaining needed information elsewhere) and the potential value of the
information when applied to an existing product, process or service or
to a projected new product, process or service. Of the 159 users surveyed, 53% were able to identify dollar benefits. They reported "current benefits" of $364,605 and "five year follow-on benefits" of
$873,500.

The methodology used by Jensen et al. was derived from an earlier study by Johnson et al. (1977), who looked at the benefits to user
organizations of another information service offered by the National
Aeronautics and Space Administration (NASA). Requests received between 1971 and mid-1976 were randomly sampled and interviews were
conducted with recipients of the information. Users were asked to
judge the information received by how it was or would be applied and
by expected economic benefits, according to the scale

0	No application.	No net benefit
1	Information acquisition only	$100 net benefit
2	Improved process, product or service	$4900 to $5000 net benefit
3	New process, product or service	$22,600 to $31,100 net benefit

The chance of each of these outcomes occurring was assessed at 34%,
54%, 11% and 1% respectively. Since mode two results, with relatively
modest net benefits, occurred relatively often, they were judged more
important than the mode three results.

A benefit cost ratio of at least 10:1 was claimed for the service.
Costs to 1976 were estimated at $6.4 million and total net benefits to
1976 were between $63.8 and $72.5 million.

Data of these kind would provide a very impressive endorsement
of an information service if they were fully credible. Unfortunately, it
is difficult to believe that anyone could come up with a realistic estimate of how long it would take to perform a particular information retrieval activity, and the results achieved by Kramer (almost 30 times
longer for an engineer to answer a question than for the librarian)
strain the bounds of credibility. It seems even less likely that the user
of an information service can put a dollar value on information received with any degree of accuracy, although Estabrook (1986) claims
that such estimates may be better than are commonly supposed.

Even if an exact dollar value cannot be placed upon a piece of information, there may be occasions when an industrial information service may prove its worth to the corporation in a dramatic way. In the
case of a research organization, the greatest benefit that the library

can provide might be the uncovering of information that prevents the company from performing research already done elsewhere. It is difficult to document events of this type (and even more difficult to prove that the company would not have found the information without the library) but a single case, if documented, might justify the cost of the library for several years. A large study of the unintentional duplication of research, and the cost of this duplication, was performed in the United Kingdom by Martyn (1964). Martyn presents impressive evidence to support the claim that large amounts of money could be saved by the performance of more complete literature searches before research projects get underway. M. Cooper (1968) presents figures on the saving of research time attributable to the informal communications distributed experimentally by the information exchange groups established by the National Institutes of Health, while Moisse (1976) and Barrett (1986) have mentioned cases in which lack of access to information brought significant research or production losses. On a larger scale, Arthur D. Little (1969) studied the economic impact of the transfer of technological information through the State Technical Services Program.

Another possible measure of benefit is the loss of production that might occur if the library were not available in a company and the scientists or engineers were forced to wait much longer for needed information. Mueller (1959), for example, discovered that the work of some engineers was actually brought to a halt while waiting for information to complete a critical task. The assumption here, of course, is that having information saves time. Solomin (1974) has argued that, under certain circumstances, having information increases company costs because it requires the expenditure of time to process and assimilate it.

Finally, a librarian might point to other positive effects on the company that can be traced to information provided by the library. These might include the development of a new product, the identification of ways to reduce the costs of existing products (e.g., by use of materials that are cheaper but equally effective), or the award of an important contract. It is not easy to prove that the library has been directly responsible for events of this kind, but a single documented example might be sufficient to justify the library's existence for some time to come.

Investigators at King Research Inc. (1982, 1984) have carried cost-benefit analysis even further in trying to determine the value of the Energy Data Base (U.S. Department of Energy). Through use of questionnaires, it was estimated that the reading of articles and reports by DOE-funded scientists and engineers resulted in the location of information yielding annual savings of \$13 billion (in avoiding duplication of work, saving time, and in other ways). This contrasts with an annual expenditure to DOE for research and development of \$5.3 billion and an expenditure of \$500 million on information processing and use.

The methods used in the Department of Energy cost-benefit analysis were later applied to other organizations (Roderer et al., 1983; Griffiths and King, 1984); they have been described in some detail by Griffiths and King (1991).

Cost-benefit analyses are very difficult to perform in the information service environment and perhaps no study of this kind has ever been fully credible. Nevertheless, one way or another, libraries and other information centers must justify their existence, so the benefits of their services, even if they seem rather nebulous, cannot be ignored in evaluative studies.

Study Questions

1. The administrator of a hospital would like to save some money by closing the hospital library. As the librarian, what evidence would you collect to persuade the administrator that this would be a shortsighted act?

2. The Russell Chemical Company has not been doing well financially for the past three years. So far the library has escaped the axe. The Director of Research, to whom the Librarian reports, is very supportive of the library and wants to shield the service from possible future attack. He wants to gather data to prove that the library provides benefits to the company that far exceed the costs of providing the service. You are the Librarian and you have been asked to undertake this cost-benefit analysis as a top priority. What approaches would you use?

3. What are the benefits of a school library? How would you conduct a cost-benefit study in this environment?

16. Continuous Quality Control

Many of the evaluation techniques described in the earlier chapters are intended for use in one-time, rather detailed studies, the objective being to gather data to aid problem solving and decision making or to identify ways in which a service might be improved. However, librarians should also be interested in the continuous monitoring of the services provided, to determine whether or not they are responsive to user needs. Such monitoring would be the equivalent in the library world of the continuous quality control activities in industry. As suggested in Chapter 1, this type of quality control is largely lacking in the library arena, and this is unfortunate.

In both the United Kingdom and the United States some segments of the library community have recently been influenced by the idea of Total Quality Management (TQM) as reflected, for example, in British Standard 5750 (British Standards Institution, 1992).* Indeed, the Association of Research Libraries has recently published a rather comprehensive bibliography on the subject (Blankenbaker, 1992) and Aslib has performed a broad survey (in 1993) on the use of TQM in information services. TQM as applied to libraries has been discussed in the literature (e.g., Usherwood, 1992; Brockman, 1992; Mackey and Mackey, 1992; and Shaughnessy, 1993), but these discussions generally fail to offer concrete suggestions relating to the continuous monitoring of the quality of services provided by libraries. Indeed, quality management of this type seems much more concerned with internal efficiency than with user satisfaction. For example, Dawson (1992) refers to the application of B.S. 5750 in terms of producing a detailed procedures manual and having the operations of the information service "audited" by an external "quality manager." While this type of activity is undoubtedly valuable, it is difficult to see how a service organization can commit itself to "quality" without collecting data reflecting the success or otherwise of its services.

Of course, some of the methods and measures discussed earlier *can* be applied on a continuous basis to collect data useful to managers. Examples include the kinds of data (relative use, turnover rate, and so on) that can be obtained from an appropriately designed circu-

---

*B. S. 5750 is the same as European Standard EN 29000 and International Standard ISO 9000.

lation system; data obtainable from the spine marking or dotting method; the ratio of borrowings to holdings; information on questions posed as recorded by reference librarians; and data from forms completed by users of interlibrary loan and database searching services.

Current Awareness Services

Beyond this, it would be entirely possible to collect user responses to some types of library services on a continuous basis. This type of monitoring could be implemented most easily with the current awareness types of services offered by some special libraries. For example, a form of the type shown in Exhibit 105 could be used to obtain continuous feedback on a bulletin of abstracts prepared by the library, and the slightly different form show in Exhibit 106 to obtain feedback on a service for the selective dissemination of information. Use of the data can be demonstrated by considering the example of the abstracts bulletin. Completed forms should be examined regularly to see if users offer valuable suggestions on how the service could be improved. Statistical data (numerical scores for relevance, novelty, value) should be recorded and averaged so that the library can monitor the service over time – e.g., is value increasing, decreasing or remaining stable? Forms should be kept on file for a period of time – perhaps two or three years – as proof of the value of the service should this ever be questioned. Should a recipient indicate that the service has little or no value, he or she should be contacted to see if his/her name should be removed from the distribution list.

The database of evaluation results should also tie responses to the identifications of recipients. If certain recipients never make use of the form, it may be worthwhile to use a standard letter to specifically request their evaluation.

The measure of *penetration* of the service will be the number of addresses on the mailing list or, better, the number of actual readers (assuming that some, at least, of the bulletins will be circulated among several people). Number of actual readers can be estimated from data on the evaluation form.

The annual costs of producing the abstracts bulletin can be related to:

1. Number of bulletins distributed in a year.

2. Number of users reached (takes into account the possibility that a single bulletin may be read by more than one person).

3. Number of abstracts included.

4. The index of relevance.

5. The index of novelty.
6. The index of value.

HELP!!

We are constantly trying to improve our services. Could you please take a few moments to tell us about your use of this publication?

1. Approximately what percentage of the items listed in this issue were directly relevant to your interests?

    Percent   0   10   20   30   40   50   60   70   80   90   100

2. <u>Of the items relevant to your interests</u>, approximately what percentage were items <u>that you were unaware of before seeing this issue</u>?

    Percent   0   10   20   30   40   50   60   70   80   90   100

3. On a scale of 1 to 10 how valuable would you judge this publication as a means of keeping up to date with new literature published in your areas of interest?

    Of no   Of very great
    value   value
      1   2   3   4   5   6   7   8   9   10

4. Are you aware of any other important literature on this subject that seems not to have been covered in this bibliography? If so, please identify the items for us:

5. Are there any other important topics that you feel should be covered by a bulletin of this type?

6. Are there any other ways in which this bulletin could be made more useful to you?

7. How many people typically examine your copy of the publication? _____

8. What use do you make of the information obtained from this bulletin (e.g., how do you apply it to your work)?

Many thanks for your help. Please identify yourself and your institution and return this form to (library address).

    Name:
    Institution:

Exhibit 105
Form for evaluation of bulletin of abstracts

Criteria four, five, and six require some explanation. Items one and two on the evaluation form allow an estimate of what percentage of the total items included in the bulletin in the year are (a) relevant to user interests and (b) new to them. For example, suppose the evalua-

SDI Service

1. This printout contains _____ items that match the profile of your
    interests. To help us improve our services to you, please indicate how
    many items fall into each of the categories below:

    A Very important items that I was not aware of before.
       The value of the search would have been greatly
       reduced if these had not been retrieved.

    B Very important items but I knew of these before.

    C Less important items that I was not aware of before.
       It is good that these were retrieved.

    D Less important items that I knew of before.

    E Relevant to my interests but not very important. It
       would not have reduced the value of the search if
       these had not been retrieved.

    F . Not relevant at all to my interests.

2.· If the search retrieved some items that are not relevant to your interests
    (category F above), please tell us why they are not relevant:

3. Are there any other subjects that you have become interested in that
    should be included in future searches for you?

4. On a scale of 1-10, please indicate how valuable this service is in
    keeping you up to date in areas of your interest.

    Of no   Of very great
    value   value
     1   2   3   4   5   6   7   8   9   10

Many thanks for your help. Please identify yourself and your institution and
return this form to (library address).
    Name:
    Institution:

Exhibit 106
Form for evaluation of SDI output

tion forms indicate that, on the average, 30% of the items included in
the bulletin are judged relevant to the interests of recipients, and that
2500 abstracts are included in the bulletin in a particular year. Then
the *cost per relevant item* distributed is derived from the formula:

$$\frac{\text{Total cost of producing the bulletin in a year}}{2500 \times \text{total number of users reached} \times (30/100)^*}$$

The *cost per new relevant item* can be calculated by a similar formula. In this calculation one must be careful to combine the results of items one and two on the evaluation form. Thus, if the relevance average is 30% and the novelty average is 50%, 15% of the items distributed on the average are both relevant and new to users. The cost per new relevant item is then derived from the formula:

$$\frac{\text{Total cost of producing the bulletin in a year}}{2500 \times \text{total number of users reached} \times (15/100)}$$

The cost of producing the bulletin can also be related to the index of value. The index of value will be derived from the average of the numerical responses to item three on the evaluation form. For example, it could be that the average value on the scale works out at 7.5. So, a cost-benefit ratio for the publication could be said to be $50,000/7.5.

Evaluation criteria one to five as enumerated above, when combined with cost, can be used to form various cost-effectiveness criteria. Thus, the cost-effectiveness of the bulletin could be said to improve if:

1. The number of bulletins distributed from year to year increases while the total costs remain the same **OR** the number of bulletins remains constant but costs are reduced.

2. The number of people reached increases but the costs remain the same **OR** the number of people reached is constant but costs are reduced.

3. The number of items produced increases but the costs remain the same **OR** the number of items remains the same but costs are reduced.

4. The number of relevant items distributed goes up without an increase in costs **OR** the number of relevant items distributed remains the same but costs are reduced.

5. The number of new relevant items distributed goes up without an increase in cost **OR** the number of new relevant items remains the same but costs are reduced.

The sixth criterion, on the other hand, can be used to form at least a crude cost-benefit ratio (where benefit is taken to be the value

---

*This formula can be justified by a simplistic example. If 2500 abstracts are distributed a year to only ten people, then there are 25,000 distributions. If our estimate is that 30% of these distributions are relevant and if the bulletin costs $50,000 a year to produce, then the cost per relevant distribution is

$$\$ \frac{50,000}{25,000 \times (3/10)} = \$ \frac{50,000}{7500} = \text{approximately } \$6.6$$

of the bulletin as perceived by users). Cost benefit improves if the index of value increases without an increase in cost or if costs are reduced without a decline in the value index.

The data collected from the SDI service (see Exhibit 106) can be used in a similar way. Precision ratios and novelty ratios (see Chapter 11) can be calculated from data supplied on the evaluation form. The higher the precision ratio and the higher the novelty ratio, the more effective is the service in keeping users current in their areas of interest. However, an SDI service is most valuable if it is able to retrieve many items that the user judges very important and that he was not aware of before receiving the search results (A items on the evaluation form), so the ratio $A/(A + B + C + D + E + F)$ would be a more refined measure of the value of the service.

Several cost-effectiveness measures for the SDI service are possible. The simplest and most obvious would be the total cost of providing the SDI service in a year divided by an estimate of the total number of relevant items retrieved in the year. This latter figure would be derived by taking the average precision ratio for all SDI outputs for which the evaluation forms were returned and using this to estimate the total number of relevant items retrieved in all SDI outputs to all users. Suppose, for example, that 10,000 bibliographic references are transmitted to users in a year and that the average precision is 62%. Then, the total number of relevant items retrieved in the year is estimated to be 6200. If the service costs $100,000 a year to provide, then the cost per relevant item retrieved would be $100,000/6200, or about sixteen dollars. An estimate of this kind is needed because not all users of the service will return all the evaluation forms they receive and some of the forms returned will probably not provide complete data.

A much more stringent cost-effectiveness measure would be the cost per important new item (A items on the evaluation form) retrieved. This could be estimated in the way mentioned above – i.e., on the basis of the average percentage of A items taken from the evaluation forms returned by users.

The cost-benefit ratio would be the same as that used for the abstracts bulletin, namely the cost of the service related to the value score.

Document Delivery

Document delivery services can be monitored through use of the type of form shown in Exhibit 107. This could be used for any service in which items are *delivered* to users (e.g., to faculty offices in an academic library) or collected by them in response to an earlier request (e.g., in the case of interlibrary loan activities).

Document Delivery

The item attached (*identify item here*) is being sent to you in response to
your recent request. As part of the evaluation of our services, we would like
to know whether or not we were able to get this item to you in time to be of
maximum value.

Would you please take a moment to indicate whether or not the value of this
item to you was reduced by any delay that may have occurred in delivery. Use
the 10-point scale provided.

Of no value now. Arrived too late to be of any use									Value to me not diminished at all by delay in delivery
1	2	3	4	5	6	7	8	9	10

Many thanks for your help. Please identify yourself and your institution and
return this form to (library address).

    Name:
    Institution:

Exhibit 107
Form for evaluation of a documeny delivery service

Question Answering

Forms completed by reference librarians and/or by library users,
as exemplified by Exhibits 50 to 52, can be used in monitoring operations. Forms that record questions received, sources used to answer
the questions, and so on, can form the basis for a follow-up evaluation
procedure. A sample of the users (say, every fifth user of the service)
could be sent a brief form to record their impressions of the service
and their assessment of its value (see Exhibit 108 for a sample form).
As an alternative, it would be possible to perform the follow-up by
telephone, asking the user the questions suggested on the form, but
this seems less desirable and would be more time-consuming since
some users might be difficult to reach.

When a user reports dissatisfaction with the service, or indicates
that it has very little value, some follow-up action will be needed in
order to identify the source of the problem. This may require a telephone call to the respondent to determine what went wrong.

Note that library personnel must fill in the question asked before
sending the form to the user, and must also indicate if the question was

answered from the library's own resources or if the user was referred
to another source for an answer. If the question was partly answered
by the library before being referred, both boxes should be checked.

Reference Services Evaluation

You recently consulted us for assistance with your question

_____(question inserted here)_____.

☐ This was answered from the library's own resources.

☐ You were referred to _____ for help with this
    question.

Would you please take a few moments to help us evaluate our services by
answering the following questions?

1. Was your question answered fully?   ☐ Yes   ☐ No

2. Was it dealt with promptly and efficiently?   ☐ Yes   ☐ No

3. On a scale of 1-10, please indicate how valuable this type of information
    service is to you.

Of no value									Of very great value
1	2	3	4	5	6	7	8	9	10

4. If you have had any problems in using this service (now or in the past),
    or if you have any suggestions as to how it may be improved, please tell
    us here:

Many thanks for your help. Please identify yourself and your institution and
return this form to (library address).

    Name:
    Institution:

Exhibit 108
Form for evaluation of a question-answering service

The cost-effectiveness of the service can be considered to be the
cost per question answered – estimated cost of the service divided by
the number of questions for which answers were found. As with other

services, the cost-benefit ratio can be the cost of the service related to the average value score taken from the value scale.

Database Searching

Searches of databases, performed in response to specific requests, can be monitored through the types of procedures discussed in relation to SDI services, using a slight modification of Exhibit 71. The cost-effectiveness ratio for the service would relate total costs to indexes of relevance and of novelty, and the cost-benefit ratio would relate costs to the value scale.

Conclusion

While libraries and other information services were once largely free from any type of performance assessment, the importance of various forms of evaluation, including continuous quality control activities, has become widely accepted in the last twenty years. Evaluation procedures can help the manager of a library to improve the quality of the services offered and also to allocate available resources more efficiently. Moreover, as long as the evaluation procedures are simple and do not place too much of a burden on the users of the services, they can be good for public relations since they indicate that the information center is genuinely interested in improving its services. Finally, the fact that an evaluation program is in place in itself reminds the staff of the information center that quality of service is important.

Study Question

1. What elements would you include in a continuous quality control program for a university library? What measures would you use to monitor changes in user satisfaction over time?

References

Abbott, C. What does good look like? The adoption of performance indicators at Aston University Library and Information Services. *British Journal of Academic Librarianship*, 5, 1990, 79-94.

Ackerson, L. G. et al. Assessing the relationship between library instruction methods and the quality of undergraduate research. *Research Strategies*, 9, 1991, 139-141.

Aguilar, W. The application of relative use and interlibrary demand in collection development. *Collection Management*, 8(1), 1986, 15-24.

Aguilar, W. *Relationship Between Classes of Books Circulated and Classes of Books Requested on Interlibrary Loan*. Doctoral dissertation. Urbana, University of Illinois, Graduate School of Library and Information Science, 1984.

Allen, G. CD-ROM training: what do the patrons want? *RQ*, 30, 1990, 88-93.

Allen, G. Patron response to bibliographic databases on CD-ROM. *RQ*, 29, 1989, 103-110.

Allen, T. J. and Gerstberger, P. G. *Criteria for Selection of an Information Source*. Cambridge, MA, Massachusetts Institute of Technology, Sloan School of Management, 1966. Another version appears in *Journal of Applied Psychology*, 52, 1968, 272-279.

Altman, E. et al. *A Data Gathering and Instructional Manual for Performance Measures in Public Libraries*. Chicago, Celadon Press, 1976.

Altuna-Esteibar, B. and Lancaster, F. W. Ranking of journals in library and information science by research and teaching relatedness. *Serials Librarian*, 23 (1/2), 1992, 1-10.

American Library Association. *Catalog Use Study*, ed. by V. Mostecky. Chicago, American Library Association, 1958.

Ankeny, M. L. Evaluating end-user services: success or satisfaction? *Journal of Academic Librarianship*, 16, 1991, 352-356.

Arthur D. Little, Inc. *Program Evaluation of the Office of State Technical Services*. Cambridge, MA, 1969. PB 186150.

Association of College and Research Libraries. Bibliographic Instruction Section. *Evaluating Bibliographic Instruction: a Handbook*. Chicago, American Library Association, 1983.

Association of College and Research Libraries. Bibliographic Instruction Section. Model statement of objectives for academic bibliographic instruction: draft revision. *College & Research Libraries News*, 48, 1987, 256-261.

Baker, S. L. The display phenomenon: an exploration into factors causing the increased circulation of displayed books. *Library Quarterly*, 56, 1986a, 237-257.

Baker, S. L. *An Exploration into Factors Causing the Increased Circulation of Displayed Books*. Doctoral dissertation. Urbana, University of Illinois, Graduate School of Library and Information Science, 1985.

Baker, S. L. Overload, browsers, and selections. *Library and Information Science Research*, 8, 1986b, 315-329.

Baker, S. L. Will fiction classification schemes increase use? *RQ*, 27, 1988, 366-376.

Baker, S. L. and Shepherd, G. W. Fiction classification schemes: the principles behind them and their success. *RQ*, 27, 1987, 245-251.

Ballard, T. *The Failure of Resource Sharing in Public Libraries and Alternative Strategies for Service*. Chicago, American Library Association, 1986.

Ballard, T. Library systems: a concept that has failed us. *Wilson Library Bulletin*, 60(4), 1985, 19-22.

Barrett, A. J. The costs of not having refined information. In: *The Value of Information as an Integral Part of Aerospace and Defence R & D Programmes*, pp. 5-1 to 5-9. Neuilly-sur-Seine, North Atlantic Treaty Organization, Advisory Group for Aerospace Research and Development, 1986. AGARD-CP-385.

Baughman, J. C. A structural analysis of the literature of sociology. *Library Quarterly*, 44, 1974, 293-308.

Baumol, W. J. and Marcus, M. *Economics of Academic Libraries*. Washington, DC, American Council of Education, 1973.

Benham, F. and Powell, R. R. *Success in Answering Reference Questions: Two Studies*. Metuchen, NJ, Scarecrow Press, 1987.

Bennion, B. C. and Karschamroon, S. Multivariate regression models for estimating journal usefulness in physics. *Journal of Documentation*, 40, 1984, 217-227.

Betts, D. A. and Hargrave, R. *How Many Books?* Bradford, England, MCB Publications, 1982.

Birbeck, V. P. Unobtrusive testing of public library reference service. *Refer*, 4 (2), 1986, 5-9.

Bland, R. N. The college textbook as a tool for collection evaluation, analysis, and retrospective collection development. *Library Acquisitions: Practice and Theory*, 4, 1980, 193-197.

Blankenbaker, A. *Resources for the Implementation of Total Quality Management (TQM): in Education, in Nonprofits and in the Service Sector*. Washington, DC, Association of Research Libraries, 1992.

Blau, P. M. and Margulies, R. Z. The reputation of American professional schools. *Change*, 6(10), 1974-1975, 42-47.

Blick, A. R. The value of measurement in decision-making in an Information Unit – a cost benefit analysis. *Aslib Proceedings*, 29, 1977, 189-196.

Blood, R. W. Evaluation of online searches. *RQ*, 22, 1983, 266-277.

Bommer, M. R. W. *The Development of a Management System for Effective Decision Making and Planning in a University Library.* Philadelphia, University of Pennsylvania, Wharton School of Finance and Commerce, 1973. (ERIC Document Reproduction Service No. ED 071 727).

Bommer, M. R. W. Review of *Performance Measures for Public Libraries*. *Library Quarterly*, 44, 1974, 273-275.

Bonk, S. C. and Pilling, D. Modelling the economics of interlending. *Interlending and Document Supply*, 18, 1990, 52-56.

Bonn, G. S. Evaluation of the collection. *Library Trends*, 22, 1973-1974, 265-304.

Borkowski, C. and Macleod, M. J. The implications of some recent studies of library use. *Scholarly Publishing*, 11, 1979, 3-24.

Bostian, R. and Robbins, A. Effective instruction for searching CD-ROM indexes. *Laserdisk Professional*, 3(1), 1990, 14-17.

Bourne, C. P. *Overlapping Coverage of Bibliography of Agriculture by 15 Other Secondary Sources*. Palo Alto, Information General Corporation, 1969.

Bourne, C. P. Some user requirements stated quantitatively in terms of the 90% library. *In: Electronic Information Handling*, ed. by A. Kent et al, pp. 93-110. Washington, DC, Spartan Books, 1965.

Bourne, C. P. and Robinson, J. *SDI Citation Checking as a Measure of the Performance of Library Document Delivery Systems*. Berkeley, University of California at Berkeley, Institute of Library Research, 1973. (ERIC Document Reproduction Service No. ED 082 774).

Bradford, S. C. *Documentation*. London, Crosby Lockwood, 1948.

Braskamp, L. A. et al. *Guidebook for Evaluating Teaching*. Urbana, University of Illinois, Office of Instructional Resources, 1983.

Braunstein, Y. M. Costs and benefits of library information: the user point of view. *Library Trends*, 28, 1979, 79-87.

Britten, W. A. A use statistic for collection management: the 80/20 rule revisited. *Library Acquisitions: Practice & Theory*, 14, 1990, 183-189.

Britten, W. A. and Webster, J. D. Comparing characteristics of highly circulated titles for demand-driven collection development. *College & Research Libraries*, 53, 1992, 239-248.

Broadus, R. N. The applications of citation analyses to library collection building. *Advances in Librarianship*, 7, 1977, 299-335.

Brockman, J. R. Just another management fad? The implications of TQM for library and information services. *Aslib Proceedings*, 44, 1992, 283-288.

Brookes, B. C. Obsolescence of special library periodicals: sampling errors and utility contours. *Journal of the American Society for Information Science*, 21, 1970, 320-329.

Brophy, P. Performance measurement in academic libraries: a polytechnic perspective. *British Journal of Academic Librarianship*, 4, 1989, 99-110.

Broude, J. Journal deselection in an academic environment: a comparison of faculty and librarian choices. *Serials Librarian*, 3, 1978, 147-166.

Brownson, C. W. Mechanical selection. *Library Resources & Technical Services*, 32, 1988, 17-29.

Bryant, V. E. An evaluation of continuing education programs based on the principles of adult learning. In: *The Evaluation of Continuing Education for Professionals: a Systems View*; ed. by P. P. LeBreton et al., pp. 326-334. Seattle, University of Washington, 1979.

Buckland, M. K. *Book Availability and the Library User*. New York, Pergamon Press, 1975.

Buckland, M. K. An operations research study of a variable loan and duplication policy at the University of Lancaster. *Library Quarterly*, 42, 1972, 97-106.

Buckland, M. K. and Hindle, A. Loan policies, duplication and availability. In: *Planning Library Services*; ed. by A. G. Mackenzie and I. M. Stuart, pp. 1-16. Lancaster, England, University of Lancaster Library, 1969.

Buckland, M. K. et al. Methodological problems in assessing the overlap between bibliographic files and library holdings. *Information Processing & Management*, 11, 1975, 89-105.

Buckland, M. K. et al. *Systems Analysis of a University Library*. Lancaster, England, University of Lancaster Library, 1970.

Bunge, C. A. *Professional Education and Reference Efficiency*. Springfield, Illinois State Library, 1967.

Burr, R. L. Evaluating library collections: a case study. *Journal of Academic Librarianship*, 5, 1979, 256-260.

Burton, R. E. and Kebler, R. W. The "half-life" of some scientific and technical literatures. *American Documentation*, 11, 1960, 18-22.

Bustion, M. and Treadwell, J. Reported relative value of journals versus use: a comparison. *College & Research Libraries*, 51, 1990, 142-151.

Bustion, M. et al. On the merits of direct observation of periodical usage: an empirical study. *College & Research Libraries*, 53, 1992, 537-550.

Buzzard, M. L. and New, D. E. An investigation of collection support for doctoral research. *College & Research Libraries*, 44, 1983, 469-475.

Byrd, G. D. et al. Collection development using interlibrary loan borrowing and acquisitions statistics. *Bulletin of the Medical Library Association*, 70, 1982, 1-9.

California State Department of Education. *Evaluation of Adult Education Programs*. Sacramento, 1979. (ERIC Document Reproduction Service No. ED 171 980).

Capital Planning Systems. *Qualitative Assessment of Public Reference Services*. Boston Spa, British Library, 1987. British Library Research Paper 21.

Carlson, G. *Search Strategy by Reference Librarians. Part 3 of Final Report on the Organization of Large Files*. Sherman Oaks, CA, Hughes Dynamics Inc., Advanced Information Systems Division, 1964. PB 166192.

Carrigan, D. P. Librarians and the "dismal science." *Library Journal*, 113(11), 1988, 22-25.

Chang, H. C. *Narrative Evaluation Report on the Institute for Training in Librarianship*. St. Croix, College of the Virgin Islands, 1976.

Charles, S. K. and Clark, K. E. Enhancing CD-ROM searches with online updates: an examination of end-user needs, strategies, and problems. *College & Research Libraries*, 51, 1990, 321-328.

Chen, C.-C. The use patterns of physics journals in a large academic research library. *Journal of the American Society for Information Science*, 23, 1972, 254-270.

Chester, L. A. and Magoss, G. Evaluating library services by sampling methods: a project at the North York public library. *Canadian Library Journal*, 34, 1977, 439-443.

Childers, T. *The Effectiveness of Information Service in Public Libraries: Suffolk County*. Philadelphia, Drexel University, School of Library and Information Science, 1978. A condensed version appears in *Library Journal*, April 15, 1980, 924-928.

Childers, T. Managing the quality of reference/information service. *Library Quarterly*, 42, 1972, 212-217.

Chrzastowksi, T. E. Journal collection cost-effectiveness in an academic chemistry library: results of a cost/use survey at the University of Illinois at Urbana-Champaign. *Collection Management*, 14 (1/2), 1991, 85-98.

Ciliberti, A. C. et al. Material availability: a study of academic library performance. *College & Research Libraries*, 48, 1987, 513-527.

Citron, H. R. and Dodd, J. B. Cost allocation and cost recovery considerations in a special academic library: Georgia Institute of Technology. *Science and Technology Libraries*, 5(2), 1984, 1-14.

Clapp, V. W. and Jordan, R. T. Quantitative criteria for adequacy of academic library collections. *College & Research Libraries*, 26, 1965, 371-380.

Clark, P. M. *A Study to Refine and Test New Measures of Library Service and Train Library Personnel in Their Use*. New Brunswick, NJ, Rutgers, the State University, Bureau of Library and Information Science Research, 1976. (ERIC Document Reproduction Service No. ED 138 262).

Coale, R. P. Evaluation of a research library collection: Latin-American colonial history at the Newberry. *Library Quarterly*, 35, 1965, 173-184.

Collette, A. D. and Price, J. A. A cost/benefit evaluation of online interactive bibliographic searching in a research and engineering organization. In: *The Value of Information: Collection of Papers Presented at the 6th Mid-Year Meeting* [of ASIS], *May 19-21, 1977*, pp. 24-34. Syracuse, NY, Syracuse University, 1977.

Comer, C. List-checking as a method for evaluating library collections. *Collection Building*, 3(3), 1981, 26-34.

Cooper, M. Current information dissemination: ideas and practices. *Journal of Chemical Documentation*, 8, 1968, 207-218.

Cooper, W. S. Expected search length: a single measure of retrieval effectiveness based on the weak ordering action of retrieval systems. *American Documentation*, 19, 1968, 30-41.

Cronin, M. T. *Performance Measurement for Public Services in Academic and Research Libraries*. Washington, DC, Association of Research Libraries, 1985.

Crowley, T. Half-right reference: is it true? *RQ*, 25, 1985, 59-68.

Crowley, T. Referred reference questions: how well are they answered? In: *Evaluation of Reference Services*; ed. by W. Katz and R. A. Fraley, pp. 83-93. New York, Haworth Press, 1984.

Crowley, T. and Childers, T. *Information Service in Public Libraries: Two Studies*. Metuchen, NJ, Scarecrow Press, 1971.

Daiute, R. J. and Gorman, K. A. *Library Operations Research*. Dobbs Ferry, NY, Oceana Publications, 1974.

Dalrymple, P. W. Clinical uses of MEDLINE on CD-ROM: a composite report of a panel discussion on five sites. In: *MEDLINE on CD-ROM*; ed. by R. M. Woodsmall et al., pp. 25-33. Medford, NJ, Learned Information Inc., 1989.

Dalton, G. M. E. Quantitative approach to user satisfaction in reference service evaluation. *South African Journal of Library and Information Science*, 60, 1992, 89-103.

Dawson, A. Quality first!: the Taywood Information Centre and BS 5750. *Aslib Information*, 20, 1992, 112-113.

De Prospo, E. R. et al. *Performance Measures for Public Libraries*. Chicago, Public Library Association, 1973.

D'Elia, G. and Walsh, S. Patrons' uses and evaluations of library services: a comparison across five public libraries. *Library and Information Science Research*, 7, 1985, 3-30.

Detweiler, M. J. Availability of materials in public libraries. In: *Library Effectiveness: a State of the Art*, pp. 75-83. Chicago, American Library Association, 1980.

Detweiler, M. J. The "best size" public library. *Library Journal*, 111(9), 1986, 34-35.

Dickson, J. An analysis of user errors in searching an online catalog. *Cataloging & Classification Quarterly*, 4(3), 1984, 19-38.

Diodato, V. and Smith, F. Obsolescence of music literature. *Journal of the American Society for Information Science*, 44, 1993, 101-112.

Dixon, J. K. *Methodological Considerations in Evaluation of Continuing Education in the Health Professions*. Paper presented at the Annual Convention of the American Educational Research Association, New York, 1977. (ERIC Document Reproduction Service No. ED 138 780).

Dolan, J. The St. Helens experience: ". . . but how many souls?." In: *Performance Indicators for Public Libraries*; ed. by M. Ashcroft and A. Wilson, pp. 35-49. Stamford, Lincolnshire, England, Capital Planning Information Ltd., 1991.

Doll, C. A. *A Study of Overlap and Duplication Among Children's Collections in Public and Elementary School Libraries*. Doctoral dissertation. Urbana, University of Illinois, Graduate School of Library and Information Science, 1980.

Domas, R. E. *Correlating the Classes of Books Taken Out Of and Books Used Within an Open-Stack Library*. San Antonio, San Antonio College Library, 1978. (ERIC Document Reproduction Service No. ED 171 282).

Douglas, I. Effects of a relegation programme on borrowing of books. *Journal of Documentation*, 42, 1986, 252-271.

Dowlin, K. and Magrath, L. Beyond the numbers – a decision support system. In: *Library Automation as a Source of Management Information*; ed. by F. W. Lancaster, pp. 27-58. Urbana, University of Illinois, Graduate School of Library and Information Science, 1983.

Drabenstott, K. M. et al. Analysis of a bibliographic database enhanced with a library classification. *Library Resources & Technical Services*, 34, 1990, 179-198.

Drone, J. M. *A Study of the Relationship Between Size of Monographic Collections and Internal Duplication in a Select Group of Libraries Using LCS (Library Computer System)*. Doctoral dissertation. Urbana, University of Illinois, Graduate School of Library and Information Science, 1984.

Drucker, P. F. Managing the public service institution. *The Public Interest*, 33, Fall, 1973, 43-60.

Dykeman, A. and King, B. Term paper analysis: a proposal for evaluating bibliographic instruction. *Research Strategies*, 1, 1983, 14-21.

Edwards, S. Effects of a self-paced workbook on students' skills and attitudes. *Research Strategies*, 9, 1991, 180-188.

Elchesen, D. R. Cost-effectiveness comparison of manual and on-line retrospective bibliographic searching. *Journal of the American Society for Information Science*, 29, 1978, 56-66.

Ellsworth, R. *The Economics of Compact Storage*. Metuchen, NJ, Scarecrow Press, 1969.

Elzy, C. A. and Lancaster, F. W. Looking at a collection in different ways: a comparison of methods of bibliographic checking. *Collection Management*, 12, 1990, 1-10.

Elzy, C. A. et al. Evaluating reference service in a large academic library. *College & Research Libraries*, 52, 1991, 454-465.

Estabrook, L. S. Valuing a document delivery system. *RQ*, 26, 1986, 58-62.

Ettelt, H. J. Book use at a small (very) community college library. *Library Journal*, 103, 1978, 2314-2315.

Evans, G. T. and Beilby, A. A library management information system in a multi-campus environment. In: *Library Automation as a Source of Management Information*; ed. by F. W. Lancaster, pp. 164-196. Urbana, University of Illinois, Graduate School of Library and Information Science, 1983.

Fairthorne, R. A. Empirical hyperbolic distributions (Bradford-Zipf-Mandelbrot) for bibliometric description and prediction. *Journal of Documentation*, 25, 1969, 319-343.

Feinberg, R. P. and King, C. Performance evaluation in bibliographic instruction workshop courses: assessing what students do as a measure of what they know. *Reference Services Review*, 20(2), 1992, 75-80.

Ferguson, D. et al. The CLR public online catalog study: an overview. *Information Technology and Libraries*, 1, 1982, 84-97.

Fjällbrant, N. Evaluation in a user education programme. *Journal of Librarianship*, 9(2), 1977, 83-95.

Flynn, R. R. The University of Pittsburgh study of journal usage: a summary report. *Serials Librarian*, 4, 1979, 25-33.

Franklin, H. Comparing quarterly use study results for marginal serials at Oregon State University. *Serials Librarian*, 16(1/2), 1989, 109-122.

Freedman, J. and Bantly, H. A. Techniques of program evaluation. In: *Teaching Librarians to Teach*; ed. by A. S. Clark and K. F. Jones, pp. 188-204. Metuchen, NJ, Scarecrow Press, 1986.

Freeman & Co. *Final Report on a Library Systems Study*. Palo Alto, Freeman & Co., 1965.

Frohmberg, K. A. et al. Increases in book availability in a large college library. *Proceedings of the American Society for Information Science*, 17, 1980, 292-294.

Fussler, H. H. and Simon, J. L. *Patterns in the Use of Books in Large Research Libraries*. Chicago, University of Chicago Press, 1969.

Gabriel, M. R. Online collection evaluation, course by course. *Collection Building*, 8(2), 1987, 20-24.

Garfield, E. Which medical journals have the greatest impact? *Annals of Internal Medicine*, 105, 1986, 313-320.

Gers, R. and Seward, L. J. Improving reference performance: results of a statewide study. *Library Journal*, 110(18), 1985, 32-35.

Getz, M. *Public Libraries: an Economic View*. Baltimore, Johns Hopkins University Press, 1980.

Gillentine, J. et al. *Evaluating Library Services*. Santa Fe, New Mexico State Library, 1981.

Glogoff, S. Using statistical tests to evaluate library instruction sessions. *Journal of Academic Librarianship*, 4, 1979, 438-442.

Goehlert, R. Book availability and delivery service. *Journal of Academic Librarianship*, 4, 1978, 368-371.

Goehlert, R. The effect of loan policies on circulation recalls. *Journal of Academic Librarianship*, 5, 1979, 79-82.

Golden, B. A method for quantitatively evaluating a university library collection. *Library Resources & Technical Services*, 18, 1974, 268-274.

Goldhor, H. Analysis of an inductive method of evaluating the book collection of a public library. *Libri*, 23, 1973, 6-17.

Goldhor, H. The effect of prime display location on public library circulation of selected adult titles. *Library Quarterly*, 42, 1972, 371-389.

Goldhor, H. Experimental effects on the choice of books borrowed by public library adult patrons. *Library Quarterly*, 51, 1981a, 253-268.

Goldhor, H. *A Plan for the Development of Public Library Service in the Minneapolis-Saint Paul Metropolitan Area*. Minneapolis, Metropolitan Library Service Agency, 1967.

Goldhor, H. A report on an application of the inductive method of evaluation of public library books. *Libri*, 31, 1981b, 121-129.

Gore, D. Let them eat cake while reading catalog cards: an essay on the availability problem. *Library Journal*, 100, 1975, 93-98.

Gouke, M. N. and Pease, S. Title searches in an online catalog and a card catalog. *Journal of Academic Librarianship*, 8, 1982, 137-143.

Greenberg, B., et al. Evaluation of a clinical medical librarian program at the Yale Medical Library. *Bulletin of the Medical Library Association*, 66, 1978, 319-326.

Griffiths, J.-M. and King, D. W. *Library Cost Benefit Analysis: a Manual Prepared for the Library Cost Benefit Analysis Seminar Presented at the SUNY/OCLC Network Annual Directors Day on February 17, 1983*. Rockville, MD, King Research, Inc., 1983.

Griffiths, J.-M. and King, D. W. *A Manual on the Evaluation of Information Centers and Services*. Neuilly-sur-Seine, North Atlantic Treaty Organization, Advisory Group for Aerospace Research and Development, 1991. AGARD-AG-310.

Griscom, R. Periodical use in a university music library: a citation study of theses and dissertations submitted to the Indiana University School of Music from 1975-1980. *Serials Librarian*, 7(3), 1983, 35-52.

Groos, O. V. Citation characteristics of astronomical literature. *Journal of Documentation*, 25, 1969, 344-347.

Grotelueschen, A. D. et al. *Evaluation in Adult Basic Education: How and Why*. Danville, IL, Interstate Printers and Publishers Inc., 1976.

Hafner, A. W. Primary journal selection using citations from an indexing service journal: a method and example from nursing literature. *Bulletin of the Medical Library Association*, 64, 1976, 392-401.

Hall, B. H. *Collection Assessment Manual for College and University Libraries*. Phoenix, Oryx Press, 1985.

Hallak, J. Cost analysis in evaluating educational programs. In *Evaluation Roles in Education*, ed. by A. Lewy and D. Nevo, pp. 475-486. London, Gordon and Breach, 1981.

Hamburg, M. et al. *Library Planning and Decision-Making Systems*. Cambridge, MA, MIT Press, 1974.

Hampton, L. A. Evaluating continuing education programs. *Adult Leadership*, 22(3), 1973, 105-107, 118-119.

Hancock-Beaulieu, M. Evaluating the impact of an online library catalogue on subject searching behaviour at the catalogue and at the shelves. *Journal of Documentation*, 46, 1990, 318-338.

Hardesty, L. Use of library materials at a small liberal arts college. *Library Research*, 3, 1981, 261-282.

Hardesty, L. et al. Evaluating library-use instruction. *College & Research Libraries*, 40, 1979, 309-317.

Harris, C. A comparison of issues and in-library use of books. *Aslib Proceedings*, 29, 1977, 118-126.

Harris, I. W. *The Influence of Accessibility on Academic Library Use*. Doctoral dissertation. New Brunswick, Rutgers, The State University, 1966.

Hatchard, D. B. and Toy, P. Evaluation of a library instruction program at BCAE. *Australian Academic and Research Libraries*, 15, 1984, 157-167.

Hawkins, D. T. The percentage distribution: a method of ranking journals. *Proceedings of the American Society for Information Science*, 16, 1979, 230-235.

Hawley, M. B. Reference statistics. *RQ*, 10, 1970, 143-147.

Hayes, R. M. The distribution of use of library materials: analysis of data from the University of Pittsburgh. *Library Research*, 3, 1981, 215-260.

Hernon, P. and McClure, C. R. Quality of data issues is unobtrusive testing of library reference service: recommendations and strategies. *Library and Information Science Research*, 9, 1987a, 77-93.

Hernon, P. and McClure, C. R. *Unobtrusive Testing and Library Reference Services*. Norwood, NJ, Ablex, 1987b.

Hindle, A. and Buckland, M. K. In-library book usage in relation to circulation. *Collection Management*, 2(4), 1978, 265-277.

Hodowanec, G. V. An acquisition rate model for academic libraries. *College & Research Libraries*, 39, 1978, 439-447.

Holland, M. P. Serial cuts vs. public service: a formula. *College & Research Libraries*, 37, 1976, 543-548.

Horton, W., Jr. Interlibrary loan turnaround times in science and engineering. *Special Libraries* 80, 1989, 245-250.

Houge, D. R. *Evaluation by Participant/Observers*. 1981. (ERIC Document Reproduction Service No. ED 206 252).

Hu, C. *An Evaluation of Online Database Selection by a Gateway System With Artificial Intelligence Techniques*. Doctoral dissertation. Urbana, University of Illinois, Graduate School of Library and Information Science, 1987.

Huang, S. T. and McHale, T. J. A cost-effectiveness comparison between print and online versions of the same frequently-used sources of business and financial information. (Proceedings of the) *National Online Meeting*; ed. by M. Williams, pp. 161-168. Medford, NJ, Learned Information, 1990.

International Federation of Library Associations. *Guidelines for Public Libraries*. Munich, Saur, 1986.

Jackson, R. Transforming the ACRL model statement of objectives into a working tool. In: *Coping With Information Illiteracy: Bibliographic Instruction for the Information Age*; ed. by G. W. Mensching, Jr. and T. B. Mensching, pp. 61-68. Ann Arbor, MI, Pierian Press, 1989.

Jain, A. K. *Report on a Statistical Study of Book Use*. Lafayette, IN, Purdue University, School of Industrial Engineering, 1967.

Jain, A. K. *A Sampled Data Study of Book Usage in the Purdue University Libraries*. Lafayette, IN, Purdue University, 1965.

Jain, A. K. Sampling and data collection methods for a book-use study. *Library Quarterly*, 39, 1969, 245-252.

Jain, A. K. Sampling and short-period usage in the Purdue Library. *College & Research Libraries*, 27, 1966, 211-218.

Jaster, F. *Assessing Corporate Training Programs in Business Communications*. 1981. (ERIC Document Reproduction Service No. ED 209 709).

Jenks, G. M. Circulation and its relationship to the book collection and academic departments. *College & Research Libraries*, 37, 1976, 145-152.

Jensen, R. J. et al. Costs and benefits to industry of online literature searches. *Special Libraries*, 71, 1980, 291-299.

Johnson, C. A. and Trueswell, R. W. The weighted criteria statistic score: an approach to journal selection. *College & Research Libraries*, 39, 1978, 287-292.

Johnson, F. D. et al. *NASA Tech Brief Program: Cost Benefit Evaluation*. Denver, University of Denver Research Institute, 1977.

Johnson, K. A. and Plake, B. S. Evaluation of PLATO library instructional lessons: another view. *Journal of Academic Librarianship*, 6, 1980, 154-158.

Jones, D. The Richmond experience. In: *Performance Indicators for Public Libraries*; ed. by M. Ashcroft and A. Wilson, pp. 5-34. Stamford, Lincolnshire, England, Capital Planning Information Ltd., 1991.

Jones, R. M. Improving Okapi: transaction log analysis of failed searches in an online catalogue. *Vine*, 62, 1986, 3-13.

Jordan, R. T. Library characteristics of colleges ranking high in academic excellence. *College & Research Libraries*, 24, 1963, 369-376.

Kantor, P. B. Availability analysis. *Journal of the American Society for Information Science*, 27, 1976a, 311-319.

Kantor, P. B. Demand-adjusted shelf availability parameters. *Journal of Academic Librarianship*, 7, 1981, 78-82.

Kantor, P. B. The library as an information utility in the university context: evolution and measurement of service. *Journal of the American Society for Information Science*, 27, 1976b, 100-112.

Kantor, P. B. Library cost analysis. *Library Trends*, 38, 1989, 171-188.

Kantor, P. B. Vitality: an indirect measure of relevance. *Collection Management*, 2, 1978, 83-95.

Kaplowitz, J. A pre- and post-test evaluation of the English 3 library instruction program at UCLA. *Research Strategies*, 4, 1986, 11-17.

Kaske, N. K. and Sanders, N. P. *Study of Online Public Access Catalogs: an Overview and Application of Findings*. Dublin, OH, Online Computer Library Center, 1983.

Kavanagh, R. TRESNET: the Trent Resource Sharing Network. *Canadian Library Journal*, 45, 1988, 283-288.

Kennedy, R. A. Computer-derived management information in a special library. In: *Library Automation as a Source of Management Information*; ed. by F. W. Lancaster, pp. 128-147. Urbana, University of Illinois, Graduate School of Library and Information Science, 1983.

Kent, A. et al. *Use of Library Materials: the University of Pittsburgh Study*. New York, Dekker, 1979.

King, D. N. The contribution of hospital library information services to clinical care: a study in eight hospitals. *Bulletin of the Medical Library Association*, 75, 1987, 291-301.

King, D. N. and Ory, J. C. Effects of library instruction on student research: a case study. *College & Research Libraries*, 42, 1981, 31-41.

King, D. W. Pricing policies in academic libraries. *Library Trends*, 28, 1979, 47-62.

King, D. W. et al. *Statistical Indicators of Scientific and Technical Communication*. Vol. 2. Rockville, MD, King Research, Inc., 1976.

King, G. B. and Berry, R. *Evaluation of the University of Minnesota Libraries Reference Department Telephone Information Service. Pilot Study*. Minneapolis, University of Minnesota, Library School, 1973. (ERIC Document Reproduction Service No. ED 077 517).

King Research Inc. *A Study of the Value of Information and the Effect on Value of Intermediary Organizations, Timeliness of Services and Products, and Comprehensiveness of the EDB*. Rockville, MD, King Research Inc., 1984. DOE/NMB-1078. DE 85003670.

King Research Inc. *Value of the Energy Data Base*. Rockville, MD, 1982.

King Research Ltd. *Keys to Success: Performance Indicators for Public Libraries*. London, Her Majesty's Stationery Office, 1990.

Kirby, M. and Miller, N. MEDLINE searching on Colleague: reasons for failure or success of untrained end users. *Medical Reference Services Quarterly*, 5(3), 1986, 17-34.

Kirkpatrick, D. L. Evaluation of training. In: *Training and Development Handbook*; ed. by R. L. Craig and L. R. Bittel, pp. 87-112. New York, McGraw-Hill, 1967.

Knowles, M. S. *The Modern Practice of Adult Education*. New York, Association Press, 1970.

Kohl, D. F. and Wilson, L. A. Effectiveness of course-integrated bibliographic instruction in improving coursework. *RQ*, 26, 1986, 206-211.

Konopasek, K. and O'Brien, N. P. *A Survey of Journal Use Within the Undergraduate Library at the University of Illinois at Urbana-Champaign*. Urbana, University of Illinois, Graduate School of Library and Information Science, 1982. (ERIC Document Reproduction Service No. ED 225 601). Another version appears in *Serials Librarian*, 9, Winter 1984, 65-74.

Kramer, J. How to survive in industry: cost justifying library services. *Special Libraries*, 62, 1971, 487-489.

Krueger, K. *Coordinated Cooperative Collection Development for Illinois Libraries*. Springfield, Illinois State Library, 1983. 3 vols.

Kuraim, F. M. *The Principal Factors Causing Reader Frustration in a Public Library*. Doctoral dissertation. Cleveland, Case Western Reserve University, 1983.

Lancaster, F. W. *Evaluation of the MEDLARS Demand Search Service*. Bethesda, MD, National Library of Medicine, 1968.

Lancaster, F. W. *Guidelines for the Evaluation of Training Courses, Workshops and Seminars*. Second edition. Paris, UNESCO, 1983.

Lancaster, F. W. *The Measurement and Evaluation of Library Services*. Washington, DC, Information Resources Press, 1977.

Lancaster, F. W. Some considerations relating to the cost-effectiveness of on-line services in libraries. *Aslib Proceedings*, 33, 1981, 10-14.

Lancaster, F. W. and Lee, J-L. Bibliometric techniques applied to issues management: a case study. *Journal of the American Society for Information Science*, 36, 1985, 389-397.

Lancaster, F. W. and Mehrotra, R. The five laws of library science as a guide to the evaluation of library services. In: *Perspectives in Library and Information Science*. Vol. 1, pp. 26-39. Lucknow, Print House, 1982.

Lancaster, F. W. and Warner, A. *Information Retrieval Today*. (Third edition of *Information Retrieval Systems: Characteristics, Testing and Evaluation*). Arlington, VA, Information Resources Press, 1993.

Lancaster, F. W. et al. The diagnostic evaluation of reference service in an academic library. In: *Evaluation of Public Services and Public Services Personnel: Proceedings of the Thirty-second Allerton Park Institute*; ed. by B. Allen, pp. 43-57. Urbana, University of Illinois, Graduate School of Library and Information Science, 1991a.

Lancaster, F. W. et al. Identifying barriers to effective subject access in library catalogs. *Library Resources & Technical Services*, 35, 1991b, 377-391.

Lancaster, F. W. et al. The relationship between literature scatter and journal accessibility in an academic special library. *Collection Building*, 11(1), 1991c, 19-22.

Lancaster, F. W. et al. *Searching Databases on CD-ROM: Comparison of the Results of End User Searching with Results from Two Modes of Searching by Skilled Intermediaries*. A report to the Council on Library Resources. Urbana, University of Illinois, Graduate School of Library and Information Science, Library Research Center, 1992. A condensed version has been submitted for publication in *RQ*.

Lawrence, G. S. and Oja, A. R. *The Use of General Collections at the University of California*. Sacramento, California State Department of Education, 1980. (ERIC Document Reproduction Service No. ED 191 490).

Lawson, V. L. Using a computer-assisted instruction program to replace the traditional library tour: an experimental study. *RQ*, 29, 1989, 71-79.

Lechner, J. V. *Bibliographic Instruction Evaluation: a Study Testing the Correlations Among Five Measures of the Impact of a Bibliographic Instruction Program on Undergraduates' Information Searching Behavior in Libraries*. Doctoral dissertation. Los Angeles, University of California, Graduate School of Library and Information Science, 1989.

Leimkuhler, F. F. Systems analysis in university libraries. *College & Research Libraries*, 27, 1966, 13-18.

LePoer, P. M. and Mularski, C. A. CD-ROM's impact on libraries and users. *Laserdisk Professional*, 2(4), 1989, 39-45.

Lester, M. A. *Coincidence of User Vocabulary and Library of Congress Subject Headings: Experiments to Improve Subject Access in Academic Library On-*

line Catalogs. Doctoral dissertation. Urbana, University of Illinois, Graduate School of Library and Information Science, 1988.

Lewis, D. W. Research on the use of online catalogs and its implications for library practice. *Journal of Academic Librarianship,* 13, 1987, 152-157.

Line, M. B. The ability of a university library to provide books wanted by researchers. *Journal of Librarianship,* 5, 1973, 37-51.

Line, M. B. Citation analyses: a note. *International Library Review,* 9, 1977, 429.

Line, M. B. Rank lists based on citations and library uses as indicators of journal usage in individual libraries. *Collection Management,* 2, 1978, 313-316.

Line, M. B. Review of *Use of Library Materials: the University of Pittsburgh Study. College & Research Libraries,* 40, 1979, 557-558.

Line, M. B. and Sandison, A. "Obsolescence" and changes in the use of literature with time. *Journal of Documentation,* 30, 1974, 283-350.

Linn, R. L. Measuring pretest-posttest performance changes. In: *Educational Evaluation Methodology: the State of the Art;* ed. by R. A. Berk, pp. 84-109. Baltimore, The Johns Hopkins University Press, 1981.

Lipetz, B.-A. Catalog use in a large research library. *Library Quarterly,* 42, 1972, 129-139.

Lipetz, B.-A. *User Requirements in Identifying Desired Works in a Large Library.* New Haven, Yale University Library, 1970.

Lipetz, B.-A. and Paulson, P. J. A study of the impact of introducing an online subject catalog at the New York State Library. *Library Trends,* 35, 1987, 597-617.

Lister, W. C. *Least Cost Decision Rules for the Selection of Library Materials for Compact Storage.* Doctoral dissertation. Lafayette, IN, Purdue University, School of Industrial Engineering, 1967. PB 174 441.

Longo, R. M. J. and Machado, U. D. Characterization of databases in agricultural sciences. *Journal of the American Society for Information Science,* 32, 1981, 83-91.

Longyear, R. M. Article citation and "obsolescence" in musicological journals. *Notes,* 33, 1977, 563-571.

Lopez, M. D. The Lopez or citation technique of in-depth collection evaluation explicated. *College & Research Libraries,* 44, 1983, 251-255.

Lowry, C. B. Resource sharing or cost shifting? The unequal burden of cooperative cataloging and ILL in network. *College and Research Libraries,* 51, 1990, 11-19.

Lynn, P. and Bacsanyi, K. CD-ROMs: instructional methods and user reactions. *Reference Services Review,* 17(2), 1989, 17-25.

MacDougall, A. F. et al. Effectiveness of a local inter-loan system for five academic libraries: an operational research approach. *Journal of Documentation*, 46, 1990, 353-358.

Mackey, T. and Mackey, K. Think quality! The Deming approach *does* work in libraries. *Library Journal*, 117, 1992, 57-61.

Magson, M. S. Techniques for the measurement of cost-benefit in information centres. *Aslib Proceedings*, 25, 1973, 164-185.

Maltby, A. Measuring catalogue utility. *Journal of Librarianship*, 3, 1971, 180-189.

Maltby, A. *U.K. Catalogue Use Survey: a Report*. London, Library Association, 1973.

Mandel, C. A. Trade-offs: quantifying quality in library technical services. *Journal of Academic Librarianship*, 14, 1988, 214-220.

Mankin, C. J. and Bastille, J. D. An analysis of the differences between density-of-use ranking and raw-use ranking of library journal use. *Journal of the American Society for Information Science*, 32, 1981, 224-228.

Mansbridge, J. Availability studies in libraries. *Library and Information Science Research*, 8, 1986, 299-314.

Mansbridge, J. *Evaluating Resource Sharing Library Networks*. Doctoral dissertation. Cleveland, Case Western Reserve University, 1984.

Markey, K. *The Process of Subject Searching in the Library Catalog: Final Report of the Subject Access Research Project*. Dublin, OH, Online Computer Library Center, 1983.

Markey, K. *Subject Searching in Library Catalogs*. Dublin, OH, Online Computer Library Center, 1984.

Marshall, J. G. The impact of the hospital library on clinical decision making: the Rochester study. *Bulletin of the Medical Library Association*, 80, 1992, 169-178.

Martyn, J. Tests on abstracts journals: coverage, overlap, and indexing. *Journal of Documentation*, 23, 1967, 45-70.

Martyn, J. Unintentional duplication of research. *New Scientist*, 21, 1964, 338.

Martyn, J. and Lancaster, F. W. *Investigative Methods in Library and Information Science: an Introduction*. Washington, DC, Information Resources Press, 1981.

Martyn, J. and Slater, M. Tests on abstracts journals. *Journal of Documentation*, 20, 1964, 212-235.

Mason, D. PPBS: application to an industrial information and library service. *Journal of Librarianship*, 4, 1972, 91-105.

McCain, K. W. and Bobick, J. E. Patterns of journal use in a departmental library: a citation analysis. *Journal of the American Society for Information Science*, 32, 1981, 257-267.

McClellan, A. W. *The Logistics of Public Library Bookstock*. London, Association of Assistant Librarians, 1978.

McClellan, A. W. New concepts of service. *Library Association Record*, 58, 1956, 299-305.

McClure, C. R. and Hernon, P. *Improving the Quality of Reference Service for Government Publications*. Chicago, American Library Association, 1983.

McClure, C. R. et al. *Planning & Role Setting for Public Libraries: a Manual of Options and Procedures*. Chicago, American Library Association, 1987.

McGrath, W. E. Correlating the subjects of books taken out of and books used within an open-stack library. *College & Research Libraries*, 32, 1971, 280-285.

McGrath, W. E. Measuring classified circulation according to curriculum. *College & Research Libraries*, 29, 1968, 347-350.

McGrath, W. E. The significance of books used according to a classified profile of academic departments. *College & Research Libraries*, 33, 1972, 212-219.

McGrath, W. E. et al. Ethnocentricity and cross-disciplinary circulation. *College & Research Libraries*, 40, 1979, 511-518.

McInnis, R. M. The formula approach to library size: an empirical study of its efficacy in evaluating research libraries. *College & Research Libraries*, 33, 1972, 190-198.

Medina, S. O. Network of Alabama Academic Libraries interlibrary loan turnaround time survey. *Southeastern Librarian*, 38, 1988, 105-107.

Mehlinger, H. D. and Patrick, J. J. *The Use of "Formative" and "Summative" Evaluation in an Experimental Curriculum Project: a Case in the Practice of Instructional Materials Evaluation*. Bloomington, Indiana University, High School Curriculum Center in Government, 1970. (ERIC Document Reproduction Service No. ED 041 443).

Metz, P. Duplication in library collections: what we know and what we need to know. *Collection Building*, 2(3), 1980, 27-33.

Metz, P. *The Landscape of Literatures: Use of Subject Collections in a Library*. Chicago, American Library Association, 1983.

Metz, P. and Litchfield, C. A. Measuring collections use at Virginia Tech. *College & Research Libraries*, 49, 1988, 501-513.

Meyer, G. R. and Jenkins, C. Preliminary studies of the effectiveness of minicourses for the in-service education of teachers and trainers. *Programmed Learning & Educational Technology*, 16, 1979, 210-218.

Miller, T. Early user reaction to CD-ROM and videodisc-based optical information products in the library market. *Optical Information Systems*, 7 1987, 205-209.

Mills, T. R. *The University of Illinois Film Center Collection Use Study.* 1982. (ERIC Document Reproduction Service No. ED 227 821).

Milne, D. and Tiffany, B. A cost-per-use method for evaluating the cost-effectiveness of serials: a detailed discussion of methodology. *Serials Review*, 17(2), 1991, 7-19.

Misanchuk, E. R. *Uses and Abuses of Evaluation in Continuing Education Programs.* Paper presented at the Adult Education Research Conference, San Antonio, Texas, 1978. (ERIC Document Reproduction Service No. ED 160 734).

Mitchell, B. J. et al. *Cost Analysis of Library Functions: a Total System Approach.* Greenwich, CT, JAI Press Inc., 1978.

Moisse, E. Costing information in an independent research organization. *Information Scientist*, 10(2), 1976, 57-68.

Molyneux, R. E. Patterns, processes of growth, and the projection of library size: a critical review of the literature on academic library growth. *Library and Information Science Research*, 8, 1986, 5-28.

Mondschein, L. G. SDI use and productivity in the corporate research environment. *Special Libraries*, 81, 1990, 265-279.

Mooers, C. N. Mooers' Law or, why some retrieval systems are used and others are not. *American Documentation*, 11(3), 1960, ii.

Morse, P. M. Demand for library materials: an exercise in probability analysis. *Collection Management*, 1, 1976-1977, 47-78.

Mosher, P. H. Quality and library collections: new directions in research and practice in collection evaluation. *Advances in Librarianship*, 13, 1984, 211-238.

Mostyn, G. R. The use of supply-demand equality in evaluating collection adequacy. *California Librarian*, 35, 1974, 16-23.

Mount, E. ed. *Weeding of Collections in Sci-Tech Libraries.* New York, Haworth Press, 1986. (Also published as *Science and Technology Libraries*, 6, Number 3, Spring 1986)

Mueller, E. Are new books read more than old ones? *Library Quarterly*, 35, 1965, 166-172.

Mueller, M. W. *Time, Cost and Value Factors in Information Retrieval.* Paper presented at the IBM Information Systems Conference, Poughkeepsie, NY, September 21-23, 1959.

Murfin, M. E. The myth of accessibility: frustration and failure in retrieving periodicals. *Journal of Academic Librarianship*, 6, 1980, 16-19.

Murfin, M. E. and Gugelchuk, G. M. Development and testing of a reference transaction assessment instrument. *College & Research Libraries*, 48, 1987, 314-338.

Myers, M. J. and Jirjees, J. M. *The Accuracy of Telephone Reference/Information Services in Academic Libraries*. Metuchen, NJ, Scarecrow Press, 1983.

Nadler, L. Improving the results of workshops. Part 3. Linkage, evaluation and follow-up. *Training and Development Journal*, 30(9), 1976, 31-35.

Nakamoto, H. Synchronous and diachronous citation distributions. In: *Informetrics 88*; ed. by L. Egghe and R. Rousseau, pp. 157-163, Amsterdam, Elsevier, 1988.

Narin, F. *Evaluative Bibliometrics*. Cherry Hill, NJ, Computer Horizons, Inc., 1976. PB 252 339.

Nash, S. and Wilson, M. C. Value-added bibliographic instruction: teaching students to find the right citations. *Reference Services Review*, 19(1), 1991, 87-92.

Neway, J. M. *Information Specialist as Team Player in the Research Process*. Westport, CT, Greenwood Press, 1985.

Newhouse, J. P. and Alexander, A. J. *An Economic Analysis of Public Library Services*. Lexington, MA, Lexington Books, 1972.

Nicholas, D. et al. Online: views on costs and cost-effectiveness. *Journal of Information Science*, 13, 1987, 109-115.

Nielsen, B. and Baker, B. Educating the online catalog user: a model evaluation study. *Library Trends*, 35, 1987, 571-585.

Nightingale, R. A. A cost-benefit study of a manually-produced current awareness bulletin. *Aslib Proceedings*, 25, 1973, 153-157.

Nimmer, R. J. Circulation and collection patterns at the Ohio State University Libraries 1973-1977. *Library Acquisitions: Practice and Theory*, 4, 1980, 61-70.

Nisonger, T. E. *Collection Evaluation in Academic Libraries: a Literature Guide and Annotated Bibliography*. Englewood, CO, Libraries Unlimited, 1992.

Nisonger, T. E. An in-depth collection evaluation at the University of Manitoba Library: a test of the Lopez method. *Library Resources & Technical Services*, 24, 1980, 329-338.

Nisonger, T. E. A test of two citation checking techniques for evaluating political science collections in university libraries. *Library Resources & Technical Services*, 27, 1983, 163-176.

Nolan, C. W. The lean reference collection: improving functionality through selection and weeding. *College & Research Libraries*, 52, 1991, 80-91.

Oberg, L. R. Evaluating the Conspectus approach for smaller library collections. *College & Research Libraries*, 49, 1988, 187-196.

Olden, A. and Marsh, S. S. An evaluation of the extent to which the holdings of four United States research libraries would have supported the writing of award-winning books on Africa. *International Journal of Information and Library Research*, 2, 1990, 177-193.

Oliveira, S. M. de. *Collection Evaluation Through Citation Checking: a Comparison of Three Sources*. Doctoral dissertation. Urbana, University of Illinois, Graduate School of Library and Information Science, 1991.

Olsen, J. K. and Coons, B. Cornell University's information literacy program. In: *Coping With Information Illiteracy: Bibliographic Instruction for the Information Age*; ed. by G. E. Mensching, Jr., and T. B. Mensching, pp. 7-20. Ann Arbor, MI, Pierian Press, 1989.

Olson, L. M. Reference service evaluation in medium-sized academic libraries: a model. *Journal of Academic Librarianship*, 9, 1984, 322-329.

Oluić-Vuković, V. and Pravdić, N. Journal selection model: an indirect evaluation of scientific journals. *Information Processing & Management*, 26, 1990, 413-431.

Orr, R. H. Measuring the goodness of library services: a general framework for considering quantitative measures. *Journal of Documentation*, 29, 1973, 315-332.

Orr, R. H. and Olson, E. E. *Quantitative Measures as Management Tools*. Materials prepared for use in a continuing education course, CE 7, of the Medical Library Association. Chicago, Medical Library Association, 1968.

Orr, R. H. and Schless, A. P. Document delivery capabilities of major biomedical libraries in 1968: results of a national survey employing standardized tests. *Bulletin of the Medical Library Association*, 60, 1972, 382-422.

Orr, R. H. et al. Development of methodologic tools for planning and managing library services. II. Measuring a library's capability for providing documents. *Bulletin of the Medical Library Association*, 56, 1968, 241-267.

Ottensmann, J. R. and Gleeson, M. E. Implementation and testing of a decision support system for public library materials acquisition budgeting. *Journal of the American Society for Information Science*, 44, 1993, 83-93.

Pacific Northwest Collection Assessment Manual. Third edition. Salem, OR, Oregon State Library Foundation, 1990.

Pan, E. Journal citation as a predictor of journal usage in libraries. *Collection Management*, 2, 1978, 29-38.

Pateman, J. Letter to the editor. *Library Association Record*, 92, 1990, 491-492.

Patton, M. Q. *Qualitative Evaluation Methods.* Second edition. Newbury Park, CA, Sage Publications, 1990.

Peat, W. L. The use of research libraries: a comment about the Pittsburgh study and its critics. *Journal of Academic Librarianship*, 7, 1981, 229-231.

Peat, Marwick, Mitchell & Co. *California Public Library Systems: a Comprehensive Review with Guidelines for the Next Decade.* Los Angeles, 1975.

Penn, P. D. *Project Born Free: Evaluation of the 1978 Born Free National Institute.* Minneapolis, University of Minnesota, College of Education, 1978. (ERIC Document Reproduction Service No. ED 193 595).

Penner, R. J. Measuring a library's capability. *Journal of Education for Librarianship*, 13, 1972, 17-30.

Perk, L. J. and Van Pulis, N. Periodical usage in an education-psychology library. *College & Research Libraries*, 38, 1977, 304-308.

Pings, V. A study of the use of materials circulated from an engineering library. *American Documentation*, 18, 1967, 178-184.

Piternick, G. Library growth and academic quality. *College & Research Libraries*, 24, 1963, 223-229.

Pizer, I. H. and Cain, A. M. Objective tests of library performance. *Special Libraries*, 59, 1968, 704-711.

Plate, K. H. *Cost Justification of Information Services.* Studio City, CA, Cibbarelli and Associates Inc., 1983.

Popovich, C. J. The characteristics of a collection for research in business/ management. *College & Research Libraries*, 39, 1978, 110-117.

Porta, M. A. and Lancaster, F. W. Evaluation of a scholarly collection in a specific subject area by bibliographic checking. *Libri*, 38, 1988, 131-137.

Porter, L. Setting inter-library loan standards in a nursing library. In: *Q.A.: Quality Assurance in Libraries: the Health Care Sector*; ed. by M. H. Taylor and T. Wilson, pp. 113-128. Ottawa, Canadian Library Association, 1990.

Postlethwait, S. N. et al. *The Evaluation of Minicourses in Undergraduate Biology.* Lafayette, IN, Purdue University, 1974. (ERIC Document Reproduction Service No. ED 193 008).

Potter, W. G. Studies of collection overlap: a literature review. *Library Research*, 4, 1982, 3-21.

Powell, R. R. *An Investigation of the Relationship Between Reference Collection Size and Other Reference Service Factors and Success in Answering Reference Questions*. Doctoral dissertation. University of Illinois, Graduate School of Library Science, 1976. A condensed version appears in *Library Quarterly*, 48, 1978, 1-19. [For another version see Benham and Powell (1987)].

Powell, R. R. Reference effectiveness: a review of research. *Library and Information Science Research*, 6, 1984, 3-19.

Power, C. J. and Bell, G. H. Automated circulation, patron satisfaction, and collection evaluation in academic libraries – a circulation analysis formula. *Journal of Library Automation*, 11, 1978, 366-369.

Prabha, C. G. and Lancaster, F. W. Comparing the scatter of citing and cited literature. *Scientometrics*, 12, 1987, 17-31.

Price, D. J. The citation cycle. In: *Key Papers in Information Science*; ed. by B. C. Griffith, pp. 195-210. White Plains, NY, Knowledge Industry Publications, 1980.

Public Library Association. *Minimum Standards for Public Library Systems, 1966*. Chicago, American Library Association, 1967.

Raffel, J. A. and Shishko, R. *Systematic Analysis of University Libraries*. Cambridge, MA, MIT Press, 1969.

Ramsden, M. J. *Performance Measurement of Some Melbourne Public Libraries*. Melbourne, Library Council of Victoria, 1978.

Ranganathan, S. R. *The Five Laws of Library Science*. Bombay, Asia Publishing House, 1931.

Rice, B. A. Selection and evaluation of chemistry periodicals. *Science and Technology Libraries*, 4(1), 1983, 43-59.

Roberts, S. A. *Cost Management for Library and Information Services*. London, Butterworths, 1985.

Roberts, S. A., ed. *Costing and the Economics of Library and Information Services*. London, Aslib, 1984.

Robertson, S. E. The parametric description of retrieval tests. *Journal of Documentation*, 25, 1969, 93-107.

Roderer, N. K. et al. *The Use and Value of Defense Technical Information Center Products and Services*. Rockville, MD, King Research Inc., 1983. AD-A 130805/5.

Rodger, E. J. and Goodwin, J. *Reference Accuracy at the Fairfax County Public Library*. Washington, DC, Metropolitan Washington Library Council, 1984.

Rogers, E. M. and Shoemaker, F. F. *Communication of Innovations*. Second edition. New York, Free Press, 1971.

Rosenberg, K. C. Evaluation of an industrial library: a simple-minded technique. *Special Libraries*, 60, 1969, 635-638.

Rosenberg, P. *Cost Finding for Public Libraries*. Chicago, American Library Association, 1985.

Rosenberg, V. *The Application of Psychometric Techniques to Determine the Attitudes of Individuals Toward Information Seeking*. Bethlehem, PA, Lehigh University, Center for Information Sciences, 1966. Another version appears in *Information Storage and Retrieval*, 3, 1967, 119-127.

Rothenberg, D. Changing values in the published literature with time. *Library Trends*, 41, 1993, 681-696.

Rothenberg, D. Diachronous and synchronous methods in the measurement of obsolescence in library circulation studies. Unpublished seminar paper. Urbana, University of Illinois, Graduate School of Library and Information Science, 1991.

Roy, L. Weeding without tears: objective and subjective criteria used in identifying books to be weeded in public library collections. *Collection Management*, 12(1/2), 1990, 83-93.

Rubin, R. *Inhouse Use of Materials in Public Libraries*. Urbana, University of Illinois, Graduate School of Library and Information Science, 1986.

Rutledge, J. and Swindler, L. Evaluating membership in a resource-sharing program: the Center for Research Libraries. *College & Research Libraries*, 49, 1988, 409-424.

Sandison, A. Densities of use, and absence of obsolescence, in physics journals at MIT. *Journal of the American Society for Information Science*, 25, 1974, 172-182.

Sandison, A. Obsolescence in biomedical journals. *Library Research*, 2, 1981, 347-348

Sapp, G. The levels of access: subject approaches to fiction. *RQ*, 25, 1986, 488-497.

Saracevic, T. et al. Causes and dynamics of user frustration in an academic library. *College & Research Libraries*, 38, 1977, 7-18.

Saracevic, T. et al. Study of information seeking and retrieving. *Journal of the American Society for Information Science*, 39, 1988, 161-216.

Sargent, S. H. The uses and limitations of Trueswell. *College & Research Libraries*, 40, 1979, 416-423.

Satariano, W. A. Journal use in sociology: citation analysis versus readership patterns. *Library Quarterly*, 48, 1978, 293-300.

Scales, P. A. Citation analyses as indicators of the use of serials: a comparison of ranked title lists produced by citation counting and from use data. *Journal of Documentation*, 32, 1976, 17-25.

Schad, J. G. Missing the brass ring in the iron city. *Journal of Academic Librarianship*, 5, 1979, 60-63.

Schauer, B. P. *The Economics of Managing Library Service*. Chicago, American Library Association, 1986.

Schloman, B. F. and Ahl, R. E. Retention periods for journals in a small academic library. *Special Libraries*, 70, 1979, 377-383.

Schmidt, J. Evaluation of reference service in college libraries, in New South Wales, Australia. In: *Library Effectiveness: a State of the Art*, pp. 265-294. Chicago, American Library Association, 1980.

Schnall, J. G. and Wilson, J. W. Evaluation of a clinical medical librarianship program at a university health sciences library. *Bulletin of the Medical Library Association*, 64, 1976, 278-283.

Schofield, J. L. et al. Evaluation of an academic library's stock effectiveness. *Journal of Librarianship*, 7, 1975, 207-227.

Schultz, K. and Salomon, K. End users respond to CD-ROM. *Library Journal*, 115, 1990, 56-57.

Schwarz, P. Demand-adjusted shelf availability parameters: a second look. *College & Research Libraries*, 44, 1983, 210-219.

Scriven, M. S. The methodology of evaluation. In: *Perspectives of Curriculum Evaluation*; ed. by R. W. Tyler, et al., pp. 39-83. Chicago, Rand McNally, 1967.

Scura, G. and Davidoff, F. Case-related use of the medical literature: clinical librarian services for improving patient care. *Journal of the American Medical Associationb*, 245, 1981, 50-52.

Seaman, S. Online catalog failure as reflected through interlibrary loan error requests. *College & Research Libraries*, 53, 1992, 113-120.

Seba, D. B. and Forrest, B. Using SDI's to get primary journals: a new online way. *Online*, 2(1), 1978, 10-15.

Segal, J. P. *Evaluating and Weeding Collections in Small and Medium-sized Public Libraries: the CREW Method*. Chicago, American Library Association, 1980.

Selth, J. et al. The use of books within the library. *College & Research Libraries*, 53, 1992, 197-205.

Setting Objectives for Public Library Services: a Manual of Public Library Objectives. United Kingdom, Office of Arts and Libraries, 1991.

Shaughnessy, T. W. Benchmarking, Total Quality Management, and libraries. *Library Administration and Management*, 7(1), Winter 1993, 7-12.

Shaw, W. M., Jr. A journal resource sharing strategy. *Library Research*, 1, 1979, 19-29.

Shaw, W. M., Jr. Longitudinal studies of book availability. In: *Library Effectiveness: a State of the Art*, pp. 338-349. Chicago, American Library Association, 1980.

Shaw, W. M., Jr. A practical journal usage technique. *College & Research Libraries*, 39, 1978, 479-484.

Silver, P. F. *The Effects of Attitudes on Quality Judgments of Inservice Programs*. Paper presented at the Annual Meeting of the American Educational Research Association, 1981. (ERIC Document Reproduction Service No. ED 203 533).

Simon, J. L. How many books should be stored where? an economic analysis. *College & Research Libraries*, 28, 1967, 93-103.

Slote, S. J. *Weeding Library Collections*. Third edition. Littleton, CO, Libraries Unlimited, 1989.

Smith, G. D. *Directing a Workshop for Implementers of Career Education*. Greeneville, TN, Greeneville City Schools, 1974. (ERIC Document Reproduction Service No. ED 105 129).

Smith, R. H. and Granade, W. User and library failures in an undergraduate library. *College & Research Libraries*, 39, 1978, 467-473.

Smith, R. H. et al. Retrieval of selected serial citations: an analysis through user interviews. *College & Research Libraries*, 50, 1989, 532-542.

Snowball, G. J. and Sampedro, J. Selection of periodicals for return to prime space from a storage facility. *Canadian Library Journal*, 30, 1973, 490-492.

Solomin, V. M. Efficiency indexes for the performance of information agencies. *Nauchno-Tekhnicheskaya Informatsiya*, series 1, number 5, 1974, 3-7. English translation appears in *Scientific and Technical Information Processing*, 1, 1974, 16-23.

Soper, M. E. *The Relationship Between Personal Collections and the Selection of Cited References*. Doctoral dissertation. Urbana, University of Illinois, Graduate School of Library Science, 1972. A condensed version appears in *Library Quarterly*, 46, 1976, 397-415.

Sparck Jones, K. *Information Retrieval Experiment*. London, Butterworths, 1981.

Spaulding, F. H. and Stanton, R. O. Computer-aided selection in a library network. *Journal of the American Society for Information Science*, 27, 1976, 269-280.

Specht, J. Patron use of an online circulation system in known-item searching. *Journal of the American Society for Information Science*, 31, 1980, 335-346.

Sprules, M. L. Online bibliometrics in an academic library. *Online*, 7(1), 1983, 25-34.

Sridhar, M. S. Is cost benefit analysis applicable to journal use in special libraries? *Serials Librarian*, 15(1/2), 1988, 137-153.

Stake, R. E. et al. *Evaluating a Regional Environmental Learning System: a Program Evaluation Manual*. Urbana, University of Illinois, College of Education, 1979.

Standards for college libraries, 1986. *College & Research Libraries News*, 47, 1986, 189-200.

Standards of Public Library Service in England and Wales. London, Her Majesty's Stationery Office, 1962.

Stankus, T. and Rice, B. Handle with care: use and citation data for science journal management. *Collection Management*, 4, 1982, 95-110.

Stayner, R. A. and Richardson, V. E. *The Cost-effectiveness of Alternative Library Storage Programs*. Clayton, Victoria, Monash University, Graduate School of Librarianship, 1983.

Steele, S. M. *Contemporary Approaches to Program Evaluation and Their Implications for Evaluating Programs for Disadvantaged Adults*. Syracuse, NY, ERIC Clearinghouse on Adult Education, 1973.

Steffey, R. J. and Meyer, N. Evaluating user success and satisfaction with CD-ROM. *Laserdisk Professional*, 2(5), 1989, 35-45.

Stelk, R. E. and Lancaster, F. W. The use of shelflist samples in studies of book availability. *Collection Management*, 13(4), 1990a, 19-24.

Stelk, R. E. and Lancaster, F. W. The use of textbooks in evaluating the collection of an undergraduate library. *Library Acquisitions: Practice and Theory*, 14, 1990b, 191-193.

Stenstrom, P. and McBride, R. B. Serial use by social science faculty: a survey. *College & Research Libraries*, 40, 1979, 426-431.

Stewart, L. and Olsen, J. Compact disk databases: are they good for users? *Online*, 12(3), 1988, 48-52.

Stinson, E. R. and Lancaster, F. W. Synchronous versus diachronous methods in the measurement of obsolescence by citation studies. *Journal of Information Science*, 13, 1987, 65-74.

Stoljarov, J. N. Optimum size of public library stocks. *Unesco Bulletin for Libraries*, 27, 1973, 22-28, 42.

Strain, P. M. A study of the usage and retention of technical periodicals. *Library Resources & Technical Services*, 10, 1966, 295-304.

Studebaker, D. P. et al. *Evaluation Training Materials: the State of the Art*. 1979. (ERIC Document Reproduction Service No. ED 177 224).

Sullivan, M. V. et al. Obsolescence in biomedical journals: not an artifact of literature growth. *Library Research*, 2, 1980-1981, 29-45.

Swanson, D. R. Subjective versus objective relevance in bibliographic retrieval systems. *Library Quarterly*, 56, 1986, 389-398.

Tagliacozzo, R. and Kochen, M. Information-seeking behavior of catalog users. *Information Storage and Retrieval*, 6, 1970, 363-381.

Taylor, C. R. A practical solution to weeding university library periodicals collections. *Collection Management*, 1(3/4), 1976-1977, 27-45.

Tiefel, V. Evaluating a library user education program: a decade of experience. *College & Research Libraries*, 50, 1989, 249-259.

Tomer, C. A statistical assessment of two measures of citation: the impact factor and the immediacy index. *Information Processing & Management*, 22, 1986, 251-258.

Torr, D. V. et al. *Program Studies on the Use of Published Indexes*. Bethesda, MD, General Electric Co., 1966. 2 vols.

Trail, M. and Gutierrez, C. Evaluating a bibliographic instruction program. *Research Strategies*, 9, 1991, 124-129.

Travillian, M. Peer coaching to improve reference performance in Maryland. *CLENEXCHANGE*, 11, 1985, 2-3.

Trochim, M. K. et al. *Measuring the Circulation Use of a Small Academic Library Collection: a Manual*. Chicago, Associated Colleges of the Midwest, 1980. [An updated version was issued by the Office of Management Studies, Association of Research Libraries in 1985.]

Trubkin, L. Building a core collection of business and management periodicals: how databases can help. *Online*, 6(4), 1982, 43-49.

Trueswell, R. W. Determining the optimal number for volumes for a library's core collection. *Libri*, 16, 1966, 49-60.

Trueswell, R. W. A quantitative measure of user circulation requirements and its possible effect on stack thinning and multiple copy determination. *American Documentation*, 16, 1965, 20-25.

Trueswell, R. W. Two characteristics of circulation and their effect on the implementation of mechanized circulation control systems. *College & Research Libraries*, 25, 1964, 285-291.

Trueswell, R. W. User circulation satisfaction vs. size of holdings at three academic libraries. *College & Research Libraries*, 30, 1969, 204-213.

University of Chicago. Graduate Library School. *Requirements Study for Future Catalogs. Progress Report No. 2*. Chicago, 1968.

Urquhart, J. A. and Schofield, J. L. Measuring readers' failure at the shelf. *Journal of Documentation*, 27, 1971, 272-286.

Urquhart, J. A. and Schofield, J. L. Measuring readers' failure at the shelf in three university libraries. *Journal of Documentation*, 28, 1972, 233-241.

Urquhart, J. A. and Urquhart, N. C. *Relegation and Stock Control in Libraries*. Newcastle upon Tyne, Oriel Press, 1976.

U.S. Civil Service Commission. *An Evaluation Model Designed to Measure the Effectiveness of a One-week Training Course "Position Classification and the Management Process"*. Washington, DC, 1970. (ERIC Document Reproduction Service No. ED 064 568).

Usherwood, R. Managing public libraries as a public service. *Public Library Journal*, 7, 1992, 141-145.

Van House, N. A. et al. *Output Measures for Public Libraries: a Manual of Standardized Procedures*. Second edition. Chicago, American Library Association, 1987.

Van Styvendaele, B. J. H. University scientists as seekers of information: sources of references to books and their first use versus date of publication. *Journal of Librarianship*, 13, 1981, 83-92.

Vickery, B. C. Bradford's law of scattering. *Journal of Documentation*, 4, 1948, 198-203.

Voigt, M. J. Acquisition rates in university libraries. *College & Research Libraries*, 36, 1975, 263-271.

Voigt, M. J. Circulation studies cannot reflect research use. *Journal of Academic Librarianship*, 5, 1979, 66.

Wainwright, E. J. and Dean, J. E. *Measure of Adequacy for Library Collections in Australian Colleges of Advanced Education*. Perth, Western Australian Institute of Technology, 1976. 2 vols.

Wallace, D. P. *An Index of Quality of Illinois Public Library Service*. Springfield, Illinois State Library, 1983.

Wanger, J. et al. *Evaluation of the Online Search Process*. Santa Monica, Cuadra Associates, 1980. PB 81-132565.

Ware, S. A. and Morganti, D. J. A competency-based approach to assessing workbook effectiveness. *Research Strategies*, 4, 1986, 4-10.

Weech, T. L. and Goldhor, H. Obtrusive versus unobtrusive evaluation of reference service in five Illinois public libraries: a pilot study. *Library Quarterly*, 52, 1982, 305-324.

Welsh, J. J. Evaluation of CD-ROM use in a government research library. *Laserdisk Professional*, 2(6), 1989, 55-61.

Wenger, C. B. and Childress, J. Journal evaluation in a large research library. *Journal of the American Society for Information Science*, 28, 1977, 293-299.

Wenger, C. B. et al. Monograph evaluation for acquisitions in a large research library. *Journal of the American Society for Information Science*, 30, 1979, 88-92.

Werking, R. H. Evaluating bibliographic education: a review and critique. *Library Trends*, 29, 1980, 153-172.

West, W. J. *The Strange Rise of Semi-Literate England: the Dissolution of the Libraries*. London, Duckworth, 1991.

Whitlatch, J. B. and Kieffer, K. Service at San Jose State University: survey of document availability. *Journal of Academic Librarianship*, 4, 1978, 196-199.

Wiberly, S. E., Jr. Journal rankings from citation studies: a comparison of national and local data from social work. *Library Quarterly*, 52, 1982, 348-359.

Wiemers, E., Jr. *Materials Availability in Small Libraries: a Survey Handbook*. Urbana, University of Illinois, Graduate School of Library and Information Science, 1981. Occasional Papers No. 149.

Williams, G. E. et al. *Library Cost Models: Owning Versus Borrowing Serial Publications*. Chicago, Center for Research Libraries, 1968.

Williams, R. An unobtrusive survey of academic library reference services. *Library and Information Research News*, 10(37/38), 1987, 12-40.

Williams, R. Weeding an academic lending library using the Slote method. *British Journal of Academic Librarianship*, 1, 1986, 147-159.

Wills, G. and Christopher, M. Cost/benefit analysis of company information needs. *Unesco Bulletin for Libraries*, 24, 1970, 9-22.

Wilsing, W. C. Program development: transforming needs into objectives. In: *The Evaluation of Continuing Education for Professionals: a Systems View*; ed. by P. P. LeBreton et al., pp. 242-264. Seattle, University of Washington, 1979.

Wilson, S. R. et al. *Use of the Critical Incident Technique to Evaluate the Impact of MEDLINE. Final Report*. Palo Alto, American Institutes for Research, 1989. PB 90-142522.

Wolf, R. M. *Evaluation in Education*. Third edition. New York, Praeger, 1990.

Wood, F. *Evaluation of a University Library's Catalogue*. Canberra, Australian National University, 1984.

Wood, J. B. et al. Measurement of service at a public library. *Public Library Quarterly*, 2(2), 1980, 49-57.

Woodsmall, R. M. et al, *eds. MEDLINE on CD-ROM*. Medford, NJ, Learned Information Inc., 1989.

Woodward, J. P. and Yeager, J. L. *Evaluation of Programs to Train Educational R & D Personnel*. Pittsburgh, University of Pittsburgh, Learning Research and Development Center, 1972. (ERIC Document Reproduction Service No. ED 064 376).

Zipf, G. K. *Psycho-Biology of Language*. Boston, Houghton Mifflin, 1935.

Zweizig, D. and Rodger, E. J. *Output Measures for Public Libraries*. Chicago, American Library Association, 1982.

Index

344